D0122588

Investment in Education

Investment in Education
The Equity-Efficiency Quandary

Edited by Theodore W. Schultz

The University of Chicago Press

Chicago and London

The University of Chicago Press, Chicago 60637
The University of Chicago Press, Ltd., London

Published 1972. All rights reserved
Published also as part 2 of volume 80, number 3, of the
Journal of Political Economy, May/June 1972
Printed in the United States of America

International Standard Book Number: 0-226-74080-3
Library of Congress Catalog Card Number: 72-84408

Contents

Contents

Prefatory Note

The core of this study deals broadly with the unsettled social question of the effects of education upon the distribution of personal income. It is strictly an economic approach to this social question. The evidence and analysis pertain primarily to higher education. All but one of the papers and comments were prepared for the workshop that convened at the University of Chicago, June 7–10, 1971. They present the results of new studies along with critical evaluations of the social and private implications of the findings.

The workshop was sponsored by the Committee on Basic Research in Education. The program of this committee is administered by the Division of Behavioral Sciences of the National Research Council, as a joint activity of the National Academy of Sciences and the National Academy of Education. A generous financial grant by the Office of Education, U.S. Department of Health, Education and Welfare, via a contract between the Office of Education and the National Academy of Sciences, made possible both the convening of the workshop and the publication of this study. It should be noted that, in accordance with the requirements of the Office of Education, this material is in the public domain.

Gary S. Becker, Edward F. Denison, W. Lee Hansen, and Theodore W. Schultz shared the task of planning and organizing the workshop. Sherman Ross, Henry David, and Barbara Meeker of the National Research Council gave generously of their time in making arrangements for the workshop and clearing the way for publication of this volume. Workshop participants whose names do not appear as authors of papers or of comments were Henry David, Richard Freeman, Bruce Gardner, Walter McMahon, Barbara Meeker, Sherman Ross, and Harry Silberman.

The pertinent paper by Marc Nerlove emerged from his thinking and study after the June workshop. He has kindly permitted me to include it.

I am very much indebted to Mrs. Virginia K. Thurner, whose editorial skills and competence have been of great value to me in shaping this volume.

THEODORE W. SCHULTZ

October 1, 1971

1

Optimal Investment in College Instruction: Equity and Efficiency

Theodore W. Schultz

University of Chicago

The allocation of resources to provide the instructional services of higher education in the United States is neither socially efficient nor equitable. The rise in personal incomes in this country, associated with economic growth, is making the traditional *financing, pricing,* and *supplying* of these instructional services ever more obsolete. There is evidence, for example, that an inordinate part of the subsidies to higher education is used to provide higher educational services below cost to the growing proportion of students who come from families who have the income and wealth to pay the full cost.

In advancing my argument that financing of higher education lacks social efficiency and equity, I approach the performance of this part of higher education under the dynamic conditions of economic growth. I treat college students as firms, behaving as entrepreneurs in allocating their own time and their other resources in investing in themselves. By and large, I contend that they do this efficiently. A considerable body of evidence shows that they respond with relatively short lags to changes in the costs that they bear in acquiring an education and to changes in job opportunities that may be available to them upon graduation.

On the other hand, institutions, as suppliers of college instruction, and government, in funding these institutions, are not socially efficient. They do not provide students with the socially appropriate scarcity signals so that the students can make socially efficient choices. On the side of equity, generous subsidies are extended to all college students, thus subsidizing, in large measure, high-income families. The educational-investment behavior of these families would not change appreciably if they paid full cost.

It could be said that higher education as it has developed in the

This paper benefited and I gained assurance from the cogent criticism of Gary S. Becker, Richard B. Freeman, W. Lee Hansen, Robert W. Hartman, and T. Paul Schultz.

United States is a "model" of competition and welfare inasmuch as college students have many subsidized options and no college or university has a monopoly of the supply of these educational services. There are more than 2,500 institutions competing for faculty and students,[1] and they compete not only with each other but also with other sectors of the economy for talent and materials. They acquire virtually all their instructional inputs in competitive markets. Moreover, to the extent that growth enhances competition, higher education has been a growth sector par excellence with enrollment rising since 1940 from 1.5 million to more than 7 million students.

With respect to equity, there is no standard comparable with that of economic efficiency. It is true, of course, that in terms of career choices higher education in the United States not only offers students many options but also subsidizes them, in part directly and nearly all of them indirectly, in large amounts. Direct financial aid to students in 1968 equalled about 4 percent of the total educational cost incurred by public institutions and about 8 percent of such cost incurred by private institutions (see table 1). But the major subsidies are indirect because tuition and fees paid by students covered only 15 percent of the total educational cost in public institutions and 45 percent in private institutions. (Indirect subsidies are also appreciable in providing room and board for students.) The welfare implications of this vast subsidization of students are far from obvious.

Since most of the direct costs of higher education in the United States are not paid for by tuition and student fees, there is a strong presumption that the economic organization of higher education has a built-in tendency in terms of efficiency to spend too much on this education socially *unless the benefits that accrue to society*—benefits the students cannot capture privately during their lifetimes—are very large. This presumption is warranted despite the competition referred to above. It is certainly true that the social rates of return and private rates of return are not proportional in all higher educational activities. Furthermore, there is a tendency to transfer wealth in the form of human capital to a select class of the population.

In general, the private rate of return to investment in higher education tends to be comparable with the private rates of return to other private investments. Whether there are long-standing disparities among private rates of return to the various higher educational opportunities awaits disaggregation and analysis. The dynamics of the economy implies that certain disparities are inevitable. Richard Freeman's study (1971) shows, however, that, as these disparities occur, the lags in adjustment are relatively short. The efficiency with which public resources are allocated to

---

[1] The number of institutions in the fall of 1969 was 2,525; see U.S. Office of Education (1970, table 113, p. 85).

TABLE 1
U.S. HIGHER EDUCATION, SELECTED DATA FOR 1940 AND 1968

	PUBLIC			PRIVATE			TOTAL			PUBLIC/PRIVATE		
	1940 (1)	1968 (2)	1968/1940 (3)	1940 (4)	1968 (5)	1968/1940 (6)	1940 (7)	1968 (8)	1968/1940 (9)	1940 (10)	1968 (11)	1968/1940 (12)
a) Number of institutions	600	940	1.6	1,150	1,440	1.3	1,750	2,380	1.4	0.5	0.6	1.2
b) Enrollment (thousands)	800	4,850	6.1	700	2,110	3.0	1,490	6,960	4.7	1.1	2.3	2.0
c) Direct total instruction costs ($ million)	300	7,900	26.5	340	4,800	14.3	630	12,700	20.0	0.9	1.6	1.9
d) Net instruction expenditures ($ million)	230	6,710	30.0	250	4,070	16.6	470	10,780	22.8	0.9	1.6	1.8
e) Implicit interest, depreciation ($ million)	71	1,190	16.7	90	730	8.1	160	1,920	11.9	0.8	1.6	2.1
f) Tuition and fees ($ million)	55	1,210	22.0	150	2,180	15.0	200	3,390	16.9	0.4	0.6	1.5
g) Student aid expenditures ($ million)	7	330	47.4	22	390	17.6	29	720	24.8	0.3	0.9	2.7
h) Enrollment per institution	1,320	5,170	3.9	610	1,460	2.4	1,170	2,920	2.5	2.2	3.5	1.6
i) Per student direct total instruction costs ($)	370	1,630	4.4	480	2,270	4.7	420	1,820	4.3	0.8	0.7	0.9
j) Per student net instruction expenditures ($)	280	1,380	4.9	350	1,930	5.5	320	1,550	4.9	0.8	0.7	0.9
k) Per student interest and depreciation ($)	89	240	2.8	130	350	2.7	110	270	2.5	0.7	0.7	1.0
l) Per student tuition and fees ($)	69	250	3.6	210	1,030	4.9	140	490	3.6	0.3	0.2	0.7
m) Per student financial aid ($)	9	69	7.6	32	180	5.7	19	100	5.4	0.3	0.4	1.3

NOTE.—Table prepared by Anne Williams. Data sources and bases of calculations are in Appendix. Col. 3 = col. 2 ÷ col. 1; col. 6 = col. 5 ÷ col. 4; col. 9 = col. 8 ÷ col. 7; col. 10 = col. 1 ÷ col. 4; col. 11 = col. 2 ÷ col. 5; col. 12 = col. 11 ÷ col. 10.

the many parts of higher education is another story. When it comes to equity consequences, the evidence is fragmentary; it is inconceivable, however, that they are neutral in their effects on the distribution of personal income.

The classical economists divided on the question of efficiency with respect to alternative ways of providing education (West 1964). This controversy is still with us (Beales et al. 1967). Nor have the proponents of "equal educational opportunities" settled the problem of equity in distributing the benefits of education. The continuing disagreements, it seems to me, suggest that we have not been asking the right questions. With respect to the United States, I have become convinced that the problems of efficiency and equity in higher education, especially as they have come to the forefront during recent decades, are in large part the consequences of the dynamics of modern growth. This view implies the following question: Under the dynamic conditions that characterize our economy, how efficient are we in allocating private and public resources to higher education and in using these resources to produce educational services? I believe the equity question should be formulated along similar lines.

Although it is obvious that these problems consist of disparities in the distribution of private and social costs and benefits, it is not obvious that these disparities are, in part, related to the developments that characterize modern growth. When an economy arrives at an equilibrium that prevails over an extended period, it is in general true that the efficiency disparities tend to become small. But under conditions of modern growth, disequilibria are the order of the day and, although adjustments are made, new disparities continue to emerge. In approaching growth via the process of investment, what is required, ideally, is a generalized optimal-investment model that encompasses both human and nonhuman capital and that accounts for all of the nonmarket benefits, including the personal satisfactions that accrue to students from their investment in higher education. But we will have to settle for less because of the limitations of the state of economic knowledge. I shall examine four interrelated issues: (1) three economic growth–education puzzles, (2) the rise in the student's opportunity cost and in his allocative benefits associated with growth, (3) the growth-related enlargement of the student's capacity to finance and to benefit from education, and (4) the equity-efficiency quandary in a growing economy.

I. Three Economic Growth–Education Puzzles

Growth is not an equilibrium state. For the purpose at hand, growth implies responses to investment opportunities in acquiring addtional income streams at a price lower than the equilibrium price. In terms of investment decisions, growth is a consequence of the allocation of investment resources in accordance with the priorities set by the relative rates of return to alternative investment opportunities. The reciprocal of the highest rate of return option is, in theory and in fact, the lowest price of additional growth. On the one hand, investment in human capital by means of higher education occurs as a response to the demand derived from growth, and, on the other, it contributes to the growth of an economy. The particular acquired ability associated with higher education is, in all probability, complementary to the new, superior material inputs that have their origin in scientific advances and the associated developments in technology. Then, too, modern research and development activities are dependent upon particular subsets of these abilities.

Thus, a satisfactory theory of economic growth should explain the mechanism that determines the formation of human and nonhuman capital, including the accumulation of knowledge.[2] Razin (1969) extended growth theory along these lines. Growth theory, however, also should explain the *sources of the investment opportunities that maintain the growth process* and keep it from settling into a stationary long-run equilibrium. This more difficult part of growth theory is lacking.

In thinking about the economics of education, I find it instructive to distinguish between the investment mechanism that determines the formation of capital and the sources of the new investment opportunities that account for growth. The mechanism appears to be sufficient to explain various puzzling interactions between growth and education. In retrospect, taking the long view, there are three such puzzles: (1) Why has the accumulation of human capital represented by education occurred at a higher rate than that of nonhuman capital? (2) Why has the difference in relative earnings between workers with little education and those with much decreased? (3) Why, as growth proceeds, does the inequality in the distribution of personal income show signs of decreasing?

There is some evidence. Human capital consisting mainly of education accounts for a smaller part of the production (income) in the less-developed countries than in those classified as developed. This implies that, as growth proceeds, the complementarity and substitution among factors are such that the role of human capital becomes increasingly important. Krueger's study (1968) is most telling on this point. In explaining the large absolute differences in per capita income between poor and rich countries in terms of factor endowments, she concludes "that the difference in human resources between the United States and the less-developed countries accounts for more of the difference in *per capita* income than all the other factors combined" (p. 658). The attribute of

---

[2] Useful knowledge that is appropriated can be treated as capital, but knowledge that enters the public domain and is available to everyone is another matter (Schultz 1971, chap. 12).

human resources that matters most in her study is education. My estimates of the average annual rates of increase of different stocks of capital in the United States between 1929 and 1957 provide some additional evidence (Schultz 1971, table 5.1): reproducible tangible wealth, 2.0 percent; educational capital in the labor force, 4.1 percent.

From 1900 to 1957 the educational capital in the labor force rose sharply relative to the stock of reproducible nonhuman capital; it was 22 percent as large as the nonhuman capital in 1900, and by 1957 it had risen to 42 percent (Schultz 1971, table 8.5). Here the implication is that the rate of return to education was sufficiently higher than the rate of return to reproducible nonhuman capital to have induced this pattern of investment. Although there are no clues in this evidence of the sources of this favorable rate of return to investment in education, it supports the presumption that investments were responding to opportunities that imply disequilibrium, and the further presumption that there have been continuing sources of new opportunities that have kept the rates of return from settling into a long-run equilibrium state.

The next puzzle for consideration is: What is it about growth that reduces the difference in relative earnings between workers who have little and those who have much education?[3] Kothari (1970) investigated the extent and the sources of the disparities in earnings in the city of Bombay, India, and the United States. His data, by occupations and education, appear in table 2. His summary of the income ratios with the earnings of unskilled workers as the base (equal to 1.0) follows:

> The relative income ratios for skilled manual occupations in Bombay as well as the United States were 1·4. The Bombay ratio for clerical personnel was 2·1, as against 1·5 for the United States, i.e., nearly 50% higher. For lower professions the Bombay ratio was 25% higher than the United States ratio. For Higher Professions the ratio in Bombay was 7·8 as against

[3] I know of no studies of the changes in relative earnings associated with differences in education during recent decades in the United States. The following data on estimated lifetime mean incomes (Bureau of the Census 1969, table 155, p. 108) suggest that the relative differences declined somewhat between 1949 and 1967.

LIFETIME MEAN INCOMES
(MALES, AGED 25 YEARS AND OLDER)

YEARS OF SCHOOLING	1949		1967	
	Thousands of Dollars	Relative Difference	Thousands of Dollars	Relative Difference
8	123	100	246	100
12	175	142	338	137
16 or more	287	233	558	227

TABLE 2

MEAN INCOME, RELATIVE INCOME RATIO, AND EDUCATION IN CITY OF BOMBAY (1955, 1956) AND IN THE UNITED STATES (1959) BY BROAD GROUPS OF OCCUPATIONS (MALES)

OCCUPATION	MEAN INCOME		RELATIVE INCOME RATIO		YEARS OF SCHOOLING	
	City of Bombay (Rupees per Month)	U.S. (Dollars per Year)	City of Bombay	U.S.	City of Bombay	U.S.
Higher professionals	622	9,890	7.78	3.00	15.1	15.7
Business and government executives in higher posts	897	7,831	11.21	2.37	13.0	12.7
Lower professionals	207	6,628	2.59	2.01	10.0	13.0
Subordinate officers in business and government	261	6,935	3.26	2.10	10.6	11.6
Clerical personnel	168	4,902	2.10	1.49	10.3	11.6
Skilled manual laborers	110	4,627	1.38	1.40	3.7	9.5
Unskilled manual laborers	80	3,301	1.00	1.00	2.0	8.2

SOURCE.—Kothari (1970, table 2, p. 609).

the United States ratio of 3. *i.e.*, nearly 2½ times as high. The differences in ratios in case of business and government executives in higher posts were even sharper. The Bombay ratio was 11·2, as against the United States ratio of 2·4. This contrast is all the more striking in the light of the educational content of different occupations. In Bombay City an unskilled worker had only 2 years of schooling while the clerical workers had 10·3 years of schooling. The corresponding figures for the United States were 8·2 years and 11·6 years. For the skilled manual occupations the years of schooling were 3·7 in Bombay and 9·5 in the United States. . . .

The real puzzle, however, is the very much higher relative income ratio in Bombay for the higher professions and the higher posts in business and government . . . [than in] the United States. [Pp. 607–8]

I see four inferences with respect to growth and education that are supported by Kothari's study: (1) As growth increases the general level of earnings, the absolute differences in earnings by level of education increase; and it is well known that the returns to education depend on the absolute, not the relative, differences in earnings. In Bombay, although college graduates were earning twice as much as matriculants, this difference was only 323 rupees per month, whereas in the United States college graduates were earning $4,158 per year more than high school graduates (Kothari 1970, p. 611); Kothari's estimates of the private rates of return for these college graduates are about the same for both locations—12 percent for the United States and 14 percent for Bombay. (2) Restrictions on entry into the "higher professions" are more telling in a less-developed country such as India than in the United States. Among the college graduates in Bombay, those who had managed to enter those professions were enjoying a 33 percent private rate of return, presumably because of such restrictions to entry as barriers associated with the caste system and the lack of facilities for engineering and medical education. (3) Higher education in the less-developed countries tends to be more elite-oriented and less subject to competition than in the United States, where higher education has become mass-oriented. (4) In adjusting education to the dynamics of growth, competition in providing educational services is an important institutional requirement.

Kuznets (1955) devoted his American Economic Association presidential address to growth and income inequality; he pointed out that there are long-term trends toward less inequality and noted that the reduction in this "inequality in the secular income structure is a puzzle" (p. 7). He later (1963) quantitatively analyzed these trends, and then in his *Modern Economic Growth* (1966) offered explanations emphasizing the relative decline in income from property, accompanied by a compensatory relative rise in income from the "greater investment in training and education" (p. 218). Thus, presumably, growth alters the functional distribution in a manner that reduces the inequality in the distribution of personal income. Mincer (1958, 1970) and Chiswick (1967, 1971) provide both theory and evidence to explain the distribution of labor incomes.

My interpretation of the role of growth in the above three puzzles can be summarized as follows: (1) As growth proceeds, investment in education occurs at a higher rate than investment in nonhuman capital, in response to the investment mechanism when the rates of return are favorable to investment in education. (2) The rise in the general level of earnings is accompanied by sufficiently large absolute differences in earnings to make the investment opportunities in education relatively attractive, even though the difference in relative earnings between unskilled and skilled workers declines; one of the long-term effects of this growth, as rates of return tend toward equality, is to reduce the income inequality within countries. (3) As growth proceeds, education becomes less elite and more mass-oriented.

Although each part of this interpretation is derived from the investment mechanism of growth, the mechanism by itself tells us nothing about the *sources* of the investment opportunities that have maintained the growth process. Despite the vast accumulation of capital from the long-continuing, ever-increasing investments, diminishing returns to investment have not prevailed in bringing about a long-run general equilibrium as traditional theory would imply. The critical unanswered question about growth is, What are the sources of the new investment opportunities that have counteracted the theoretically expected tendency toward diminishing returns to investment? Let me advance the following hypothesis: The acquisition of additional knowledge that becomes useful in reducing the cost of production and in enlarging consumer choice accounts in large part for the continuation of growth. Since the "production" of knowledge also requires scarce resources, it has the attributes of an investment.[4] Research-oriented universities are among the major contributors to the advances in knowledge (Schultz 1971).

II. Rise in Opportunity Costs and Allocative Benefits Associated with Growth

One of the attributes of economic growth is that it increases the value of time; thus the *earnings foregone* by students tend to rise. Another attribute of growth is that it affords new production and consumption opportunities and, as a result, there are *allocative benefits* to be had by responding promptly to these opportunities. Education is not organized to take account of earnings foregone, and our studies of the returns to education tend to omit these allocative benefits. Moreover, both components have efficiency and equity implications.

Although most economists include earnings foregone as a cost in analyzing the rates of return to investment in education, such costs are not taken into account in educational planning. Nor do earnings foregone appear in official educational statistics. It is fair to say that, in determining educational policy, in authorizing programs, and in allocating resources to finance education, we go on ignoring earnings foregone although they are well over half of the real cost of higher education. Despite the marked upward trend in the value of the time of students, educational administrators and faculties appear to be virtually unaware of this development. There is no search for ways of economizing on the

---

[4] My critics urged me to extend my comments on this issue, but I shall forego this opportunity because a major paper would be required to develop the analysis and because earlier (Schultz 1971, chaps. 1, 2, 12) I examined some aspects of the issue. Suffice it to say here that the argument that has been underway in *Science* among scientists, beginning with Bentley Glass on "Science Education—Process or Contents?" (March 5, 1971, p. 851), is not helpful. While it is obviously true that the acquisition of additional knowledge is, in some ultimate sense, subject to diminishing returns, merely to argue that the "exponential growth (of science) is self-limiting" is rather pointless in clarifying the funding of science in a world of scarce resources.

time of students. The standard of 4 years for a bachelor's degree is enforced regardless of differences in the capacity of students to learn and regardless of the increases in value of their time. Such a standard is inefficient. Students stand in long lines to get what is subsidized; it is rationing by queuing instead of by pricing the instructional services at cost.

Among the benefits of education there is an *allocative benefit* that is determined by the ability to respond to the opportunities afforded by growth. This particular benefit increases as the level of education rises, with the least-educated persons slowest in responding to the new opportunities. In production, the allocative benefit accrues initially to those persons who are among the first to respond; then, under competition, it is transferred and accrues to consumers sooner than it would have if the production response had occurred more slowly. Economists in their studies of education, with a few exceptions, have put this class of benefits aside although they are of major economic importance. The approach has been, in estimating the lifetime-earnings function from cross-sectional earnings data associated with education, to adjust this function downward for growth over time on the assumption that the rate of growth is wholly independent of the allocative behavior of educated people.

While I have argued that growth favors investment in education, it is also plausible that if the economy were to experience no growth for an extended period the benefits from education would decline. Less education would suffice as economic life became more placid. The disequilibria that are the result of growth would diminish, and fewer economic adjustments would be required because the domain of economic activity would become more routine in character. It follows that the economic value of one of the abilities developed by education is not only dependent upon growth but also contributes to growth. This is the ability *to discern the new opportunities, to evaluate them, and to act promptly and effectively* in taking advantage of them. These are opportunities that are inherent in the disequilibria associated with growth. I contend that the contribution of this particular ability to growth is omitted in reckoning the benefits of education.

The discovery of the allocative benefit here under consideration owes much to Welch's perceptive treatment (1970) of the "allocative effects" of education. His conceptual distinction between the worker effect and the allocative effect of education in production is clear and cogent. To the extent that increases in "education enhance a worker's ability to acquire and decode information about costs and productive characteristics of other inputs" (p. 42), there is an allocative effect. He argues that, in a technically dynamic economy, educated persons are more adept than less-educated individuals at critically evaluating new opportunities because they can distinguish more quickly between the systematic and random elements in such an economy; thus they are more productive than uneducated persons. In addition to Welch's evidence (drawn from U.S. agriculture) in support of the allocative-effects hypothesis, there is the evidence provided by Chaudhri's studies (1968, 1969) of education and the productivity of agriculture in India.

The allocative benefits from this particular ability developed by education are not restricted to farmers in the modernization of agriculture. There are reasons for believing, and there is some evidence, that they are pervasive under the dynamic conditions of growth. Schwartz (1968) found that differentials in lifetime earnings provide a better explanation of migration than do the differentials in current earnings and also that the response to the differences in lifetime earnings is lowest for the least-educated persons and increases monotonically with education. His findings are consistent with the hypothesis that one of the effects of education is to reduce the cost of obtaining information about job opportunities. O'Neill (1969) confirms Schwartz's results with respect to responses to job opportunities. She also found that the effects of consumption opportunities upon migration show a comparable pattern of response by level of education.

I interpret Freeman's finding (1971) of relatively short lags by college students in adjusting to changes in job opportunities among the fields in which they specialize as also supporting the argument that there are allocative benefits associated with education.

In studying the effects of education upon the management of the household, Michael (1969) showed that efficiency is lowest for the heads of households with the least education and increases with education. Here, too, one of the effects of education would appear to be a reduction in the cost of acquiring information to respond to new consumer opportunities which come with growth. At every turn in the application of the new micro (household) approach to fertility (population), the level of the woman's education appears to be a strong explanatory factor in connection with the wage effect, the efficiency effect in the household, and the contraception effect.

What then are the efficiency and equity (income-distribution) implications of these allocative benefits? In production, as better production possibilities become available, the allocative benefits are the sum of two parts: (1) the benefits that accrue to the educated person as a reward for his expeditious response to the opportunity, and (2) the benefit that accrues to the consumer sooner than it would have if the production response had occurred with a longer lag. The logic of economics implies that, under the assumption of competition, the opportunities arising as a result of growth disequilibria will be fully realized when equilibrium is attained. The educated person who is capable of exploiting such opportunities first (fastest) stands to gain relative to those who respond less expeditiously. Then, as these opportunities are realized under competition, the gains from a set of better production possibilities for example, are transferred to the intermediate, and through them to the final product, where they become consumer surpluses. The consumer acquires these surpluses soonest where the responses in production occur with the shortest lag. Herein is the consumer's part of the gain from the allocative benefit attributed to the education of producers.

Welch's study (1970) provides a useful framework by way of summary. In production, the distribution of the allocative benefits among producers depends on the differences in their ability to respond. Welch found that more-educated farmers have an advantage compared with less-educated farmers in responding to the dynamics of growth. The sooner the better production possibilities are attained, the sooner the additional efficiency from them is added to the real income of the economy. Resulting reductions in real factor cost are thus transferred to consumers in terms of lower food prices, and, as a special case, when this occurs in agriculture it tends to improve the income position of low-income families relatively more than that of higher-income families. Thus, to some extent for agriculture, this process under competition reduces the inequality in the distribution of personal income in general, *although it tends to widen the inequality among farm families.*[5]

III. Enlarging the Student's Capacity for Educational Finance and Benefits

Turning to the investment by college students in their own human capital, I will examine a set of attributes of economic growth with the view of determining their effects upon the capacity of students to finance and to benefit from higher education. I will treat *the student (family) as a firm, his capacity to finance as the supply, and his capacity to benefit as the demand.* Although institutions and policy also are altered by growth, I will abstract from these alterations. I will concentrate on the investment decisions of college students (families) in acquiring human capital by means of some form of higher education for which they incur costs and from which they obtain benefits. The primary growth attributes to be examined are (1) the rise in the personal income of families, (2) the enlargement of the student's capacity to learn, (3) the increase in the

[5] It may be true, in general, that less-educated persons experience losses in terms of the earnings they would have received had not those with more education been present to exploit new opportunities more quickly than they could. Since this may be what happens, I have not treated the particular consumer surplus on which the above paragraph concentrates as one of the social benefits of higher education.

value of time, and (4) the improvements in the entrepreneurial ability of students, including the allocative benefits they obtain in managing their investment decisions.

The connection between the value of the student's time and his *earnings foregone* has been examined briefly in Part II. Likewise, the importance of the *allocative benefits* that increase with education under conditions of growth is formally clear and consistent with a growing body of evidence. Earlier, in accounting for a higher rate of investment in education than in nonhuman capital, we found that economic growth favors the investment in education. In solving the puzzle of the narrowing difference in relative earnings between those with little and those with much education, we were led to reaffirm that the difference in absolute earnings, not the relative difference, accounts for the investment opportunities in successive levels of education.

My approach to the changing pattern of the supply curve and demand curve here under consideration is basically the optimal-investment-in-human-capital model developed by Becker (1967). The demand curve represents the marginal benefit measured by the rate of return to the student on each additional dollar of investment, and the supply curve, the marginal financing cost measured by the rate of interest on each additional dollar invested. I will extend the Becker model somewhat in treating the attributes of economic growth.

The rise in the personal income of families is the key that alters these supply and demand curves over time. The number of students and their respective marginal-financing cost account for the aggregate supply curve; their respective marginal benefits account for the aggregate demand curve. The general direction of the changes in supply and demand as income rises can be inferred. If social and legal institutions and policy remain constant and if the distribution of personal income remains unchanged, or becomes less unequal, it follows that, as incomes rise, the marginal-financing cost declines, and the per student supply curve shifts down and becomes more elastic.[6] More important, however, in determining the increases in investment in higher education associated with growth, is that the rise in income under these conditions increases the marginal benefits from higher education and the per student demand curve shifts up.[7] The inference with respect to the supply as personal incomes rise is fairly evident, but that pertaining to the demand is far from obvious and is generally neglected in examining the economics of higher education.

[6] I focus on the supply or demand curve of the per student, a composite of all students, and leave aside the increases in the number of students that occur over time.

[7] The logic and evidence on this shift will be presented shortly.

Changing Supply Curves

The supply curves, following Becker, do not reveal the cost of producing college education. They represent the marginal cost borne by students (families) in financing additional units of education. To simplify the analysis, I shall treat the distribution of personal income as a dichotomy consisting of families who are rich and those who are not rich. Thinking in terms of U.S. 1969 incomes, I shall arbitrarily classify all families who have had over a period of years a permanent income of $15,000 or more as being rich, and all of the families with less income than this as not rich.[8] I shall assume that the families who are here classified as rich have sufficient resources to finance their students and that their own capital is the cheapest source for the purpose. Moreover, the financial resources of these families would be sufficient even if college students from these families were to pay the full cost of providing the education with no scholarships, fellowships, or subsidized student loans. The characteristics of the per student supply curve of this set of families are as follows: (1) it is below that of families who are not rich, (2) it is relatively elastic, and (3) it is not segmented.

It is evident that many families who are not rich, in contrast, lack sufficient income and wealth to finance from their own resources the full cost of higher education for their children. Accordingly, they must depend, for a part of the capital required, on borrowed funds that entail relatively high transaction costs because of legal restrictions on lending funds to invest in human capital. It is for these reasons that the per student supply curve of students from families who are not rich is segmented, less elastic, and above that of students of rich families.[9]

Although the value of the time of students rises with growth, actual earnings foregone are held in check by more part-time work by students. This has occurred during recent years in the United States; such work may, however, impair a student's education (Schultz 1971, chap. 7). Thus, the dominant factors shifting the per student supply curve down and making it more elastic are: (1) the increase in the proportion of all

[8] Of full-time college students as of October 1969, one-fourth were dependents of families with $15,000 and over of family income during the preceding 12 months, while over one-half were accounted for by families with $10,000 and over of family income. For a detailed specification of concepts and characteristics of the sample, see Bureau of the Census (1971). In considering policy choices, families with incomes between $10,000 and $15,000 may be viewed as "comfortably" rich in terms of their ability to finance the education of their dependents.

[9] The increase in the value of the time of students, as earnings rise with growth, obviously increases the student's cost of acquiring a college education. Thus, even if the cost of producing a unit of education by universities and colleges were to remain constant, the total cost that the student would have to finance would rise. For many students from families who are not rich, the supply implications of the rise in earnings foregone are real and harsh.

families who become rich with growth, and (2) the rise in the personal incomes of the rest of the families that reduces their marginal cost of financing education.

Changing Demand Curves

The interactions between economic growth and the marginal benefits measured by the rate of return to students on each additional dollar of investment in higher education are complex, and they have received all too little analytical attention. The key to the analysis is in the enlargement of the capacities of potential and actual students made possible by the rise in personal incomes. In examining this process with respect to changes in demand, I again appeal to the simplified dichotomy of rich and not-rich families.

Both the students' *capacity to learn* in benefiting from college work and their *entrepreneurial capacity* in combining their own time with the services of teachers and with other resources come into play. I contend that the rise in personal incomes associated with growth results in parents making additional expenditures to enlarge these capacities in their children; as this occurs, the per student demand curve shifts up.

Presumably it is the task of geneticists, psychologists, and students of education to explain the changes and the differences among students in their capacity to learn. While it is exceedingly hard for economists to interpret their findings, it would be naïve to treat the capacity to learn as if it were identical with innate ability. To do so can only lead to a serious misspecification of the factors that account for the observed differences in the capacity of the youth of college age to learn. A convenient framework, albeit a much oversimplified one, is to treat this capacity as a product of both innate ability and acquired ability. The amount of acquired ability is obviously dependent not only upon the years of schooling, but, importantly, upon the quality of the elementary and secondary schooling. Equally, if not more, important is the preschool home environment and experience of the child; this is in no small part determined by the education of the mother. It is nevertheless true that the rate at which these acquired abilities are accumulated depends in part on the innate ability that each child inherits.

The proposition is here advanced that the *proportion* of the youth of college age who have this capacity to learn *increases* as relatively more of the members of this age group benefit from precollege investments that add to their acquired ability. At some point, however, as this process continues, the innate abilities that are required to benefit from college work will become exhausted. But it is hard to believe that we are close to this point, even though high schools have improved and most teenagers complete high school, preceded by improved elementary schooling and preschool training and experience as the schooling of mothers moves up. All things considered, my interpretation of the available evidence is that the supply of the relatively high level of innate ability distributed among the college-age population is as yet less scarce than the supply of acquired abilities that is necessary to a sufficient capacity to learn enough to warrant the investment in college work.

In supporting the above proposition, it is not necessary to assume that the distribution of innate ability of students from rich families is the same as that of students from families who are not rich. This interpretation by no means implies that all youth of college age or all who now enter college have enough innate ability to benefit from college work, measured in terms of the going rate of return, to undertake such an investment compared with alternative investment opportunities. On this score, my view of the facts is that the lack of sufficient innate ability is somewhat greater in the United States among college students from rich families than among students from families who are not rich. This difference between them is concealed, however, because students from rich families are long on acquired ability whereas those from the other set tend to be short on the necessary acquired abilities. As of October 1969, 66 percent of U.S. rich families with dependent members 18–24 years old had dependents in college full time contrasted with only 16 percent from the very poor families. Surely no one would argue that this difference of four to one implies that the genetic difference between them is equally wide. The complete classification of families by income (Bureau of the Census 1971, table 17, p. 21) is shown in table 3.

Becker, in his perceptive and cogent argument on why the demand curves for human capital are negatively inclined and not horizontal (1967, pp. 5–9), digresses to suggest that persons investing in human capital are "firms." Since entrepreneurial time is required by students

TABLE 3

CLASSIFICATION OF FAMILIES BY INCOME

Family Income	No. of Families with 18- to 24-Year-Old Dependents (in Thousands)	Families with Dependents in College Full Time (%)
Under $3,000	690	16
$3,000–$4,999	940	24
$5,000–$7,499	1,440	33
$7,500–$9,999	1,470	42
$10,000–$14,999	2,100	49
$15,000 and over	1,410	66
Not reporting	720	39
Total	8,770	42

in combining their learning time with the services of teachers and with other resources, the differences among students in their entrepreneurial capacities alter their respective demand curves. A part of the "profit" attributed to this capacity is an allocative benefit of the type presented in Part II. This particular benefit increases for the same reasons advanced earlier, namely, from both improvements in the quality and quantity of the schooling and in preschool investments, that enlarge this part of the student's entrepreneurial capacity. But the primary attribute of entrepreneurship is the capacity to cope with risk and uncertainty, and the source of it is far from settled. It is probably true, in general, that students from poor families who have managed despite all manner of difficulties to acquire a college capacity to learn possess more entrepreneurial capacity than students from rich families who have had at their disposal without stint or effort the best facilities and instruction in acquiring such a capacity to learn.

In summary, the first conclusion of Part III is that the per student supply curve that represents the financing cost of students who come from rich families is not altered by additional increases in their personal income resulting from economic growth. Their supply curve remains low, unsegmented, and relatively elastic. Since relatively more families, however, become rich, the general per student supply curve is altered to that extent. The important change in the supply curve occurs as a consequence of the rise in the personal income of families who are not rich. For this class of families the supply curve shifts down and becomes less segmented and more elastic as growth proceeds toward the arbitrary $15,000 dividing line that I have imposed. It should be noted, once again, that this analysis rests on the assumptions that social and legal institutions and policies remain constant and that the distribution of personal income does not become more unequal with growth.

The second conclusion is that the demand curve representing the marginal benefits measured by the rate of return to students on each additional dollar of investment depends on their capacity to learn and on their entrepreneurial capacity. The sources of the capacity to learn are innate abilities coupled with acquired abilities; the supply of the first component presently in our college-age population is less restrictive than the supply of the second. Here, too, the per student demand curve of dependents from rich families is not altered appreciably by additional increases in personal incomes that come to them from growth. Their demand curve remains high and relatively inelastic. Since relatively more families become rich as growth proceeds, to this extent the general per student demand curve shifts up. The larger change in the demand curve takes place, however, as a consequence of the rise in the personal incomes of families who are not rich. The per student demand curve of this class rises and probably becomes less elastic. The allocative benefits arising from the entrepreneurial capacities of students in managing their college affairs suggest a similar pattern of effects on the demand. But the sources and the consequences of the entrepreneurial capacity required to cope with risk and uncertainty are not clear.

IV. The Equity-Efficiency Quandary

Are we, because of our commitment to economics, not seeing the beauty of the higher education rainbow? Our concern about allocative efficiency and the welfare implications of the distribution of personal income serves us in choosing those issues that are amenable to our analytical skills. But this convenience does not make economics the right forum if the issues are matters of taste in appreciating beauty. It is undoubtedly true that the perplexities of higher education reach far beyond the economic calculus; higher education is an involved state of affairs that has become embodied in a large number of public and private institutions strongly rooted both socially and politically.

Although higher education has long been institutionalized in our society, there is much disagreement on the essentials of an ideal model of higher education. This lack of consensus arises primarily out of basic inconsistencies associated with the attributes that are deemed to be essential for higher education. The view that higher education should be free of any manner of government control and that public bodies should appropriate most of the funds for it is inconsistent because government cannot abdicate its responsibility in accounting for uses of public funds. The view that, ideally, the services of higher education should be free to all qualified students is inconsistent with the will and capacity of private donors and public bodies to pay the bill. The incompatibility between "free" and "scarce" is paramount in understanding this lack of agreement. It is little wonder that a major controversy is underway with regard to those goals of higher education appropriate to our democracy with its strong equalitarian values. The two goals at the center of the controversy may best be identified as "predominantly free higher education" and "optimal investment in higher education." The proponents of the first of these goals still dominate public discussions, mainly because the investment approach has emerged out of economics only fairly recently. The proponents of predominantly free higher education appeal to the political process as the means for attaining their goal—primarily to the legislatures for appropriations and secondarily to the courts for legal standards and their enforcement. They overlook the *limits* of the enforcement powers of the courts and of the taxing and spending powers of the legislatures. As these limits become increasingly evident, the optimal-investment goal gains ascendancy in this controversy. While it is clear (to economists) that this shift with respect to goals sets the stage for more allocative efficiency, it still is a matter of doubt that it also could serve to reduce the inequality in the distribution of personal incomes.

The argument for predominantly free higher education is postulated basically as a "social principle"—an established preference of society revealed by widely held and consistent social values of our people.[10] The political process is the means by which it is to be attained. Thus it is an appeal to the legislative bodies and to the courts to maintain and extend predominantly free higher education.

I shall not belabor the weakness of the foundation of the "social principle." Suffice it to say that it is built on shifting sand because our social values as they are in fact revealed by the political process are not only far from consistent but fluctuate and change over time. This argument also fails to take account of the *limits* of the judicial process in enforcing, and of the legislatures in financing, such a goal—and that is the critical reason it leads to false conclusions.

In *Brown* v. *Board of Education*, the Supreme Court in a rare unanimous decision declared that education today is perhaps the most important function of state and local governments and that success in life depends on the opportunity of an education. It said: "Such an opportunity, where the state has undertaken to provide it, is *a right which must be made available to all on equal terms.*"[11]

The lucid and cogent analysis of Kurland (1968) when applied to higher education in the United States leaves little room for doubt that "the Supreme Court is the wrong forum for providing a solution" (p. 592) to the problem of inequality in higher educational opportunities. A part of the legal argument presented by Kurland is that there are three necessary conditions for the success of any fundamental decision of the Court: The constitutional standard must be a simple one, as it is in the reapportionment cases: one man—one vote. Also the public must acquiesce. Clearly, in reapportionment, there has been an "unwillingness of any large segment of the population to do battle with it" (p. 593). The third condition is that "the judiciary have adequate control over the means of effectuating enforcement" (p. 592). In satisfying this condition, the problem of enforcement of the "one man—one vote" principle has thus far not arisen; should a case arise that applied this principle to the U.S. Senate, however, the Court would be in difficulty. Turning to equal opportunity in higher education, there is no simple standard. Universities are made to resist governmental authority, and it is inconceivable that

[10] The prestigious reports of the Carnegie Commission on Higher Education are most explicit in propounding this principle; see, for instance, Carnegie Commission (1970). The concept of equal opportunity in this connection is ever so imprecise and elusive.

[11] As cited by and with emphasis added by Kurland (1968, p. 584). Original source is 347 U.S., p. 493 (1954).

the judiciary could enforce such a fundamental decision in the area of higher education.

I take it to be obvious that the judiciary does not have the means of effectuating the enforcement of the principle, for example, that all public colleges and universities provide the *same quality* of educational services. If the courts could enforce all public colleges and universities throughout the United States to be the same in this respect, the results would be absurd. Moreover, if this principle could be enforced, students (families) who wanted higher quality could escape by retreating to private colleges and universities, and the courts would be incapable of preventing it. The powers of the courts are essentially negative, not affirmative. Kurland's quotation from Hamilton is indeed pertinent in considering the possibilities of attaining equal opportunity in higher education via the decisions of the judiciary: "The judiciary . . . has no influence over either the sword or the purse; no direction either of the strength or the wealth of society."[12] *Herein lie the limits of the judiciary.*

The legislatures hold the power of the public purse that consists of two parts: taxing power and spending power. The reports of the Carnegie Commission on Higher Education have not examined the limits of these two powers. According to the commission, it is all very simple: the state and local authorities should increase their appropriation for higher education to $7 billion by 1976–77 and the federal government should jump its contribution from $3.5 billion (1967–68) to $13 billion by 1976–77— as if there were no limits to the taxing powers of the respective legislatures. Nor is there any analysis of the effects of this financing proposal upon the control by the federal authority over the affairs of higher education. The current confusion over the sharing of federal revenue brings to the fore the problem of developing politically acceptable standards of control, along with the problem of the federal government administering, over the whole of the United States, the spending of vast federal funds in accordance with such standards. Clearly, the spending power of the government also has its limits. Since these limits arise out of the scarcity of resources, their allocation, and the uses to which they are put, economics is to this extent not the wrong forum for providing solutions for the problems here under consideration.

Returning to the quandary, surely the instructional service of higher education embodied in the student is not a public good inasmuch as a "pure public good is one for which enjoyment by one individual does not in any degree exclude the enjoyment" by others.[13] With somewhat less assurance, I would contend that a college graduate generates only a few externalities that accrue as benefits to other persons, with one major

[12] From *The Federalist*, no. 78, as cited by Kurland (1968, p. 595).
[13] See "A Geometrical Note on General Equilibrium with Public Goods" (Johnson, in press, appendix 3).

exception, namely, the important benefit the education of a woman gives her children in terms of preschool training and experience. It is internalized in the family, however. I take it to be self-evident that the differences in the quality of educational services among colleges and universities are inconsistent with the "principle" of equality of opportunity, and on practical grounds it can be argued that preferential treatment of qualified students who are in need has a priority over the equal treatment of all students. If these conditions and propositions are granted, a good deal of progress can be made in clarifying the underlying perplexities of higher education that account for the existing inequities and inefficiencies.

Higher education is not organized to bring about an optimal investment in its instructional services. The source of the difficulty is in the *financing*, *pricing*, and *supplying* of these services. The financing tends to subsidize the wrong educational activities. The pricing bears no meaningful relation to the differences in the costs of producing the services, and the suppliers of these services are, therefore, substantially sheltered from the discipline of competition, notwithstanding the large number of colleges and universities in the United States. Current endeavors to cope with the financial adversities arising out of the pause in the educational boom of the sixties are efforts to "save" the existing organization. They are not seeking solutions for the basic underlying difficulty that has become increasingly acute, especially so since World War II, as a consequence of the economic growth revealed by the doubling since 1940 of personal per capita disposal income (in 1958 prices).

The reasons for the failure to comprehend the sources of organizational difficulties confronting higher education can be put quite simply. It is obvious that most families in the United States, who have members (students) enrolled in higher education, now have the income and wealth to pay the full cost of the education. What has not been perceived clearly are the following points: (1) the allocation of public revenue (even if all of it were collected by means of progressive income taxes) to subsidize *all* publicly supported college and university instruction is bound to be socially inefficient; (2) the optimal investment in this form of human capital is basically dependent upon the micro decisions of students functioning as firms, and these are as efficient as any other large set of private firms; (3) the underpricing of the instructional services to all students in supplying them with these services thwarts the possibility of the privately efficient investment decisions of students bringing this sector of the economy into a socially efficient state; and (4) in the area of instruction, the practical function of private gifts and public funds is in financing and subsidizing, in accordance with some socially agreed-upon standards, the qualified students from low-income families (and of on-campus research).

In support of the proposition that private educational choices of college students are privately efficient, there is a growing body of evidence that shows that the private rates of return tend to be equal among educational options and comparable with the private rates of return to other private investment, that range in general between 10 and 15 percent (Becker 1964; Schultz 1971). The widely held belief of the critics of this interpretation who maintain that college-oriented students are too immature to be informed with respect to the economic value of the fields in which they might best specialize is far from valid. The short lags in their responses to changes in job opportunities for the various specialized skills leave little room for doubt that college students become informed about these opportunities and respond to them fairly promptly, as Freeman's study (1971) clearly shows. The large shifts, during the sixties, by Negro college students from specializing in teaching to preparing for business, law, and engineering careers where this option is available, as Freeman's ongoing work reveals, strongly support the responsiveness of these students to changes in job opportunities.

In citing this evidence, I am *not* implying that all of the youth of college age who have the necessary innate ability have had the opportunity in their precollege schooling to accumulate the necessary acquired ability to qualify for college, or that all who have the necessary capacity to learn at that age can finance the cost of a college education, or that those who enter college can obtain adequate information to determine fully the differences in the quality of the educational services among fields and among the institutions that provide these services.

To see more clearly the extent to which our system of higher education is socially inefficient in terms of optimal investment, it may be helpful to compare it with a hypothetical system designed to be "perfectly" inefficient socially.[14] The requirement would be free tuition, free board and room, free transportation, and a monthly payment to each student to compensate him fully for his earnings foregone, adjusted, of course, for the difference between the free board and room and the cost of living were he to take a job. On-campus living would become a way of life for students, and it would have lifetime possibilities once terminal dates were abolished and free child-care centers for the children of students were assured! Unless some social purpose were served by maintaining college

---

[14] I am prompted in suggesting this hypothetical system by the example of higher education in Turkey. Krueger (1971) informs us that in Turkey "the costs of a university education borne by the student are probably negative." Tuition charges in public universities are nominal, and there "are a host of special concessions available to students; special low fares on intracity bus transportation; subsidized lunches, and sometimes even highly subsidized housing; half-price cinema tickets, etc. Scholarships average about 50 percent of foregone income." Thus it comes as no surprise that "the disparity between the private return and the social return is remarkable. . . . While it does not pay, socially, . . . it is privately very profitable to attend college."

students in this privileged manner, the rate of return to the cost borne by society would be zero.

Compared with Turkey, higher education in the United States must be grossly antisocial! In the United States tuitions and fees charged by private instiutions have risen from $210 in 1940 to $1,030 in 1968, per student.[15] Even the cherished free-tuition banner of public institutions has become slightly tattered, for their tuitions and fees have risen from $69 to $250 per student during this period. (Four state universities, however, still charge no tuition.) Tuition and fees minus financial aid per student in 1968 averaged $850 in private and $182 in public institutions. Board and room are generally subsidized, more so at public than at private institutions, but the amount of the subsidization is a well-kept secret. But, all told, what students pay the colleges and universities is the smaller part of the direct educational costs per student (see table 1).

Although it may not be obvious, the logic of economics clearly implies that *the solution of the inefficiencies and inequities here under consideration is not in simply allocating more state and federal funds in support of higher education, even if all such funds were collected by highly progressive taxation.*[16] The problem to be solved is in the choice of educational activities that are to be subsidized by such funds. For example, since university research that is primarily "basic" in character is indeed a public good, it must be subsidized if it is to be undertaken. In supporting needy students, subsidies are required.[17] But, to be allocatively efficient, such subsidization must go directly to the students and not into the funds of colleges and universities, leaving it to them to distribute the financial aid to students by all manner of standards. Until those educational activities that require subsidization are identified and the amounts required deter-

---

[15] Not all private institutions charge anywhere near this much. At Berea College, for example, there are upper income limits on the admission of students and there are no tuition charges. Income limits start at $4,000 for a family with one child and go up to $8,500 for a family with seven children, with two exceptions: children of the Berea faculty and from families in the town of Berea (population, 6,000) also may attend tuition-free. The income levels of parents of Berea students are: less than $4,000 for 36 percent of the students; between $4,000 and $6,000, 31 percent; $6,000–$8,000, 19 percent; and between $8,000 and $10,000, 10 percent. This accounts for 96 percent of enrollment. Thus Berea's enrollment is concentrated at the lower tail of the income distribution, whereas higher education is, in general, heavily weighted toward the middle and upper range of family incomes.

[16] Surely economists would agree that the economic inefficiencies and gross inequities associated with the several billion dollars of federal funds allocated annually to U.S. farmers cannot be remedied by increasing the progressivity of federal taxation. The same logic applies here to higher education.

[17] The point was made repeatedly in the discussions of these COBRE papers that the subsidization of needy qualified college students would in principle discriminate on equity grounds against those who could not qualify as college students. Thus, to treat all such youth equally, what is called for would be a subsidy to every youth from a low-income family, comparable in amount with that provided to the needy college student.

mined, to simply proceed in allocating even more funds to subsidize *all* students is not only socially inefficient but grossly inequitable.

One of the necessary conditions in developing a socially efficient system of higher education is full-cost pricing of each of the different classes of instructional services, modified (reduced) in the amount of known social benefits if, and only if, the social benefits are ascertainable and worthwhile in terms of the going rate of return to alternative investment opportunities (Hansen and Weisbrod 1971).

Yet, for all manner of reasons, it is widely held that the economic logic of full-cost pricing, as modified above, is impractical, unrealistic, and contrary to all historical experience. It is deemed to be wrong by the proponents of predominantly free higher education. It is viewed with suspicion by the rank and file of faculty, by college and university administrators, and probably by many legislators. The students' self-serving interests (however rich the students may be) in demanding that everything they want be free is understandable, if they do not see that this would be at the expense of other persons in society.

It may be true that virtually all colleges and universities have always been subsidized and that there may have been good and sufficient reasons for institutionalization of this traditional practice. But it is also true that institutions that perform economic functions, as I have attempted to show in "Institutions and the Rising Economic Value of Man," become obsolete (Schultz 1971, chap. 13). Higher education clearly is not an exception. Another strongly held view is that it is impossible to determine the real costs of each of the many classes of the services (educational) that students receive from the university. It is true that the economic accounting within a university is not designed for this purpose. But it is no more impossible than it is for firms that are producing a complex set of different products, many of which are joint products of many different production activities within such firms. *Necessity imposed by competition makes it possible.*

There is then the argument that full-cost pricing of the instructional services would reduce the supply of college graduates far below the demand for persons with these particular high skills. Recent graduates who specialized in the sciences may now be entertaining the thought that the supply is all too large, but these ex post thoughts in view of the present depressed market for these particular skills have no bearing on the argument. The full-cost implications of the direct educational expenditures per student in 1968 (assume that students from rich families paid it) are that average tuition and fees per student would be increased from $490 to $1,820 (see table 1). When earnings foregone are taken into account, it would increase the cost to these students about two-fifths. Meanwhile, the approach taken here is that more students from low-income families would be subsidized. Even so, the supply of particular skills may be reduced sufficiently to bring the intercept up along the demand curve where the returns to the investment would again assure the going rate of return to alternative investment opportunities. The adjustments would take place with a relatively short lag in view of the known responsiveness of students to changes in the economic value of these forms of human capital.

As a last resort, there is always the argument that the social benefits of higher education are not only ever present, but that they are large and all-pervasive, both in bringing about gains in productivity from which the noncollege population benefits and in improving the quality of life. Although these claims have been with us for ever so long, they continue, with the exception of benefits to children from a mother's education, to remain unsubstantiated. They have the ring of special pleading for more funds to maintain the existing system of higher education. The exception noted is not among those social benefits commonly cited. It has been advanced only recently as a result of the extension of economic theory to analyze the microeconomics of the household. Even this important "social" benefit accures in large part to the parents in terms of satisfactions. Moreover, and to repeat, most families have sufficient income and wealth to pay for this particular value added to the female members of their families. But the existence of this class of "social" benefits argues for the subsidization of needy students, whether they are males or females.

Conclusion

My analysis implies that the rise in personal incomes associated with economic growth, which has doubled real personal incomes in the United States since 1940, makes the traditional financing, pricing, and supplying of the instructional services of higher education ever more obsolete. The general conclusion is that the instructional part, especially undergraduate instruction, has become increasingly less efficient socially, and that an inordinate part of the subsidies to higher education is used to provide these educational services below cost to students from families who have the income and wealth to pay the full cost. Thus, in providing instruction, higher education is in general both socially inefficient and inequitable.

I am aware that my analysis at a number of points rests on evidence that is still fragmentary. A critical point throughout the analysis is the interpretation of the evidence at hand that college students are privately fairly efficient in investing in themselves. Then, too, if the personal distribution of income, as per capita income has risen, has become in fact more unequal, it would undermine a part of my argument. If colleges and universities were allocating a substantial, and an increasing, part of the funds they receive from public and private sources to provide college instruction in subsidizing needy students, it would impair my conclusions with respect to social inequities. If the supply curves—the capacity of students to finance the cost of their education—were becoming more segmented, less elastic, and were moving upward over time, despite the rise in personal incomes, it would weaken my argument appreciably. Similarly, if the demand curves—the capacity of students to benefit sufficiently from the education to warrant the investment—were not moving upward as personal incomes rose, the argument would lose some of its strength. Although the allocative benefits associated with education imply that there are gains from them that are transferred to consumers, I have not treated these particular gains as social benefits because, in the process of adjusting to the dynamics of a growing economy, less educated persons may become less well-off in competing with more educated persons. If this were not true, there would be a part of these allocative benefits that should be treated as one of the social benefits of education. My argument rests squarely on the concept that students behave as economic firms. The validity of the underlying assumption of this concept implies a hypothesis that awaits more complete testing.

Appendix

Table 1 Data Sources and Bases of Calculations

Data for 1940 are for the continental United States only; those for 1968 are for the "aggregate U.S." (fifty states, District of Columbia, Canal Zone, Guam, Puerto Rico, and the Virgin Islands). They are for the school years ending in 1940 and 1968. Totals may not add due to rounding.

  a) *Number of institutions.*—1940 (cols. 1, 4, and 7): U.S. Office of Education (1947, vol. 2, chap. 1, table 2, p. 3). 1968 (cols. 2, 5, and 8): U.S. Office of Education (1970, table 9, p. 7).

  b) *Enrollment (opening fall).*—1940 (cols. 1, 4, and 7): resident degree-credit enrollment; Bureau of the Census (1970, table 146, p. 104). 1968 (cols. 2, 5, and 8): degree-credit enrollment includes both resident and extension students; it is available for the United States (fifty states and District of Columbia) in U.S. Office of Education (1970b, table 6, p. 23). For total enrollment (United States and outlying areas), see U.S. Office of Education (1970a, table 84, p. 65). Degree-credit enrollment for aggregate United States is estimated by applying the U.S. degree credit/total enrollment ratio to total enrollment in outlying areas (see table A1).

  c) *Direct total instruction costs.*—Calculated as $(d) + (e)$.

  d) *Net instruction expenditures.*—These are educational and general costs, excluding extensions and public service, other sponsored activities, and 50 percent of organized research. 1940 (cols. 1, 4, and 7): source is U.S. Office of Education (1947, vol. 2, chap. 4, table 16, p. 90). 1968 (cols. 2, 5, and 8): from U.S. Office of Education (1970a, table 129, p. 96).

  e) *Implicit interest and depreciation.*—Calculated as 8 percent of value of physical property, multiplied by ratio of net instruction expenditures to sum of

TABLE A1

	ENROLLMENT (IN THOUSANDS)		
	Total	Public	Private
1. U.S. degree credit	6,390	4,350	2,040
2. U.S. total	6,910	4,820	2,100
3. Degree credit/total ratio (= col. 1 ÷ col. 2)	0.9	0.9	0.9
4. Outlying areas, total	52	34	18
5. Outlying areas, degree credit (= col. 4 × col. 3)	48	31	18
6. Aggregate U.S. degree credit (= col. 1 + col. 5)	6,960	4,850	2,110

educational and general expenditures and expenditures on auxiliary enterprises (see table A2).

f) Tuition and fees.—1940 (cols. 1, 4, and 7): U.S. Office of Education (1947, vol. 2, chap. 4, table 13, p. 68). 1968 (cols. 2, 5, and 8): U.S. Office of Education (1970a, table 126, p. 5).

g) Student aid expenditures.—1940 (cols. 1, 4, and 7): data are for "other noneducational activities" (U.S. Office of Education 1947, vol. 2, chap. 4, table 16, p. 90). The same figures are given as "Scholarships, Fellowships and Prizes" in Bureau of the Census (1970, table 191, p. 127). 1968 (cols. 2, 5, and 8): U.S. Office of Education (1970a, table 129, p. 96).

h) Enrollment per institution.—Calculated as $(b) \div (a)$.

i) Per student direct total instruction costs.—Calculated as $(c) \div (b)$.

j) Per student net instruction expenditures.—Calculated as $(d) \div (b)$.

k) Per student interest and depreciation.—Calculated as $(e) \div (b)$.

l) Per student tuition and fees.—Calculated as $(f) \div (b)$.

m) Per student financial aid.—Calculated as $(g) \div (b)$.

TABLE A2

	TOTAL		PUBLIC		PRIVATE	
	1940	1968	1940	1968	1940	1968
1. Value ($ million)	2,750	34,590	1,260	21,180	1,490	13,410
2. 8 percent of col. 1	220	2,770	100	1,690	120	1,070
3. Ratio of net instruction expenditures to those for educational and general and auxiliary enterprises	0.7	0.7	0.8	0.7	0.7	0.7
4. Implicit interest and depreciation chargeable to instruction (= col. 2 × col. 3)	160	1,920	71	1,190	90	730

SOURCE.—1940: U.S. Office of Education (1947, vol. 2, chap. 4, table 17, p. 92). 1968: U.S. Office of Education (1970a, table 133, p. 99).

References

Beales, A. C. F.; Blaug, Mark; Veale, Sir Douglas; and West, E. G. *Education: A Framework for Choice.* London: Inst. Econ. Affairs, 1967.

Becker, Gary S. *Human Capital: A Theoretical and Empirical Analysis with Special Reference to Education.* New York: Nat. Bur. Econ. Res., 1964.

————. *Human Capital and the Personal Distribution of Income: An Analytical Approach.* W. S. Woytinsky Lecture no. 1. Ann Arbor: Inst. Public Admin., Univ. Mich., 1967.

Bureau of the Census. *Statistical Abstract of the United States.* Washington: Government Printing Office, 1969, 1970.

————. *Current Population Reports.* Special Studies, Series P-23, no. 34. Washington: Government Printing Office, February 1, 1971.

Carnegie Commission on Higher Education. *Quality and Equality: New Levels of Federal Responsibility for Higher Education.* New York: McGraw-Hill, 1968.

————. *A Chance to Learn: An Action Agenda for Equal Opportunity in Higher Education.* New York: McGraw-Hill, 1970.

Chaudhri, D. P. "Education and Agricultural Productivity in India." Ph.D. dissertation, Univ. Delhi, 1968.

————. "Farmers' Education and Productivity: Some Empirical Results from Indian Agriculture." Investment in Human Capital Paper no. 69:4. Mimeographed. Chicago: Univ. Chicago, 1969.

Chiswick, Barry R. "Human Capital and the Personal Income Distribution by Regions." Ph.D. dissertation, Columbia Univ., 1967.

————. "Earnings Inequality and Economic Development." *Q.J.E.* 85 (February 1971): 21–39.

Freeman, Richard B. *The Market for College-Trained Manpower: A Study in the Economics of Career Choice.* Cambridge, Mass.: Harvard Univ. Press, 1971.

Hansen, W. Lee, and Weisbrod, Burton A. "A New Approach to Higher Education Finance." In *Financing Higher Education: Alternatives for the Federal Government,* edited by M. D. Orwig, pp. 117–42. Iowa City: American Coll. Testing Program, 1971.

Johnson, Harry G. *The Two-Sector Model of General Equilibrium.* London: Allen & Unwin, in press.

Kothari, V. N. "Disparities in Relative Earnings among Different Countries." *Econ. J.* 80 (September 1970): 605–16.

Krueger, A. O. "Factor Endowments and per Capita Income Differences among Countries." *Econ. J.* 78 (September 1968): 641–59.

————. "Rates of Return to Turkish Higher Education." Mimeographed. Minneapolis: Univ. Minn., 1971.

Kurland, Philip B. "Equal Educational Opportunity: The Limits of Constitutional Jurisprudence Undefined." *Univ. Chicago Law Rev.* 35 (Summer 1968): 583–600.

Kuznets, Simon. "Economic Growth and Income Inequality." *A.E.R.* 45 (March 1955): 1–28.

————. "Quantitative Aspects of the Economic Growth of Nations. VIII. Distribution of Income by Size." *Econ. Development and Cultural Change,* vol. 11, pt. 2 (January 1963).

————. *Modern Economic Growth.* New Haven, Conn.: Yale Univ. Press, 1966.

Michael, Robert T. "Effects of Education on Efficiency in Consumption." Ph.D. dissertation, Columbia Univ., 1969.

Mincer, Jacob. "Investment in Human Capital and Personal Income Distribution." *J.P.E.* 66 (August 1958): 281–302.

———. "The Distribution of Labor Incomes: A Survey with Special Reference to the Human Capital Approach." *J. Econ. Literature* 8 (March .1970): 1–26.

———. "Schooling, Age, and Earnings." In *Human Capital and Personal Income Distribution.* New York: Nat. Bur. Econ. Res., in press.

O'Neill, June. "The Effects of Income and Education on Interregional Migration." Ph.D. dissertation, Columbia Univ., 1969.

Razin, Assaf. "Investment in Human Capital and Economic Growth: A Theoretical Study." Ph.D. dissertation, Univ. Chicago, 1969.

Schultz, Theodore W. *Investment in Human Capital: The Role of Education and of Research.* New York: Free Press, 1971.

Schwartz, Aba. "Migration and Lifetime Earnings in the U.S." Ph.D. dissertation, Univ. Chicago, 1968.

U.S. Office of Education. *Biennial Survey of Education in the United States, 1938–40.* Washington: Government Printing Office, 1947.

———. *Digest of Educational Statistics, 1970.* Washington: Government Printing Office, 1970. (*a*)

———. *Projections of Educational Statistics to 1978–79.* Washington: Government Printing Office, 1970. (*b*)

Welch, Finis. "Education in Production." *J.P.E.* 78 (January/February 1970): 35–59.

West, E. G. "Private versus Public Education." *J.P.E.* 72 (October 1964): 465–75.

Comment

Anne O. Krueger

University of Minnesota

I can only agree with T. W. Schlutz's positive analysis of higher education: there are undoubtedly large social inefficiencies in the present pattern of financing higher education, and that pattern is surely inequitable. In terms of positive analysis, there is one additional ground for arguing that the present system is inefficient: given taxpayer financing of the state universities and the degree of monopoly power that in-state tuition charges give individual institutions, it is doubtful whether universities have significant incentives to minimize cost. Despite the large number of colleges and universities, it is not obvious that competitive forces are strong enough to induce competitive efficiency among institutions.

That consideration only adds force to Schultz's argument that traditional financing patterns are outmoded. The real question, therefore, is what alterations ought to be made in the system. Evaluation of policy alternatives must start with two fundamental questions: First, what are the governmental goals for which education is an instrument? Second, what are the constraints upon "first-best" optimization in terms of the policy choices?

There are two distinct considerations which suggest that Schultz's policy conclusions—let the rich self-finance and subsidize the education of the poor—can be challenged. First and most important, while it is obvious that there can be no defense of the present inequitable financing pattern, that does not imply that public educational policy should be the instrument for achieving society's equity goals. A negative income tax is a far superior instrument for that purpose. Second, since those among the "poor" who do go on to higher education will receive the benefits of that education, why should they be subsidized at the expense of the children of the poor who do not attend college? There is a fundamental issue of the unit of equity: Is it the present value of the lifetime income of the college attender, or is it the family income of the student? Of course, the imperfection of the capital market requires *some* government intervention, but the logic of a "first-best" efficient solution—and of the equity argument—suggests that a student loan program is more likely than a subsidy scheme to be efficient *and* equitable.

As to a "first-best" optimum and the constraints upon attaining it, it is clear that investment in human capital should be made to the point where the rate of return to that investment is equated with rates of return available to other types of investments. Since human capital is not a salable asset, the loan market is imperfect because of either the unenforceability of loan-repayment contracts or the high cost of enforcing them. A "first-best" solution would involve government intervention in the form of removing the imperfection from the loan market. Then, accepting Schultz's argument that students are privately efficient in their education choices, students would be able to maximize the present value of their future net earnings stream and to select their preferred lifetime consumption stream by appropriate choice of the amount of borrowing. Such a solution, of course, implies that some students would borrow in excess of the amount of their direct costs of college education.

Schultz's argument—that the rich can self-finance—essentially implies that the rich have enough net wealth, or are saving sufficiently, so that their budget constraint already enables them to attain a "first-best" optimum. If that is empirically correct, a general student loan program, at rates of interest equal to those attainable on other assets, would not be utilized by the rich.

The essential issue, therefore, is how the capital market can be improved so that those whose self-financing abilities are insufficient to attain a "first-

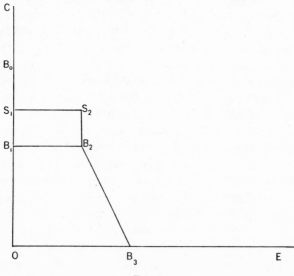

Fig. 1

best" optimum can be enabled to do so.[1] A subsidy scheme for the "poor" can be analyzed with the aid of figure 1. On the horizontal axis is the amount of higher education (E) purchased. The amount of all other goods consumed (C) is on the vertical axis. In the absence of either subsidies or a loan program, the budget constraint of a "poor" student can be represented by the point B_0 and the line B_2B_3. The point B_0 represents attainable consumption if the student does not buy any higher education and enters the labor force. The vertical distance B_0B_1 represents the foregone income and direct costs of attaining higher education in the amount B_1B_2. Clearly, it is likely that many poor students will choose points such as B_0, although some will choose B_2 and points on the line segment B_2B_3.

Now, a subsidy in the amount of direct costs of college education will shift the horizontal portion of the budget constraint upward—for example, to the new budget line $B_0S_1S_2B_2B_3$, where the amount of the subsidy is B_1S_1. It is evident that such a subsidy might influence some to move from a choice such as B_0 to S_2. However, the presence of a subsidy does not guarantee an optimal solution: some may be unwilling to accept the low present consumption implied by the loss of foregone income, while others may accept the subsidy although the rate of return is below market alternatives. Yet, on a subsidy basis, Schultz himself has pointed out the folly of largely or completely providing subsidies to offset foregone income.

A loan program, by contrast, would enable poor students to undertake higher education and to choose their preferred lifetime consumption path, without the distortions shown in figure 1. Insofar as poor students attending college are increasing the present value of their lifetime earnings, their budget constraint between present and future income will shift outward, which is Pareto superior. In principle, then, a loan program would enable more present and more future income, a possibility not attainable with a subsidy program.

The question remains only as to whether loans should be at subsidized or at market-alternative rates of interest. If loans are at subsidized rates, the "rich" would avail themselves of them—which is inequitable—or else a means test would have to be imposed. Moreover, the subsidy component of the loan would only accrue to those buying education, thus discriminating against other "poor," and would be a subsidy equivalent, as in figure 1.

I conclude, therefore, that Schultz's own argument suggests the logic of a loan scheme on efficiency and equity grounds, and that subsidies to the poor should be independent of their college attendance.

---

[1] Since secondary education is publicly financed, there would be a distortion between perceived private rates and social rates of return to investments in secondary education and in college education. I have ignored this throughout, on the grounds that the magnitude of that distortion is likely to be small empirically.

Time-Series Changes in Personal Income Inequality in the United States from 1939, with Projections to 1985

Barry R. Chiswick

City University of New York and National Bureau of Economic Research

Jacob Mincer

Columbia University and National Bureau of Economic Research

Data on the distribution of personal income of adult males in the United States indicate that relative inequality declined between 1939 and the early postwar years but has subsequently remained almost unchanged.[1] In contrast, average real income grew substantially during the same period. Although these data have been subject to investigation, we still lack a unified theory to explain the pattern of change or stability in time-series income inequality. The absence of a theoretical structure also may have inhibited the prediction of inequality into the future.[2]

Some insights into the theoretical structure of income inequality over time may be obtained through what has been called the human-capital approach (Mincer 1970). While theoretical and empirical investigations of the relation between human capital and income distribution have been limited to cross-sectional analyses, there is nothing inherent in the analy-

The research reported here is part of a continuing study of income distribution conducted by the National Bureau of Economic Research. It has not undergone NBER review. The skillful research assistance of Sara Paroush and Susan Crayne is greatly appreciated.

[1] The increasing importance of females and students in the labor force whose employment is more intermittent creates upward trends in the personal inequality of annual income for the total labor force, though not in wage rates (Schultz 1971) nor in the annual incomes of families (Metcalf 1969). See also Miller (1966, pp. 15–28), Lydall (1968, pp. 176–79), and Schultz (1969, p. 98).

[2] One exception is Soltow, who used 1956 as a base to predict inequality in 1970 and 1980 by assuming an unchanged income-concentration ratio between classes and within classes; he used projected schooling and age distributions to obtain class weights (1960, pp. 450–53).

sis to prohibit its application to a time-series study. In this study, we employ the human-capital earnings function to analyze changes in male income inequality over time in the United States. Though less appropriate, the empirical analysis is for income rather than earnings, in the absence of annual data on earnings distributions.

Due to the paucity of data for earlier years, most of the empirical analysis focuses on the past two decades. We have, however, extrapolated backward to 1939 and forward to 1985. Our predicted inequality for 1939 can be compared with the actual inequality.

In Part I, an earnings function is generated which relates personal earnings to human capital and employment variables. By taking the variance of the earnings function, relative inequality becomes a function of the variances, levels, and intercorrelations among the human-capital and employment variables.

In Part II, we decompose the earnings-inequality function to ascertain the effects of changes in the explanatory variables on the income inequality of males. Postwar changes in the explanatory variables are examined and we find that their relative stability did not allow for significant changes in inequality.

In Part III, we utilize the relative earnings function to predict the income inequality for each year from 1949 to 1969. When the predicted and actual values are compared, the model is found to have substantial explanatory power.

In Part IV, we compare the actual and predicted differences in earnings inequality from 1939 to 1965 and find that the depression in 1939 is in large part responsible for the greater inequality of earnings during that year. United States Department of Commerce projections of schooling and age distributions for 1985 are used to predict the difference in income inequality between 1965 and 1985. For 25- to 64-year-old males, no change is foreseen, but for males 35 to 44 years old, we may anticipate a small decline in income inequality.

I. The Earnings Function

The relation between gross earnings[3] and investment in human capital for the ith person in year j can be written as

$$E_{ji} = E_{oi} + \sum_{t=1}^{j-1} r_{ti}C_{ti},\qquad(1)$$

where the gross earnings (E_{ji}) are a function of the "original" endow-

[3] Gross earnings are earnings before the costs of contemporaneous investments in training are subtracted. Investments, of course, are net of depreciation. Part I relies heavily on Mincer (1972).

ment (E_{oi}) and the sum of the returns on previous investments (C_{ti}), r_{ti} being the average rate of return to the investment in the tth year. In this expression, earnings are a linear function of dollars of investment.

An alternative specification of the relation between gross earnings and investment can be obtained by expressing C_{ti} as a fraction of E_{ti} (that is, $C_{ti} = k_{ti}E_{ti}$). If the original endowment is assumed constant across years and individuals (E_0), we can write[4]

$$E_{ji} = E_o + \sum_{t=1}^{j-1} r_{ti}k_{ti}E_{ti} = E_o \prod_{t=1}^{j-1} (1 + r_{ti}k_{ti}). \qquad (2)$$

By taking the natural log of both sides of equation (2), since r_tk_t is small, we obtain (approximately)

$$\ln (E_{ji}) = \ln E_o + \sum_{t=1}^{j-1} r_{ti}k_{ti}. \qquad (3)$$

For the purpose of this analysis, equation (3) is superior to equation (1) as the basic earnings function. First, there appears to be more interest in changes in the relative rather than in the absolute inequality of earnings, and equation (3) is better suited to an investigation of relative inequality. Second, the available data sources permit us to measure investment in human capital by years of schooling and years of labor-market experience rather than in terms of dollar investment, and equation (3) is more easily converted into a years-of-training formulation. Finally, if earnings are more closely approximated by a log-normal than a normal distribution, the structure in equation (3) will have residuals which are more homoscedastic than the structure in equation (1).

The number of periods of investment in training ($j - 1$) can be decomposed into S years of schooling and $j - S - 1$ years of labor-market experience. By assuming that an individual invests in experience each year after leaving school, experience is measured as age minus schooling minus 5 ($T = A - S - 5$). Due to data limitations, an additional approximation is that the direct costs of formal schooling are equal to the

---

[4] For the ith person,

$$E_j = E_o + \sum_{t=1}^{j-1} r_tC_t = E_o + \sum_{t=1}^{j-1} r_tk_tE_t,$$

for $j = 1$, $E_1 = E_o$. For $j = 2$, $E_2 = E_o (1 + r_1k_1)$. For $j = 3$,

$$E_3 = E_o + r_1k_1E_1 + r_2k_2E_2,$$

$$E_3 = E_o(1 + r_1k_1)(1 + r_2k_2),$$

and so on.

actual earnings of students at that level. This means we can write $k_{ji} = 1$ for the schooling years.

Equation (3) implicitly assumes full-year employment. If E^* is weekly earnings, annual earnings are $E_i = E_i^* (W_i)^\gamma$, where W_i is the number of weeks worked and γ is the elasticity of earnings with respect to weeks worked. Empirically, γ is greater than unity,[5] which implies that average weekly wages are higher for those who work more weeks per year. We assumed constant γ across individuals. We included W_i in the earnings function not merely as a standardizing variable; the theory of human capital predicts greater stability of employment for workers whose investments are firm specific. Thus, both the time variation in W and the fact that $\gamma > 1$ are, in part,[6] reflections of human-capital investments.

When these modifications of the human-capital earnings function are incorporated into equation (3), we obtain

$$\ln E_{ji} = \ln E_o + r_i S_i + \sum_{t=s+1}^{j-1} r_{ti} k_{ti} + \gamma(\ln W_i). \qquad (4)$$

To evaluate the expression $r_t k_t$, we must make some assumption concerning the temporal behavior of k_t, the fraction of gross earnings invested, and r_t, the rate of return on the investment in the tth period. We assume the latter is constant, $r_{ti} = r_i^*$. There are several reasons to believe that k_t declines over time (Becker 1967; Ben-Porath 1967). First, if additional experience increases the productivity of time devoted to employment more than that devoted to the production of additional experience, the opportunity cost of time invested in experience rises with additional experience. This decreases the profitability of additional investment. Second, additional experience reduces the length of the remaining working life. Finally, if an investment is profitable, it is more profitable (highest net present value) the earlier it is undertaken. For simplicity, then, we assume that k_t declines linearly with respect to time. Therefore, $\Sigma_t r^* k_t$ is a parabolic function of the number of years of experience (T).[7] Its maximum is reached at T^*, when $k_t = 0$.

Available data sources document earnings net of the opportunity cost

[5] Mincer (1972, Pt. II) found $\gamma = 1.2$ for white nonfarm males with earnings who were not enrolled in school in 1959.

[6] Additional possible factors are: a rising supply curve of labor, and a positive correlation between hours worked per week and weeks worked per year (see Fuchs 1967, p. 4).

[7] If $k_{ti} = k_o [1 - (Ti/T^*)]$ for $j \geq S + 1$, where T^* is the number of years of positive net postschool investment, converting to continuous time,

$$\int_0^{T_i} r_i^* k_{ti} dT = r_i^* k_o T_i - \frac{r_i^* k_o}{2T^*} T_i^2.$$

of training (Y_j) rather than gross earnings (E_j). By definition, $Y_j = E_j$ $(1 - k_j)$ or $\ln Y_j = \ln E_j + \ln (1 - k_j)$. Evaluating $\ln (1 - k_j)$ by using a Taylor expansion around T^* taken to the third term, $\ln (1 - k_j) = -k_o [1 + (k_o/2)] + (k_o/T^*) (1 + k_o) T + (-k_o^2/2T^{*2}) T^2$. Incorporating the net-earnings relation and the linear decline in the experience term into equation (4) results in

$$\ln Y_{ji} = \left[\ln E_o - k_o \left(1 + \frac{k_o}{2} \right) \right] + r_i S_i + \left[r_i^* k_o + \frac{k_o}{T^*} (1 + k_o) \right] T_i$$

$$- \left(\frac{r_i k_o T^* + k_o^2}{2(T^*)^2} \right) T_i^2 + \gamma \ln (W_i) + U_i, \quad (5)$$

where U_i is a residual. Data are available for an individual's net earnings, years of schooling, age, and weeks worked, but not for the coefficients of the explanatory variables. The equation, however, quite powerfully explains differences in earnings. When the log of earnings is regressed on S_i, T_i, T_i^2, and $\ln W_i$ for white nonfarm males from the 1960 U.S. census 1/1,000 sample, the coefficient of determination is over 50 percent (Mincer 1972, Pt. II). Such high explanatory power is rather exceptional in microdata analyses.

Further simplifications or assumptions are made before calculating the variance of both sides of the earnings equation. First, the squared experience term is deleted. Its inclusion would be computationally cumbersome (requiring third and fourth moments of experience), while the addition to explanatory power is not likely to be large. The deletion of the squared experience term, however, biases downward the slope coefficient of experience. For example, if the age distribution of the population under study is more or less uniform, the slope of the experience term is cut in half, to approximately $(r^* k_o)/2$.

Second, note that the experience variable is simply age minus schooling minus 5. Public policy can change the distribution of schooling independent of age, but if it does so, the distribution of experience is necessarily altered. There also is more concern with the distribution of earnings by age group than by experience group. Thus, it would be desirable to express earnings as a function of schooling and age. Fortunately, this is easy to do.

Finally, it will be assumed that across individuals the coefficients of schooling and experience in equation (5) are random variables independent of S and T. This assumption is not as strange as it might at first seem. Thinking in terms of the model for the supply and demand for funds for investment in human capital developed by Becker (1967), those with greater "training ability" have, for a given cost-of-funds schedule, a higher average and marginal rate of return, and thus tend to invest more. Those with higher levels of wealth, holding "training ability" constant, invest more but have a lower average and marginal rate of return. Greater wealth and greater "ability" are positively correlated, resulting in an ambiguous a priori relation between level of investment and marginal and average rates of return. Empirical evidence for this ambiguity is the absence of a significant slope coefficient for the quadratic term when the log of earnings is regressed on schooling, schooling squared, and the log of weeks worked (Mincer 1972, Pt. II).

Using these modifications, equation (5) becomes

$$\ln Y_i = x + r_i S_i + r'_i (A_i - S_i - 5) + \gamma (\ln W_i) + U_i, \qquad (6)$$

where r'_i is the coefficient of experience and x is the constant intercept.

The residual, U_i, reflects individual differences in earnings for given levels of schooling, age, and employment. It includes the effects of discrimination, differences in the nonpecuniary aspects of jobs, nonlabor income (if this is included in the income concept), and errors of measurement. For simplicity, we assume that the residual is a random variable.

By taking the variance of both sides of equation (6), we can express relative-income inequality as a function of schooling, age, employment, and rate-of-return parameters. The assumption that the rate of return to schooling is a random variable independent of the level of schooling and a similar assumption for experience simplify the algebra.[8] It is also assumed that r_i and r'_i are uncorrelated. Then:

$$
\begin{aligned}
\sigma^2 (\ln Y) = \ &[(\bar{r} - \bar{r}')^2 + \sigma^2 (r) + \sigma^2 (r')] \, \sigma^2 (S) \\
&+ [(\bar{r}')^2 + \sigma^2 (r')] \, \sigma^2 (A) + \gamma^2 \sigma^2 (\ln W) \\
&+ [\overline{2r'}(\bar{r} - \bar{r}') - \sigma^2 (r')] \, R_{as} \, \sigma (A) \, \sigma(S) \\
&+ [2\gamma \, (\bar{r} - \bar{r}')] \, R_{sw} \, \sigma (S) \, \sigma (\ln W) \qquad (7) \\
&+ (2\overline{\gamma r'}) \, R_{aw} \, \sigma (A) \, \sigma (\ln W) \\
&+ \sigma^2 (r) \, \overline{S^2} + \sigma^2 (r') \, (\overline{A} - \overline{S} - 5)^2 + \sigma^2 (U).
\end{aligned}
$$

The relative variance of earnings is now expressed as a function of the variances and correlations among schooling, age and the log of weeks worked, and the levels of schooling and age. An interesting feature of the model is that relative-earnings inequality is a function of the relative inequality in weeks worked. Previous time-series studies of earnings inequality included the unemployment rate as an explanatory variable (Metcalf 1969; Schultz 1969). For the United States, the unemployment

[8] If X and Y are independent random variables, $\mathrm{var}(XY) = \overline{X}^2 \, \mathrm{var} \, (Y) + \overline{Y}^2 \, \mathrm{var}(X) + \mathrm{var}(X) \, \mathrm{var}(Y)$ (see Goodman 1960).

rate is highly correlated with the inequality of weeks worked over the busines cycle but is weakly correlated across states at a moment in time (Hashimoto 1971). Inequality of weeks worked, $\sigma^2(\ln W)$, is the appropriate variable to use in the analysis of income inequality. In analyses of interstate differences in income inequality, Aigner and Heins (1967) used the unemployment rate and found it insignificant, while Chiswick (1972) found $\sigma^2(\ln W)$ to have a significant positive effect. The unemployment rate is a substitute ("proxy") for $\sigma^2(\ln W)$ over the business cycle only because $\sigma^2(\ln W)$ widens when demand for labor declines; employment declines relatively more at lower skill (hence wage) levels. This is a consequence of specific human-capital investment.[9]

The intercorrelations have economic meaning. A negative correlation between age and schooling reflects a secular trend in schooling.[10] Upward secular trends in schooling have a narrowing effect on earnings inequality. This is because the young, whose few prior but relatively large contemporaneous investments would tend to lower their net earnings, also have greater than average schooling, which tends to raise their earnings. Inequality decreases when the trend in schooling increases, that is, when R_{as} becomes more negative.

Nonzero correlations of weeks worked with schooling and age, respectively, can be explained by both supply of labor and demand for labor factors. On the demand side, increased investments in specific training with higher levels of schooling and age, until older ages, diminish the firm's incentive to lay off such workers, and thereby increase the number of weeks worked. On the supply side, investments specific to the firm

[9] If employment declined at the same rate for all grades of labor on a cyclical downswing, unemployment would increase, but $\sigma^2(\ln W)$ would remain fixed. It is the systematically greater declines at lower skill (wage) levels which cause $\sigma^2(\ln W)$ to move in the same direction as unemployment. Note also that more than proportionate declines in employment rates at lower levels are entirely consistent with proportionate declines in unemployment rates, as the table below shows.

	PEAK		TROUGH	
SKILL	U	E	U	E
High	2	98	4	96
Middle	4	96	8	92
Low	6	94	12	88

Here U is the unemployment rate (in percentage points) and $E = (1 - U)$ is the employment rate.

[10] For males 25–64 in 1965, the correlation was $R = -0.22$. Lower mortality and higher migration rates for persons with more schooling affect the correlation but are not important for the United States as a whole during the period under study.

(for example, training and nonvested pension funds) also increase with schooling and age, again until older ages, thereby lowering quit rates. In addition, those with higher opportunity costs of time have an incentive to economize on search time, and therefore tend to work more weeks per year. One factor generating lower levels of weeks worked by the young may be a higher turnover rate due to their searching for information about the nature of jobs. When older males are included, the correlation between age and weeks worked declines.[11]

II. Decomposition Analysis

The income-inequality function is now decomposed into parts attributable to the human-capital and employment variables.[12] The contribution of schooling, age, and employment to inequality is identified. Effects of changes in the explanatory variables are examined to indicate future sources of change in inequality. The data are for civilian labor-force males age 25 to 64 years.

Let us first look at a simplified version of equation (7), one in which the rate of return to schooling (r_i) and the experience coefficient (r_i') are assumed to be constant for all individuals rather than random variables. The coefficients $\bar{r}$, $\bar{r}'$, and γ were computed by a regression analysis on individual data of the log of earnings on schooling, experience, experience squared, and the log of weeks worked, yielding values of $\bar{r} = 0.11$, $\bar{r}' = 0.04$, and $\gamma = 1.2$.[13] Using 1959 data, equation (7), and the assumption $\sigma^2 (r) = \sigma^2 (r') = 0$, the income inequality of adult males in 1959 can be expressed as

$$\sigma^2(\ln Y) = (\bar{r} - \bar{r}')^2 \sigma^2(S) + (\bar{r}')^2 \sigma^2(A) + \gamma^2 \sigma^2(\ln W)$$

[11] For labor-force males in 1965, the correlation between age and the log of weeks worked was:

Age Group	Correlation
25–64	−0.06
25+	−0.22
18+	+0.12

The correlation between schooling and the log of weeks worked in 1959 for labor-force males 25–64 was +0.14.

[12] Data sources are in Appendix A; computed means, variances, and correlations are shown in Appendix B.

[13] They were calculated from a regression analysis for white nonfarm, nonenrolled males under age 65 in the 1960 U.S. census 1/1,000 sample. The value of 0.04 for $\bar{r}'$ is one-half of the slope coefficient of experience in the regression (see Mincer 1972, Pt. II).

$$+ [2\bar{r}'(\bar{r} - \bar{r}')] \, R_{as} \, \sigma(A) \, \sigma(S)$$

$$+ [2\gamma(\bar{r} - \bar{r}')] \, R_{ws} \, \sigma(\ln W) \, \sigma(S) + 2\gamma\bar{r}' \, R_{aw} \, \sigma(A) \, \sigma(\ln W)$$

$$+ \sigma^2(U) = (0.0049) \, \sigma^2(S) + (0.0016) \, \sigma^2(A) + (1.44) \, \sigma^2(\ln W)$$

$$+ (0.0056) \, R_{as} \, \sigma(A) \, \sigma(S) + (0.168) \, R_{ws} \, \sigma(\ln W) \, \sigma(S) \qquad (8)$$

$$+ (0.096) \, R_{aw} \, \sigma(\ln W) \, \sigma(A) + \sigma^2(U) = 0.0637 + 0.1808$$
$$\phantom{+ (0.096) \, R_{aw} \, \sigma(\ln W) \, \sigma(A) + \sigma^2(U) = } (S) \qquad (A)$$

$$+ 0.2160 + (-0.0493) + 0.0468 + (-0.0198) + \sigma^2(U)$$
$$ (W) (A,S) (W,S) (A,W)$$

$$= 0.4383 + \sigma^2(U).$$

The observed income inequality was 0.6483. The model "explains" 68 percent (0.4383/0.6483) of individual differences in the log of income. Note that the direct contribution of schooling inequality is small compared with that of age and employment. It should be understood, however, that by holding the variance of age constant, the effect of an increase in the variance in schooling on income inequality is therefore reduced by the effect of the change in the variance of experience.

Based on equation (7), table 1 shows the effect of a change in the explanatory variables on the inequality of earnings. The effect of a unit change in the explanatory variables can be computed using the previously computed values of $\bar{r}$, $\bar{r}'$, and γ, assuming the coefficients of variation in r_i and r'_i are one-third, and using 1959 observed values for the other variables.[14]

For the means, standard deviations, and correlations,

$$\frac{\partial \, \sigma^2(\ln Y)}{\partial \, \sigma(S)} = 0.046 \qquad \frac{\partial \, \sigma^2(\ln Y)}{\partial \, \bar{S}} = 0.013 \qquad \frac{\partial \, \sigma^2(\ln Y)}{\partial \, R_{as}} = 0.194$$

$$\frac{\partial \, \sigma^2(\ln Y)}{\partial \, \sigma(A)} = 0.031 \qquad\qquad\qquad \frac{\partial \, \sigma^2(\ln Y)}{\partial \, R_{aw}} = 0.390$$

[14] There is some evidence that one-third may be an upper limit to the coefficient of variation of r. The earnings function can be written as $\ln Y = a + rH$, where H is accumulated human capital measured in time equivalents. Then, $\sigma^2(\ln Y) = \bar{r}^2 \sigma(H) + \bar{H}^2 \, \bar{\sigma}^2(r) + \sigma^2(r) \, \sigma^2(H)$. From regressing $\ln Y$ on H, $R^2 \simeq 1/2$ and $CV(H) \simeq 1/3$. Thus:

$$R^2 = \frac{\bar{r}^2 \, \sigma^2(H)}{\bar{r}^2 \, \sigma^2(H) + \bar{H}^2 \, \sigma(r) + \sigma^2(r) \, \sigma^2(H)}$$

$$= \frac{1}{1 + [CV(r)/CV(H)] + [CV(r)]^2} = 1/2$$

and $CV^2(r) = 1/10$, or $CV(r) \simeq 1/3$. If there is a true residual in the regression such that in $Y = a + rH + U$, then $1/3.3 \simeq 1/3$ is an upper limit of $CV(r)$. For an elaboration, see Mincer (1972, Pt. II).

TABLE 1

PARTIAL EFFECTS OF THE EXPLANATORY VARIABLES ON INCOME INEQUALITY

$$\frac{\partial \sigma^2 (\ln Y)}{\partial \, \sigma(S)} = 2[(\bar{r} - \bar{r'})^2 + \sigma^2(r) + \sigma^2(r')]\sigma(S)$$

$$+ [2r'(\bar{r} - \bar{r'}) - \sigma^2(r')]R_{as} \, \sigma(A) \qquad (1)$$

$$+ [2\gamma(\bar{r} - \bar{r'})]R_{ws} \, \sigma(\ln W)$$

$$\frac{\partial \sigma^2 (\ln Y)}{\partial \, \sigma(A)} = 2[\bar{r'} + \sigma^2(r')] \, \sigma(A) + [2\bar{r'}(\bar{r} - \bar{r'}) - \sigma^2(r')]R_{as} \, \sigma(S)$$

$$+ (2\bar{r'}\gamma)R_{aw} \, \sigma(\ln W) \qquad (2)$$

$$\frac{\partial \sigma^2 (\ln Y)}{\partial \sigma(\ln W)} = 2(\gamma^2) \, \sigma(\ln W) + [2\gamma(\bar{r} - \bar{r'})]R_{ws} \, \sigma(S) + (2\gamma\bar{r'})R_{aw} \, \sigma(A) \qquad (3)$$

$$\frac{\partial \sigma^2 (\ln Y)}{\partial \, \bar{S}} = 2[\sigma^2(r) - \sigma^2(r')] \, \bar{S} - 2 \, \sigma^2(r')(\bar{A} - 5) \qquad (4)$$

$$\frac{\partial \sigma^2 (\ln Y)}{\partial \, A} = 2(\bar{A} - \bar{S} - 5) \, \sigma^2(r') \qquad (5)$$

$$\frac{\partial \sigma^2 (\ln Y)}{\partial \, R_{as}} = [2\bar{r'}(\bar{r} - \bar{r'}) - \sigma^2(r')] \, \sigma(A) \, \sigma(S) \qquad (6)$$

$$\frac{\partial \sigma^2 (\ln Y)}{\partial \, R_{ws}} = 2\gamma \, (\bar{r} - \bar{r'}) \, \sigma(\ln W) \, \sigma(S) \qquad (7)$$

$$\frac{\partial \sigma^2 (\ln Y)}{\partial \, R_{wa}} = 2\gamma(\bar{r'}) \, \sigma(\ln W) \, \sigma(A) \qquad (8)$$

$$\frac{\partial \, \sigma^2 (\ln Y)}{\partial \, \bar{A}} = 0.009$$

$$\frac{\partial \, \sigma^2 (\ln Y)}{\partial \, \sigma(\ln W)} = 1.185 \qquad \frac{\partial \, \sigma^2 (\ln Y)}{\partial \, R_{ws}} = 0.234.$$

These eight partial deviatives are employed to assess the effects of changes in the distributions of schooling, age, and employment on the relative variance of income.

The standard deviation of schooling changes slowly over time. For the study group, it fell fairly steadily from 3.70 years in 1949 to 3.04 years in 1970. A decline of one unit, or approximately 30 percent, reduces the relative variance of income by 0.046 points, or about 7 percent. The observed decline by 0.66 years in the standard deviation of schooling from 1949 to 1970 would be responsible for a 4 percent decline in the variance of the log of income, or a 2 percent decline in its standard deviation.

A unit increase in the level of schooling increases inequality of 0.013 points. Average schooling has risen 2 years, from 9.66 years in 1949 to 11.66 years in 1970. This would have increased inequality over the period by 0.026 points. Thus, the net effect of the postwar decline in the standard deviation of schooling by 0.66 years and the rise in level by 2 years is to leave the relative variance of income virtually unchanged.[15]

The income distribution is also affected by the correlation of age with schooling. The stronger the upward secular trend in schooling, the more negative is the correlation and the smaller is the inequality of income. The correlation ranged from a high of —0.2340 in 1949 to a low of —0.2070 in 1970, indicating a slight decline in schooling trends. Its effect on inequality would be small, a rise of 0.0052 points, or a rise of less than 1 percent in the variance of logs. If, in 1959, the correlation were zero instead of —0.23, but the level and inequality of schooling were unchanged, inequality would have been greater by 0.0447 points, or by nearly 7 percent of the variance of logs.

Even a drastic change in the distribution of schooling would not necessarily have a large effect. If the dispersion of schooling were reduced to zero but its mean level were unchanged, income inequality would decline by 0.1656 points compared with 1959. However, a uniform level of schooling would change the correlation between schooling and age from —0.23 to zero. The net effect of the decreased variance and increased correlation would be to reduce the income variance by 0.1683 points, a 26 percent decline from 1959.[16]

If, however, the zero dispersion were due to a uniform level of schooling

---

[15] The change of $(0.046) \ (-0.66) + (0.013) \ (2.0) = -0.004$ points is less than 1 percent of the 1959 level of inequality. Soltow examined the effect of actual and projected (1970 and 1980) changes in the schooling distribution of adult family heads and unrelated individuals on the concentration ratio of household income. Using the income distribution in 1956, he found that changes in the distribution of schooling predicted a decline in inequality from $R = 0.420$ in 1940 to $R = 0.387$ in 1980. For the period 1950 $(R = 0.416)$ to 1970 $(R + 3.96)$, Soltow (1960) predicted a 4.8 percent decline in the concentration ratio.

[16] The reduction in variance is:

Variable	Change in Variable	Contribution to Change in Inequality
$\sigma(S)$	—3.6	—0.1656
R_{as}	+0.23	0.0446
$\sigma(S) \ R_{as}$ (joint effect)	...	—0.0473
Predicted difference	...	—0.1683

at 16 years, so that everyone were a college graduate, the increase in average schooling would be 5.37 years. Inequality would increase by 0.1074 points. The net effect is a decline of 0.0609 points. This represents a 9.4 percent decrease in the variance of income.

The standard deviation of age of adults changes slowly over time as a result of long fluctuations in birth rates. For civilian labor-force males age 25–64, it declined from 10.65 in 1949 to 10.52 in 1964, and then rose to 10.72 in 1970. Since a unit change in the standard deviation of age affects the variance of the log of income by only 0.0313 points, the two-tenths of a unit range during the past 20 years would have had a trivial influence on overall inequality.

Again using 1959 data as the base, the effect of an increase in the level of age by 1 year is to increase inequality by only 0.009 points. During the postwar period the average age of the study group increased slightly more than 1 year.[17] This too would tend to produce a small increase in inequality. The predicted change in income inequality due to the change in the age distribution from 1949 to 1970 is $+0.0125$, or 2 percent of the 1959 income variance.[18]

If the current decline in the rate of growth of the population continues but the rate remains nonnegative, and if retirement patterns are un-altered, the level and dispersion of age of labor-force males will increase. With a uniform distribution near zero population growth, the mean and standard deviation of age for those 25–64 would be 45 and 11.18 years, respectively.[19] Compared with the 1959 values, the income variance would be higher by 0.038 points, representing a 6 percent increase in the relative variance of income or a 3 percent increase in the standard deviation of

---

[17] The increase was fairly continuous, from 42.52 in 1949 to 43.67 in 1970.

[18] Using U.S. data, Soltow (1960) studied the effect of actual and projected (1970 and 1980) changes in the age distribution of household heads (family and unrelated individuals) on the concentration coefficient of household income. Using the 1956 distribution of income by age, he found a rising concentration coefficient, due to the aging of the population, from 1900 ($R = 0.384$) to 1970 ($R = 0.418$) and a slight decline to 1980 ($R = 0.414$). The change from 1959 ($R = 0.405$) to 1970 is 0.13 points, or 3 percent of the 1960 level. Soltow also studied income inequality in eight Norwegian cities (1940 to 1960) and found that the rate of growth of the male labor force had a significant negative partial correlation (holding constant the labor-force size, an occupational index, a wealth-income ratio, and time) with income inequality. A more rapidly growing labor force, due either to a higher birth rate or to migration, implies a lower level and lower dispersion of age. Soltow's findings (1965, pp. 42–45) are consistent with our analysis.

[19] Standard deviations of age used in this paper are computed from four age groups (25–34, 35–44, 45–54, and 55–64 years) on the assumption that all individuals are at the midpoint of the group. If the distribution of age for those 25–64 is uniform and continuous, the standard deviation is 13.0. The difference between 11.18 and 13.0 reflects the losses of within-interval variability. For the analysis of males in the 35–44 group, a continuous distribution is assumed and the variance of age is 8.33 years squared.

logs.[20] In the absence of negative population growth rates or catastrophic age-specific changes in mortality, this small change may be viewed as the maximum likely increase in inequality for males 25–64 due to changes in age structure caused by slowing population growth.

The standard deviation in the log of weeks worked in 1959 was 0.3872, while the average standard deviation for 1965–68, years of low unemployment, was 0.3445. Let us attribute this difference to cyclical factors. Then, if there had been no cyclical unemployment in 1959, the variance in income would have been lower by 0.051 points, or almost 8 percent.[21]

The year 1958 shows the highest dispersion [$\sigma(\ln W) = 0.4371$] and the lowest level of weeks worked during the postwar period, as well as a relatively large income variance (0.6447). If the dispersion in weeks worked were at the 1965–68 level, inequality in 1958 would have been lower by 0.1097.[22] Thus, 17 percent of the variance of income in 1958 could be attributed to a cyclical increase in the dispersion of employment. While the elimination of all differences in weeks worked would reduce annual income inequality by a substantial amount, it is clearly not a reasonable objective.

The correlations of the log of weeks worked with schooling and age also influence the income distribution. During the period 1949–70 the range of the correlation of age and employment was from −0.0236 to −0.0746. The correlation is more negative in years of high unemployment due to the relatively lower levels of employment for older males. The range, however, is associated with a small difference in inequality.[23]

Data on the correlation of schooling with the log of weeks worked are not available for this period on a year-by-year basis. In 1959, however, the correlation was 0.142 for males 25–64. If it were cut in half, which would presumably represent a substantial change in employment patterns, inequality would decline by 0.0242 points, or nearly 4 percent of the variance of logs. Thus, it is unlikely that the correlation had a significant effect on post–World War II income inequality.

At present, therefore, it appears that changes in the levels, dispersions, and intercorrelations of schooling, age, and employment have not been major sources of change in relative-income inequality during the postwar period, nor are they likely to produce much change in the future. If the current decline in the rate of population growth continues, the level and dispersion in age will increase, tending to generate a slight increase in aggregate inequality. The distribution of schooling is relatively less important; even a drastic change in its level and dispersion need not have a

---

[20] $(45.00 - 43.06) \ (0.009) + (11.18 - 10.55) \ (0.031) = 0.081 + 0.020 = 0.038.$

[21] $1.185 \ (0.3872 - 0.3445) = +0.051.$

[22] The reduction would be $(1.185) \ (0.3872) = 0.46$ points.

[23] $0.390 \ (0.0746 - 0.0236) = 0.0199.$

large effect. Cyclical unemployment significantly increases income in-equality. The correlations among age, schooling, and employment have a small effect. Viewing as a possible source of change the deceleration of secular trends in schooling, we find a small rise (7 percent) in the income variance in the limit.

Let us turn our attention to the effects of possible changes in rates of return to training. Assume the same percentage change in $\bar{r}$ and $\bar{r}'$ and no change in the coefficients of variation in the rates of return. Suppose the rate of return declines by 30 percent. This implies a 50 percent $[(0.7)^2 = 0.49]$ decrease in $\bar{r}^2$, $\bar{r}'^2$, $\sigma^2(r')$, and $\sigma^2(r')$. In equation (7), each of the terms is cut in half, except the covariance terms involving weeks worked which are cut by 30 percent, and the variances of weeks worked and the residual, which are unchanged. The variance of income falls by 0.1535 points, or by 23.7 percent of the 1959 level.[24] It is not clear, however, whether average rates of return are as much as 30 percent above the equilibrium level, so that a cut of such magnitude would be a desirable policy objective. As for actual postwar experience, the rate of return to high school may have increased but the return to college investment was unchanged during the 1950s (Becker 1964, pp. 124–31). At present there is no information on changes in rates of return during the 1960s. Thus, we have no basis for speculating about the future magnitudes of the rate of return. Yet it is the parameter to which income inequality is most sensitive.

In summary, the changes in aggregate relative income inequality of adult males are due primarily to changes in the distributions of age and employment, with the schooling distribution playing a smaller role. During the post–World War II period there has been no significant secular change in income inequality because changes in the levels and inequalities of schooling and age have been small and their effects have been offsetting. This suggests that other factors which have not been quantified for the postwar period (for example, the rate of return, its coefficient of varia-tion, and the residual variance) either have been fairly constant over time or have been self-canceling in their effects.

The decomposition analysis indicates the importance of the relative inequality of weeks worked for interpreting cyclical fluctuations in income inequality. This suggests that the large relative dispersion in employment in 1939 may have been responsible for the high earnings inequality in that year.

Looking into the future, if full employment is maintained, if job search behavior is unchanged, and if the level and dispersion of the rate of return are also constant, personal-income inequality can be expected to remain

[24] From equation (7), $\Delta\sigma^2 (\ln Y) = (-0.5) (0.0832 + 0.2000 - 0.0478 + 0.1538 + 0.1285) + (-0.3) (-0.0235 - 0.03277) = -0.1535$.

at the present level during years of full employment. The dispersion of weeks worked and the rate of return to schooling and on-the-job training are the most important vehicles for altering the distribution of income[25] from a purely quantitative point of view. For normative considerations, these variables matter only to the extent that dispersion in employment is involuntary and the (marginal) rates of return are above (or below) equilibrium.

III. Predicted and Observed Inequalities: 1949–69

We proceed to apply earnings function (7) to year-by-year predictions of income inequality for adult males in the postwar period. The observed income inequalities are the variances of the natural log of income for labor-force males in three age groups, 25 years and over, 25–64, and 35–44.

Two procedures are adopted for estimating the parameters for which data do not exist on a yearly basis. The first is to use the 1959 cross-section earnings equation for these parameters. The second is to let a regression analysis covering the entire period select the parameter values.

By definition, the regression approach maximizes the R^2, so that we would expect it to have greater predictive power than the cross-section-based method. Moreover, the regression predictions are unbiased even though the implicit parameter estimates may be unreliable in view of the substantial multicollinearity among the variables in our time-series data. The coefficients, however, should stabilize and their reliability improve as the length of the time series increases. In the first approach, the parameters have coefficients which are fixed for the particular base year, as estimated in the 1959 cross-section.

A. Method I

Under the first, or cross-section-based, approach the predicted measure of income inequality for each year and age group is derived from equation (7) by: (a) using observed data on the level and inequality of schooling, age, and the log of weeks worked, and the correlations of age with schooling and the log of weeks worked; (b) assuming the correlation between schooling and the log of weeks worked in 1959 for each age group is un-

---

[25] The dispersion of weekly wages within age and schooling groups, which is treated as a constant residual variance in this analysis, appears to be a substantial component of aggregate inequality. In principle, the residual inequality is a matter of the otherwise unaccounted inequalities in human-capital investments outside of schooling as well as in the quality of schooling, initial endowments, and rates of return to each of these. Although it is beyond the scope of this paper, this dispersion warrants investigation, as it represents both a substantial source of income inequality and possibly an avenue for changes in inequality in the future.

changed over time; (c) assuming the values of $\bar{r}$, $\bar{r}'$, and γ are equal to those for white nonfarm, nonenrolled males with earnings in the 1960 U.S. census 1/1,000 sample and that the coefficients of variation of rates of return are one-third; and (d) assuming the residual variance in each year is the same as in 1959 for each age group.

In a comparison of the observed and predicted inequality for the three age groups from 1949 to 1969, the predicted value is nearly always within 10 percent of the observed value for the 25-and-over and the 25–64 age groups.[26] For those 35–44, the model substantially underpredicts the observed inequality. The larger predictive error for the 35–44 group is not surprising. One reason is that the age distribution for those 35–44 is assumed constant over time. In addition, the relative variance in weeks worked is small and varies less over the business cycle for this group than for others. Thus, there is greater scope for the variation in residual factors to influence the overall inequality. The simple correlations of observed and predicted inequality are $R(25+) = 0.65$, $R(25–64) = 0.78$, and $R(35–44) = 0.62$, all of which are significant at the 0.5 percent level.

Table 2 shows the results of a multiple regression of observed inequality on predicted inequality, time (1949 = 1), and time squared. The time variables are included to reveal the presence of the net effect of secular trends in the variables assumed constant. The Durbin-Watson statistic indicates the absence of significant autocorrelation.

The slope coefficient for predicted inequality is significantly greater than zero and less than 1 at the 2.5 percent level in all cases. Compared with the hypothesized value of unity, the coefficient is biased downward. The bias may be due to errors of measuring the predicted inequality or to misspecifications in the equation. As will be shown below, this bias disappears in the more efficient regression prediction of inequality.

For the age group 25 years and over, time is significant at the 5 percent level and time squared is significant at the 10 percent level (two-tailed tests). Holding predicted inequality constant, the coefficients imply a small secular rise in inequality of 0.0630 points from 1949 to 1960 and then a decline of 0.0488 points to 1969. For the 25–64 group, time is barely significant at the 10 percent level and time squared is not significant at that level. However, the coefficients imply a rise of 0.0456 points from 1949 to 1961 and then a decline of 0.0176 points. The 35–44 group shows no time trend.

The magnitude of residual secular effects during the period under study is small or insignificant. At most, these effects suggest a per annum rise in income inequality of less than 1 percent for the broader age groups from 1949 to approximately 1960 and thereafter a similar annual rate of

[26] See comparison in tables B1–B3. Budd (1970) discusses the sampling variability and quality of the *Current Population Reports* income data.

TABLE 2

Time-Series Analysis of Observed and Predicted Income Inequality, 1949–69

Regression for (Value of γ) (1)	Intercept (2)	Predicted Inequality (3)	Time (1949 = 1) (4)	Time Squared (5)	$\bar{R}^2$, Multiple R d^* (6)
1. Age 25+					
(γ = 1.2)	0.3850	0.4078	0.0108	0.0005	0.48
		(0.1627)	(0.0041)	(0.0002)	0.75
		2.51	2.62	−2.41	1.66
2. Age 25–64					
(γ = 1.2)	0.1545	0.6783	0.0077	−0.0004	0.57
		(0.1760)	(0.0046)	(0.0002)	0.80
		3.85	1.67	−1.78	1.33
3. Age 35–44					
(γ = 1.2)	0.2519	0.6003	−0.0024	0.0001	0.25
		(0.2355)	(0.0061)	(0.0003)	0.61
		2.55	−0.39	0.25	1.80
4. Age 25+					
(γ = 1.1)	0.3228	0.4852	0.0110	−0.0005	0.49
		(0.1920)	(0.0041)	(0.0002)	0.75
		2.53	2.69	−2.47	1.66
5. Age 25–64					
(γ = 1.1)	0.0805	0.7953	0.0075	−0.0004	0.57
		(0.2076)	(0.0046)	(0.0002)	0.80
		3.83	1.63	−1.80	1.33
6. Age 35–44					
(γ = 1.1)	0.2008	0.7026	−0.0025	0.0001	0.25
		(0.2763)	(0.0061)	(0.0003)	0.60
		2.54	−0.41	0.24	1.80

Note.—1959 is deleted from the data. In cols. 3–5, the first figure for each age group is the slope coefficient, the second is the standard error, and the third is the student's t-ratio. For sixteen degrees of freedom, one-tailed test, $t(0.05) = 1.75$, $t(0.025) = 2.12$, $t(0.01) = 2.58$.
* For three explanatory variables—twenty observations, a 5 percent level of significance, and a two-tailed test—the range for accepting the null hypothesis of no autocorrelation is $d = 1.55$ to 2.00 and the range for neither accepting nor rejecting the null hypothesis is $d = 0.89$ to 1.55.

decline to the end of the period under study. The rise in inequality in the 1950s is consistent with an observed increase in the rate of return to high school during this period. It is also consistent with the rising trend in unemployment over the period.

It is known that skill differentials in weekly earnings and in weeks worked are countercyclical. Therefore, the elasticity of earnings with respect to weeks worked and the covariance of schooling with the log of weeks worked are likely to vary inversely with the business cycles. Because of the scarcity of data, the parameters are assumed to have their 1959 values for the entire period. Since 1959 was a year of higher than average unemployment, overestimates of these parameters are assigned in nonrecession years, and these may be responsible for the downward bias of the slope coefficient. Thus, the observed time trends may be no more than a reflection of the omitted effects of cyclical changes on the parameters.

The analysis is recomputed under the assumption of a constant $\gamma = 1.1$ rather than $\gamma = 1.2$. The value 1.1 is presumed to be closer to the true value in a year with average unemployment. The simple correlations between observed inequality and the new predicted inequality are $R(25+) = 0.64$, $R(25-64) = 0.77$, and $R(35-44) + 0.61$.[27] These correlations are similar to those obtained under the assumptions of $\gamma = 1.2$.

Rows 4–6 in table 2 present the regression of observed inequality on the new predicted inequality, time and time squared. The only difference in the two sets of regressions is an increase in the slope coefficient of predicted inequality. Under a two-tailed test and a 5 percent level of significance, the slope coefficient is now not significantly different from unity for the 25–64 and 35–44 groups. While the coefficient remains significantly less than unity for those 25 and over, the t-ratio is less under the assumption $\gamma = 1.1$ than when $\gamma = 1.2$. Note that the trends are not altered by the change in γ. These results suggest that the model's explanatory power would be greater and the slope coefficient of predicted inequality would be closer to unity if annual observations were available for the elasticity of earnings with respect to weeks worked and the covariance of schooling and the log of weeks worked.

B. *Method II*

In the absence of annual data for several parameters, the alternative approach we use is to compute a multiple regression of observed income inequality on the explanatory variables for which data are available. The variables are entered in the manner suggested by equation (7). Because the explanatory variables are highly correlated, the regression coefficients lose their separate interpretation, but the predicted variances are unbiased estimates of income inequality.[28] Predicted values are obtained for each year from 1949 to 1969. In general, the percentage error is much smaller for the regression-predicted inequality than for the procedure used before. The percentage error is, once again, largest for the group 35–44. The *simple* correlations of observed inequality with the regression-predicted inequality are $R(25+) = 0.85$, $R(25-64) = 0.94$, and $R(35-44) = 0.65$.

For comparative purposes, the observed inequality is regressed on the predicted inequality, time and time squared (see table 3). The slope coefficient of predicted inequality is now near unity, and the observed t-ratios in a test of significance from unity are all less than 1.0. The time-trend variables are almost significant at the 10 percent level for the age

[27] The new predicted inequalities and the percent error are in tables B1–B3.

[28] The multiple regressions and correlation matrices for the three age groups are shown in tables B4–B9. Tables B1–B3 contain the regression-predicted values and the percentage error.

TABLE 3

TIME-SERIES ANALYSIS OF OBSERVED AND REGRESSION-PREDICTED
INCOME INEQUALITY, 1949–69

Regression (1)	Intercept (2)	Predicted Inequality (3)	Time (1949 = 1) (4)	Time Squared (5)	$\bar{R}^2$, Multiple R d (6)
1. Age 25+	−0.0001	1.0002 (0.1411) 7.09	...	...	0.71 0.85 2.17
2. Age 25+	0.0992	0.8378 (0.1681) 4.99	0.0055 (0.0033) 1.67	− 0.0002 (0.0001) − 1.67	0.72 0.87 2.39
3. Age 25–64	−0.0001	1.0002 (0.0859) 11.64	...	...	0.87 0.94 1.41
4. Age 25–64	0.0208	0.9511 (0.1050) 9.06	0.0024 (0.0027) 0.92	− 0.0001 (0.0001) − 0.92	0.86 0.94 1.48
5. Age 35–44	0.0001	0.9999 (0.2621) 3.81	...	...	0.40 0.65 1.47
6. Age 35–44	−0.0108	1.0012 (0.3094) 3.24	0.0024 (0.0050) 0.47	− 0.0001 (0.0002) − 0.45	0.34 0.66 1.50

NOTE.—1959 is included in the data. See notes to table 2.

group 25 and over (with an implied peak in 1961–62) and are not significant in the other two regressions. Among the three age groups, the income inequality of males 25 and over is most sensitive to the business cycle. The regression computation of predicted inequality does not permit variations over the cycle in the parameters that are estimated. Thus, it is consistent with our interpretation of γ and the covariance of schooling and weeks worked that, if any age group shows significant time effects with a peak around 1961, it would be the group most sensitive to cyclical forces.

In the regression procedure for predicting income inequality, the explanatory power is highest for males 25–64. The lower explanatory power for the other age groups is consistent with the model. Because of the lack of appropriate age data, four variables—the level and variance of age for males 35–44 and the covariance of age with schooling and weeks worked—could not be included in the analysis. Yet surely these variables experience secular or cyclical changes. The model was not designed to explicitly include the effects of the depreciation of earning power with age, and this may account for the poorer explanatory power of the regression that includes persons 65 and older.

IV. Predicted Changes in Inequality: 1939 and 1985

In this section the income inequality function, equation (7), is used to predict changes in inequality from 1965, a year of low unemployment, to 1939 and 1985. The components of the predicted change are examined.

A. 1939

As cited in the Introduction, earnings inequality in 1939 was larger than in the postwar period.[29] Was this larger inequality due to a different age and schooling distributon of adult males, to the depression, or to a higher rate of return?[30]

Table 4 compares the components of earnings inequality for males 20–64 in 1940 and labor-force males 18 and over in 1965. The net effect of the different age and schooling distributions is to predict a slightly lower

TABLE 4

COMPARISON OF PREDICTED INCOME INEQUALITY IN 1939 WITH 1965

Variables	1939	1965	1939 − 1965	Contribution to Change in Income Inequality
$\bar{A}$	39.38	41.84	−2.46	−0.02149
$\sigma(A)$	14.21	13.65	+0.56	0.02822
$\bar{S}$	8.83	11.16	−2.33	−0.03332
$\sigma(S)$	3.70	3.41	+0.29	0.01235
$\sigma(\ln W)$	0.737	0.565	+0.232	0.43517
R_{as}	−0.26	−0.23	−0.03	−0.00758
$\sigma(S)\ \sigma(\ln W)$ (joint effect)	...	...	...	0.011323
$\sigma(A)\ \sigma(\ln W)$ (joint effect)	...	...	...	0.01249
$R_{as}\ \sigma(S)\ \sigma(A)$ (joint effect)	...	...	...	−0.00119
Predicted difference ...	...	...	...	0.43597

NOTE.—With one exception. the 1965 data are for civilian labor-force males age 18 and over. The correlation of schooling and employment is for labor-force males age 25 and over in 1959. Using 1965 as the base year, the rate-of-return data for 1959, and $\gamma = 1.2$, the partial effects on the variance in the log of income for males are: $\bar{A}$, +0.009; $\sigma(A)$, +0.050; $\bar{S}$, +0.014; $\sigma(S)$ +0.043; $\sigma(\ln W)$, +1.876; and R_{as}, +0.253.

[29] The variance in the log of wage and salary income in 1939 of experienced members of the labor force 14 and over in 1940 was 2.16. The relative inequality of earnings of males 14 and over in 1965 was 1.31 (computed from sources shown in Appendix A). Data on earnings in 1965 are available only for this age group.

[30] In explaining the substantial decline in inequality from 1938 to 1957 in Great Britain, Lydall (1959, p. 33) wrote: "It seems that several different forces have been at work. The most important of these, without any doubt, has been the achievement and maintenance of full employment."

earnings inequality in 1939 than in 1965.[31] This is due mainly to the lower level of schooling in 1939. When the relative inequality of weeks worked is considered, the picture changes. The employment effect outweighs the net effect of the changed distributions of schooling and age, and consequently, a large increase in income inequality over the 1965 level is predicted. The model predicts an earnings inequality larger in 1939 than in 1965 by 0.44 points.

The relative inequality of wage and salary income for experienced labor-force males was 2.16 in 1939; in 1965 it was 1.31 for wage and salary workers 14 years old and over. The observed difference is 0.85.

The predicted difference of 0.47 is computed with γ assumed to be equal to 1.2 in both 1939 and 1965 and with the correlation of the log of weeks worked with schooling and age assumed the same in both years. Since γ is likely to vary inversely with the business cycle, the 1959 value of 1.2 is lower than the 1939 value and higher than the 1965 value. The predicted difference is recomputed using $\gamma = 1.1$ in 1965 and $\gamma = 1.3$ or 1.4 in 1939.[32] The predicted difference is 0.54 for $\gamma = 1.3$ and 0.79 for $\gamma = 1.4$. The predicted difference would be increased if data were available for 1939 and 1965 for the correlation of log of weeks worked with schooling and age. This suggests that if the data specified by the model were available in both 1939 and 1965, the gap between the observed and the predicted difference in income inequality might be relatively small.

B. 1985

We have used age and schooling distributions for labor-force males projected by the U.S. Department of Commerce for 1985 as the basis for predicting the income inequality of labor-force males 25–64 and 35–44 years old in that year. The projected data permit us to calculate the level and inequality both of age and of schooling, and their intercorrelation. The variance in the log of weeks worked in 1985 has been computed on the assumption that the mean and variance of the log of weeks worked for each age group in 1985 will be the same as in 1965. Thus, we assume 1985 will be a year of low unemployment. The correlation between age and the log of weeks worked was assumed to be the same as in 1965. The 1959 data used previously for the other parameters were assumed to have the same value in 1985.

Table 5 contains the value of the schooling, age, and employment

[31] Data are not available to correlate weeks worked with schooling or age in 1939, but it is assumed that these values are the same as in 1965. We also have assumed that the other parameters for which there are no time-series data are constant over the interval.

[32] Year-specific observed values are used except for the correlation of schooling with the log of weeks worked for both years and the correlation of age with the log of weeks worked in 1939, for which 1959 data are employed.

TABLE 5

COMPARISON OF PREDICTED INCOME INEQUALITY IN 1985 WITH 1965 FOR MALES 25–64

Variables	1985	1965	1985 — 1965	Contribution to Change in Income Inequality
$\bar{A}$	41.31	43.60	−2.29	−0.02061
$\sigma(A)$	10.76	10.54	+0.22	0.00682
$\bar{S}$	12.50	11.17	+1.33	0.01689
$\sigma(S)$	3.05	3.48	−0.43	−0.01978
$\sigma(\ln W)$	0.359	0.364	+0.005	−0.00593
R_{as}	−0.10	−0.22	+0.12	0.02328
$\sigma(S)\ \sigma(\ln W)$ (joint effect)	...	...	...	−0.00051
$\sigma(A)\ \sigma(\ln W)$ (joint effect)	...	...	...	−0.00001
$R_{as}\ \sigma(A)\ \sigma(S)$ (joint effect)	...	...	...	−0.00240
Predicted difference ...	...	...	...	−0.00231

variables for labor-force males 25–64 in 1985 and 1965. A lower level, but a wider dispersion of age, is predicted, presumably due to an assumed decrease in the retirement age for many older males. The change in age structure also is expected to produce a small reduction in the standard deviation of the log of weeks worked. The level of schooling is projected to increase by 1.33 years and its standard deviation to decrease by almost half a year. The most dramatic projected change is a substantial increase in the correlation of age and schooling from $R_{as} = -0.22$ to $R_{as} = -0.10$. This increase implies a slowing of the secular growth in the level of schooling.

Using 1959 values as the base, table 5 also indicates the effects of these variables singly and jointly on the change of income inequality from 1965 to 1985. Taken as a whole, changes in the levels and inequalities of age and schooling will have a small negative impact, while the change in the correlation of age and schooling increases inequality by a larger amount. The influence of the small change in the relative inequality of weeks worked is minor.

The net effect is to decrease predicted inequality by 0.0023 points, or about four-tenths of 1 percent of the variance in the log of income in 1965. Thus, if the rate of return to schooling and the residual inequality remain unchanged, and if 1985 is a year of full employment, no change in income inequality from the 1965 level is predicted.

Although Part III indicated that the model was less successful for predicting inequality for those 35–44, we decided to examine the change for that group. The data appear in table 6. We assumed that the level and dispersion of age will not change, and the correlation between age and schooling for a given year is the same as that for males 25–64. It also was

TABLE 6

COMPARISON OF PREDICTED INCOME INEQUALITY IN 1985 WITH 1965 FOR MALES 35–44

Variables	1985	1965	1985 − 1965	Contribution to Change in Income Inequality*
$\bar{S}$	12.81	11.58	+1.23	+0.01722
$\sigma(S)$	2.85	3.34	−0.49	−0.02499
R_{as}	−0.10	−0.22	+0.12	+0.00660
$R_{as}\ \sigma(S)$ (joint effect)	...	...	...	−0.00077
Predicted difference ...	...	...	...	−0.00194

* For males 35–44 years old, using 1965 as the base year and the rate-of-return data for 1959, the partial effects on the variance in the log of income for males are: S, 0.014; $\sigma(S)$, 0.051; and R_{as}, 0.055.

assumed that the dispersion in employment and the correlations of employment with schooling and age are unchanged.

With 1965 as the base year, we have calculated the contribution of each variable assumed to change through time. The differences in the partial slopes shown in table 6 and in Part II for males 25–64 are due mainly to the different values of the variables held constant for the two age groups. The effect of the projected change in the distribution of schooling is to decrease inequality, but its influence is partially offset by the rise in the correlation of age and schooling. The net effect is a projected decrease in inequality by 0.0019 points, representing a decline of three-tenths of 1 percent below the observed variance in 1965. Thus, in the absence of cyclical unemployment in 1985, and if the variables assumed constant do in fact remain constant, the relative-income variance in 1985 among males 35–44 is expected to be the same as it was in 1965.

V. Conclusions

This paper represents a first attempt to use a human-capital earnings function as an instrument for the analysis of time-series changes in income inequality. The model relates income inequality to the distributions of age, schooling, employment, and rates of return, and to the intercorrelations among these variables.

Although greatly oversimplified, the model achieves high explanatory power in the analysis of annual-income inequality in the period 1949–69. For the age group for which the model is best suited, males 25–64, the adjusted coefficient of determination is 87 percent. The average error of prediction is less than 2 percent and it never exceeds 5 percent. It is reassuring that an empirical analysis based on the human-capital approach substantially surpasses in predictive performance previous ad hoc empirical efforts.

For adult males in the United States, changes in the income distribution are affected mainly by changes in distributions of schooling, age, and employment. During the past 20 years, changes in the level and inequality of age and the inequality of schooling have been small and could not have greatly influenced the overall distribution, especially since they tend to have canceling effects. The stronger influence has been the business cycle through its effects on the dispersion of weeks of employment.

Although employment variation explains about a half of the variation in income inequality over time, the other variables account for over 60 percent of the remaining half of the variation, according to our more efficient predictions produced by Method II.[33]

For the age group 25 and over, there was a barely significant upward trend in observed income inequality, holding the predicted inequality constant, of less than 0.5 percent per year from 1949 to 1962, and thereafter a similar rate of decline. These time trends may reflect changes in the rates of return from high school and/or changes in unemployment during this period. The other age groups showed no time trends.

The model was used to explain the observed earnings inequality in 1939 and to predict income inequality in 1985. The different age and schooling distributions in 1939 compared with 1965 would have resulted in a smaller earnings inequality in the former year. But the larger dispersion in weeks worked in 1939 outweighed the effect of the age and schooling distributions and led to a prediction of a substantially larger inequality in 1939 than in 1965. Most of the observed difference in inequality between 1939 and 1965 is explained by changes in employment conditions. The remainder is a decline in the inequality of wage rates, possibly due to a decline in the rate of return to schooling.[34]

Predicted changes in income inequality from 1965 to 1985 are computed for labor-force males 25–64 and 35–44, on the assumption that age-specific employment is the same in both years. No net change is anticipated for either age group. These predictions, however, assume that the rate of return to training and the residual variance do not change in the interim.

A substantial decline in inequality in the future during years of full employment could occur if there is a reduced dispersion in full-employment weeks worked or if there is a decline in the rate of return to human capital. Thus, an understanding of the determinants of the distribution

---

[33] The poor showing of Method I in this respect is something of a puzzle at this stage of our work.

[34] There is some evidence of the former in Schultz (1971) and of the latter in Rahm (1971).

of work time and of the levels of rates of return is of primary importance for an understanding of the income distribution. The analysis also suggests that the residual variance, the inequality of weekly incomes within age and schooling groups, deserves further study. It represents a substantial proportion of income inequality, and the unexplored factors underlying the residual may constitute avenues for some degree of change in overall inequality in the future. Since we studied income in the absence of a continuous series on earnings distributions, one obvious factor in the residual is the share and dispersion of nonemployment income. This factor may be lurking behind some of the obscurities in our empirical data, but it is largely outside the scope of the human-capital model.

Appendix A

Data Sources

1. *Income Inequality:* Interval Midpoints and Pareto Estimate for Upper Open-End Interval.

1949–64: *Trends in the Incomes of Families and Persons in the United States: 1947–1964.* Technical Paper no. 17, table 14. Washington: U.S. Dept. Commerce, 1967. 1949–50, ten groups; otherwise eleven groups. Money income.

1965–69: *Current Population Reports,* ser. P-60, nos. 51, 53, 60, 66, and 75. Washington: U.S. Bur. Census. Eleven groups. Money income. (1965, earnings, sixteen groups.)

1939: *U.S. Census of Population, 1940.* Vol. 3, *The Labor Force,* table 71. Washington: U.S. Bur. Census. Fourteen groups. Wage and salary income for the civilian labor force.

2. *Schooling and Age:* Averages, Variances, and Correlation: Civilian Labor-Force Males.

1949: *U.S. Census of Population, 1950.* Special Report no. 58, "Education," table 9.

1952 and 1957: *Current Population Reports,* ser. P-50, nos. 49 and 78.

1959–68: *Educational Attainment of Workers.* Special Labor Force Reports nos. 1, 30, 53, 65, 83, 92, and 103. Washington: U.S. Dept. Commerce.

Missing observations for age distribution obtained from *Handbook of Labor Statistics: 1970,* table 1. Washington: U.S. Dept. Labor.

Missing observations for schooling distribution and correlation obtained from linear interpolations.

1985: *U.S. Labor Force: Projections to 1985.* Special Labor Force Report no. 119. Washington: U.S. Dept. Commerce, 1970. Also, *Education of Adult Workers: Projections to 1985.* Special Labor Force Report no. 122. Washington: U.S. Dept. Commerce 1970.

1939: *U.S. Census of Population: 1940.* Vol. 3, *The Labor Force,* tables 28 and 32. Vol. 4, *Characteristics by Age,* table 18. Schooling data and the correlation for males age 25–69 in 1940. Age data for males in the labor force in 1940.

3. *Weeks Worked:* Variance of the Log of Weeks Worked and Correlation with Age for Civilian Labor-Force Males: Five Employment Groups for 1949, 1950, and 1969, Otherwise Six Groups.

1950–58: *Current Population Reports,* ser. P-50, nos. 35, 43, 48, 54, 59, 68, 77, and 91.

1959–68: *Work Experience of the Population.* Special Labor Force Reports nos. 11, 19, 25, 38, 48, 62, 76, 91, 107, and 115.

1969: *Current Population Reports,* ser. P-60, no. 75.

Missing observations, 1949, assumed equal to 1950; 1957 interpolated.

1985: Projected age distribution in 1985, and level and variance of the log of weeks worked by age group for 1965.

1939: *U.S. Census of Population: 1940.* Vol. 3, *The Labor Force,* p. 13 and table 88. The "months worked" data (table 88) were converted to weeks worked (p. 13).

4. *Correlation between Schooling and Employment. U.S. Census of Population: 1960.* Subject report, "Employment Status and Work Experience," table 20. For labor-force males in 1959.

5. *Other Parameters*

Rates of return ($\bar{r}$ and $\bar{r}'$). and the elasticity of earnings with respect to weeks worked (γ). Computed from *U.S. Census of Population: 1960,* 1/1,000 sample, for white nonfarm, nonenrolled males 14 years of age and over with earnings.

Appendix B

TABLE B1

Observed and Predicted Income Inequality, Males 25 and Over

Year	Observed	Predicted ($\gamma = 1.2$) Value	Predicted ($\gamma = 1.2$) Error	Predicted ($\gamma = 1.1$) Value	Predicted ($\gamma = 1.1$) Error	Predicted (Regression) Value	Predicted (Regression) Error
1949	.7422	.8191	10.4	.8156	9.9	.7682	3.4
1950	.7552	.8193	8.5	.8158	8.0	.7542	−0.1
1951	.6968	.7537	8.2	.7604	9.1	.6938	−0.4
1952	.6657	.7447	11.9	.7520	13.0	.6976	4.6
1953	.7411	.7365	−0.6	.7450	0.5	.7260	−2.1
1954	.7821	.7945	1.6	.7945	1.6	.7698	−1.6
1955	.7699	.7482	−2.8	.7551	−1.9	.7456	−3.3
1956	.7691	.7534	−2.0	.7592	−1.3	.7650	−0.5
1957	.7694	.8035	4.4	.8015	4.2	.7532	−2.2
1958	.7699	.8569	11.3	.8468	10.0	.7685	−0.2
1959	.7842	.7842	...	.7842	...	.7989	1.8
1960	.7893	.8077	2.3	.8037	1.8	.8016	1.5
1961	.8219	.8365	1.8	.8294	0.9	.7845	−4.8
1962	.7626	.8330	9.2	.8259	8.3	.7890	3.6
1963	.7531	.8053	6.9	.8014	6.4	.7654	1.6
1964	.7627	.7855	3.0	.7852	3.0	.7445	−2.4
1965	.7551	.7683	1.8	.7716	2.2	.7487	−0.9
1966	.7450	.7474	0.3	.7531	1.1	.7366	−1.1
1967	.7319	.7347	0.4	.7430	1.5	.7325	0.1
1968	.7048	.7363	4.5	.7457	5.8	.7263	3.0
1969	.7294	.7418	1.7	.7514	3.0	.7315	0.3

TABLE B2
Observed and Predicted Income Inequality, Males 25–64

Year	Observed	Predicted ($\gamma = 1.2$) Value	% Error	Predicted ($\gamma = 1.1$) Value	% Error	Predicted (Regression) Value	% Error
1949	.6533	.6759	3.5	.6693	2.4	.6562	0.4
1950	.6341	.6786	7.0	.6720	6.0	.6351	0.2
1951	.5570	.6117	9.8	.6159	10.6	.5737	2.9
1952	.5295	.6034	14.0	.6090	15.0	.5402	2.0
1953	.5844	.5922	1.3	.5991	2.5	.5810	—0.6
1954	.6545	.6514	—0.5	.6498	—0.7	.6425	—1.9
1955	.6387	.6075	—4.9	.6131	—4.0	.6139	—4.0
1956	.6312	.6084	—3.6	.6139	—2.7	.6163	—2.4
1957	.6334	.6634	4.7	.6612	4.4	.6406	1.1
1958	.6447	.7221	12.0	.7114	10.3	.6492	0.7
1959	.6483	.6483	...	.6483	...	.6827	5.0
1960	.6635	.6689	0.8	.6664	0.4	.6653	0.3
1961	.6858	.7014	2.3	.6949	1.3	.6615	—3.7
1962	.6413	.6951	8.4	.6892	7.5	.6477	1.0
1963	.6318	.6686	5.8	.6669	5.6	.6370	0.8
1964	.6307	.6459	2.4	.6478	2.7	.6201	—1.7
1965	.6282	.6303	0.3	.6349	1.1	.6135	—2.4
1966	.5808	.6134	5.6	.6206	6.9	.5675	—2.3
1967	.5675	.6040	6.4	.6135	8.1	.5734	1.0
1968	.5609	.6076	8.3	.6171	10.0	.5794	3.2
1969	.5813	.6117	5.2	.6213	6.9	.5844	0.5

TABLE B3
Observed and Predicted Income Inequality, Males 35–44

Year	Observed	Predicted ($\gamma = 1.2$) Value	Error	Predicted ($\gamma = 1.1$) Value	Error	Predicted (Regression) Value	Error
1949	.6229	.5287	—15.1	.5246	—15.8	.5832	— 6.8
1950	.5477	.5295	— 3.3	.5254	— 4.1	.5753	4.8
1951	.4865	.4692	— 3.6	.4745	— 2.5	.5181	6.1
1952	.4777	.4826	1.0	.4860	1.7	.5335	10.5
1953	.5231	.4833	— 7.6	.4867	— 7.0	.5330	1.9
1954	.5949	.5112	—14.1	.5104	—14.2	.5551	— 7.2
1955	.5212	.4525	—13.2	.4608	—11.6	.4956	— 5.2
1956	.5299	.4526	—14.6	.4610	—13.0	.4954	— 7.0
1957	.5531	.5065	— 8.4	.5067	— 8.4	.5504	— 0.5
1958	.5311	.5723	7.8	.5631	6.0	.5710	6.9
1959	.5164	.5164	...	.5164	...	.5360	3.7
1960	.5886	.5248	—10.8	.5240	—11.0	.5376	— 9.5
1961	.5993	.5744	— 4.1	.5664	— 5.5	.5607	— 6.9
1962	.5317	.5514	3.7	.5473	2.9	.5496	3.2
1963	.5157	.5101	— 1.1	.5124	— 0.6	.5343	3.5
1964	.5400	.5051	— 6.5	.5082	— 5.9	.5454	1.0
1965	.5629	.4816	—14.4	.4884	—13.2	.5386	— 4.5
1966	.4866	.4778	— 1.8	.4855	— 0.2	.5184	6.1
1967	.4952	.4538	— 8.4	.4652	— 6.1	.4977	0.5
1968	.4826	.4459	— 7.6	.4589	— 4.9	.4949	2.5
1969	.5231	.4469	—14.6	.4599	—12.1	.5065	— 3.3

TABLE B4

REGRESSION OF OBSERVED INCOME INEQUALITY ON EXPLANATORY VARIABLES,
MALES 25 AND OVER, 1949–69

Variable	Regression Coefficient	Standard Error	t-Ratio
$\sigma^2(S)$	− 0.1258	0.1560	−0.81
$\sigma^2(A)$	0.0037	0.0034	1.08
$\sigma^2(\ln W)$	−13.1808	9.1885	−1.43
$\mathrm{Cov}(A, S)$	0.0101	0.0404	0.25
$\sigma(\ln W)\ \sigma(S)$	3.3376	2.2560	1.48
$\mathrm{Cov}(A, \ln W)$	− 0.0685	0.0806	−0.85
$(\bar{S})^2$	0.0016	0.0043	0.37
$(\bar{A} - \bar{S} - 5)^2$	− 0.0011	0.0009	−1.16
Intercept	− 0.1100	...	...

NOTE.—Multiple $R = 0.8518$; adjusted $R^2 = 0.54$; and Durbin-Watson statistic $= 2.17$.

TABLE B5

REGRESSION OF OBSERVED INCOME INEQUALITY ON EXPLANATORY VARIABLES,
MALES 25–64, 1949–69

Variable	Regression Coefficient	Standard Error	t-Ratio
$\sigma^2(S)$	− 0.1486	0.0961	−1.55
$\sigma^2(A)$	− 0.0106	0.0071	−1.50
$\sigma^2(\ln W)$	−20.2190	8.1312	−2.49
$\mathrm{Cov}(A, S)$	0.0660	0.0276	2.39
$\sigma(\ln W)\ \sigma(S)$	4.5080	1.7269	2.61
$\mathrm{Cov}(A, \ln W)$	0.1072	0.1581	0.68
$(\bar{S})^2$	− 0.0004	1.7269	−0.19
$(\bar{A} - \bar{S} - 5)^2$	− 0.0026	0.0008	−3.16
Intercept	3.1691	...	...

NOTE. Multiple $R = 0.9365$; adjusted $R^2 = 0.87$; and Durbin-Watson statistic $= 1.41$.

TABLE B6

REGRESSION OF OBSERVED INCOME INEQUALITY ON EXPLANATORY VARIABLES,
MALES 35–44, 1949–69

Variable	Regression Coefficient	Standard Error	t-Ratio
$\sigma^2(S)$	−0.0920	0.0859	−1.07
$\sigma^2(\ln W)$	−4.5414	6.1199	−0.74
$\sigma(\ln W)\ \sigma(S)$	1.1369	1.2042	0.94
$(\bar{S})^2$	0.0549	0.0383	1.43
S	−1.2056	0.8443	−1.43
Intercept	7.4506	...	...

NOTE.—Multiple $R = 0.6585$; adjusted $R^2 = 0.25$; and Durbin-Watson statistic $= 1.47$.

TABLE B7
Correlation Matrix, Males 25 and Over, 1949–69

	$\sigma^2(\ln Y)$	$\sigma^2(S)$	$\sigma^2(A)$	$\sigma^2(\ln W)$	Cov(A, S)	$\sigma(\ln W)\,\sigma(S)$	Cov($A.\ln W$)	S^2
$\sigma^2(S)$	0.22	...	...	...	...	...	...	...
$\sigma^2(A)$	−0.11	0.75	...	...	...	...	...	...
$\sigma^2(\ln W)$	0.67	0.29	−0.24	...	...	...	...	...
Cov(A, S)	−0.06	−0.96	−0.82	−0.09	...	...	...	...
$\sigma(\ln W)\,\sigma(S)$	0.65	0.58	0.05	0.95	−0.03	...	...	...
Coc($A, \ln W$)	−0.30	0.61	0.84	−0.28	−0.33	−0.81	...	...
$\bar{S}^2$	0.01	−0.94	−0.89	−0.03	−0.08	−0.79	0.77	...
$(\bar{A} - \bar{S} - 5)^2$	−0.05	0.93	0.80	0.08	−0.93	0.63	0.27	−0.96

TABLE B8

CORRELATION MATRIX, MALES 25–64, 1949–69

	$\sigma^2(\ln Y)$	$\sigma^2(S)$	$\sigma^2(A)$	$\sigma^2(\ln W)$	$\mathrm{Cov}(A, S)$	$\sigma(\ln W)\,\sigma(S)$	$\mathrm{Cov}(A.\ln W)$	S^2
$\sigma^2(S)$	0.34	...	...	...	...	...	...	...
$\sigma^2(A)$	−0.37	0.03	...	...	...	...	...	...
$\sigma^2(\ln W)$	0.75	0.57	0.35	...	...	...	...	...
$\mathrm{Cov}(A, S)$	−0.19	−0.94	−0.02	−0.48	...	...	...	...
$\sigma(\ln W)\,\sigma(S)$	0.71	0.74	−0.29	0.97	−0.64	...	...	...
$\mathrm{Cov}(A, \ln W)$	0.43	0.28	−0.22	0.68	−0.21	0.63	...	...
$\bar{S}^2$	−0.18	−0.96	−0.22	−0.43	0.90	−0.60	−0.19	...
$(\bar{A} \cdot \bar{S} - 5)^2$	0.13	0.88	−0.15	0.48	−0.84	−0.37	0.72	−0.87

63

TABLE B9

Correlation Matrix, Males 35–44, 1949–69

	$\sigma^2(\ln Y)$	$\sigma^2(S)$	$\sigma^2(\ln W)$	$\dfrac{\sigma(\ln W)}{\sigma(S)}$	$\overline{S^2}$
$\sigma^2(S)$	0.43	...	...	...	...
$\sigma^2(\ln W)$	0.59	0.66	...	...	...
$\sigma(\ln W)\ \sigma(S)$	0.60	0.75	0.99	...	...
$\overline{S^2}$	−0.29	−0.78	−0.47	−0.55	...
$\overline{S}$	−0.29	−0.78	−0.46	−0.54	0.99+

TABLE B10

Data on the Mean and Standard Deviation of Schooling and the Correlation of Schooling with Age

	Age 25+			Age 25–64			Age 35–44	
Year	$\overline{S}$	$\sigma(S)$	R_{sa}	$\overline{S}$	$\sigma(S)$	R_{sa}	$\overline{S}$	$\sigma(S)$
1949	9.54	3.7421	−0.2527	9.66	3.6980	−0.2340	9.90	3.5908
1950	9.66	3.7250	−0.2581	9.79	3.6820	−0.2357	10.08	3.5410
1951	9.80	3.7100	−0.2636	9.93	3.6660	−0.2374	10.26	3.4912
1952	9.93	3.6975	−0.2690	10.07	3.6504	−0.2391	10.43	3.4413
1953	9.99	3.6910	−0.2654	10.13	3.6400	−0.2352	10.48	3.4325
1954	10.05	3.6850	−0.2617	10.19	3.6300	−0.2313	10.53	3.4236
1955	10.12	3.6796	−0.2581	10.25	3.6200	−0.2274	10.58	3.4148
1956	10.18	3.6739	−0.2544	10.31	3.6120	−0.2235	10.63	3.4059
1957	10.24	3.6682	−0.2507	10.37	3.6007	−0.2196	10.68	3.3971
1958	10.36	3.6700	−0.2535	10.49	3.5998	−0.2250	10.83	3.4179
1959	10.50	3.6721	−0.2564	10.63	3.5991	−0.2304	10.98	3.4386
1960	10.59	3.6694	−0.2558	10.72	3.5960	−0.2311	11.08	3.4502
1961	10.69	3.6610	−0.2552	10.81	3.5932	−0.2318	11.18	3.4618
1962	10.79	3.6549	−0.2546	10.90	3.5900	−0.2324	11.29	3.4733
1963	10.89	3.5969	−0.2545	11.00	3.5350	−0.2299	11.39	3.4298
1964	11.00	3.5408	−0.2445	11.10	3.4823	−0.2275	11.48	3.3863
1965	11.07	3.5420	−0.2445	11.17	3.4815	−0.2237	11.58	3.3428
1966	11.14	3.5039	−0.2445	11.23	3.4438	−0.2287	11.60	3.3905
1967	11.27	3.4827	−0.2401	11.37	3.4218	−0.2186	11.67	3.3583
1968	11.40	3.4418	−0.2355	11.49	3.3872	−0.2149	11.79	3.3424
1969	11.52	3.4020	−0.2310	11.61	3.3620	−0.2112	11.86	3.3265

Source.—See Appendix A.

TABLE B11

DATA ON THE MEAN AND STANDARD DEVIATION OF AGE

| | Age 25+ | | Age 25–64 | |
YEAR	$\bar{A}$	$\sigma(A)$	$\bar{A}$	$\sigma(A)$
1949	44.34	12.35	42.52	10.65
1950	44.50	12.31	42.70	10.64
1951	44.66	12.27	42.88	10.64
1952	44.83	12.24	43.07	10.63
1953	44.55	12.33	42.74	10.65
1954	44.59	12.31	42.81	10.66
1955	44.59	12.28	42.83	10.65
1956	44.74	12.29	42.94	10.64
1957	44.98	12.09	43.32	10.56
1958	44.73	12.11	43.10	10.59
1959	44.62	12.02	43.06	10.55
1960	44.81	12.00	43.26	10.56
1961	44.85	11.96	43.36	10.57
1962	45.04	11.98	43.48	10.55
1963	44.96	11.86	43.54	10.53
1964	44.99	11.82	43.59	10.52
1965	45.04	11.86	43.62	10.54
1966	44.98	11.81	43.64	10.57
1967	44.94	11.81	43.63	10.59
1968	44.88	11.89	43.54	10.66
1969	44.88	12.01	43.48	10.73
1970	45.00	11.93	43.67	10.72

SOURCE. See Appendix A.

TABLE B12

DATA ON THE MEAN AND STANDARD DEVIATION OF THE LOG OF WEEKS WORKED
AND THE CORRELATION OF THE LOG OF WEEKS WORKED WITH AGE

| | Age 25+ | | | Age 25–64 | | | Age 35–44 | |
YEAR	$\ln \bar{W}$	$\sigma(\ln W)$	R_{wa}	$\ln \bar{W}$	$\sigma(\ln W)$	R_{wa}	$\ln \bar{W}$	$\sigma(\ln W)$
1949	...	0.4554	−0.1302	...	0.4198	−0.0407	...	0.3653
1950	3.75	0.4554	−0.1302	3.77	0.4198	−0.0407	3.80	0.3653
1951	3.79	0.4066	−0.1472	3.81	0.3615	−0.0450	3.84	0.3078
1952	3.79	0.4089	−0.1730	3.81	0.3561	−0.0604	3.83	0.3203
1953	3.79	0.4051	−0.1853	3.82	0.3512	−0.0746	3.84	0.3204
1954	3.76	0.4465	−0.1650	3.79	0.3970	−0.0577	3.81	0.3463
1955	3.78	0.4141	−0.1861	3.81	0.3544	−0.0519	3.85	0.2874
1956	3.78	0.4255	−0.2075	3.81	0.3587	−0.0683	3.85	0.2868
1957	3.75	0.4597	−0.1830	3.79	0.3979	−0.0459	3.82	0.3403
1958	3.72	0.4940	−0.1646	3.76	0.4371	−0.0236	3.79	0.3938
1959	3.75	0.4532	−0.2009	3.79	0.3872	−0.0524	3.82	0.3416
1960	3.75	0.4755	−0.2129	3.79	0.3999	−0.0471	3.80	0.3468
1961	3.74	0.4829	−0.1790	3.78	0.4168	−0.0254	3.80	0.3874
1962	3.74	0.4893	−0.2077	3.78	0.4175	−0.0471	3.81	0.3652
1963	3.75	0.4766	−0.2207	3.80	0.3961	−0.0497	3.83	0.3273
1964	3.77	0.4589	−0.2211	3.81	0.3771	−0.0534	3.84	0.3225
1965	3.78	0.4407	−0.2196	3.82	0.3635	−0.0641	3.85	0.2984
1966	3.79	0.4316	−0.2374	3.83	0.3474	−0.0633	3.86	0.2914
1967	3.80	0.4165	−0.2362	3.84	0.3335	−0.0645	3.86	0.2644
1968	3.80	0.4079	−0.2223	3.84	0.3336	−0.0644	3.87	0.2524
1969	...	0.4079	−0.2223	...	0.3336	−0.0644	...	0.2524

SOURCE.—See Appendix A.

66

References

Aigner, D. J., and Heins, A. J. "On the Determinants of Income Equality." *A.E.R.* 57 (March 1967): 175–84.

Becker, Gary S. *Human Capital: A Theoretical and Empirical Analysis with Special Reference to Education.* New York: Nat. Bur. Econ. Res., 1964.

——. *Human Capital and the Personal Distribution of Income: An Analytical Approach.* W. S. Woytinsky Lecture no. 1. Ann Arbor: Inst. Public Admin., Univ. Mich., 1967.

Ben-Porath, Yoram. "The Production of Human Capital and the Life Cycle of Earnings." *J.P.E.* 75, pt. 1 (August 1967): 352–65.

Budd, Edward C. "Postwar Changes in the Size Distribution of Income in the U.S." *A.E.R.* 60, no. 2 (May 1970): 247–60.

Chiswick, Barry. "Interstate Analysis of Income Distribution." In "Human Capital and Personal Income Distribution." Mimeographed. New York: Nat. Bur. Econ. Res., 1972.

Fuchs, Victor R. *Differentials in Hourly Earnings by Region and City Size, 1959.* Occasional Paper no. 101. New York: Nat. Bur. Econ. Res., 1967.

Goodman, Leo. "On the Exact Variance of a Product." *J. American Statis. Assoc.* 55 (December 1960): 708–13.

Hashimoto, M. "Factors Affecting State Unemployment." Ph.D. dissertation, Columbia Univ., 1971.

Lydall, Harold. "The Long-Term Trend in the Size Distribution of Income." *J. Royal Statis. Soc.* 122, ser. A, pt. 1 (1959): 1–37.

——. *The Structure of Earnings.* Oxford: Clarendon, 1968.

Metcalf, Charles E. "The Size Distribution of Personal Income during the Business Cycle." *A.E.R.* 59 (September 1969): 657–68.

Miller, Herman P. *Income Distribution in the United States.* 1960 Census Monograph. Washington: U.S. Dept. Commerce, 1966.

Mincer, Jacob. "Schooling, Age, and Earnings." In *Human Capital and Personal Income Distribution.* New York: Nat. Bur. Econ. Res., 1972.

——. "The Distribution of Labor Incomes: A Survey with Special Reference to the Human Capital Approach." *J. Econ. Literature* 8 (March 1970): 1–26.

Rahm, Carl M. "Human Capital and the Occupational Wage Structure." Ph.D. dissertation, Columbia Univ., 1971.

Schultz, T. Paul. "Secular Trends and Cyclical Behavior of Income Distribution in the United States: 1944–1965." In *Six Papers on the Size Distribution of Wealth and Income,* edited by Lee Soltow, pp. 75–100. Studies in Income and Wealth, vol. 33. New York: Nat. Bur. Econ. Res., 1969.

——. "Long Term Changes in Personal Income Distribution." Paper presented at the meetings of the American Economic Association, December 1971.

Soltow, Lee. "The Distribution of Income Related to Changes in the Distributions of Education, Age, and Occupation." *Rev. Econ. and Statis.* 42 (November 1960): 450–53.

——. *Toward Income Equality in Norway.* Madison: Univ. Wis. Press, 1965.

Comment

Mary Jean Bowman

University of Chicago

Barry Chiswick and Jacob Mincer show that a human-capital earnings function is a promising approach for the analysis of income inequality. The model relates income inequality to the distributions of earnings by age, schooling, employment, and rates of return, and to the interrelationships among these variables.

It is important to recognize just what this does and does not mean. It does not entail any sort of dynamic or developmental theoretical framework; time-series distributions are "explained" by applying the coefficients from a static model to one year after another. Nor is this a test of behavioral theory, although prior theoretical applications of capital theory to analysis of human-investment decisions are drawn upon in the specification of the human-capital earnings functions as particular forms of the "general" training case, with gross earnings equal to potential marginal products at full employment. The observed earnings are, of course, net, and the rates of return used are not rates of return proper but, rather, slopes of the logarithms of earnings on schooling—hence, quite directly an empirical measure of relationships between earnings and schooling (or earnings and experience), whatever the theoretical argument. The employment variable (weeks worked), which is treated as extraneous to the human-capital earnings function, adds significantly to the predictive power of the regressions. In brief, the empirical analysis is not a "causal" analysis, either theoretically or in econometric form, and it could stand on its own as a model of national distributive accounting regardless of the modern theory of investment in human beings and its ramifications. "Explanation" in this context is descriptive of components of inequality, not a behavioral analysis of how these things come to be what they are or how they interact. But the paper is greatly enriched by the theoretical background against which it is developed.

This is the second time that I have been cast in the role of discussant

(1970) of a paper by Chiswick (1970), again on a closely related subject. I therefore omit earlier comments that I deem applicable here except incidentally to other remarks. My comments deal with three topics: (1) what is relevant about "inequality" and why; (2) some dubious digressions in the Chiswick-Mincer paper; and (3) further thoughts concerning the theoretical base of the paper and some of its limitations. In view of substantial changes from the original, I have eliminated my initial comments concerning projections into the future (and back to 1939). Other comments have also been modified, although it is possible that I have let some remarks that are no longer applicable slip by.

1. Inequality and Its Meaning

Even if we keep our attention focused on inequalities in earnings, ignoring other aspects of income inequality, of wealth, or of poverty, it would seem appropriate to ask just what facets of inequality may be of greatest interest and how the paper relates to them.

   a) A first consideration must be which populations were included, or which were omitted, and how important these are for analysis of income distribution. Chiswick and Mincer were working with earnings or incomes of white nonfarm males only; excluded were all nonwhites, all farm people, and all females. The importance of the omitted categories for analysis of income distribution, either at a point in time or over time, is evident. Limitation of the population studied had decided advantages for the formulation and interpretation of the Chiswick-Mincer empirical model, but this also is the reason why Mincer could explain only a third of 1959 income variance with schooling and experience as independent variables and over half of that variance by adding weeks worked (Mincer 1972, Pt. II, table 11). Perhaps the limitation to nonfarm white males also is one of the several reasons for projected changes in distributions of earnings being so narrowly bounded; but to attack this question would require another study with a more complex and genuinely dynamic distributive development model. The present paper, with other recent and current work by Mincer on income distribution, constitutes a valuable step toward the larger analysis of how earnings are distributed across the entire adult population and over time.

   b) Despite their careful and sophisticated treatment of life-earnings streams and their takeoff from the theory of investment in human beings, Chiswick and Mincer gave no attention in this paper to the question of inequalities in entire life-income streams; they looked only at inequalities at each point in time. Yet if all individuals had the same expected or realized life-earnings paths, the whole idea of inequality in earnings surely would have quite different economic, social, and political connotations. The data problem in construction of distributions of life-income prospects or experience is a severe one, to be sure; we do not have longitudinal histories of individuals that would permit direct evaluation of distributions of individual life-income experiences adequate even for a single cohort. However, it would be possible to construct cohort approximations by schooling categories and to simulate distributions of earnings around those means for the construction of life-earnings distributions, past and projected into the future. Such explorations would be a natural extension of human-investment decision theory treated as a probabilistic expectational phenomenon. But again, this would be another study. More simply, it would have been interesting to see an analysis of inequalities within educational categories at Mincer's "over-take point" (1972, Pt. II) and at other experience or age levels, even without analysis of autocorrelations.

2. Some Minor Digressions

a) A relatively minor matter with respect to this paper in particular, but perhaps not so minor in a broader view, is a proposition that was introduced in support of the assumption that the coefficients on schooling (*r*) and on experience (*r'*) in equation (5) are random variables independent of *S* and *T*.[1] Citing the argument presented by Becker in his Woytinsky Lecture, Chiswick and Mincer assert that "greater wealth and greater 'ability' are positively correlated, resulting in an ambiguous a priori relation between level of investment and marginal and average rates of return." There are two things wrong with this statement. First, it does not take a positive correlation between wealth and "ability" to get ambiguous results in relations between level of investment and marginal or average rates of return; similar ambiguity can arise with negative correlation between wealth and "ability." Second, it is not nearly so obvious that association between wealth and the marginal rate-of-return schedule (misleadingly labeled "ability") will be positive, as has been assumed. A positive correlation must mean that the easier the access to funds ("wealth"), the greater the marginal rates of return to investments in schooling *despite* higher foregone earnings and access to family and class advantages that are independent of schooling. This set of relationships calls for more careful examination.

b) Chiswick and Mincer evoke the hypothesis of associations between "specific" training at work and years of schooling to explain observed nonzero correlations between weeks worked and age or schooling, although elsewhere their analysis is developed in terms of a "general" rather than a "specific" training model. It is argued further that the high opportunity cost among the better schooled constitutes an incentive to economize on

---

[1] Note that this does *not* say that marginal rates of return to investments are independent of *S* and *T*, although Chiswick and Mincer do tend to read investments into the age-earnings curve.

job search, thereby further contributing to the positive correlations between schooling and weeks worked. However, seniority rules and customs are ignored, as is the operation of different channels of information which serve different individuals. It may be, for example, that what keeps the better educated from losing time in job search is not so much the cost of that time as the greater efficiency of their information networks and the associated chance of placement in a new job before leaving an old one; these are almost certainly causally interdependent phenomena. There would seem to be extremely interesting possibilities in pursuing some of these themes further, both as a way of breaking into the unexplained residual variance in earnings and as a way to trace ways in which schooling may affect labor-market participation and earnings paths.

c) I was a bit startled to discover, in the original version of this paper, that "an older worker" is anyone over 25! While this phraseology has been changed and a regression including men over 65 has been added, there is still little consideration of the real oldsters, despite their importance among populations under one or another "poverty line" and their distinctive situation with respect to choices between work and leisure.

3. The Basic Earning Functions and the Findings Reconsidered

In the end, Chiswick and Mincer conclude that among nonfarm white males in the United States, the distribution of income is dominated by the distributions of age and of employment. Schooling per se plays only a minor part. They also conclude that a substantial decline in inequality in the future could come about through decreased dispersion of employment or a decline in rates of return to training.

These results flow not only from the data but also from their interpretation, which treats postschool increments to earnings over the life-span as independent of prior schooling. Mincer argued an empirical justification for that interpretation in his observations of parallelism in the shapes of logarithmic earnings curves by years of work experience for white men at each level of educational attainment in 1959 (Mincer 1972, Pt. II). He has justified it theoretically by his opportunity-cost model of on-the-job investment in "general" skills. But this sort of an argument entails particular ways of viewing how schooling enters into production. It ignores employer demands for *learning* power and the extent to which schooling is preparation for learning and adapting in a dynamic setting. Also ignored is the fanning out in earnings streams with experience among men in particular schooling categories and the roles of ability in relation to schooling in that process. Although, at the end, the authors stress the importance of looking into the residual variance in earnings, there is a curious selectivity in what is mentioned as within the residual. In particular, the omissions of differences in ability and in the characteristics and explanations of divergent coefficients on weeks worked seem surprising.

Not so surprising, because it has been very generally neglected by economists despite the recent interest in the economics of information, is disregard of the notion that education to various levels and in various sorts of schools provides differential chances to enter working life through a favored *information field*. We could think of this not merely as the certificate phenomenon, which has evoked increasing attention, but as a two- or three-stage information and selection system. At each stage a certain range of potential prospects and contracts is opened up, and this is followed by a subsequent sorting and sifting by both the individual and his employer. If this is in fact the way in which careers evolve, a more fundamental explanation of the distribution of earnings must entail examination of associations among schooling, entry occupations, ability, and communication networks; all of these operate to further or impede the accumulation of learning and of enlarged career opportunities. Once this view of the process is adopted, its dynamic core is immediately evident. So, too, is the critical question of what determines opportunities and the uses made of them over a life-span. The most important questions with respect to distributions of earnings then appear in their true colors: as distributions of life-earnings expectations rather than of earnings across all age groups at a particular point or points in time.

References

Bowman, Mary Jean. "Comment." In *Education, Income and Human Capital*, edited by W. Lee Hansen, pp. 184–89. Studies in Income and Wealth, vol. 35. New York: Nat. Bur. Econ. Res., 1970.

Chiswick, Barry R. "An Interregional Analysis of Schooling and the Skewness of Income." In *Education, Income and Human Capital*, edited by W. Lee Hansen, pp. 157–84. Studies in Income and Wealth, vol. 35. New York: Nat. Bur. Econ. Res., 1970.

Mincer, Jacob. "Schooling, Age, and Earnings." In *Human Capital and Personal Income Distribution*. New York: Nat. Bur. Econ. Res., 1972.

Comment

Thomas Johnson
Southern Methodist University

Barry Chiswick and Jacob Mincer use the basic human-capital model to represent the earnings capacity and observed earnings of males 25 and older. They allow for postschooling investment (OJT) and an effect of aggregate economic activity in the weeks-worked term. It is impressive indeed that with only three variables—schooling, age, and weeks worked—they are able to account for more than 60 percent of the variations in the logarithm of earnings (income) in the 1960 1/1,000 U.S. census sample. The decomposition of this variance is interesting. The most important conclusion, however, is that changes in the level of schooling can be expected to have little effect (by this measure) on the overall distribution of income.

In this comment I will first examine the major approximations which are made in departing from the basic model. I will then raise some questions about the dispersion of weeks worked and, finally, pose a more fundamental inquiry.

After assuming that k_t declines linearly with time, $k_t = k_0[1 - (T/T^*)]$, $\ln(1 - k_t)$ is approximated by a three-term (quadratic) Taylor's series expansion in T about the value T^*. If k_0 is 0.5, this approximation is within 7 percent of the true value of $(1 - k_t)$ at $T = 0$. The error declines to zero at $T = T^*$ and is less than 1 percent for $T = 2T^*$. Thus, if T^*, the age of zero net investment, is halfway between the end of schooling and death (or retirement), we can accept this as a good approximation.

We cannot be too concerned with the quadratic approximation for $\ln(1 - k_t)$ in this paper because the t^2 term is quickly dropped with the justification that "its inclusion would be computationally cumbersome (requiring third and fourth moments of experience), while the addition to explanatory power is not likely to be large." I would like to see some further investigation of this point. Deleting the squared experience term prevents the model from tracking the decline of earnings of older workers

72

which one observes in cross-sectional data. I have found the coefficient of the squared experience term to be significant in the analysis of cross-section data. Might not this deletion be one cause of the problem of underpredicting the inequality in the 35–44 age group (see Sec. III)?

The effect of exogenous depreciation or growth in earnings would also be associated with the experience term. It is of course well known how this exogenous growth in earnings can bias the cross-sectional profile. Including a constant exogenous growth rate in this model would add a term $- g(A - 5)$ to the expression for $\ln Y_t$. This would result in a reduction in the estimate of the variance contribution of A, since the $(\bar{r})^2$ multiplier of $\sigma^2(A)$ would be replaced by $(\bar{r} - g)^2$ in equation (7). The authors note that this phenomenon may be a source of poorer explanatory power when persons 65 years of age and older are included in the regression.

The authors do a good job of justifying dropping the covariance between weeks worked and both schooling and age. Data limitations then overcome our concern for the forms of the r and r' covariance terms, as both r and r' are taken as constant rather than variables with individuals. As long as we are considering white males in the labor force, constancy of r and r' seems reasonable. However, this may be a source of intergroup variation when we start comparing white with nonwhite and male with female earnings.

Moving now to conclusions and policy recommendations, we find that the dispersion of weeks worked does seem to offer an attractive target. It is undoubtedly desirable to reduce among all age groups the dispersion in weeks worked. But programs improving training, health, information, and mobility which would contribute to a reduction of dispersion of weeks worked would be the same programs undertaken to reduce the residual in this model, so weeks worked may not be a source of variation to be attacked separately. When we consider these programs for reducing the residual variation, we realize that even the remarkable 60 percent explanation does not exhaust the explanatory power of the human-capital approach.

Finally, I must voice some misgivings about the meaningfulness of the variation in earnings or income. Actual concern and programs focus on the bottom of the distribution more than the dispersion. Relevancy, therefore, compels us to consider the power of the human-capital model in explaining the lower end of the distribution.

References

Johnson, Thomas. "Returns from Investment in Human Capital." *A.E.R.* 60 (September 1970): 546–60.

Mincer, Jacob. "Schooling, Age, and Earnings." In *Human Capital and Personal Income Distribution.* New York: Nat. Bur. Econ. Res., 1972.

Education, Income, and Ability

Zvi Griliches
Harvard University

William M. Mason
Duke University

I. Introduction

Current estimates of the contribution of education to economic growth have been questioned because they ignore the interaction of education with ability. Whether the neglect of ability differences in the analyses of the income-education relationship results in estimates that are too high was considered in an earlier paper by one of the authors (Griliches 1970), and a negative answer was conjectured. In this paper, we pursue this question a bit further, using a new and larger body of data. Unfortunately, a definitive answer to this question is hampered both by the vagueness and elasticity of "education" and "ability" as analytical concepts and by the lack of data on early (preschooling) intelligence.

The data examined in this paper are based on a 1964 sample of U.S. military veterans. The variables measured include scores on a mental ability test, indicators of parental status, region of residence while growing up, school years completed before service, and school years completed during or after service. These have allowed us to inquire into the separate effects of parental background, intelligence, and schooling.

The basic problem and analytical framework can be set out very simply. Let income be a linear function of education and ability, or, $Y = \alpha + \beta_1 E + \beta_2 G + u$, where Y is income, E is education, G is ability,

This work has been supported by National Science Foundation grant no. GS2762X. This paper was originally prepared for the Social Science Research Council Conference on Structural Equations Models, Madison, Wisconsin, November 1970. We are indebted to Paul Ryan for research assistance and to Edward F. Denison, O. D. Duncan, A. S. Goldberger, A. C. Kerckhoff, and K. O. Mason for comments on earlier drafts.

and u represents other factors affecting income, which are assumed to be random and uncorrelated with E and G. The relation is presumed to hold true for cross-sectional data. If education and ability are positively associated, then a measure of the contribution of education to income that ignores the ability variable (most commonly, the simple least-squares coefficient of Y on E) will be biased upward by the amount $\beta_2 b_{GE}$, where b_{GE} is the regression coefficient of ability on education in the particular sample. The first substantive section of this paper (Section III) investigates the magnitude of this bias via the estimation of income-generating equations containing measures both of education and ability.[1]

In our data the output of the educational process is measured by the number of school grades completed in the formal education system, while ability is measured by the performance on a test at an age when most of the schooling has already been completed. Both of these measures are far from ideal for our purposes. Consider the education variable: What we would like to have is a measure of education achieved (E); what we have is years of schooling completed (S) without reference to the conditions under which individuals obtained their formal schooling and the kinds of schooling pursued. Let us call the discrepancy between these two variables "quality" $(Q,$ where $E = S + Q)$ and assume that it is uncorrelated with the quantity of schooling (S).[2] At the same time, the quality of schooling is likely to be correlated with ability because (1) there is some correlation between socioeconomic status and ability, (2) more able students are more likely to get into better schools, and (3) performance on intelligence tests taken at age 18 or so also reflects in part differences in both the quantity and quality of education.

Allowing for differences in the quality of education makes the assessment of the bias in the estimated education coefficient somewhat more complicated. The true income-generating equation becomes $Y = a + \beta_1 E + \beta_2 G + u = a + \beta_1 S + \beta_1 Q + \beta_2 G + u$.

In this framework, ignoring not only G but also Q leads to the same result as before since b_{QS} (the regression coefficient of quality on quantity of schooling) is zero by assumption. But when a measure of ability is included in the estimating equation, the estimated education coefficient becomes $b_{YS.G} = \beta_1 + \beta_1 b_{QS.G}$, where $b_{QS.G}$ is the partial regression co-

---

[1] Concern with the accuracy of the education estimate due to the omission of ability may, of course, be readily extended to other factors associated with educational attainment and known also to contribute to the determination of socioeconomic outcomes. Denison (1964), for instance, notes the salience of race, inherited wealth, family position, and diligence, and the list can easily be lengthened. In the present analysis we control for these factors to a considerable degree.

[2] This is not too unreasonable an assumption since there is a wide variation in quality of education at all levels of schooling. It is possible, however, that children going to better schools also are more likely to accumulate more years of schooling. If that is the case, we define Q to be that part of the "quality" distribution which is uncorrelated with "quantity." The rest follows in a similar manner.

efficient of quality on quantity of schooling, holding ability constant.[3] Given our assumptions, it can be shown (see the Appendix) that $b_{QS \cdot G} = -b_{QG} \cdot b_{GS}/(1 - r^2_{GS})$, where r^2_{GS} is the square of the correlation coefficient between the quantity of schooling and ability. Since we expect both b_{QG} (the regression coefficient of educational quality on individual ability) and b_{GS} (the regression coefficient of individual ability on quantity of schooling) to be positive, $b_{QS \cdot G}$ will be negative. Substituting this expression for $b_{QS \cdot G}$ back into the expression for $b_{YS \cdot G}$ gives $b_{YS \cdot G} = \beta_1 - \beta_1 b_{QG} \cdot b_{GS}/(1 - r^2_{GS})$. Since $b_{YS} = \beta_1 + \beta_2 b_{GS}$, it is clear that by going from b_{YS} to $b_{YS \cdot G}$ we reduce the coefficient of schooling for two reasons. First, we eliminate the upward bias due to the earlier omission of ability. Second, however, we *introduce* another bias due to the correlation of ability with the left-out quality variable. This new bias is partly a function of the magnitude of the correlation between quantity of schooling and ability. We solve the problem of this second bias by concentrating our attention on that part of schooling occurring during or after military service (SI—schooling increment), which turns out to be almost entirely uncorrelated with our measure of ability and hence is not subject to this type of bias.

The availability of the schooling-increment variable also helps us to solve another vexing problem—how to disentangle the question of causality when the available measure of ability may itself be in part the result of schooling. Since the intelligence test available in these data is administered pior to entering service, performance on it cannot be affected by the schooling increment. Thus, because our measure of ability is causally prior to SI, and because using SI reduces the bias problem in estimating the effects of education on income, we shall be putting most of the stress on the results for only a *part* of schooling (SI) in the subsequent sections.

We have already noted that our ability measure is not ideal because it is obtained after most of the formal schooling has been completed. What we would like is a measure of ability obtained before the major effects of the school system have been felt. Although it is possible using data such as ours to construct models which incorporate estimates of the effects of *early* ability (see Duncan 1968; Bowles 1970), we have chosen to work exclusively with our measure of *late* ability. Given this decision, the ability variable we work with still is not ideal for our purposes. For it is possible that our measure of ability, *taken as a measure of late ability*, has errors in it. These errors may have a number of sources, and some may be random, others nonrandom. To the extent the errors are random, we know that a direct application of least squares in their presence may understate the effect of ability on income and simultaneously bias the estimated education

---

[3] These formulae hold as computational identities between least-squares coefficients. They also can be interpreted as expectations of computed least-squares coefficients from random samples from a population satisfying our assumptions.

coefficient upward. To circumvent this effect of random errors we devise, in Section IV, a model of income determination that contains an unobserved achievement variable in place of measured ability. Manipulation of this model leads to equations estimable by means of a two-stage or instrumental-variables approach and secures a reading of the effect of ability freed of random errors.[4]

In Section V our results are summarized and compared with previous work in this field. Unlike other studies, we can focus on a relatively independent part of total schooling—that gained during or after military service. This gives us a less-biased estimate of the effect of a change in schooling than was possible before.

II. The Sample and the Variables

Our analysis is based on a sample of post–World War II veterans of the U.S. military, contacted by the Bureau of the Census in a 1964 Current Population Survey (CPS). The population consists of men who were then in the age range of 16–34 years, primarily the ages of draft eligibility. The sample includes about 3,000 veterans for whom supplementary information from individual military records was collated with the CPS questionnaire responses.[5] Of special interest to us is that a substantial proportion of the veterans' military records contain individual scores on the Armed Forces Qualification Test (AFQT), which we use here in lieu of standard civilian mental ability (IQ) tests.

The men who serve in the U.S. military do not represent any recent cohort of draft-age men, since those at either extreme of the ability and socioeconomic distributions are less likely to serve than those in the middle.[6] Thus, conclusions based on our analysis of these data apply only to the veterans' population. But, since this population is sizable, the data are of interest despite their obvious limitation. Moreover, this is one of the few relatively large sets of data combining information on income, education, demographic characteristics, mental test scores, and family socioeconomic background. The latter three are important as controls in estimating the income-education relationship.

---

[4] Ideally we would like to correct all of our variables for random errors. But although it is possible to adjust some others besides ability for random errors (Siegel and Hodge 1968), we do not have enough information to adjust them all. Since our major interest is with changes in the education coefficient due to the inclusion of the ability measure, the errors in the latter are most crucial to our analysis.

[5] See Rivera (1965) and Klassen (1966) for a description of the sample. Duncan (1968) and Mason (1968, 1970), among others, used these data.

[6] Educational deferments have channeled substantial numbers of young men into entirely civilian careers, and a low score on the AFQT reduces the probability of being drafted. For a general discussion of this aspect of the Selective Service System see U.S. President's Task Force on Manpower Conservation (1964). Davis and Dolbeare (1968) give an overview of Selective Service.

Within the veterans' sample, the individuals on whom we base our conclusions are 1,454 men who were employed full time when contacted by the CPS; who were between the ages of 21 and 34 and not then enrolled in school; who were either white or black; who provided complete information about their current occupation, income, education, family background; and for whom AFQT scores were available.[7]

The major characteristics of our sample and the variables we used are summarized in table 1. The definition and measurement of most of the

TABLE 1

MEANS AND STANDARD DEVIATIONS OF VARIABLES:
VETERANS AGE 21–34 IN 1964 CPS SUBSAMPLE

Variable	Mean or Fraction in Sample	SD	Symbol in Subsequent Tables	Group Name
Personal background:				
Age (years)	29.0	3.5	Age	
Color (white)	0.96	*	C	
Schooling before service (years)	11.5	2.3	SB	
Total schooling (years) ..	12.3	2.5	ST	
Schooling increment (years)	0.8	1.4	SI	
AFQT (percentile)	54.6	24.8	AFQT	
Length of active military service (months)	30.7	16.9	AMS	
Father's schooling (years)	8.7	3.2	FS	Fa. stat.
Father's occupational SES	29.0	20.6	FO	
Grew up in South	0.29	*	ROS	
Grew up in large city	0.22	*	POC	Reg. bef.
Grew up in suburb of large city	0.05	*	POS	
Current location:				
Now living in the South ..	0.27	*	RNS	
Now living in the West ..	0.15	*	RNW	Reg. now
Now living in an SMSA ..	0.68	*	SMSA	
Current achievement:				
Length of time in current job (months)	54.3	42.8	LCJ	Curr. exp.
Never married	0.14	*	NM	
Current occupational SES	39.2	22.7	...	
Log current occupational SES	3.47	0.68	LOSES	
Actual income (weekly, dollars)	122.5	52.4	...	
Log actual income	4.73	0.40	LINC	

NOTE.—$N = 1,454$, for this and subsequent tables based on the 1964 CPS. Fa. stat. = father's status; reg. bef. = region before; reg. now = region now; curr. exp. = current experience.
  * The standard deviation for a dummy variable is equal to $\sqrt{f(1-f)}$, where f is the fraction in the sample having the requisite characteristic. Thus, it is computable from the numbers given in the first column.

[7] The variables noted above account for the greatest reduction in sample size, but

variables is standard, and we shall comment here only on a few of the more important ones.

Income is gross weekly earnings in dollars. It is an answer to the request: "Give your usual earnings on this job before taxes and other deductions." The data provide also another concept of income, "earnings expected from all jobs in 1964." We experimented at some length with both concepts of income, getting somewhat better (more stable) results for the first (actual) income measure. Since the major results were similar for both measures of income, we shall report here only those for the first (actual) income measure. We also experimented a bit with functional form before settling on the semilog form for the "income-generating" function leading to the use of the logarithm of income (LINC) as our main dependent variable.

Education is measured in years of school (highest grade) completed and is recorded at two points in time: before entry into military service and at the time of the survey. By taking the difference between total grades of school completed (ST) and grades of school completed before military service (SB) we get a measure of the increment in schooling (SI) acquired during or after military service.[8] The minimum value of this variable is zero (no increment in schooling), and the maximum is six grades. As noted above, this incremental measure of education is central to our analysis both because it occurs after the time at which ability was measured and because it is so little correlated with our measure of ability.

Performance on the AFQT is scaled as a percentile score estimated from eight grouped categories.[9] This test includes questions on vocabulary, arithmetic, and spatial relations, but also contains a section on tool knowledge. The AFQT has been treated by other investigators (including Duncan 1968; and Jensen 1969) as an intelligence test, so that we are following in the footsteps of others in this regard. We are unaware, though, that the comparability of the AFQT with civilian intelligence tests has ever been documented.[10]

---

the data file used also contains a number of other variables of interest and is consequently slightly smaller than it would be solely on the basis of the above-mentioned variables.

[8] Each of the education measures is based on eight categories of school years completed and is scored as follows: Less than 8 years = 4; 8 years = 8; 9–11 years but not high school graduate = 10; high school graduate = 12; some college but less than 2 years = 13.5; 2 or more years of college but no degree = 15; B.A. = 16; and graduate study beyond the B.A. = 18. As a matter of convenience we will hereafter refer to SI as *post*service schooling, ignoring the possibility that some of the increment may have occurred while the man was in service.

[9] The percentile scores are the midpoints of each of the eight categories provided in the data. For a number of individuals in the sample there were records of results for mental tests other than the AFQT. Prior to our acquisition of the data these scores were converted to AFQT-equivalents following instructions provided by the Department of Defense. Despite use of the AFQT to select individuals into the armed forces, all levels of performance on the AFQT are represented in our sample.

[10] We would welcome information on this point. Our own review turned up nothing about the reliability of the AFQT or about correlations between it and civilian IQ

It is clear from even this brief discussion of the AFQT that *some* error may arise from using the AFQT as an intelligence test in addition to the kinds of errors which could be present in using one of the standard civilian IQ tests.[11] Another difficulty with the use of the AFQT in our analysis, a difficulty which is inherent in the use of *any* global IQ test for purposes such as ours, is that IQ by definition is an aggregation of several different traits (for example, verbal and mathematical ability) sampled from some larger population of traits. The weights used in combining these traits to obtain a global IQ score are not necessarily those which would maximize the contribution of each trait to some other variable (such as income). Therefore, the use of AFQT instead of the separate traits which comprise it, and the use of only those traits, may lead to attenuation in our estimate of the effect of ability on income. This explains our interest in the errors-in-variables approach to be taken up in Section IV.

The long list of other variables considered can be divided, somewhat imperfectly, into personal background and current location and success variables. In the first group, we have the usual variables for age (in years), color dummy (white = 1, black = 0), and region and place of *origin* dummies (these are in terms of places "you lived most until age 15") that record growing up in the South, in a large city (over 100,000 in population), or in a suburb of such a city. In addition to these, we also have two measures of parental status: father's schooling (in years of school completed—FS) and father's occupation (FO, coded according to Duncan's 1961 SES scale).[12]

The age variable is usually included in such studies because older men (within the range of our data) are likely to have had more training on the job and more opportunity to find the better jobs that are appropriate to their training. This, however, is probably measured better not by calendar time but by the actual time spent in the civilian labor force accumulating

---

tests. Karpinos (1966, 1967), the only articles we found discussing the AFQT, focused on characteristics of those failing the test, not the test itself. We have seen fragmentary evidence about the AGCT, predecessor of the AFQT, but to extrapolate from experiences with the former to the latter would be merely to speculate.

[11] If the AFQT is not virtually interchangeable with the standard civilian IQ tests, then Jensen (1969) could well be wrong in assuming that the heritability of the AFQT is the same as for the standard civilian tests. Griliches (1970, pp. 92–104) suggests that the heritability of the AFQT may be lower than Jensen supposes, and pursues related issues.

[12] These are, of course, only incomplete measures of the family's socioeconomic status and are subject moreover to the possibility of recall error and misperception by respondents (sons) from whom this information was elicited. Blau and Duncan (1967, appendices D and E) take up the issue of recall error for these two variables in their occupational changes in a generation (OCG) sample. Conclusions drawn from their discussion should apply here, since the OCG sample is comparable with ours in the same age group. For evidence on this see Duncan (1968), who reports virtually identical correlations between father's education and occupation for the OCG and the CPS sample from which we draw.

work "experience."[13] We can estimate this roughly by defining: potential experience = age — 18 — (education before service — 12) — education after service — (total months in service)/12. Since this measure is a linear function of variables that we include anyway (age and schooling), there is no need to compute it explicitly. It does provide, however, an interpretation for the role of time spent in military service (AMS), when the latter variable is introduced separately.[14]

The "current location and success" variables are represented by a regional dummy variable classification of current location as south, northeast-northcentral and west (RNS and RNW); a dummy variable for current residence in a Standard Metropolitan Statistical Area (SMSA); a measure of the length of time on current job (LCJ, in months); a dummy variable for never married (NM) as opposed to other possibilities; and a measure of the socioeconomic status of the individual's current occupation (LOSES, the logarithm of Duncan's occupational SES scale). Each of these factors intervenes between education and income and helps to explain the relationship between these two variables. For example, more education may lead to greater interpersonal competence and other socially desirable characteristics which in turn may lead to a greater likelihood of being married. Individuals in this status may be expected to have the incentive of responsibility for others, and this may in turn lead to higher income.

Although we present some results that take into account factors intervening between education and income, they are not of central interest to us. We shall, therefore, not emphasize them in our discussion but concentrate instead on the contribution of the education and ability estimates in the presence of background factors alone.

Table 1 presents means and standard deviations for the variables to be used. Note that this group of veterans is young and hence will not exhibit differentials in income by education as large as those occurring in later, peak-earnings years. Also, because the number of blacks is quite small, white-black income differences will be characterized only by the multiplicative coefficient for the *color* dummy variable (since we are using the logarithm of income as our dependent variable). Although there are "interactions" between the color dummy variable and some of the other variables in the income-generating equation (Duncan 1969), there are too few blacks to estimate reliably the coefficients of the interaction terms. Observe, finally, that the average increment in schooling for this group of men is nearly one complete grade (0.8). Actually, 68 percent of the group did not return to school after service, so that those with additional schooling must have completed on average more than one additional grade. Since the

[13] The use of such a measure was suggested to us by Jacob Mincer.

[14] There is scant reason (Mason 1970) to believe that military service conveys a subsequent advantage in the civilian labor force. Thus we expect the AMS variable to have a negative coefficient in the income-generating equation.

grades completed range from a high school grade to a graduate school grade, it appears that the incremental-schooling variable may justifiably stand alone in the income-estimating equations.

In table 2 we list the simple correlation coefficients between the major variables of our sample. Note that there is very little correlation between the increment in schooling (SI) and various personal background variables such as color, father's schooling and occupation, and the respondent's AFQT score. None of these accounts for more than 1 percent of the variance of the schooling-increment variable. We have in this variable something as close to a well-designed experimental situation as we are likely to get in social science statistics.

III. Direct Results

A major objection to the usual estimates of the contribution of education to economic growth is their dependence on cross-sectional income-schooling relationships. The latter are likely to overestimate the "true" effect of schooling because of its intercorrelation with the omitted measures of social status and mental ability. Our sample provides two ways of meeting this objection. First, we do have measures of ability and parental status and can thus attempt to control for these biases directly. But more importantly, we can break down our schooling variable into two, the second part of which, the schooling increment (SI), is much less related to such other factors and hence also much less subject to such bias.

The causal model we use to guide our assessment of the relationships between income, education, ability, and other variables at our disposal can be stated as follows (using the variable labels given in table 1): (1) $SB = F(\text{fa. stat., reg. bef., } C)$; (2) $AFQT = G(\text{fa. stat., reg. bef., } C, SB)$; (3) $AMS = H(\text{fa. stat., reg. bef., } C, \text{age, } SB, AFQT)$; (4) $SI = J(\text{fa. stat., reg. bef., } C, \text{age, } SB, AFQT, AMS)$; (5) $LINC = K(\text{fa. stat., reg. bef., } C, \text{age, } SB, AFQT, AMS, SI)$; where each of these functional relationships indicates a (linear) structural equation. Figure 1 provides a slightly more globally stated graphic equivalent to (1)–(5). As it stands, the model is given by a set of recursive equations. Including other functional relationships linking current achievement and location variables to income and other factors would lead to some simultaneous relationships, and in any case would complicate the model unnecessarily for our purposes. Thus, since we are primarily interested in the *total* effects of schooling and ability *net* of potential labor-force experience and background factors, we will not report on all the structural equations that inclusion of occupational SES, marital status, and other variables would entail.[15] For

[15] At one point (see table 5), though, we do use some of these additional variables to expand the list of regressors in order to determine the maximum ability of our data to predict income.

TABLE 2

CORRELATIONS (r) BETWEEN SELECTED VARIABLES IN THE 1964 CPS SUBSAMPLE

VARIABLES	(1)	(2)	(3)	(4)	(5)	(6)	(7)	(8)	(9)	(10)
(1) Age	1.000	...	...	...	...	...	...	...	...	...
(2) Color	−.055	1.000	...	...	...	...	...	...	...	...
(3) Schooling before AMS ...	−.010	.011	1.000	...	...	...	...	...	...	...
(4) Schooling increment ...	.109	−.028	−.170	1.000	...	...	...	...	...	...
(5) Total schooling	.052	−.006	.832	.405	1.000	...	...	...	...	...
(6) AFQT	−.056	.174	.469	.098	.490	1.000	...	...	...	...
(7) Log income	.216	.116	.264	.149	.329	.235	1.000	...	...	...
(8) Log occupational SES ...	.120	.031	.397	.216	.490	.311	.338	1.000	...	...
(9) Father's schooling ...	−.093	.004	.283	.103	.321	.229	.114	.250	1.000	...
(10) Father's occupational SES ...	−.004	.089	.307	.085	.333	.242	.229	.266	.431	1.000

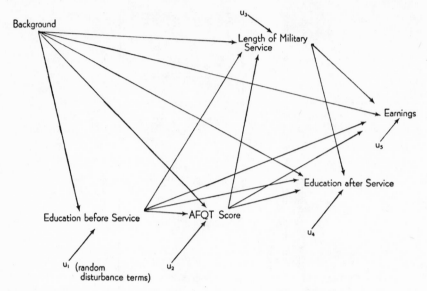

Fɪɢ. 1.—Basic causal model for determination of earnings. u_i = random disturbance terms.

the same reason, we concentrate in this section on the income equation, using the actual estimates for the rest of the causal model only to obtain a few secondary results.

The organization for the rest of this section is as follows: First we describe the sensitivity of the education coefficients to inclusion of ability and personal background characteristics in the income-generating equation. At this point we also appraise more generally the contribution of education to income. Next we describe the contributions of ability, background, color, and other variables in the income-generating equation, and, to some extent, their contributions in the model taken as a whole. Finally, we summarize some of the relationships between variables other than income.

Education.—We began this paper with a concern about the bias in the schooling coefficient due to the omission of ability. There are, however, several different ways of measuring this bias. We have already stated the need to take into account personal background factors. Doing so means that the estimated bias in the schooling coefficient due to omitting ability can be computed before or after the inclusion of personal-background factors in the regression. We also are including two schooling variables, so that there are two schooling coefficients to examine for each assessment of bias, although we have emphasized that the coefficient of schooling after service is preferable to the coefficient of schooling before service. Therefore, to derive the needed bias figures, our procedure is to regress income on (1) education; (2) education and ability; (3) education and personal-background factors; (4) education, personal-background factors, and ability. Comparisons made among these four regressions will provide the necessary figures for assessing bias.

Table 3 presents a number of regression results relating the logarithm of income to selected variables at our disposal. All of the regressions include age, length of military service, and color, so that the education, ability, and background effects are all net of color and the potential experience variable defined earlier. The first four regressions are directly relevant to deriving the reduction of the schooling coefficients due to the inclusion of personal-background factors and ability. For comparative purposes, regressions 5–8 parallel regressions 1–4 but use total schooling instead of the two separate schooling components.

Regression 1 provides the "baseline" estimates of the two schooling coefficients, estimates that do not allow for the effects of ability, father's status, and region of origin. Regressions 2 and 3, respectively, add AFQT and personal-background factors to the baseline regression. Regression 4 includes both AFQT and personal-background factors. By taking one minus the ratio of the education coefficient after including the factor to the corre- sponding education coefficient before including the factor, we get the proportionate bias in the schooling coefficients due to the omission of a relevant factor as a proportion. These calculations applied separately to regressions 1–4 and 5–8 provide the estimates shown in table 4.

Looking first at the figures for SB and SI, the introduction of the AFQT variable leads to a drop of 7–10 percent in the coefficient of SI and 13–17 percent in the coefficient of SB. The drop in the SB coefficient (22–25 percent) is, however, much greater than in the SI coefficient (3–6 percent) when the personal-background factors are included. Moreover, the total decline in the SB coefficient (35 percent) is nearly three times the decline in the SI coefficient (12 percent). These results were to be expected. Education before service is more highly correlated to personal-background factors and ability than education after service and more likely to be biased downward because of the absence of a measure of school quality.[16] This is why

---

[16] The argument concerning the effects of the left-out variable of schooling quality is slightly more complicated than that outlined in the Introduction because of the presence of *two* schooling variables. Considering only differences in the quality of schooling before military service and assuming that they are uncorrelated with both SB and SI leads to the conclusion that the introduction of the AFQT variable will bias the estimated SB coefficient downward (due to the assumed positive correlation of quality of schooling, Q, with AFQT and the observed positive correlation of AFQT with SB). The estimated coefficient of SI would remain unbiased provided that it really was uncorrelated with SB, AFQT, and the unobserved Q. The correlation of SI with AFQT is effectively zero ($r^2 = .007$), but it does have a nonnegligible negative correlation with SB. This leads also to a downward but smaller bias in the coefficient of SI; the ratio of the two biases (in the coefficient of SI relative to the bias in the co-efficient of SB) is equal to $b_{SB,SI}$, which is about .3 in our data (see Appendix).

TABLE 3

Regression Equations with Log Income as Dependent Variable

Regression No.	Color	SB	SI	ST	AFQT	Other Variables in Equation*	R^2
1	.2548 (.0472)	.0502 (.0042)	.0528 (.00702)	...	...	Age, AMS	.1666
2	.2225 (.0479)	.0418 (.0049)	.0475 (.0072)	...	.00154 (.00045)	Age, AMS	.1732
3	.1904 (.0473)	.0379 (.0045)	.0496 (.0070)	...	...	Age, AMS, fa. stat., reg. bef.	.2129
4	.1714 (.0479)	.0328 (.0050)	.0462 (.0071)	...	.00105 (.00045)	Age, AMS, fa. stat., reg. bef.	.2159
5	.2544 (.0471)	...	...	.0508 (.0039)	...	Age, AMS	.1665
6	.22245 (.04793)	...	...	.0433 (.0044)	.00150 (.00045)	Age, AMS	.1729
7	.1907 (.0473)	...	...	.0408 (.0041)	...	Age, AMS, fa. stat., reg. bef.	.2115
8	.1732 (.0479)	...	...	.0365 (.0046)	.00097 (.00044)	Age, AMS, fa. stat., reg. bef.	.2141
9	.1335 (.0487)	...	...	...	.00252 (.00041)	Age, AMS, fa. stat., reg. bef.	.1794
10	.1742 (.0488)	...	...	...	...	Age, AMS, fa. stat., reg. bef.	.1578
11	.2052 (.0456)	.0320 (.0048)	.0445 (.0068)	...	.00115 (.00045)	Age, fa. stat., reg. bef., reg. now, curr. exp., AMS	.2979
12	.2240 (.0449)	.0372 (.0046)	.0468 (.0068)	...	.00129 (.00043)	Age, reg. now, curr. exp., AMS	.2851

Note.—See table 1 for definitions.

* Variable groups are denoted as follows: fa. stat. = fa. occ. and fa. schooling; reg. bef. = RUS, POC, POS; reg. now = RNS, RNW, SMSA; curr. exp. = NM, LCJ.

TABLE 4

ESTIMATED BIAS IN SCHOOLING COEFFICIENTS

PROPORTIONAL CHANGE IN THE COEFFICIENT OF			
SB	SI	ST	VARIABLES ADDED
.17	.10	.15	AFQT
.25	.06	.20	Fa. stat., reg. bef.
.35	.12	.28	AFQT, fa. stat., reg. bef.
.13	.07	.11	AFQT added after fa. stat., reg. bef.
.22	.03	.16	Fa. stat., reg. bef. added after AFQT

we prefer the coefficient of SI as an estimate of the effect of an incremental change in schooling. But, even using total schooling, the decline (28 percent) in the education coefficient is not all that great. Of the total decline in the coefficient for ST, 11–15 percent can be attributed to the introduction of the AFQT variable; the rest is due to parental background and region and size of city of origin, variables that are likely to be closely related to the omitted school-quality dimension.

For analysis of the contribution of education to economic growth, the most appropriate estimate is that given by the coefficient of incremental schooling in regression 4, a regression which includes background and ability measures but does not contain any later current experience and success variables. The value of this coefficient is .0462, and we have already observed that this is only 12 percent lower than the .0528 given by the first regression, which includes no background or ability measures. Thus, while the usual estimates of the contribution of education may be biased upward due to the omission of such variables, this bias does not appear to be large and is much smaller than the 40 percent originally suggested by Denison (1962).

Education does, of course, make some significant independent contribution to the explanation of income, as may be seen by comparing regression 9 with regression 4. And comparison of regressions 4 and 8 indicates that even though the two schooling variables are acquired at different times and under different circumstances, their effects on income are similar. In fact, the difference between the two schooling coefficients in regression 4 is not statistically significant at the conventional 5 percent level, although this difference is significant at about the 8 percent level (which the computed $F = 3.2$ satisfies). We would expect the difference to be more highly significant with a larger sample, and we also would expect the inclusion of a school-quality measure to eliminate it completely.

Finally, recall that our model postulates the dependency of postservice schooling, length of service, and performance of the AFQT on schooling before service. It might be argued, quite apart from SB's sensitivity to the omission of school quality from regression 4, that the correct comparison of the effects of SB and SI on income would take account of SB's indirect contribution to income through SI, AMS, and AFQT, and that if we made this comparison we would discover SB's effect on income to be greater than SI's. As it turns out, the hypothesis that excluding the paths of SB through SI, AMS, and AFQT to income stacks the cards in favor of the coefficient of SI is incorrect. For, taking into account SB's effects on SI, AMS, and AFQT, we obtain a total coefficient of .0319 for SB's effect on income, which is slightly less than the direct coefficient of .0328 for SB in regression 4.[17] The explanation for this is, of course, that there is a negative relationship between SI and SB; the further a man goes in school before service, the less he needs to go after leaving service, and the less he *can* go after leaving service.

AFQT.—Given the current resurgence of interest in the role of intelligence in the achievement process and the common use of the AFQT as a measure of IQ, the performance of this variable is more modest than we had expected. While it is relatively highly intercorrelated with schooling before military service and with the other personal-background variables, its own *net* contribution to the explanation of the variance in the income of individuals is very small. For example, introducing AFQT into regression 2 increases the R^2 by only .007 (relative to regression 1). Introducing it into regression 4 would only increase the R^2 by .003 (relative to regression 3). Even if one attributed all of the joint schooling-intelligence effects (including schooling before service and hence before the date of these tests) to the AFQT variable, one would raise its contribution to the R^2 to only .022 (regression 9 vs. regression 10).[18]

[17] Given the causal ordering embodied in equations (1)–(5), the total effect of SB on income net of all prior factors can be decomposed into a direct contribution (given in regression 4) and an indirect contribution, obtained by computing the contribution of SB to income *through* SI, AMS, and AFQT. Decompositions of this sort are part of the results of the method of path regressions or path coefficients (Duncan 1966). Or, as we demonstrate later, they also can be derived by application of the excluded-variables formula given in the introduction. Dividing the variables listed in (1)–(5) into SI (S), SB (B), AFQT (T), AMS (M), other (O), and calling income y, we can think of the total effect of SB on y as given by $b_{yB.O}$. The decomposition of this coefficient implied by our model is given by the following expression: $b_{yB.O} = b_{yB.TOMS}$ $+ b_{SB.TOM} \cdot b_{yS.TOMB} + b_{MB.TO} \cdot (b_{yM.TOBS} + b_{yS.TOMB} \cdot b_{SM.TOB}) + b_{TB.O}$ $[b_{yT.MOBS} + b_{ST.MOB} \cdot b_{yS.TOMB} + (b_{yM.TOBS} + b_{yS.TOMB} \cdot b_{SM.TOB}) b_{MT.BO}]$. The first term on the right-hand side gives the net, direct effect of SB on income, and is equal to .0328 as indicated by regression 4. Each of the other terms on the right-hand side gives the indirect contribution of SB to income through SI, AMS, and AFQT, respectively. The sum of these indirect effects is −.0009. Therefore $b_{yB.O} = .0319$.

[18] Another way to look at the relation between income and AFQT is to decompose the correlation between them into components, using path coefficients. Doing so is equivalent to a repeated application of the excluded-variables formula, with all the variables scaled to have mean zero and a unit standard deviation. The advantage of such a decomposition is that it is additive, whereas a decomposition in terms of changes in R^2 is not. This decomposition does presuppose a causal ordering, for which we shall

One final consideration is of interest here in discussing the role of AFQT in determining earnings. The literature on the "residual factor" and economic growth (Denison 1964, for example) has frequently involved adjusting, rather arbitrarily, observed income distributions for variation presumed due to a genetic substrate. Relevant variation on this substrate is usually held to be measured best by variation in performances on intelligence tests and to some extent by variation in parental social status. Since, in this paper, we have measures of these variables, we are in a position to question how much they contribute, taken together, to the explanation of income differences. We can then use our estimate as an upper bound for the (presently) measurable effects of this part of genetic heredity on income. This, in turn, provides us with another way of looking at the bias in education due to omitting intelligence and parental status.

With our data, adding AFQT and fa. stat. to this list of regressors in a regression of income on age, color, and reg. bef. increases the R^2 by only .052; while adding *color*, AFQT, and fa. stat. to the list of regressors in a regression of income on age and reg. bef. increases the R^2 by only .061. The increment in explained variance due to these "heredity"-associated variables is thus only about a fifth of the total "explainable" variance in income (the maximal R^2 in predicting income is given in table 5 as .31). And this makes no allowance for the effects of quality of schooling and discrimination that are confounded with color, regional origin, and parental-status variables. The *measurable* potential effects of genetic diversity on income, in the sense described above, appear to be much smaller than is usually implied in debates on this subject. And it follows, therefore,

---

use equations (1)–(5) (our model). Dividing and labeling our variables into AFQT (T), SI (S), AMS (M), and other (O), calling income y, and using the left-out variables formula repeatedly, we get the path coefficients decomposition of: $r_{yT} = \beta_{yT.MSO} + \beta_{yM.SOT} \cdot \beta_{MT.O} + \beta_{yS.TOM} (\beta_{ST.MO} + \beta_{SM.OT} \cdot \beta_{MT.O}) + r_{OT} [\beta_{yO.TSM} + \beta_{yS.TOM} (\beta_{SO.TM} + \beta_{SM.TO} \cdot \beta_{MO.T}) + \beta_{yM.SOT} \cdot \beta_{MO.T}]$, where the "$\beta$'s" are the standardized partial regression coefficients and $\beta_{ij} = r_{ij}$. The first term of the right-hand side is the net effect of T on y, the second and third terms together give the effect of T via M and S, and the last term gives the effect of T which is "due to" or "joint with" the other variables (O).

The decomposition of r_{yT} via path coefficients yields the conclusion that more than half of the observed simple correlation between income and AFQT is "due to" or "joint with" the logically prior variables of color, fa. stat., reg. bef., SB, and age. The estimates for equations (1)–(5) of our model imply that $r_{\text{earnings}\cdot\text{AFQT}} = .2355 =$ (.0657 net) + (.0361 through SI and AMS) + (.1337 joint with, or due to, other factors) = (.102 attributable to AFQT net of prior factors) + (.133 attributable to correlations between AFQT and prior factors). In terms of the model used here, over half of the initial correlation between income and AFQT is explained by factors in the model which are prior to AFQT. And, even if schooling before service and the background variables were not taken as predetermined with respect to AFQT, over half of the zero-order correlation still would be allocated to *joint* influence with these other independent variables. Note also that $r = .1$ (the approximate role of AFQT net of prior factors) is equivalent to $r^2 = .01$.

TABLE 5

REGRESSION OF LOG INCOME ON ALL AVAILABLE
RELEVANT VARIABLES

Variable	Coefficient	t-Ratio
Age	.0126	(4.3)
Color	.1970	(4.4)
FO	.0016	(3.2)
FS	−.0038	(−1.2)
POC	.0325	(1.4)
POS	.0971	(2.4)
ROS	−.0238	(−0.7)
SB	.0244	(4.9)
AFQT	.00095	(2.2)
SI	.0352	(4.8)
RNS	−.0751	(−2.3)
RNW	.1173	(4.5)
SMSA	.1365	(6.7)
LCJ	.0013	(5.7)
NM	−.1496	(−5.7)
LOSES	.0804	(5.3)
AMS	−.0011	(2.0)
(Constant)	3.6483	...
(R^2)	.3114	...

that since most of the effects of heredity are indirect, there is little bias
in an estimate of a schooling coefficient that does not take heredity into
account. Heredity will affect the distribution of schooling attained, but
the estimated schooling coefficient measures its contribution correctly, whatever the source of a change in schooling.

Additional details and relationships.—By including almost all of the
variables available to us (see table 5) we can account for about a third
of the observed variance in the logarithm of income. This is comparable
with the results of other studies based on observations of individuals (for
example, Hanoch 1967), but it is clear that the bulk of the variance in
individual income is not accounted for by our equations, even when using
a rather long list of variables.

We may use the regression displayed in table 5 to provide some more
information on our results. Since the dependent variable is the logarithm
of income, these coefficients (times 100) give the percentage effect of a
unit change in the respective variables on income. The more interesting
findings here are: (1) The nonsignificance of the father's schooling variable
in the presence of father's occupational SES score. This is also true in
most of the other regressions. (2) The relative importance of current
location (being in an SMSA and in the West). (3) The rather surprising
strong negative effect of not having married. And (4), the negative effect
of time spent in the military and the implied positive effect of potential
experience in the labor force on income.[19]

[19] Since, except for constants, potential experience = age − SB − SI − AMS/12,
in a regression that already contains age, SB, and SI, its coefficient is given by *the*

In table 6 we gather some results on the interrelationships between the other variables in our model. Among the more interesting of these are the highly significant (and rather large) effects of region, color, and schooling before service on AFQT, and the barely significant (and minor) effects of the parental-status variables. This is hardly consistent with Jensen's (1969) treatment of variance in AFQT scores as primarily heritable. The other interesting fact is that using occupational status rather than income as the dependent variable gives similar results: significance for the schooling variables, and only marginal importance for parental status and AFQT.

IV. Errors in the AFQT Variable and Other Extensions

In this section we reestimate the income-generating equation assuming that AFQT is subject to random errors to get an idea of the results we might obtain with a better measure of ability.[20] To do so, we shall have to revise somewhat the model sketched out in the previous section and introduce an unobservable ability or achievement variable. Since we have no direct knowledge of the errors in the AFQT, the discussion which follows is an essay: We assume the AFQT measures adult ability with random errors. We specify a model for the explanation of earnings that takes into account these random errors. If these assumptions are correct then the results of our reestimation also are correct.

Let us postulate the following simple linear model, summarized in table 7 and diagrammed in figure 2, where the time subscripts 0, 1, 2, represent measurements taken before the start of formal schooling (approximately age 6), before entering military service (approximately age 18), and at the

---

negative of the coefficient of AMS times 12. In this case, it comes out to .0132, and this is also the predicted coefficient for age. Since the actual coefficient for age is .0126, the two are consistent and support the interpretation that both calendar age and time spent in military service influence income via their effect on "experience." Another way of testing this is to constrain the coefficient of age to equal 12 times minus the coefficient of AMS. The computed F-statistics for such constrained versions of regressions 1 and 4 are 3.7 and 2.8, respectively, indicating that the data are consistent with the validity of such a constraint at the conventional 5 percent significance level (the critical F is 3.8). For regression 4, the constrained version implies that a year of experience is worth a 2.3 percent increase in income, on the average, and that holding "experience" (but not age) constant leads to estimated 7.3 and 7.8 percent increases in income per year of schooling, for pre- and postservice schooling, respectively.

[20] The sources of random error in the AFQT are presumed to be grouping, reliability, aggregation, and left-out components of ability. Grouping would create random errors if the actual scores are distributed evenly within intervals. Reliability errors, though doubtless present, probably are minor because of the grouping procedure. Aggregation, in the sense of using a global index instead of its separate components, could create random differences between the ability index which maximally predicts income and the AFQT index. Left-out components of ability also could differ randomly from the AFQT. Nonrandom errors could be due to the differential distribution by parental SES of test-wiseness, motivation, and experience with the kinds of material the test uses (culture-boundedness of the test). We are unable to adjust for nonrandom errors.

TABLE 6

Interrelations between Determinants of Income
(t-Ratios)

Dependent Variable	Color	FO	FE	POC	POS	ROS	SB	SI	AFQT	AGE	AMS	R^2
SB	*	8	6	4	*	5						.152
SB	−4	6	4	3	*	3			17			.289
AFQT	5	5	5	2	*	6	17					.139
AFQT	6	2	3	*	*	4	5			9		.271
AMS	*	*	2	4	*	*	11		*	4		.083
SI	*	3	4	*	*	3	*		8	4	4	.130
NM	*	−2	*	*	*	−3	*	*	*	−9	*	.073
LCJ	3	*	*	*	*	2	3	3	*	18	4	.208
RNS	*	*	*	*	*	46	*	*	*	*	*	.625
RNW	−3	*	*	−4	*	−5	3	2	*	*	3	.051
SMSA	*	*	*	12	6	−4	2	3	*	3	2	.145
LOSES	*	2	3	5	*	*	12	10	3	5	*	.290

* In the equation but estimated t-ratio less than 2.

TABLE 7

Schematic Model of Interrelationships between Schooling, Ability, and Income

(1)	$G_0 = a_1B + a_2H$
(2)	$T_0 = G_0 + t_0$
(3)	$S_1 = b_1B + b_2H + e$
(4)	$G_1 = G_0 + \gamma S_1$
(5)	$T_1 = G_1 + t_1$
(6)	$S_2 - S_1 = c_1S_1 + c_2B + w$
(7)	$G_2 = G_1 + \gamma(S_2 - S_1)$
(8)	$I_2 = \beta G_2 + u$

Note. G = achievement, or ability to earn income, unobservable directly; B = background factors including social class of parents (fa. stat.) and location of adolescence (reg. bef.); H = heredity, or genotype, unmeasured; T = test score, purporting to measure G (T_1 = AFQT); S = schooling (S_1 = SB, S_2 = ST, $S_2 - S_1$ = SI); I income (LINC); e,t,w,u = random forces, uncorrelated with each other and with the causally prior exogenous variables of the system, that is, the t's are assumed to be uncorrelated with each other and with all the other variables in the model except the T's; e is assumed to be uncorrelated with B and H, w also with S_1 and u also with $S_2 - S_1$.

time of the survey (age in 1964), respectively. The symbols are intended to be mnemonic; random disturbances appear only in equations with observable dependent variables. We also assume that all variables are measured around their mean levels, obviating the need for constants in these equations. Basically we have an unobservable ability or achievement (or human-capital) variable, which is augmented by schooling, and the stock of which (G) is estimable (subject to error) via test scores (T). We assume in this model that all of the influence of class and heredity is indirect, via the early-achievement variable. Note that we assume equal contributions of a unit change in SI $(S_2 - S_1)$ to achievement and of a unit change in S_1 (SB), and we also assume that the schooling increment is uncorrelated with the error in observed test scores (t_1) and with that part of heredity (H) not already reflected in S_1 or correlated with B. These assumptions (equality of the coefficients of S_1 and S_2 and no correlation between $S_2 - S_1$ with t_1 and H net of S_1 and B) are the important identifying restrictions in our model.

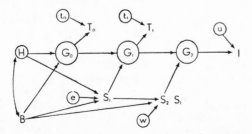

Fig. 2.—Revised causal model of income determination. Circled items = unobservables.

The present data are not sufficient to estimate this model in its entirety. We have no measures of A, T_0, and H. Yet, we can mesh our data with this model in a way which may allow us to escape the effect of errors in AFQT. Substituting equations (4) and (1) into (5) (see table 7) gives

$$T_1 = \gamma S_1 + a_1 B + a_2 H + t_1,\qquad(9)$$

and substituting equations (7) and (5) into (8) results in

$$I_2 = \beta[\gamma(S_2 - S_1) + (T_1 - t_1)] + u$$
$$= \beta\gamma(S_2 - S_1) + \beta T_1 + u - \beta t_1.\quad(10)$$

Since the error (t_1) in T_1 is not observable, we have again an errors-in-variables problem (or a simultaneity problem in the sense of a nonzero correlation of T_1 with the new disturbance $u - \beta t_1$). To solve this problem we can use the observable predetermined variables $(S_1$ and $B)$ not appearing in equation (10) in a two-stage instrumental-variables procedure. In the first stage we estimate equation (9), ignoring the unavailable H variable and get a predicted value of T_1, $\hat{T}_1$ (AFQT *Hat*), based on the observed predetermined variables. This predicted value replaces T in equation (10). In the second stage, we regress I_2 (LINC) on $S_2 - S_1$ (SI) and $\hat{T}_1$ (AFQT *Hat*) to estimate $\beta\gamma$ and β.[21] This procedure solves the problem of error in T_1, assuming that our model is correctly specified, but does little about the effect of the omitted variable H (except for its influence via S_1). Here we have to count on the presumed relative independence of the increment in schooling from H, net of their joint relationship with S_1 and the variables contained in B.

Table 8 summarizes the two-stage calculations. Comparing regressions 13 and 14 with 4, 11, and 12 (table 3), we note that the estimated coefficient of incremental schooling does not decrease. Constraining the model so that background factors and schooling before service work through the unobserved achievement variable gives the same results for the remaining schooling variable as the unconstrained regressions. Allowing for direct effects of measured AFQT, schooling before service, and social background improves the fit only marginally (regressions 4 vs. 13 or 11 vs. 14). Thus, the approach taken here suggests that our initial estimate of the schooling effect on income is robust with respect to the presence of (random) measurement errors in AFQT. Moreover, the comparable levels of fit in the error model and the unconstrained regressions support the model outlined in table 7.

Considering next the AFQT *Hat* variable, note that its coefficient in regressions 13 and 14 is much larger and more highly significant than those

---

[21] Note that color, age, and AMS also are included because they are assumed to have an independent effect on income. As in Section I, AMS also could be entered explicitly into the model. To do so, however, would not change the results of interest and would detract from the clarity of the model's central features.

TABLE 8
Two-Stage and Other Regressions

Regression No.	Coefficient (Standard Error) of				Other Variables in Equation	R^2
	Color	SI	AFQT *Hat**	AFQT		
Dependent variable = Log Income:						
13	.0351 (.0494)	.0504 (.0069)	.01051 (.00078)	...	Age, AMS	.1876
14	.0730 (.0468)	.0483 (.0065)	.00889 (.00078)	...	Age, reg. now, curr. exp., AMS	.2855
15	.1982 (.0458)	.0331 (.0067)	...	.00298 (.00038)	Age, reg. now, curr. exp., AMS	.2526
Dependent variable = Log Occupation SES:						
16	−.3979 (.0815)	.1320 (.0114)	.02554 (.00129)	...	Age, AMS	.2636
17	−.3517 (.0809)	.1277 (.0113)	.02626 (.00134)	...	Age, reg. now, curr. exp., AMS	.2880
18	.0157 (.0831)	.0843 (.0121)	...	.00809 (.00069)	Age, reg. now, curr. exp., AMS	.1779
19	.1014 (.0787)	.1151 (.0117)	...	.00253 (.00073)	Age, reg. now, curr. exp., fa. stat., reg. bef., SB, AMS	.3034

* The equation used to define this variable is:

$$\text{AFQT } Hat = -19 + 17.85 \text{ color} + .0735 \text{ FO} + .5505 \text{ FS} + 4.434 \text{ SB} - 5.472 \text{ ROS}$$
$$\quad\quad\quad\quad (2.83) \quad\quad (.0309) \quad\quad (.1481) \quad\quad (.262) \quad\quad (1.282)$$

with $R^2 = .271$.

for the original AFQT measure (table 3). "Purging" AFQT of errors thus increases its contribution to income, even though it does not modify the estimated contribution of education. Observe also that a bound can be set on the effect of ignoring the H variable in equations (9) and (10) derived from the error model. In particular, the gain in predicting income with the estimate of error-free AFQT more than offsets the loss due to lack of a measure of the direct influence of H. That is, the *ignored* systematic part of ability, the part of heredity that is uncorrelated with the variables defining AFQT *Hat,* has a smaller variance than the variance of error in observed AFQT, since the R^2 in regression 15 is greater than in regression 14.[22]

The only novel result in table 8 pertains to the coefficient of the white-black dummy variable in the presence of the AFQT *Hat* variable. It is insignificant now, indicating that all of the color effects were captured by AFQT *Hat.* Taken at face value, this result implies that discrimination against blacks does not affect white-black differences in income once person-to-person differences in ability and achievement are adjusted for random-measurement error. This outcome could not have been forecast on the basis of any previous literature. Since the number of blacks in the sample is very small, the result cannot be taken for anything more than an invitation to further work along the above lines.

Having set up the model outlined in table 7, we could add additional equations connecting other indicators of success, such as occupational SES, to the unobserved G_2 (achievement in 1964) variable. Such an extension is presented in figure 3. It implies a proportionality of coefficients in

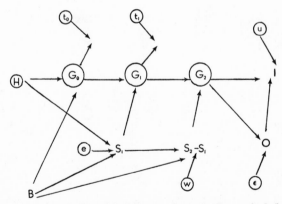

FIG. 3.—Extension of revised model of income determination to include current success variables. $O =$ occupational SES or other measures of current success.

[22] Let $G = S + H$, and H be defined so as to be uncorrelated with S. Then using the observed T as a variable implies leaving out from the regression $- \beta t$, the error of measurement in T. Using $\hat{T} = S$ implies the leaving out of βH. The latter causes a smaller reduction in the explained variance than the former.

equations with different success measures as dependent variables that could be used in another estimation round to get a constrained but more efficient set of estimators for the coefficients of the independent variables (see Zellner 1970; Goldberger 1971). Since we are primarily interested in the effect of these variables on earnings, we have not pursued this further here. We doubt, however, that it is reasonable to impose such a proportionality assumption across the coefficients of *all* the variables in our data. It would not be surprising if variables such as marital status or color have different relative effects on income and occupational status. The last set of regressions in table 8 points up the problem. With log occupational SES as the dependent variable, the coefficients of incremental schooling and AFQT (or AFQT *Hat*) are roughly proportional to those with log income as the dependent variable. Comparing regression 16 with regression 13, the coefficients stand in the ratio 2.6 and 2.4 for the SI and AFQT *Hat* variables, respectively. In regressions 18 and 15 the ratios are 2.5 and 2.7, respectively. This is not too bad. But the color coefficients stand in a ratio of .5 for the second comparison, and they are actually of opposite sign for the first. Thus, proportionality across *all* the coefficients is not apparent in the data and is also unlikely for such variables as color and marital status. Procedures are available for dealing with these more complicated models but we do not pursue this topic further here.[23]

V. Discussion and Summary

We have tried to compare our results with those of other similar studies but without too much success. None of the other studies uses an incremental-schooling variable, a distinction on which much of our results rest. Also, such studies tend to treat years of school as the conceptually right and error-free measure of educational attainment, a position that is hardly tenable in light of the extreme diversity of the education system in the United States.

Duncan's (1968) major study uses the same basic data set as we do, but defines the subsample of interest as white males ages 25–34, includes both veterans and nonveterans, and introduces early intelligence and

---

[23] See Hauser and Goldberger (1970) for more details. To rationalize these facts we must assume that there also is some direct effect of variables such as color and marital status on income outside and beyond their contribution to the unobserved achievement variables. In terms of figure 3, color would be contained in B but might have additional independent and different paths to I_2 and 0. Similarly, marital status could be interposed between G_2 and I_2 and 0, having differential effects on the latter two variables. In general, if income and occupational success depend not only on cognitive achievement (AFQT, schooling, and related measures) but also on "motivation" where motivation may be a function of previous achievement, some of the same background variables, and other random variables, then only smaller subsets of coefficients are subject to proportionality constraints.

number of siblings from other sources. Instead of actual income, he uses expected income. For this sample so defined, the coefficient of total schooling declines about 31 percent when parental status, number of siblings, and early intelligence variables are introduced into a regression with expected income as the dependent variable. We cannot, however, be sure that this difference between Duncan's study and ours is due to the difference in populations sampled, because expected and actual income are imperfectly correlated (in our sample the correlation between the logarithms of these two variables is about .7), and his results do not control for differences in labor-force participation or the effects of different regions of origin nor do they allow for the correlation of the parental-status variables with the left-out school-quality variable.[24]

Hansen, Weisbrod, and Scanlon (1970) analyze a sample of 17–25-year-old men rejected by the Selective Service System because of low AFQT scores, and conclude that schooling is a relatively unimportant income determinant. In their data, the education coefficient drops about 50 percent when the AFQT variable is introduced into the regression of income on age, color, size of family of origin, whether the family of origin was intact, and education. The education coefficient drops even further when such current-success variables as job training and marital status are added. Their sample is peculiar in that it concentrates on the very young and on blacks (about half of their sample is nonwhite vs. 9 percent in our subsample). It is well known that schooling-income differentials are rather low at the beginning of the labor-force experience and that there is little evidence for a strong schooling-income relationship among blacks (see Hanoch 1967). Both facts could help to explain the differences between these two samples. Moreover, the correlation between AFQT and the omitted variable of school quality is likely to be higher for this population than for higher-ability groups, so that including AFQT in the regression overstates the bias in the education coefficient due to neglecting ability. For these reasons, then, we are not ready to conclude that using a larger number of low-ability men than was available to us within our own sample would alter our estimate of the bias in the education coefficient due to omitting ability. All of these considerations do remind us again, though, that we cannot take our sample as representative of the entire labor force.[25]

[24] In addition to collating information from several samples, Duncan's study also uses correlations between the AFQT and other variables based on an extrapolation from the veterans' subsample to the total sample. The use of these adjusted correlations would seem to partly explain the discrepancy between our own results and those implied by Duncan's data. Although the assumptions which underlie the adjusted correlations appear reasonable, they do remain open to question.

[25] Several studies of high-SES samples have also shown a relatively small bias in the schooling coefficient due to left-out ability variables (Ashenfelter and Mooney 1968; Weisbrod and Karpoff 1968; Rogers 1969; Taubman and Wales 1970). This last study also can be interpreted so as to show a rather significant effect of variation in the quality of college schooling.

Our findings support the economic and statistical significance of schooling in the explanation of observed differences in income. They also point out the relatively low independent contribution of measured ability (AFQT scores). Holding age, father's status, region of origin, length of military service, and the AFQT score constant, an additional year of schooling would add about 4.6 percent to income in our sample. At the same time a 10 percent improvement in the AFQT score would only add about 1 percent to income.

Using a "clean" schooling variable, incremental schooling, we concluded that the bias in its estimated coefficient due to the omitted ability dimension is not very large (on the order of 10 percent). The earlier (before military service) schooling coefficient falls more, but we interpret this to be the consequence of the interrelationship between test scores and father's status variables with the other important omitted variable—the quality of schooling. Unfortunately, given the nature of our sample, restricted as it is by the selectivity inherent in being a veteran and the relatively young (under 35) age of males included, these results cannot be taken as representative for all males. Nevertheless, this is one of the largest samples ever brought to bear on this problem and we would expect it to survive extension to a more complete population.

Our results also throw doubt on the asserted role of genetic forces in the determination of income. If AFQT is a good measure of IQ and if IQ is largely inherited, then the direct contribution of heredity to current income is minute. Its indirect effect also is not very large. Of course, the AFQT scores may be full of error and heredity may be very important, but then previous conclusions about the importance of heredity are also in doubt since they were drawn on the basis of similar data.

Appendix

All of the formulae used in the text are repeated variations on the "left-out variable" formula.[26] Let the true equation be

$$y = \beta_1 x_1 + \beta_2 x_2 + e,$$

where all the variables are measured around their means (and hence we ignore constant terms) and e is a random variable uncorrelated with x_1 and x_2.

Now, consider the least-squares coefficient of y on x_1 alone:

$$b_{y1} = \Sigma x_1 y / \Sigma x_1^2 = \Sigma x_1 (\beta_1 x_1 + \beta_2 x_2 + e) / \Sigma x_1^2$$

$$= \beta_1 + \beta_2 \Sigma x_1 x_2 / \Sigma x_1^2 + \Sigma x_1 e / \Sigma x_1^2.$$

Since the expectation of the last term is zero, we can write

[26] These formulas are given, in a different context, in appendix C of Griliches and Ringstad (1971). See Yule and Kendall (1950, chap. 12) for the notation used here.

$$E(b_{y1}) = \beta_1 + \beta_2 b_{21},$$

where

$$b_{21} = \Sigma x_1 x_2 / \Sigma x_1^2$$

is the (auxillary) least-squares coefficient of the left-out variable x_2 on the included x_1.

Moreover, if e were to refer to the computed least-squares residuals, $\Sigma x_1 e$ would equal zero by construction. Hence, the same formula also holds as an *identity* between computed least-squares coefficients of different order. That is,

$$b_{y1} = b_{y1 \cdot 2} + b_{y2 \cdot 1} b_{21}.$$

This same formula, with a suitable change in notation, applies also to higher-order coefficients:

$$b_{y1 \cdot 2} = b_{y1 \cdot 23} + b_{y3 \cdot 12} \cdot b_{3 \cdot 12}.$$

In what follows we shall assume that we are talking either about least-squares coefficients or about population parameters, and we will not carry expectation signs along. The discussion could be made somewhat more rigorous by inserting the plim (probability limit) notation at appropriate places.

The model we deal with can be written as

$$\begin{aligned} y &= \beta_1 E + \beta_2 T + e \\ &= \beta_1 S + \beta_2 T + \beta_1 Q + e, \end{aligned}$$

where $E = S + Q$ is education, S is quantity of schooling, Q is quality of schooling, and T is a measure of ability (here assumed to be error-free); Q is uncorrelated with S but is correlated with T. Then, estimating the equation with both T and Q out, leads to

$$b_{yS} = \beta_1 + \beta_2 b_{TS} + \beta_1 b_{QS} = \beta_1 \beta_2 b_{TS}$$

since $b_{QS} = 0$ by assumption. Including T in the equation also gives

$$b_{yS \cdot T} = \beta_1 + \beta_1 b_{QS \cdot T}.$$

Now, while b_{QS} is zero, $b_{QS \cdot T}$ need not be zero. Given our assumptions we can write,

$$b_{QS} = b_{QS \cdot T} + b_{QT \cdot S} b_{TS} = 0,$$

which implies that

$$b_{QS \cdot T} = -b_{QT \cdot S} b_{TS} < 0,$$

since both $b_{QT \cdot S}$, the partial relationship of school quality to test scores, and b_{TS}, the relationship between test scores and levels of schooling, are expected to be positive. We also have

$$b_{QT} = b_{QT \cdot S} + b_{QS \cdot T} \cdot b_{ST}.$$

Substituting the formula for $b_{QT \cdot S}$ into the formula for b_{QT}, we get

$$b_{QT} = b_{QT \cdot S} - b_{QT \cdot S} b_{TS} \cdot b_{ST}.$$

Solving for $b_{QT \cdot S}$ and remembering that $b_{TS} b_{ST} = r^2_{ST}$ gives

$$b_{QT \cdot S} = b_{QT}/(1 - r^2_{TS}),$$

which then gives

$$b_{QS \cdot T} = -b_{QT} \cdot b_{TS}/(1 - r^2_{TS}).$$

The algebra gets a bit more complicated when S is divided into two components, which for notational convenience will be called B (before) and A (after) here. The model now is

$$y = \beta_1 B + \beta_1 A + \beta_2 T + \beta_1 Q + e.$$

Then

$$b_{yB \cdot AT} = \beta_1 + \beta_1 b_{QB \cdot AT}$$

and

$$b_{yA \cdot BT} = \beta_1 + \beta_1 b_{QA \cdot BT}.$$

Assume, as is approximately true in our sample, that A is uncorrelated with T. Since we have already assumed that Q is uncorrelated with both A and B, we have:

$$b_{QB \cdot A} = b_{QB \cdot AT} + b_{QT \cdot AB} \cdot b_{TB \cdot A} = 0;$$
$$b_{QA \cdot B} = b_{QA \cdot BT} + b_{QT \cdot AB} \cdot b_{TA \cdot B} = 0;$$

and hence

$$b_{QB \cdot AT} = -b_{QT \cdot AB} b_{TB \cdot A};$$
$$b_{QA \cdot BT} = -b_{QT \cdot AB} b_{TA \cdot B}.$$

Thus we can see immediately that the relative magnitude of the biases in the two schooling coefficients depends on the size of $b_{TB \cdot A}$ relative to $b_{TA \cdot B}$. Now because

$$b_{TA} = b_{TA \cdot B} + b_{TB \cdot A} b_{BA} = 0,$$

by assumption, we have

$$b_{TA \cdot B} = -b_{TB \cdot A} b_{BA},$$

which we can substitute in

$$b_{TB} = b_{TB \cdot A} + b_{TA \cdot B} \cdot b_{AB}$$

to yield

$$b_{TB \cdot A} = b_{TB}/(1 - b_{AB} b_{BA}) = b_{TB}/(1 - r^2_{AB})$$

and

$$b_{TA \cdot B} = -b_{TB} b_{BA}/(1 - r^2_{AB}).$$

Now, if A (schooling after service) were entirely uncorrelated with B (schooling before service), $b_{BA} = 0$, and its coefficient in the income-generating equation $(b_{yA \cdot BT})$ would be unbiased:

$$b_{QA \cdot BT} = -b_{QT \cdot AB} \cdot b_{TA \cdot B}$$
$$= +b_{QT \cdot AB} \cdot b_{TB} \cdot b_{BA}/(1 - r_{AB}^2),$$
$$= 0$$

while the coefficient of schooling before service in the income-generating equation would be biased downward. In our sample, however, b_{BA} is actually negative and on the order of -.3, implying that the coefficient of A is also biased downward, but only by about a third of the bias in the coefficient of B.

References

Ashenfelter, Orley, and Mooney, Joseph D. "Graduate Education, Ability and Earnings." *Rev. Econ. and Statis.* 50 (February 1968): 78–86.

Blau, Peter M., and Duncan, Otis Dudley. *The American Occupational Structure.* New York: Wiley, 1967.

Bowles, Samuel. "Schooling and Inequality from Generation to Generation." Unpublished paper presented at the eastern meetings of the Econometric Society, Tokyo, June 1970.

Davis, James W., Jr., and Dolbeare, Kenneth M. *Little Groups of Neighbors: The Selective Service System.* Chicago: Markham, 1968.

Denison, Edward F. *The Sources of Economic Growth in the United States and the Alternatives before Us.* Supplementary Paper no. 13. New York: Committee Econ. Development, 1962.

———. "Measuring the Contribution of Education." In *The Residual Factor and Economic Growth*, pp. 13–55, 77–100. Paris: Org. Econ. Co-operation and Development, 1964.

Duncan, Otis Dudley "A Socioeconomic Index for All Occupations," and "Properties and Characteristics of the Socioeconomic Index." In Albert J. Reiss. Otis Dudley Duncan, Paul K. Hatt, and Cecil C. North, *Occupation and Social Status*, chaps. 6 and 7, pp. 109–61. New York: Free Press, 1961.

———. "Path Analysis: Sociological Examples." *American J. Sociology* 72 (July 1966): 1–16.

———. "Ability and Achievement." *Eugenics Q.* 15 (March 1968): 1–11.

———. "Inheritance of Poverty or Inheritance of Race?" In *On Understanding Poverty*, edited by Daniel P. Moynihan, pp. 85–110. New York: Basic, 1969.

Goldberger, A. S. "Maximum-Likelihood Estimation of Regression Models Containing Unobservable Variables." Social Systems Research Institute, Unpublished paper, EME 7101, Univ. Wis., 1971.

Griliches, Zvi. "Notes on the Role of Education in Production Functions and Growth Accounting." In *Education, Income and Human Capital*, edited by W. Lee Hansen, pp. 71–127. Studies in Income and Wealth, vol. 35. New York: Nat. Bur. Econ. Res., 1970.

Griliches, Zvi, and Ringstad, V. *Economies of Scale and the Form of the Production.* Amsterdam: North-Holland, 1971.

Hanoch, Giora. "An Economic Analysis of Earnings and Schooling." *J. Human Resources* 2 (Summer 1967): 310–29.

Hansen, W. Lee; Weisbrod, Burton A.; and Scanlon, W. J. "Schooling and Earnings of Low Achievers." *A.E.R.* 60 (June 1970): 409–18.

Hauser, Robert M., and Goldberger, A. S. "The Treatment of Unobservable Variables in Path Analysis." Social Systems Research Institute Workshop Paper, EME 7030. Univ. Wis., 1970.

Jensen, Arthur R. "How Much Can We Boost IQ and Scholastic Achievement?" *Harvard Educ. Rev.* 39 (Winter 1969): 1–123.

Karpinos, Bernard D. "The Mental Qualification of American Youths for Military Service and Its Relationship to Educational Attainment." *Proc. of Social Statis. Sect. American Statis. Association, 1966.* Washington: ASA, 1966.

———. "Mental Test Failures." In *The Draft*, edited by Sol Tax, pp. 35–53. Chicago: Univ. Chicago Press, 1967.

Klassen, A. D. *Military Service in American Life since World War II: An Overview.* Report no. 117. Chicago: Nat. Opinion Res. Center, Univ. Chicago. 1966.

Mason, William. "Working Paper on the Socioeconomic Effects of Military Service." Unpublished paper, Univ. Chicago, 1968.

———. "On the Socioeconomic Effects of Military Service." Ph.D. dissertation, Univ. Chicago, 1970.

Rivera, Ramon J. "Sampling Procedures on the Military Manpower Surveys." Chicago: Nat. Opinion Res. Center, Univ. Chicago, 1965.

Rogers, Daniel C. "Private Rates of Return to Education in the U.S.: A Case Study." *Yale Econ. Essays* 9 (Spring 1969): 89–134.

Siegel, Paul M., and Hodge, Robert W. "A Causal Approach to the Study of Measurement Error." In *Methodology in Social Research*, edited by Hubert M. Blalock, Jr., and Ann B. Blalock, pp. 28–59. New York: McGraw-Hill, 1968.

Taubman, Paul, and Wales, Terence. "Net Returns to Education." In *Economics —a Half-Century of Research, 1920–1970; 50th Annual Report*, pp. 65–66. New York: Nat. Bur. Econ Res., 1970.

U.S. President's Task Force on Manpower Conservation. *One-third of a Nation: A Report on Young Men Found Unqualified for Military Service.* Washington: Government Printing Office, 1964.

Weisbrod, Burton A., and Karpoff, Peter. "Monetary Returns to College Education, Student Ability, and College Quality." *Rev. Econ. and Statis.* 50 (November 1968): 491–97.

Yule, G. Udny, and Kendall, M. G. *An Introduction to the Theory of Statistics.* 14th ed., rev. London: Griffin, 1950.

Zellner, Arnold. "Estimation of Regression Relationships Containing Unobservable Independent Variables." *Internat. Econ. Rev.* 11 (October 1970): 441–54.

Comment

Paul Taubman

University of Pennsylvania

Some of you may have noticed that Zvi Griliches and William Mason mention briefly, at the end of their paper, the work by Terence Wales and me but make no comparisons with it. I think that comparisons would have been appropriate for several reasons: First, we have a much richer body of data, though for a much narrower range of education. Second, in one of our samples all of the conditions set forth by Griliches and Mason in terms of separation of pre- and posttest schooling are met; in the other sample, the conditions are nearly met. Those of you who believe that the slight to my work might color my comments are good judges of character.

Their paper has much to recommend it. There have been far too few studies of the importance of ability (properly defined) and socioeconomic standing (SES) in determining income and in calculating the bias on education coefficients. Thus, any competent study would be welcome. Of course, given the authors, the study is in many ways more than competent. The discussion of the effects of omitting the quality of schooling is well done and quite important, as is the general extension to errors-in-variable problems. I have, however, some objections to the assumptions made to achieve identifiability.

As a whole, however, I find the paper less useful than I had hoped because the sample used by the authors is too small and too lacking in detail to answer the important questions in this area of human capital. Nevertheless, within the confines of their sample space, the authors have done a reasonable job and have provided some interesting results.

Basic questions in the human capital area connected with ability would seem to be these: What are the appropriate measures of education and ability? How do the extra income and the internal rate of return vary with successive education levels? How do the benefits vary with education, and what is the relative importance of education and ability at various levels? Finally, how do the age-income profiles vary by education and ability?

Let us examine the sample and method used by Griliches and Mason to see which of these questions they answer reliably. The sample consists of 1,454 male veterans, aged 21–34 years and employed full time in 1964, who provided complete information on necessary variables and for whom the Armed Forces Qualification Test (AFQT) was available. As noted by the authors, the sample is not representative of the population, since the extremes of ability and SES are underrepresented. It is not stated if the sample is representative of the population of veterans, or if there are response and success biases.

In their analysis, the authors represent education by years of school attended, but use midpoints of certain spans (for example, more than 9 years but less than high school graduation is set equal to 10). This variable, however, is approximately linear. The ability measure is the AFQT (in percentile form) that is like an IQ test but contains material on mechanical-tool knowledge. As the authors indicate, the education variable omits quality while the ability variable captures only a particular type of ability. Both, moreover, are scaled somewhat arbitrarily. The dependent variable is the log of normal gross weekly earnings on the main job.

The functional form used is:

$$\ln y = a + b + c + d \, \text{AFQT} + e \, \text{age} + f \, \text{SES}. \qquad (1)$$

With this functional form which was chosen after "some experimentation," every independent variable has positive, but diminishing, effects, and the marginal impact is independent of every other variable. Thus, with this functional form it is impossible to *test*: for nonlinear effects of schooling or ability on $\ln y$ (or y) except those implied by the semilog form, for interactions between ED and Ab and for such variables as age. Given the data, it is not possible to examine alternative definitions of schooling and ability except through the authors' errors-in-variable approach. They basically can only examine, for males, the average effect of ability and the bias over all schooling and ability levels (assuming that their scaling is correct). (The authors do not have enough observations to test properly for interactions and nonlinearities, but they did experiment with cruder tests.)

To test for nonlinearities and interactions, various statistical tests can be employed. While one can define new variables such as education squared, education (ability), it seems to me that the best way to proceed is to divide the sample into various cells and use the analysis of covariance. It also is helpful to divide education and ability into a set of dummy variables. (For example, in our work we used a separate dummy for each fifth of the ability distribution and each educational level—high school, some college, bachelor's degree, graduate student, master of arts degree, doctor of philosophy, bachelor of law degree, and doctor of medicine.)

Unfortunately, this method probably would not yield useful results for Griliches and Mason since, with the eight education groups in their scale, there would be an average of 180 persons in each educational cell. Given the wide range of income, even within an education group, this number probably is too small to give reliable results and to test for nonlinearities of ability.

The authors, who describe the ability variable as an IQ plus mechanical-tool knowledge, indicate its limitations. However, the title of the paper is certainly misleading, since something like "mental ability" should be used (and, I might add, "in the early years"). It also is important, however, to realize, as the authors do, that other types of cognitive abilities that are imperfectly correlated with AFQT may be relevant for earning income. Indeed, in my samples, which include high school graduates and the higher education levels noted above, when a verbal IQ-type measure (with mechanical-tool knowledge added) is used in equations with general functional forms for education and ability, much smaller biases are obtained than when mathematics is used. Robert Thorndike, who is familiar with our tests, has suggested that, in our sample, mathematical ability is a better measure of true IQ than the combination of verbal, mathematical, and mechanical abilities; thus, our result may be for IQ rather than mathematical ability. However, the question about the authors' measure still must be raised.

In our work, Wales and I have concentrated on two samples in each of which everyone has at least a high school degree. First, with the aid of Dael Wolfle, we obtained some unpublished details of the Wolfle-Smith sample of Minnesota high school graduates of 1938. We found in this sample that, for people about 33 years old, each year of education above high school gave smaller absolute and percentage amounts of y (not $\ln y$), that the ability effects were important but not linear nor continuous, and that there was an interaction for high-ability people with at least a bachelor's degree. Incidentally, everyone in the sample was tested as a high school senior, hence all other education was subsequent to the tests—the condition Griliches and Mason consider necessary to eliminate certain statistical problems. The bias in this sample from omitting ability would be less than 4 percent.

The other sample, however, is bigger, better, and more important. Wales and I, with funds from the National Bureau of Economic Research, updated the Thorndike-Hagen sample and obtained the NBER-TH sample. Of the nearly 4,000 people in the sample, each was at least a high school graduate. While there is a response bias, there is no important success bias in NBER-TH. If the people are examined at a mean age of 33 when most had been working for seven or more years, we find: (1) Except for holders of doctor of philosophy, medical, and law degrees, mean income at all other education levels is 10–15 percent above that of a high school graduate with the same characteristics. Thus, mean y should not be described by a semilog function. (2) Mathematical ability, not IQ, is important, indeed as important as education, in explaining the range in earnings.[1] (3) The bias is about 30–35 percent at various education levels for mathematical ability and 9 percent for other types of mental ability. Thus, from our work it seems that mathematical ability is the most important type of mental ability for determining income. There is not much evidence of interactions between education and ability, but because ability has little effect on initial salaries, the rates of return do not vary with ability. Finally, neither the effects of education nor of ability are linear or log-linear.

Returning to Griliches and Mason, I think it appropriate to point out that their analysis would yield information only on private returns. Suppose education is used as a credential rather than being an augmentor of productivity.[2] The social benefits in this instance can be obtained only by a more complicated analysis.

On the two-stage analysis, I do not see why I should accept the "identifying restrictions" that either S-S_2 or the test-score error is not correlated with residual H (after all, why should not scholastic ability, as opposed to the ability needed to succeed in business, determine $S_2 - S_1$?). Second, the model implies that residual heredity effects are much smaller than test-measurement effects, but test-retest reliability is high, so this result implies that AFQT is a poor measure of the ability useful in earning a living. I also might note that there is a dimensionality problem, since it is assumed that a change in schooling adds to scores linearly. Finally, the Griliches-Mason approach assumes that the cognitive and not the affective impact of education determines income.

Thus, I conclude that while the authors have done a good job with the material on hand, more is to be gained from the use of larger samples with more information. I would so conclude even if it were necessary that the various samples not have the same information nor span as large an education range as those of Griliches and Mason.

---

[1] Note, however, Thorndike's objection discussed earlier.
[2] Wales and I have shown that the social benefits would not equal the private benefits in this instance.

Earnings Profile: Ability and Schooling

John C. Hause

National Bureau of Economic Research and University of Minnesota

I. Theory and Hypotheses about the Role of Ability

This study examines the role played by ability in determining earnings differentials along both the earnings profile for given levels of schooling attainment and across schooling levels. Information about these relationships is important for determining more precisely the quantitative contribution of schooling to earnings as well as the "technology" by which schooling increases earnings. The net earnings increment from schooling has been subject to some uncertainty because most studies have lacked data on ability. If people of higher ability have the capacity to earn more (at a given schooling level) and if they also tend, significantly, to acquire more schooling than others, the failure to take ability differences explicitly into account has two consequences: it leads one to overstate the gross contribution of schooling to earnings and to understate the opportunity cost of foregone earnings to high-ability persons who attain high levels of schooling.

There is a well-documented, strong, positive relationship between earnings and schooling attainment, and the rising demand for (and expansion of) formal schooling seems to be significantly motivated by the expectation of higher earnings. However, there is little decisive evidence,

This paper is a major extension of an earlier one (Hause 1971). Much of the initial work was supported by National Science Foundation grant GS-1797. Robert Thorndike was most cooperative in making available to the National Bureau of Economic Research his massive data from 1955. I am greatly indebted to Torsten Husén for letting me use the Swedish sample, and to Daniel C. Rogers for use of the basic data tape from his 1967 study. Ingemar Fägerlind carefully coordinated collection of the Swedish earnings data, and Holger Wichman made that task feasible. Mia Thorpe and Rita Kristensen carried out most of the search in the Swedish archives. Computations were made by J. Sanguinetty, M. Sternfeld, and A. L. Norman. Margareta Forselius and Karlis Goppers provided valuable assistance with the Swedish statistics. The American Institute of Research prepared the Project Talent data tape. I have benefited from the comments by Finis Welch on an earlier draft.

much less consensus, on what schooling actually does to (or for) people to increase their postschool earnings. The search for significant complementarity between ability, schooling attainment, and job experience as those are related to earnings is a promising way of getting some evidence on this important question.

The preceding paragraphs are studiously imprecise (if not downright evasive) about ability as a determinant of earnings and raise the following questions: In the analysis of choices that alter earnings capacities, what theoretical role should be assigned to ability? In empirical work, how is ability to be measured? What plausible hypotheses can be made about the effect of measured ability on the earnings profile?

Becker (1967) suggested an attractive theoretical definition of ability for some purposes. Consider the (negatively sloping) schedules of marginal rates of return of two persons as functions of the amount invested to increase earnings. If one schedule lies above the other for all levels of investment, Becker proposes saying that the person with the higher schedule has greater ability. In common usage, "ability" means the power to perform something. In Becker's definition, this power is the capacity to increase future earnings by current investments in oneself. This definition has the appealing feature of not committing one to explain the higher schedule of the individual of greater ability. Such a capacity could be due to a combination of genetic factors, previous investment, experience (including schooling), and other elements that might be difficult to unravel theoretically (or statistically). If some of these elements, such as previous schooling, can be identified, there will still, presumably, be some difference in the rates-of-return schedules which can be attributed to "ability."

If the rates-of-return schedules were observable, one could define in some manner a "distance" between the schedules, call this measure "ability," and use it as one factor in the analysis of differences in investment in earnings capacity between the two persons or of the differences in the rates of return to their investments.

There are two difficulties in going from this definition to the empirical study of schooling and its returns. First, available data usually provide information only on a single point from the rate-of-return schedule of each person.[1] Additional information or an independent measure of ability is necessary to estimate the rate-of-return schedule passing through the observed point; without such estimates, one cannot empirically link differences in investment to differences in ability. A second difficulty with Becker's definition for our purposes is that we are interested in getting some idea from observable interactions among ability, schooling attainment, and work experience of the technology relating schooling and earnings. Becker's

---

[1] In fact, the available data are usually annual earnings for one or several points from the earnings profile as related to schooling attainment, not the rate of return related to investment cost.

level of abstraction precludes hypotheses about *why* ability affects the earnings profile, and this reduces the possibility of learning about the role of schooling from these interactions.

In this theoretical framework, any observable measure of ability should be restricted to variables which are, plausibly, positively correlated with the height of the rate-of-return schedule. Further conjectures are required as to why this positive correlation exists if one hopes to throw any light on the technological relations of schooling and earnings by observing interactions with ability and job experience. These hypotheses may depend partly on how ability is measured. For example, in this study, ability is measured by IQ or by closely related test scores. Recent work by psychologists using the speed of brain-wave responses to light stimulus as a measure of intelligence is quite a different variable, although it appears to be significantly correlated with IQ. Presumably conjectures as to why these two measures of intelligence are correlated with the rate-of-return schedule would not be identical.[2]

How and why should ability, measured by IQ, interact with schooling and alter the earnings profile? This question lies largely outside the competence of economists. William Garner (1971), in commenting on an earlier paper, argues that IQ and similar tests measure ability in terms of both the achievement of specific skills and the speed with which these skills can be applied. The strong correlations, apparent in this study, of IQ with the level of final educational attainment and with subsequent achievement tests in school indicate that IQ measures (or is correlated with) potential capacity to contend successfully with subsequent schooling. To the extent that the capacity so measured is directly useful in performing a job, or is correlated with the ability to acquire job-specific skills, one would expect measured IQ to have a positive partial correlation with earnings, holding schooling attainment constant.

Although we do not understand well the primary components of the schooling output that affects earnings, much less how to measure them, the strong correlation between IQ and schooling makes the dependence of some of these schooling components on the cognitive ability measured by IQ highly plausible. These components presumably include the specific mental skills required for some jobs, school-acquired "learning to learn" skills, and knowledge and practice in locating and utilizing information. A number of specific skills that are required for certain jobs (for example, as tax lawyers, nuclear physicists, or counterinsurgency experts) can be identified by employers from school transcripts. Learning capacity, information-handling ability, and the potential value of both to an employer are less easy to evaluate for persons who have just completed their schooling.

---

[2] Note that conjectures as to why a particular measure of ability affects earnings do not require one to decompose the ability measure into underlying determinants. I emphasized this point earlier (Hause 1971).

The latter skills probably play a larger role in earnings differentials over time as employers see improvement in the performance of people as they gain experience. Casual observation of the distribution of occupations by schooling attainment suggests that these skills become increasingly important for jobs requiring high levels of education. At the lowest levels of schooling attainment, subsequent jobs consist largely of well-defined tasks in which output is readily measured and which do not require great cognitive ability. Following high levels of education, more jobs require responsible decisions in which the consequences are both more important and less easy to evaluate in the short run. There is no reason for the marginal returns to the skills used in these jobs becoming negligible over time.

This impressionistic discussion suggests two important hypotheses to be considered empirically. First, there is an increase, with schooling attainment, in the relative effect of measured ability on earnings. That is, schooling and ability have a significant complementary effect on earnings. Indeed, there is a plausible theoretical argument supporting this hypothesis. Let us suppose that schooling is measured in time units and that the opportunity cost of foregone earnings is a significant part of the investment cost of schooling.[3] The strong positive relationship between schooling attainment and measured ability suggests there is a greater incentive for persons of more ability to obtain more schooling.[4]

Suppose that earnings could be expressed as the sum of a function of ability and a function of schooling: $Y = f(A) + g(S)$. (We assume dY/dA and dY/dS are both positive.) In this form, the marginal product of schooling, dg/dS, is independent of ability. This result does not seem plausible, since it implies that people of low ability have a greater incentive to invest in schooling. The increase in earnings from an increment of schooling is the same for all, regardless of ability, but the opportunity cost of foregone earnings while acquiring the schooling is lower for those with less ability. This argument implies that the earnings function is misspecified unless ability increases the marginal product of schooling. In fact, it requires that ability increase the marginal product of schooling on earnings rapidly enough to more than offset the rise in opportunity cost associated with higher ability up to the optimal level of schooling investment. If *all* higher-level schooling costs were opportunity costs of foregone earnings (*and a perfect capital market existed*), an earnings function of the form $\log E = f(A) + g(S)$ would still not provide sufficient complemen-

[3] Schultz (1968) indicated that the opportunity costs are more than half of the private costs of education.

[4] Scholarships and similar financial biases favor highly able students. However, this support is not great enough now, much less at the time members of the Thorndike and Rogers samples were in college, to explain the strength of the association between ability and schooling.

tarity to explain the strong tendency for more-able people to acquire more schooling.

This expected positive interaction of schooling and ability on earnings can be rationalized in a slightly different way. Suppose we consider ability as an index of the quality of a student and assume that students of differing ability apply the same amount of time to schooling. The higher earnings of the student with greater ability may be considered the greater output, corresponding to a higher-quality input applied to the educational process.

The second hypothesis is concerned with the effect of ability over time on earnings for a given level of educational attainment. It holds that there is no tendency for the coefficient on ability to attenuate with time in the labor force (at least, any, over the first half of the life cycle of earnings), and there may well be a tendency for it to increase, especially at high levels of education. Behind this hypothesis lies the idea of abler people being more effective than the less able in raising productivity through job experience, that is, measured ability and learning ("experience") in the labor force are complements in producing earnings. The persistence (or increase) in the ability coefficient over time implies the existence of productivity differentials in earnings even after individuals reach peak-level earnings. Such differentials are compatible with the large observable dispersion in personal earnings, even after standardizing for age, schooling, and occupation. To the extent that these productivity differences are due to differences in measured ability, these considerations suggest that ability is more than the capacity to acquire job-relevant skills rapidly. It also enables people to use the skills more rapidly and acquire more-complex skills or both.

II. Empirical Analysis of Ability, Schooling, and Earnings

Four samples of cohort data are examined to explore the ability-schooling-earnings relationship. The samples differ substantially in size, populations from which they are drawn, and supplementary independent variables (see details of each in Appendix, and also Husén 1969; Rogers 1967; and Thorndike and Hagen, 1959).

Two statistical caveats are in order. First, the sample populations in this study are more homogeneous than is usually the case, especially for regressions within schooling classes. Consequently, the coefficients of determination are sometimes relatively small. The standard error of estimate is a much more relevant summary than the coefficient of determination for indicating residual ignorance when comparing the results obtained with those from other studies. The second caveat is related to the small sample base of many of the regressions. Since there is little theory predicting the interaction between various background variables and schooling as these affect earnings, many regressions are computed within schooling class to obtain a point estimate of the ability coefficient. In some smaller samples, this results in large computed standard errors for the coefficients on ability. The calculation of within-schooling-level regressions seems reasonable for estimating the ability coefficients, especially since the ability coefficients appeared to be stable when going from test runs for part of a sample to the full sample. However, one should avoid the pitfall of testing hypotheses on *patterns* of the coefficients by looking at the statistical significance of the coefficients one at a time, since this inappropriate test makes it difficult to reject any null hypothesis when sample size is small. The correct testing procedure is to pool samples or results to get greater statistical discrimination among hypotheses.

A.   Results from the NBER-Thorndike Sample

The NBER-Thorndike sample includes about 2,300 white males who passed a battery of tests given to potential American pilots and navigators in 1943. Earnings data and additional information were obtained from questionnaires in 1955 and 1969. The results discussed here restrict attention to those born in the period 1921–25, so most of the men in the sample had completed high school but had little if any additional schooling when they took the Air Force tests. This restriction circumvents the substantial schooling-when-tested problem that Griliches and Mason (in this Supplement) faced, since the measured-ability differentials cannot be attributed to major schooling differentials prior to the 1943 tests.

The means and standard deviations of the (natural) logarithm of earnings by schooling attainment are given in table 1. The six schooling classes are: E_1, high school graduate; E_2, some college; E_3, college graduate with one degree (and perhaps some past-B.A. schooling with no additional degree awarded; E_4, college graduate with two or more degrees; E_5, lawyer; and E_6, medical doctor. The last three classes are mutually exclusive. Because of the higher schooling and training investment required to become a lawyer or (especially) a doctor, these two occupations are usually distinguished for separate analysis. Both the earnings means and the measured-ability means (TST43) rise significantly over the first four schooling levels. In this sample, the two professional groups (E_5 and E_6) have about the same measured ability as the college graduates with one degree.

The background variables in table 1 are subpopulation dummy variables for father's education (FEDH = 1 if father has at least one college degree; FEDL = 1 if father did not graduate from high school), religion (RC = 1 if Catholic, RJ = 1 if Jewish); and marital status (NM = 1 if not married in 1969); and region (S = 1 if from U.S. Office of Education Region 5 [Southeast]).

No attempt is made to rationalize the precise role of these variables in

TABLE 1

Means and Standard Deviations of Log Earnings, Ability, and Background Variables by Education Level
(NBER-Thorndike Sample)

Education Level	Sample Size (N)*	LE69	LE56	TST43†	FEDL (Father's Education, Low)	FEDH (Father's Education, High)	RC	RJ	NM	S
E₁ (high school grad.)	489	9.128 (.362)	8.645 (.292)	109.3 (13.1)	.760	.035	.309	.022	.045	.121
E₂ (col. nongrad.)	535	9.301 (.403)	8.743 (.312)	111.9 (13.2)	.600	.077	.230	.034	.047	.151
E₃ (col. grad., 1 deg.)	900	9.517 (.376)	8.849 (.419)	118.2 (15.2)	.536	.133	.231	.040	.044	.174
E₄ (col. grad., 2 deg.)	211	9.600 (.436)	8.842 (.337)	122.3 (15.9)	.530	.137	.180	.081	.047	.114
E₅ (lawyer)	128	9.885 (.494)	8.872 (.328)	117.7 (15.2)	.515	.250	.266	.094	.047	.227
E₆ (doctor)	53	10.061 (.387)	9.094 (.694)	118.7 (13.5)	.472	.245	.264	.057	.057	.151

Source.—NBER-Thorndike data tape.
Note.—Numbers in parentheses are standard deviations.
* Sample size is for 1969 earnings. Sample sizes for the original 1955 earnings for the six education classes are: 475, 520, 873, 209, 105, and 36.
† Scaled to an approximate IQ equivalent by the linear transformation TST43 = 114.5 + 8.33 TST43, when TST43 is the factor-analyzed ability measure.

the earning function. In most cases, they have very low correlations with measured ability (within schooling class). The highest correlation of a father's education dummy and ability is .36 (FEDH for medical doctors); in all other cases, the correlations of a father's-education dummy and ability is .14 or less. The use of these background variables in earnings regressions eliminates some sources of differential earnings which complicate the estimation of an ability effect from the smaller samples. Some of these variables are correlated with level of schooling, and their inclusion in regressions that pool the different schooling classes helps to prevent an exaggerated effect of ability on earnings. The entire set of background variables is denoted by X^*.

To test the hypothesis that schooling and measured ability are significantly complementary in their effect on earnings, all observations were pooled (excluding medical doctors), and a regression of 1969 earnings was run on X^*, TST43, years of schooling (YS), and the product of TST43 and years of schooling (TST43 $\times$ YS). The coefficients of the last three variables are shown in table 2.

Despite the high multicollinearity among these three variables, the coefficient on the interaction term is positive and significant (almost at 1 percent for a one-tail t-test), which supports the hypothesis that measured ability and educational attainment have significant complementarity.[5] These coefficients imply that the difference in earnings of college graduates with one degree who differ by one standard deviation in IQ (fifteen points) is about $800, while the corresponding difference for high school graduates is $250.

When a pooled regression is run with the logarithm of earnings as the

TABLE 2

LINEAR AND INTERACTION COEFFICIENTS ON MEASURED ABILITY AND
YEARS OF SCHOOLING FROM REGRESSIONS OF 1969 EARNINGS
ON TST43, YS, TST43 $\times$ YS, AND X^*
(NBER-Thorndike Sample)

Dependent Variable	Sample Size (N)	TST43	YS	TST43$\times$YS	SE	R^2
Earnings (1969) ...	2,263	−.094 (.063)	−.020 (.466)	.009 (.004)	6.671	.196
Log earnings (1969) ...	2,263	−.001 (.004)	.038 (.027)	.0003 (.0002)	.383	.250

NOTE.—Numbers in parentheses are standard errors. Earnings are in thousands of dollars.

[5] The simple correlations between the variables are: $r_{\text{TST43} \times \text{YS, TST43}} = .755$, $r_{\text{TST43} \times \text{YS, YS}} = .825$, and $r_{\text{TST43, YS}} = .262$.

dependent variable, the interaction coefficient is again positive, although, in this case, the intercorrelations make it impossible to associate high statistical significance with any single coefficent. When either the linear YS or TST43 term is dropped from the regression, the remaining two coefficients are highly significant (with t's lying between 6.7 and 19.5), and the interaction term is always positive.

To determine the relative effect of ability on earnings over time, simple within-schooling-class regressions were calculated of the log of 1969 earnings on the log of 1955 earnings. The residuals were then regressed on the measured-ability variable (again within schooling class). The purpose of this procedure is to determine whether the earnings in a relatively early year in the life cycle capture most of the effect of measured ability, with ability then having a negligible effect on later earnings once the effect of early earnings is netted out by the first regression. Table 3 gives the coefficients on TST43 from this second round of regressions.

All of the ability coefficients from these regressions are positive, which indicates an increasing role played by ability over time (given the influence it has on earnings in 1955). A natural way of testing the hypothesis of the increasing effect of ability pools the results of the individual regressions. The null hypothesis (of no increase in effect) at the .001 level is rejected when a procedure developed by Fisher is used.[6]

Although this calculation implies an increasing role for ability over time, for some purposes it is desirable to obtain unconstrained point estimates of the ability coefficient at a given age within schooling class. These coefficients are convenient for estimating the significance of omitting a measure of ability from earnings regressions. The results of regressions of

TABLE 3

COEFFICIENTS ON MEASURED ABILITY FROM REGRESSIONS
OF LOGARITHMIC EARNINGS RESIDUALS ON TST43
(NBER-Thorndike Sample)

	EDUCATION LEVEL				
	E_1	E_2	E_3	E_4	E_5
Coefficient	.264	.148	.135	.354	.253
	(.102)	(.114)	(.073)	(.152)	(.311)
Sample size (N)	467	516	868	204	102

NOTE.—Numbers in parentheses are standard errors. Coefficients and standard errors are multiplied by 100.

[6] Fisher's test (see Hald 1952, pp. 408–9) is used in the following way: Let P_i be the significance level of the ith schooling-level-ability coefficient, based on a one-tail t-test (for positive effect). Then $\Sigma^n \log (P_i)^2$ has a χ^2 distribution with $2n$ degrees of freedom, where n is the number of schooling classes, and natural logarithms are used. Table 3 yields a χ^2 of 33.9 with 10 df, which is significant at .001.

the log of earnings in both 1969 and 1955 on X^* and measured ability (TST43) within schooling-attainment classes are in table 4. The bracketed figures in the 1969 column are the products of the TST43 coefficient and one standard deviation of the test score (within the corresponding schooling level). Since the dependent variable is the natural logarithm of earnings and the product is usually small, this product approximates the relative change in earnings associated with a one-standard-deviation change in measured ability. Since the tests used to measure ability in the different samples in this study are not identical and do not have identical scaling, this product also is convenient for comparing results from the different samples.

For classes E_4 and E_5 (persons with two or more degrees, and lawyers), one standard deviation in measured ability (see table 4) increases earnings by about 13.7 and 8.0 percent, respectively—modest but empirically nontrivial amounts. The ability coefficient is positive for all schooling levels with the exception of doctors in 1955. It has been suggested that ability and job experience may be complementary in increasing earnings, and the calculation with table 3 indicates this is the case. Given this complementarity, it is possible that more-able people, in contrast with those

TABLE 4

COEFFICIENTS ON 1943 ABILITY FROM REGRESSIONS OF LOG
EARNINGS ON TST43 AND OTHER VARIABLES (X^*)
(NBER-Thorndike Sample)

EDUCATION LEVEL	SAMPLE SIZE (N)	YEAR	
		1969	1955
E_1 (high school grad.)	489	.321 (.122) [.042]	.073 (.102)
E_2 (col. nongrad.)	535	.256 (.132) [.033]	.247 (.103)
E_3 (col. grad., 1 deg.)	900	.318 (.080) [.048]	.329 (.064)
E_4 (col. grad., 2 deg.$^+$)	211	.858 (.173) [.137]	.720 (.136)
E_5 (lawyer)	128	.529 (.291) [.080]	.303 (.212)
E_6 (doctor)	53	.364 (.403) [.049]	−.768 (1.248)

NOTE.—Numbers in parentheses are standard errors. Coefficients and standard errors are multiplied by 100. The bracketed figures are the product of the TST43 coefficient and standard deviation of the test score at the corresponding schooling level. The product is *not* multiplied by 100. It indicates, for example, that the 15.7 standard deviation on TST43 is associated with a 13.7 percent earnings differential for the E_4 class.

of less ability, choose jobs in which work experience contributes significantly to future productivity. It seems plausible that competition tends to equalize returns from different jobs, thus reducing earnings in early years in such productivity-enhancing jobs. However, the positive ability coefficients in 1955 indicate that this competition does not reduce early earnings of the more able below the earnings of others. The negative coefficient for medical doctors in 1955 could arise because the more able invest in more-specialized training and have not caught up with others by this time. The small sample size (thirty-six) precludes strong conclusions.

The coefficients in table 4 can be used to characterize a bias in earnings and schooling relationships when ability is not included. Taking the sample means of the ability measure, TST43, for the E_1, E_2, and E_4 cohorts and multiplying them by the ability coefficients for college graduates with one and two or more degrees reveals that neglecting ability differences in this sample would lead one to overstate the potential (1969) earnings gain to (average) terminal high school graduates by 2.8 and 11.1 percent, respectively.

Because persons in the Thorndike sample had been prescreened before taking the Air Force battery of tests, the lower tail of the ability distribution is partially truncated. Consequently, there is an upward bias in the ability means, which is largest for high school graduates.

B. Results from the Rogers Sample

The sample obtained by Daniel C. Rogers includes 343 white males, for the most part Connecticut eighth-graders in 1935 when they were tested for IQ. Table 5 gives the logarithm of earnings for several years, IQ, and background variables. The five schooling variables used are E_1^+, high school nongraduates; E_2^+, high school graduates; E_3^+, college nongraduates; E_4^+, college graduates with one degree (and perhaps additional study); and E_5^+, graduate-degree holders. The background variables include family socioeconomic status (SESH$^+$ = 1 for the two highest social classes out of five; SESL$^+$ = 1 for the two lowest), religion (RC = 1 if Catholic; RJ = 1 if Jewish), marital status (NM = 1 if not married in 1965), and private school attendance (PS = 1 for precollege private schooling). This set of variables is denoted by X^{*+}. Generally, earnings means increase with schooling, except in 1959, when the E_5^+ graduate-degree group had little postschool job experience. Furthermore, IQ means increase significantly with level of schooling attained, paralleling the results from the NBER-Thorndike sample as given in table 1. Relative to the standard deviation of IQ within schooling class, the differences in IQ means for high school and college graduates are larger in the Rogers sample than in the NBER-Thorndike sample, probably because of the

TABLE 5

Means and Standard Deviations of Log Earnings, IQ, and Background Variables by Education Level
(Rogers Sample)

Education Level	Sample Size (N)	LE65	LE60	LE55	LE50	LDE4%	IQ	SESH+	SESL+	RC	RJ	PS	NYI
E^+_1 (high school nongrad.)	60	8.857 (.326)	8.708 (.281)	8.664 (.279)	8.569 (.335)	11.836 (.221)	95.9 (11.8)	.033	.917	.750	...	.033	.050
E^+_2 (high school grad.) ...	117	9.001 (.392)	8.764 (.336)	8.662 (.320)	8.550 (.338)	11.872 (.324)	102.3 (11.1)	.034	.829	.650	.017	.094	.077
E^+_3 (col. nongrad.)	51	9.262 (.557)	9.057 (.439)	8.900 (.428)	8.668 (.478)	12.070 (.429)	107.8 (9.59)	.196	.529	.431	.039	.235	.039
E^+_4 (col. grad., 1 deg.) ...	68	9.466 (.539)	9.253 (.479)	9.008 (.432)	8.689 (.535)	12.211 (.519)	115.8 (11.00)	.412	.427	.325	.059	.470	.059
E^+_5 (col. grad., 2 deg.) ...	47	9.640 (.574)	9.414 (.607)	9.061 (.502)	8.525 (.624)	12.262 (.445)	117.3 (10.0)	.446	.319	.298	.170	.383	.042

Source.—Rogers data tape.
Note.—Numbers in parentheses are standard deviations.

partial truncation in the NBER-Thorndike sample of people of lower ability. The patterns of the other background variables across schooling level are similar in the two samples.

A test for the complimentarity of ability and schooling is reported in table 6. As expected, the interaction coefficient is positive. The relatively small sample size and high multicollinearity among IQ, years of schooling (YS), and the product IQ $\times$ YS make attaching high statistical significance to any of the three coefficients impossible, although the interaction term has the most statistical power. As is always true of multicollinearity, the indeterminancy results partly from the small sample. For example, if the Rogers sample could be expanded to the same size as the NBER-Thorndike sample while maintaining covariances, the interaction coefficient would have a t-value exceeding 2.5. When the interaction term and either IQ or YS is included, the interaction term is highly significant, but the linear coefficient is not. This result also is obtained when the logarithm of earnings is the dependent variable. The socioeconomic-status dummies have moderate correlations with IQ, YS, and IQ $\times$ YS.[7] When they are excluded, the interaction coefficient is statistically significant ($t = 2.03$). The coefficients from the first regression in table 6 imply that fifteen points difference in IQ increases earnings of high school graduates by \$990 and those of college graduates by \$1,820.[8] These differentials are somewhat larger than those obtained from the NBER-Thorndike sample.

Table 7 gives results analogous to table 3 for the effect of ability on earnings over time. In this case, the logarithm of 1965 earnings is regressed on the logarithm of 1950 earnings, and the residuals from this calculation

TABLE 6

LINEAR AND INTERACTION COEFFICIENTS ON MEASURED IQ AND YEARS OF SCHOOLING FROM REGRESSIONS OF 1965 EARNINGS ON IQ, YS, IQ$\times$YS, AND X*†
(Rogers Sample)

Dependent Variable	Sample Size (N)	IQ	YS	IQ$\times$YS	SE	R^2
Earnings	343	−.101 (.141)	−.731 (1.134)	.014 (.010)	6.276	.336
Log earnings	343	−.001 (.010)	.008 (.078)	.001 (.001)	.430	.379

NOTE.—Numbers in parentheses are standard errors. Earnings are in dollars.

[7] The simple correlations are $r_{IQ \times YS, IQ} = .816$; $r_{IQ \times YS, YS} = .937$; $r_{IQ, YS} = .574$. The t-ratio on the interaction coefficient is approximately twice the t-ratio of either of the linear terms.

[8] The corresponding earnings differentials, omitting the socioeconomic-status dummy variables from the regressions, are \$1,260 and \$2,530.

TABLE 7

COEFFICIENTS ON IQ FROM REGRESSIONS OF LOGARITHMIC
EARNINGS RESIDUALS ON IQ
(Rogers Sample)

	EDUCATION LEVEL				
	E_1^+	E_2^+	E_3^+	E_4^+	E_5^+
Coefficient	.13	.82	.41	.75	.79
	(.35)	(.30)	(.58)	(.48)	(.82)
Sample size (N)	60	117	51	68	47

NOTE. Numbers in parentheses are standard errors. Coefficients and standard errors are multiplied by 100.

are regressed on IQ. Once again, all the IQ coefficients are positive, indicating an increasing effect over time. The Fisher χ^2 test rejects the hypothesis of a nonincreasing ability effect at the .01 level.

Unconstrained point estimates of the IQ coefficient from within-schooling-class regressions of the logarithm of earnings on IQ and X^{*+} are in table 8. The data in the table show that by 1965 IQ had a negligible effect on earnings of E_1^+, the high school nongraduates, with one standard deviation affecting earnings only by 0.26 percent. It is possible that high

TABLE 8

COEFFICIENTS ON IQ FROM REGRESSIONS OF LOG EARNINGS ON IQ AND
OTHER VARIABLES (X^*) BY YEAR
(Rogers Sample)

Education Level	Sample Size (N)	1965	1960	1955	1950	Other Variables
E_1^+ (high school nongrad.) ..	60	.024 (.35) [.003]	.14 (.29)	.20 (.29)	—.27 (.36)	X^*
E_2^+ (high school grad.)	117	.70 (.32) [.078]	.36 (.29)	.32 (.28)	.28 (.30)	X^*
E_3^+ (col. nongrad.)	51	.36 (.78) [.035]	.17 (.66)	.32 (.62)	.04 (.68)	X^*
E_4^+ (col. grad., 1 deg.)	68	.92 (.63) [.101]	.70 (.55)	.53 (.51)	.74 (.69)	X^*
E_5^+ (col. grad., 2 deg. +)	47	1.32 (.90) [.132]	1.01 (.99)	—.18 (.97)	—.17 (1.11)	X^*

NOTE. Numbers in parentheses are standard errors. Coefficients and standard errors are multiplied by 100. The bracketed figures are the product of the IQ coefficient and one standard deviation of IQ from table 1. It has not been multiplied by the 100 factor of the other lines in the table.

school nongraduates with very low IQ scores did not respond to the sample questionnaire and that the inclusion of such individuals would indicate that some minimal level of cognitive skill is required for most jobs in contemporary society. One standard deviation of the within-schooling-class samples makes a larger difference in earnings for high school and college graduates with one degree in the Rogers sample than in the NBER-Thorndike sample; the 10.1 percent earnings differential for the Rogers college graduate is more than twice the 4.8 percent for the NBER-Thorndike sample. This difference might result from statistical variability of the smaller Rogers sample. The earnings differential from one standard deviation of tested ability leads to very similar earnings differentials (between 13 and 14 percent) for those with two or more college degrees. In a more disaggregated form, these results tend to confirm the positive interaction between schooling and measured ability on earnings. In the Rogers sample, the strong trend in the size of the IQ coefficient over time for the E_5^+ group with two or more college degrees could be partly due to sizable earnings by professional men of high ability after their lengthy schooling and initial training is completed, although occupational information is not readily available to verify this possibility.

In correcting for the apparent bias in the increase in earnings attributed to schooling when ability is not accounted for, in tables 5 and 8 we take the βIQ in 1965 for college graduates times the sample difference in mean IQ of college graduates and high school graduates, and this indicates that IQ-typical terminal high school graduates would earn 13 percent less than college graduates with one degree. The corresponding differential for college graduates with two degrees and high school graduates is 18 percent. The truncation of low-ability high school graduates in the NBER-Thorndike data explains in part the larger bias from the neglect of ability in the Rogers sample.

C. Results from the Project Talent Sample

The Project Talent data used in this study include 8,840 white males who had full-time employment in 1966, who were high school juniors when they took the Project Talent battery of ability and achievement tests and provided information on home background and interests in 1959, and who answered a mail questionnaire in 1966. This large sample differs in two ways from the preceding samples and the calculations based on them: First, the available earnings data are for very early points in the lifetime earnings profile (1 and 5 years after high school graduation for most members in the sample). Second, results are presented from several general cognitive as well as more-specific achievement tests.[9]

---

[9] The NBER-Thorndike data contain seventeen specific tests whose relationship with earnings can be studied.

The tests reported on include C001 (a composite test score which is reported to be highly correlated with IQ), C004 (a composite quantitative test score), R410 (arithmetic computation), and R430 (clerical checking). Means and standard deviations of these test scores are reported by schooling level in table 9, with the logarithm of 1966 and 1962 earnings and background variables. The five schooling levels for this sample are: E'_1, high school nongraduates; E'_2, high school graduates; E'_3, college nongraduates (with 2 or less years of college completed); E'_4, college nongraduates (with 3 or 4 years of college), and E'_5, college graduates (with one degree). The background variables include family high and low socioeconomic status (SESH' and SESL', obtained from a composite socioeconomic-status variable P*801, developed by Project Talent), religion (RC = 1 if Catholic; RJ = 1 if Jewish); nonpublic school attendance prior to college (PAR = 1 for parochial; PRV = 1 for private school attendance in 1959), marital status (NM = 1 if not married in 1966), region (S = 1 if school attended in 1959 was in U.S. Office of Education Region 5 [Southeast]); and the logarithm of weeks worked the past year (LNWK). The collection of background variables is denoted by $X*'$.

At this early point in earnings careers, the logarithmic mean earnings for 1966 are more irregular than in the other samples discussed in this paper. The mean for high school nongraduates is trivially larger than the mean of the high school graduates. This result may be due to a differential response bias favoring nongraduates with high earnings, although there is no direct evidence. The differences in the means of the logarithm of weeks worked is partly responsible for the lower earnings means of the two highest schooling levels. If one assumes that earnings per week are not affected by the number of weeks worked and standardizes all 1966 earnings to the mean of 3.90 (log) weeks worked by the high school nongraduates, the five earnings figures for E'_1 through E'_5 become 8.54, 8.47, 8.42, 8.38, and 8.56, respectively.[10] Only the rank of college graduates is changed by this adjustment. It seems plausible that the ranking is significantly affected by productivity gains achieved by those with lower levels of schooling who have been in the civilian labor force for a longer time. Other samples suggest that the ranking will be altered in favor of those with more schooling in the future, when data become available from the 11-year Project Talent follow-ups.

The two more abstract measures of cognitive ability, C001 and C004, rise significantly with schooling attainment, similar to the Rogers and NBER-Thorndike samples. The more-specific ability and achievement-test scores (R410 and R430) also tend to rise with schooling, but the within-schooling standard deviations for these variables are relatively much larger

---

[10] This adjustment appears to be too large for the Project Talent sample. Within-schooling-level regressions yield coefficients on the log of weeks worked of about 0.7 instead of the 1.0 implied by this adjustment.

TABLE 9

MEANS AND STANDARD DEVIATIONS OF LOG EARNINGS, ABILITY AND ACHIEVEMENT VARIABLES, AND BACKGROUND VARIABLES BY EDUCATION LEVEL
(Project Talent Sample)

Education Level	Sample Size (N)	LE66	LE62*	LNWK (Log of Weeks Worked)	C001 (IQ Composite)	C004 (Quantitative Composite)	R410 (Arithmetic Computation)	R430 (Clerical Checking)
E'_1 (high school nongrad.)	183	8.535 (.404)	7.913 (.555)	3.90 (.14)	139 (50)	72 (31)	38 (13)	39 (18)
E'_2 (high school grad.)	3,853	8.475 (.454)	7.833 (.580)	3.91 (.13)	166 (44)	95 (36)	40 (10)	40 (16)
E'_3 (col. nongrad., 1–2 yr)	1,914	8.411 (.514)	...	3.89 (.20)	192 (42)	121 (42)	42 (9)	41 (15)
E'_4 (col. nongrad., 3–4 yr)	793	8.302 (.598)	...	3.81 (.32)	202 (38)	135 (42)	44 (9)	41 (14)
E'_5 (col. grad., 1 deg.)	2,097	8.271 (.597)	...	3.61 (.50)	217 (31)	156 (40)	47 (9)	42 (13)

Education Level	SESL'	SESH'	RC	RJ	NM	S	PAR	PRV
E'_1 (high school nongrad.)	.399	.279	.328	.016	.284	.137	.022	.011
E'_2 (high school grad.)	.314	.283	.331	.015	.398	.165	.061	.012
E'_3 (col. nongrad., 1–2 yr)	.169	.465	.315	.041	.462	.159	.099	.026
E'_4 (col. nongrad., 3–4 yr)	.107	.603	.282	.062	.484	.160	.106	.039
E'_5 (col. grad., 1 deg.)	.113	.621	.266	.078	.502	.157	.102	.044

SOURCE.—Project Talent data tape on high school junior subsample.
NOTE.—Numbers in parentheses are standard deviations.
* Sample sizes for these two education levels are 63 and 1,854.

than the mean differences between schooling levels. This result is not surprising if one considers the particular skills the latter tests are intended to measure.

Table 10 presents the coefficients on the four ability and achievement tests when the logarithm of 1966 earnings is regressed on the background variables $X^{*\prime}$ and the corresponding ability-test score. It is interesting to discover that the coefficients on C001 and C004 are negative in the 1962 earnings regressions for high school graduates 1 year out of high school, with the C001 coefficient significant at .05. This result could arise if jobs requiring greater cognitive ability of high school graduates also require more training and experience time to acquire job-specific skills. However, even if this is the correct explanation, the effect is small. One standard deviation of the sample high school graduate C001 score reduces mean earnings by 3.2 percent. By 1966, none of the ability coefficients for any of the schooling levels is significant and negative. Two of the ability and achievement measures, quantitative ability (C004) and clerical checking (R430), are statistically significant and positive for the high school graduates. Neither of the more-general cognitive-ability measures (C001 and C004) is significant for college dropouts. However, the clerical checking measures (R430) for college dropouts and R410 for the higher-level drop-

TABLE 10

COEFFICIENTS ON ABILITY AND SKILL MEASURES FROM REGRESSIONS OF LOG
EARNINGS (1966) ON AN ABILITY OR SKILL AND OTHER VARIABLES (X'^*)
(Project Talent Sample)

EDUCATION LEVEL	SAMPLE SIZE (N)	ABILITY OR SKILL VARIABLE			
		C001	C004	R410	R430
E'_1 (high school nongrad.) ...	183	.04 (.059) [.012]	.02 (.125) [.006]	—.06 (.222)	.00 (.30)
E'_2 (high school grad.)	3,853	.02 (.013) [.009]	.06 (.018) [.022]	.11 (.073) [.011]	.12 (.044) [.019]
E'_3 (col. nongrad., 1–2 yr) ...	1,914	—.03 (.025)	.00 (.100)	.16 (.114) [.014]	.30 (.071) [.045]
E'_4 (col. nongrad., 3–4 yr) ...	793	.04 (.051)	—.03 (.054)	.44 (.200) [.040]	.44 (.126) [.062]
E'_5 (col. grad., 1 deg.)	2,097	—.01 (.030)	.06 (.027) [.024]	.47 (.117) [.041]	.19 (.080) [.025]

NOTE.—Numbers in parentheses are standard errors. Coefficients and standard errors are multiplied by 100. The bracketed figures are the product of the ability or skill coefficients and are standard deviations of the corresponding test by schooling level. It has *not* been multiplied by the 100 factor of the other lines in the table. For completeness, the 1961 coefficients for the first two schooling levels and four tests are as follows: E ($N = 63$): .17 (.16); .08 (.25); —.83 (.57;); and —.25 (.39). For E'_2 ($N = 1,854$): —.08 (.033); —07 (.037); .05 (.13); and .11 (.089). (These regressions omit, of course, the log of weeks worked in 1966 as an independent variable.)

outs are statistically significant and are associated with modest earnings differentials for one standard deviation of the test measure (within schooling class), lying between 4 and 6.5 percent. That these specific variables play a more-important role for college dropouts than for high school graduates may reflect differences in the occupational distributions for these levels of educational attainment. Additional regressions should be run within "blue-collar" and "white-collar" occupations to test this possible explanation.

That more-specific ability measures have a larger effect than the general cognitive measures at early points in the earnings profile is not particularly surprising. The former are probably better indicators of differences in current productivity in certain jobs than the more-general measures (at least before people have acquired highly specific skills from job experience). Although these more-specific skills are associated with modest earnings differentials, omitting them is unlikely to be a significant source of bias in estimating the returns from schooling, since they are not highly correlated with the level of schooling attainment.

D. Results from Husén's Sample

The Husén sample discussed here includes some 450 Swedish males who were third-graders in Malmö when they were originally tested in 1938. They replied to a questionnaire in 1964 and earnings data were obtained by searching records partially summarizing income tax returns. The distribution of schooling attainment and the structure of Swedish education differed substantially from those in the United States while the Malmö students were still in school, making this sample an interesting one to contrast with the three American samples used in this study. Table 11 gives the available earnings data and ability and background variables by schooling level. The seven schooling levels and, roughly, their U.S. equivalence are: E_1'', *folkskola* not completed (elementary school); E_2'', *folkskola* completed (usually at age 14); E_3'' some *realskola* (secondary school); *realexamen* (*realskola* completed, usually at age 16 or 17) and technical school graduate; E_5'', *studentexamen* (completion of the gymnasium, roughly junior college, at ages 19–21, including a test required for admission to Swedish universities); E_6'', university degree (excluding E_7''); and E_7'', doctor or dentist. The ability measure, TST38, is the total score from four subtests similar in content to IQ tests. The IQ48 is a measure of IQ in 1948 for part of the sample, tested when the men were in military service. The background variables include dummy variables for social class (SCH"=1 for the highest of four classes of a discrete class variable, SCL" = 1 for the lowest); marital status (never married as of 1964); and serious, prolonged illness during the person's late teens or thereafter (PHLTH=1). This set of background variables is denoted by $X*''$.

TABLE 11

MEANS AND STANDARD DEVIATIONS* OF LOG EARNINGS, ABILITY, AND BACKGROUND VARIABLES BY EDUCATION LEVEL
(Husén Swedish Sample)

Education Level	Sample Size (N)†	LE68	LE64	LE59	LE54	LE49	TST38	IQ48	SCH"	SCL"	NM	PHLTH
E''_1 (folk. nongrad.)	18	9.494 (.278)	9.249 (.223)	8.833‡ (.267)	8.986 (.232)	8.154§ (.458)	34.1 (12.7)	···	···	.428	.111	.056
E''_2 (folk. grad.)	235	9.455 (.318)	9.203 (.305)	8.996 (.229)	9.033 (.182)	8.225 (.349)	44.3 (13.5)	93.5 (11.5)	.017	.404	.089	.127
E''_3 (real. nongrad.)	59	9.515 (.380)	9.328 (.266)	9.058 (.239)	9.035 (.259)	8.234 (.450)	50.9 (13.9)	101.3 (10.5)	.068	.203	.068	.051
E''_4 (real. grad.)	66	9.849 (.393)	9.562 (.322)	9.191 (.283)	9.042 (.245)	8.133 (.393)	56.3 (12.5)	109.7 (10.2)	.152	.136	.106	.091
E''_5 (gym. grad.)	51	10.061 (.346)	9.574 (.491)	9.260‖ (.376)	···	···	59.6 (11.8)	···	.294	.156	.098	.078
E''_6 (univ. grad.)	26	10.236 (.286)	···	···	···	···	60.6 (9.2)	···	.539	.039	.077	.077
E''_7 (doctors and dentists)	5	10.529 (.167)	···	···	···	···	66.8# (4.6)	···	···	···	···	···

* Earnings means are deflated by the Swedish Consumer Price Index (1949 = 100). Numbers in parentheses are standard deviations.
† N is for 1968 earnings and all other nonearnings variables. Numbers of observations decline for earlier years. Cells with very few observations are indicated.
‡ 120 observations.
§ 7 observations.
‖ 20 observations.
8 observations.

Table 11 shows the strong correlation of earnings with schooling attainment, with substantial increases over the full range of schooling attainment. The slightly larger value of the logarithm of *folkskola* nongraduate over *folkskola* (E_1'' over E_2'') is apparently due to response bias in answering the 1964 questionnaire. Another calculation (of the logarithmic means) not limited to questionnaire respondents yielded means of 9.401 and 9.320 to E_2'' and E_1'' respectively, in 1968.

Although substantial changes have been taking place in the Swedish educational system, at the time members of this sample cohort were in school, most children terminated their education with the completion of the *folkskola* at age 14, and relatively few completed university training. The attrition rate of those starting the *realskola* is high, and only slightly more than half obtained the secondary *realexamen* degree (or a degree from the more vocationally oriented alternative institution). These differences in the educational system probably explain the modest rise in the TST38 ability for levels beyond *realexamen*, (E_4''), relative to the standard deviation of the test within schooling-attainment class (except for the very small sample of doctors and dentists). There is a very strong tendency for the highest social class to become an increasingly important source of students acquiring schooling beyond *realexamen*. At this time, the Swedish government absorbed most of the direct costs of university attendance. All those passing the *studentexam* were eligible for university admission, yet less than 40 percent completed the university (or became doctors and dentists). Thus, it appears that a relatively small proportion of those from the middle or low social classes found getting a university degree worthwhile even though they were eligible. This suggests that the expected increase in earnings associated with a university degree was not large enough to offset the opportunity cost of foregone earnings and the out-of-pocket living costs required of a student. This argument suggests that the investment for higher earnings of university graduates may have played a less important role in Sweden than in the United States during this period.

Table 12 shows the ability coefficient over time and for different schooling levels from regressions of the logarithm of earnings on TST38 and X^*''. A substantial fraction of members of this sample was retested in 1948 during their required military service. The results from 1968 and 1954 log earnings for this test IQ48 also are recorded in the table for the larger samples. This second test score may be satisfactory for studying the effect of measured ability over time within a schooling class, but it runs into the difficulties of the Griliches-Mason study for the comparison of different levels of schooling attainment since it is measured after all schooling levels through E_5'', *studentexamen*, are completed. Although the *means* of IQ48 by schooling class may be affected by the schooling level achieved, this does not necessarily imply the observed greater statistical power and em-

TABLE 12
COEFFICIENTS ON 1938 ABILITY FROM REGRESSIONS OF LOG EARNINGS ON TST38 AND OTHER VARIABLES ($X''*$)
(Husén Swedish Sample)

EDUCATION LEVEL	SAMPLE SIZE (N)	YEAR						
		1968	1964	1959	1954	1949	1968*	1954*
E''_1 (*folk.* nongrad.)	18	.39 (.61) [.049]	−.23 (.78)	−.86† (.68)	...	...	...	...
E''_2 (*folk.* grad.)	235	.05 (.80)	.13 (.16)	.14 (.14)	.19 (.12)	.12 (.27)	.32 (.19) [.037]	.12 (.14)
E''_3 (*real.* nongrad.)	59	.22 (.38) [.031]	.32 (.29)	.11 (.27)	−.54 (.33)	.04 (.71)	.40 (.47) [.050]	−.52 (.42)
E''_4 (*real.* grad.)	66	.43 (.39) [.054]	.46 (.38)	.35 (.36)	.62 (.51)	−.84‡ (.81)	1.03 (.58) [.105]	.13 (.52)
E''_5 (gym. grad.)	51	.58 (.41) [.068]	1.19 (.86)	1.09 (.83)	...	...	1.06 (.78) [.106]	...
E''_6 and E''_7 (univ. deg.; doctors, dentists)	26§	.42 (.67) [.038]	...	...	...	...	...	...

NOTE.—Numbers in parentheses are standard errors. Coefficients and standard errors are multiplied by 100. The bracketed figures are the product of the TST38 coefficient and one standard deviation of TST38 by schooling level. It has *not* been multiplied by the 100 factor of the other lines in the table.

* These columns give regression coefficients on IQ measured in 1948, 10 years after the 1938 tests. The scaling is different from the 1938 tests, so the coefficients are not strictly comparable, although the bracketed products are.

† Sample size, 12.

‡ Sample size, 22.

§ Pooled sample of E''_5 and E''_6, includes dummy variable for doctors and dentists.

pirical effect of one standard deviation of within-schooling-class 1948 IQ as contrasted with the 1938 measure. For the schooling levels with more than twenty observations for both ability measures $(E_2''-E_5'')$, the coefficients increase monotonically for both measures in 1968. The drop in the coefficient of the university graduates for the TST38 coefficient could be a peculiarity of the quite small sample, or it could arise from decisions to get a university degree being less dependent on expected earnings. Scatter diagrams of earnings and ability were plotted for this group, and no extreme observations lowering or raising the regression slope were noted. Nor were any extreme occupational peculiarities detected that would account for this result.

Although the large modal class of *folkskola* graduates, E_2'', contains people who were only 14 years old when they completed their academic training, the product of the IQ48 coefficient and one standard deviation of sample mean measured ability within E_2'' gives an increment to earnings closer to that for the NBER-Thorndike-sample high school graduates than to the negligible effect for Rogers high school nongraduates. This result seems plausible. Because of the large fraction of the population in the Swedish E_2'' group, postacademic institutions and job experience may leave greater latitude for cognitive ability to influence earnings differentials. However, the 3.7 percent implied by this calculation is very modest relative to the observed standard deviation of earnings for this class, that is, larger than 32.8 percent of the mean (table 11). Using IQ48, the earnings differential of 10 percent or more for those passing the *realexam* or *studentexam* is in line with that for college graduates in the Rogers sample, and substantially larger than that for the NBER-Thorndike college graduates with one degree. Again, this result suggests that postschool experience has more room for cognitive ability in producing larger earnings differentials with given years of schooling in Sweden than the same number of years of schooling in the United States.

E. Summary of Statistical Calculations from the Samples

The first part of the paper presented the economic rationale for a strong theoretical presumption that measured ability has significant complementarity with schooling and job experience on earnings. The argument focuses on education as an investment, notes the important role of foregone earnings as the main cost of this investment, and appeals to the strong empirical collinearity between measured ability and schooling.

Both the statistical tests based upon pooling the schooling-attainment classes and the pattern of coefficients on measured ability from regressions run within schooling class strongly support these hypotheses on complementarity of ability with schooling and postschool experience in producing earnings. For low levels of schooling (less than high school graduate in the U.S. data), ability differentials are of negligible importance in creating earnings differentials. For high levels of schooling, one standard deviation of within-sample-schooling-class measured ability is associated with earnings differentials ranging from 10 to 13 percent by the time males are 35–40 years old.

In considering biases in imputing increased earnings to schooling when ability is not observed, two results are especially worth noting. In both the Thorndike and Rogers samples, the ability coefficient is very small for the first year of available earnings data for high school graduates and the Project Talent data even suggest the coefficient may be negative 1 year out of high school, and quite small (but positive of foregone earnings) 4 years later. This result indicates that the net opportunity cost of people of higher ability who acquire one or more college degrees, relative to the actual earnings profiles of higher-ability people leaving school after high school graduation, is not significantly raised by differences in ability. Hence, the overstatement of rates of return to a college education (compared with high school) due to an understatement of ability-related opportunity costs does not appear to be a serious source of bias if ability data are unavailable. The bias in stating what the earnings of a terminal high school graduate of average ability would be if he acquired one or more college degrees 15 or 20 years after school completion is larger. A calculation using the Thorndike coefficients and ability means indicated a bias of at least 2.8 percent for one college degree and 11.1 percent for two or more college degrees for average high school graduates. The corresponding calculation with Rogers data indicated a bias of 13 and 18 percent, respectively. These differences are large enough to be of empirical interest.

The modest contribution of measured ability to explaining differences in earnings, in contrast with the strong association of measured ability and schooling attainment, is not very surprising, since most of the ability measures studied in this paper are designed to forecast academic potential and achievement. Despite the relative sample homogeneity due to the narrow age range, the criteria for omitting observations, and, given the background variables used in the regression calculations, the standard error of estimate of the within-schooling-group regressions is still substantial, as the total regression equations summarized in table B1 indicate. In no regression with the log of annual earnings does it fall below .24. Although it is important and interesting to have better information on the ability–earnings profile relationship, the further decomposition of this residual is still a major task that should prevent students of the distribution of earnings from becoming mentally unemployed in the near future.

Appendix A

Description of the Samples

The following descriptions of the four samples and the procedures used in this study are intended to permit assessment of the role of population differences in the results. (Detailed descriptions are, of course, available at the data sources.)

A. NBER-Thorndike Sample

This sample is based on male Air Force volunteers for pilot, navigator, and bombardier programs who had passed an initial screening test and were given an additional set of seventeen tests to measure various abilities in the last half of 1943. Thorndike and Hagen in 1955 sent a questionnaire, including a question on 1955 earnings, to a sample of 17,000 of these men. In 1969 the National Bureau of Economic Research sent a subsequent questionnaire. From usable coded responses, the sample was reduced to exclude independent proprietors, doctors, lawyers, and teachers (occupational groups raising particular problems which will be studied separately). The grossly overrepresented pilots also were eliminated from the sample. Heterogeneity was reduced by restricting the sample to the central group between ages 44 and 47 in 1969. Heteroscedasticity in earnings was reduced by eliminating those in poor health. Those reporting earnings of less than $500 were eliminated, and the earnings figures were truncated at $99,999. A three-standard-deviation rejection criterion from the empirical log of earnings distribution for each education level was then imposed. Original 1955 earnings were obtained by inflating monthly salary to an annual basis. Earnings for other years were reported on an "annual full-time basis salary." Final sample size is 2,316.

B. The Rogers Sample

The Rogers sample is based on respondents to a 1966 questionnaire survey Rogers (1967) designed and carried out. The modal group consists of Connecticut eighth-graders in 1935, tested for IQ in the eighth grade. Age has a tight distribution with a standard deviation of 1.2 years. All earnings data are retrospective and were obtained from the questionnaire. The 1965 figure is intended to be a reasonably precise measure of total earnings for the year. The 1960, 1955, and 1950 figures are full-time equivalent earnings based on inflated salary or wage rate recall information.

The original sample contained 364 observations. By eliminating those reporting zero salary or wage for any year, those not working full-time in 1965, those with a severe handicap, and three extreme observations (which were more than 3.00 standard deviations from the corresponding schooling means), the final sample size in this study was reduced to 343. The purpose in rejecting these observations is to reduce the extreme heteroscedasticity of individual earnings data which makes estimation of parameters of interest difficult in small samples.

Rogers's measure of socioeconomic status is based on a two-factor index of social position devised by A. B. Hollingshead. This index assigns scores to father's occupation and father's schooling attainment. Rogers then allocated total scores to five social classes. The high and low social class dummy variables used in this study assigned the two top and two bottom classes of Rogers, respectively.

C. Project Talent Sample

The Project Talent subsample is based on some 14,000 male high school juniors who took the Project Talent battery of tests in 1960, and who indicated positive earnings in 1966. For the calculations in this study, all still attending school, all indicating part-time work in 1966, all farmers and men in the military, and all those reporting poor health in 1960 were rejected. Nonwhites were also removed for separate analysis. For each of the five education levels for the remaining observations, the mean and standard deviation of the log of 1966 earnings was computed, and observations lying more than 2.75 standard deviations beyond the mean were discarded. The first group of criteria removes individuals not full-time members of the civilian labor force and specific groups with heteroscedastic or difficult-to-interpret earnings. The second criterion was imposed to eliminate observations in the extreme tails of the log-earnings-distribution. This brutal treatment of the data further reduces heteroscedasticity and is probably a low-cost way of improving the efficiency of the estimates (relative to no adjustments). This procedure left 8,840 observations.

Missing independent variables are obtained either by assignment of modal class for discrete, nonordered variables or by estimation from subregressions, using a flexible program written by A. L. Norman. No observation with more than five missing independent variables is used in subsequent calculations.

The dummy variables for "high and low" socioeconomic status (SESH' and SESL') are obtained from the Project Talent variable, P*801, which is an index weighting breadwinner's income, parents' education, and a number of other items on family background from the original 1960 questionnaire. A person is assigned to the higher status SES' if P*801 > 111, and to the lower status SESL' if P*801 < 91.

D. The Husén Sample

The Husén data is based on all (male) third-graders in Malmö who were given a series of four tests in 1938. Additional information was obtained from school and social records and a 1964 questionnaire (to which the response rate exceeded 80 percent). Information on earnings was obtained for 1968, 1964, 1959, 1954, and 1949 directly from archives containing a summary of individual income tax data. Thus, these earnings are realized earnings rather than the full-time equivalents reported in most of the other samples. No information was available on weeks worked per year or hours per week except for a questionnaire item that distinguished part-time and full-time workers in 1964. A 2.75 rejection criterion for log of earnings exceeding 2.75 standard deviations of the corresponding mean (by schooling level) was applied and iterated once. Only questionnaire respondents are included in this paper. The sample size of those with 1968 earnings passing these criteria is 458.

The high and low socioeconomic class variables SCH" and SCL" are obtained from the highest and lowest of four "classes" developed in 1939. Criteria include father's income, occupation, and social welfare status.

The "continental schooling system" in which relatively few attain high levels of formal schooling prevailed when the Malmö cohorts were third-graders. This difference explains the very different distribution of individuals by schooling attainment as well as the weaker tendency for ability to separate schooling attainment once *realexamen* attainment is achieved.

Appendix B

Summary of Full Regression Equations of Log Earnings by Schooling Level on Measured Ability and Other Variables

Table B1 summarizes, for the different samples and different schooling levels, regressions of the log of earnings for a single year on some ability measure and a more or less standard set of background variables. The education levels are

TABLE B1

COEFFICIENTS FROM FULL REGRESSIONS OF THE LOGARITHM OF EARNINGS ON AN ABILITY MEASURE, AND BACKGROUND VARIABLES

Education Level	Sample Size (N)	Ability Test*	LNWK (Log of Weeks Worked)	SESH (Socio-economic Status High)	SESL (Socio-economic Status Low)	RC (Religion Catholic)	RJ (Religion Jewish)
NBER-Thorndike (Dependent Variable: Log of 1969 Earnings; $R^2 = .28$)†							
E_1 (high school grad.)	489	.321 (.122)	...	−.059 (.092)	−.034 (.040)	−.039 (.035)	.564 (.101)
E_2 (col. nongrad.)	535	.256 (.132)	...	−.039 (.069)	−.118 (.038)	.003 (.042)	.291 (.096)
E_3 (col. grad., 1 deg.)	900	.318 (.080)	...	.003 (.039)	−.082 (.027)	.002 (.029)	.372 (.062)
E_4 (col. grad., 2 deg.)	211	.858 (.173)	...	−.011 (.086)	−.217 (.060)	.182 (.073)	.274 (.102)
E_5 (lawyer)	128	.529 (.291)	...	−.237 (.126)	−.233 (.112)	.037 (.112)	.122 (.157)
E_6 (doctor)	53	.364 (.403)	...	−.356 (.148)	−.207 (.123)	.122 (.126)	.040 (.225)
Rogers (Dependent Variable: Log of 1965 Earnings; $R^2 = .46$)							
E_1^+ (high school nongrad.)	60	.024 (.35)	...	−.262 (.278)	−.351 (.202)	.202 (.099)	...
E_2^+ (high school grad.)	117	.70 (.32)	...	.050 (.210)	−.233 (.107)	.067 (.081)	.679 (.275)
E_3^+ (col. nongrad.)	51	.36 (.78)	...	.062 (.262)	.144 (.174)	.040 (.153)	.696 (.376)
E_4^+ (col. grad., 1 deg.)	68	.92 (.63)	...	−.106 (.174)	−.119 (.182)	.114 (.139)	.170 (.270)
E_5^+ (col. grad., 2 deg. +)	47	1.32 (.90)	...	.180 (.221)	.020 (.222)	.566 (.210)	.636 (.245)

TABLE B1 (Continued)

Education Level	Sample Size (N)	NM (Not Married)	S (Southern U.S.)	PHLTH (Serious Illness since Mid-Teens)	PS (Private School)	SE
NBER-Thorndike (Dependent Variable: Log of 1969 Earnings; $R^2 = .28$)†						
E_1 (high school grad.) ···············	489	−.180 (.077)	−.024 (.049)	...	...	.351
E_2 (col. nongrad.) ···············	535	−.058 (.081)	−.022 (.048)	...	...	.395
E_3 (col. grad., 1 deg.) ···············	900	−.167 (.059)	−.084 (.032)	...	...	.361
E_4 (col. grad., 2 deg.) ···············	211	−.176 (.128)	−.060 (.086)	...	...	.388
E_5 (lawyer) ···············	128	.118 (.208)	−.065 (.106)	...	...	.487
E_6 (doctor) ···············	53	−.420 (.230)	.129 (.159)	...	...	.368
Rogers (Dependent Variable: Log of 1965 Earnings; $R^2 = .46$)						
E_1^+ (high school nongrad.) ···············	60	−.473 (.180)	...	...	−.057 (.298)	.300
E_2^+ (high school grad.) ···············	117	−.045 (.132)	...	...	.072 (.134)	.369
E_3^+ (col. nongrad.) ···············	51	−.744 (.390)	...	...	.556 (.238)	.504
E_4^+ (col. grad., 1 deg.) ···············	68	−.843 (.251)	...	...	.338 (.162)	.462
E_5^+ (col. grad., 2 deg. +) ···············	47	−.695 (.386)	...	...	.063 (.245)	.514

NOTE.—Standard errors are in parentheses except for Project Talent, where the regression program gives t-values.
* Different ability tests are used for each major sample cohort. These are: Rogers, IQ test scores; Project Talent, 0004 (quantitative composite); NBER-Thorndike (a general ability factor from Air Force test battery); and Husén, TST38 (total test score 1938).
† The R^2 for the different samples are obtained from pooled regressions, letting every variable in the basic set interact with schooling-level dummies.

TABLE B1 (*Continued*)

Education Level	Sample Size (N)	Ability Test*	LNWK (Log of Weeks Worked)	SESH (Socio-economic Status High)	SESL (Socio-economic Status Low)	RC (Religion Catholic)	RJ (Religion Jewish)
Project Talent (Dependent Variable: Log of 1966 Earnings; $R^2 = .26$)†							
E'_1 (high school nongrad.)	183	.02 (.16)	.489 (2.36)	.038 (.49)	−.083 (1.20)	.042 (.67)	.203 (.88)
E'_2 (high school grad.)	3,853	.06 (3.24)	.488 (9.51)	.067 (4.00)	−.046 (2.84)	.041 (2.57)	.050 (.91)
E'_3 (col. nongrad., 1–2 yr)	1,914	.00 (.03)	.514 (9.25)	.059 (2.44)	.012 (.38)	.068 (2.45)	.093 (1.66)
E'_4 (col. nongrad., 3–4 yr)	793	−.03 (.56)	.702 (12.0)	.062 (1.49)	.010 (.15)	.066 (1.38)	.132 (1.64)
E'_5 (col. grad., 1 deg.)	2,534	.06 (2.24)	.719 (34.3)	.038 (1.57)	−.006 (.172)	.055 (1.92)	.027 (.67)
Husén Swedish Sample (Dependent Variable: Log of 1968 Earnings; $R^2 = .43$)							
E''_1 (*folk.* nongrad.)	18	.392 (.607)	...	...	−.105 (.195)	...	...
E''_2 (*folk.* grad.)	235	.050 (.800)	...	−.138 (.161)	−.049 (.042)	...	...
E''_3 (*real.* nongrad.)	59	.219 (.379)	...	−.291 (.208)	−.072 (.129)	...	...
E''_4 (*real.* grad.)	66	.427 (.386)	...	.049 (.136)	−.111 (.141)	...	...
E''_5 (*gym.* grad.)	51	.586 (.409)	...	.255 (.106)	−.086 (.137)	...	...
E''_6 and E''_7 (univ. deg., doctors, dentists)	26	.420 (.670)	...	−.026 (.125)	...	...	...

TABLE B1 (*Continued*)

Education Level	Sample Size (N)	NM (Not Married)	S (Southern U.S.)	PHLTH (Serious Illness since Mid-Teens)	PS (Private School)		SE
					Par	Prv	
Project Talent (Dependent Variable: Log of 1966 Earnings)							
E'_1 (high school nongrad.)	183	−.166 (2.53)	−.236 (2.74)	...	.023 (.11)	.026 (.09)	.387
E'_2 (high school grad.)	3,853	−.298 (21.3)	−.068 (3.57)	...	−.030 (.99)	.224 (3.59)	.419
E'_3 (col. nongrad., 1–2 yr)	1,914	−.320 (14.5)	−.095 (3.11)	·	−.017 (.42)	.001 (.02)	.474
E'_4 (col. nongrad., 3–4 yr)	793	−.330 (8.06)	−.082 (1.58)	...	−.052 (.76)	.165 (1.73)	.515
E'_5 (col. grad., 1 deg.)	2,534	−.105 (4.98)	.038 (1.28)	...	−.069 (1.71)	−.031 (.62)	.472
Husén Swedish Sample (Dependent Variable: Log 4 1968 Earnings)							
E''_1 (*folk.* nongrad.)	18	−.112 (.241)	...	−.061 (.349)	...		.301
E''_2 (*folk.* grad.)	235	−.163 (.072)	...	−.025 (.062)	...		.316
E''_3 (*real.* nongrad.)	59	−.121 (.394)	...	−.116 (.237)	...		.389
E''_4 (*real.* grad.)	66	−.277 (.157)	...	−.238 (.166)	...		.384
E''_5 (gym. grad.)	51	−.071 (.161)	...	−.098 (.176)	...		.384
E''_6 and E''_7 (univ. deg., doctors, dentists)	26	.011 (.312)	...	−.028 (.227)	...		.293

not directly comparable for the different samples, and the coding should be checked in the main text. The scaling of the different ability tests makes direct comparison among samples meaningless, and the tests themselves would not be perfectly correlated. However, since earnings are expressed in logarithms, multiplying the ability coefficients by the standard deviation of the ability measure indicates the proportion (approximate) by which earnings are altered by this size of change in measured ability.

The scaling and criteria used to produce dummy variables for high and low socioeconomic status differ greatly among samples and make comparison of coefficient magnitudes in the four samples meaningless.

The R^2 given for the four samples are from total regressions that allow for interaction of all independent variables with level of schooling attainment.

References

Becker, Gary S. *Human Capital and the Personal Distribution of Income: An Analytical Approach.* W. S. Woytinsky Lecture no. 1. Ann Arbor: Inst. Public Admin., Univ. Mich., 1967.

Garner, William T. "Discussion." *A.E.R.* 61 (May 1971): 299–301.

Griliches, Zvi. "Notes on the Role of Education in Production Functions and Growth Accounting." In *Education, Income and Human Capital,* edited by W. Lee Hansen. Studies in Income and Wealth, vol. 35. New York: Nat. Bur. Econ. Res., 1970.

Hald, Anders. *Statistical Theory, with Engineering Applications.* New York: Wiley, 1952.

Hause, John C. "Ability and Schooling as Determinants of Lifetime Earnings or If You're So Smart, Why Aren't You Rich?" *A.E.R.* 61 (May 1971): 289–98.

Husén, Torsten. *Talent, Opportunity, and Career.* Stockholm: Almquist & Wiksell, 1969.

Rogers, Daniel C. "Private Rates of Return to Education in the United States: A Case Study." Ph.D. dissertation, Yale Univ., 1967. A shortened version is in *Yale Econ. Essays* 9 (Spring 1969): 89–134.

Schultz, Theodore W. "Resources for Higher Education: An Economist's View." *J.P.E.* 76 (May 1968): 327–47.

Thorndike, Robert L., and Hagen, Elizabeth. *Ten Thousand Careers.* New York: Wiley, 1959.

Comment

Burton A. Weisbrod

University of Wisconsin

John Hause's paper is addressed to the perplexing matters of how to disentangle the effects of ability and schooling on worker earnings, and of the effect of ability on earnings over a worker's lifetime.[1] His emphasis on "ability" and schooling as determinants of earnings is surely not intended to deny that other variables also affect earnings—or to deny that these other variables may also interact with ability and schooling level—but he barely touches on other variables or the possibility of interactions. Instead, Hause chooses to include in his regressions a variety of "background" variables, such as father's education, religion, and marital status. The a priori relevance, however, of each of these variables to the problem at hand—the ability-schooling nexus—is by no means clear. More serious is the matter of omitted variables or omitted interaction terms which may be correlated with the included independent variables. When Hause examines the relationships between ability and earnings within schooling levels, he is estimating regression coefficients under the implicit assumption that other determinants of earnings are uncorrelated with the included ability, schooling level, and background variables. One omitted variable in particular, however, is not likely to fulfill the test of noncorrelation: "motivation." Why do high-ability students become dropouts from high school or college? Why do many people with modest ability do well in college? In general, why do people with widely varying abilities attain the same level of schooling? There are surely many plausible answers, but one of them focuses on differences in motivation, and motivation is likely to be correlated negatively with ability for persons with a given level of educational attainment. Persons having relatively high ability for their particular educational level group may well have modest or even relatively low levels of motivation. Such a negative correlation would lead to downward-biased parameter estimates of the importance of ability for persons stratified by level of schooling, since the estimates for ability will actually reflect the effects of

[1] Comments are on Hause's revised COBRE paper.

both ability and motivation. It is conceivable that the assorted "background" variables utilized by Hause constitute proxies for motivational forces which are, after all, likely to influence educational attainment as well as earnings. However, Hause makes no such claim for the background variables he uses, nor does he even mention motivational forces.

Motivation is important for another reason. If it affects both ability (as measured) and level of educational attainment (LEA) but is not included explicitly in the model as estimated, then ability and LEA will be correlated. The interpretation may then be that those variables interact, when the truth can be that they do not, both being effects of a third factor.

A still more fundamental problem is the definition of "ability." It should be clear that we cannot hope to unravel the knotty, interrelated effects of ability and schooling on earnings until we define ability. Hause provides little help or guidance, however, in developing a "useful" definition. In fact, he uses "ability" and "measured ability" in quite a variety of ways in his literary discussion and empirical work. At one point he describes as "attractive" a "theoretical" definition of ability, based on differences among people in marginal rate-of-return functions, but he later finds it wanting. Subsequently, he mentions a physiological definition, involving brain-wave responses, and this is followed by a reference to IQ. In the empirical work, a variety of scores on different tests are taken as indicating (passim) "ability," "cognitive ability," "specific ability," and "measured ability," while still other test scores, we are told, measure "specific achievement," "IQ," "clerical checking" facility, or other things whose relationships to ability and, hence, to the subject of the paper are obscure. What, one wonders, is the relationship between ability and the "battery of tests given to potential American pilots and navigators in 1943" (Thorndike sample)? Whatever those tests measured, does the IQ test given to Connecticut eighth-graders in 1935 (the Rogers sample) measure the same thing? Of the four tests—two "general cognitive" and two "specific achievement"— used in the Project Talent sample, why are the two former ones identified with ability? How can we decide which is a better measure of the concept of ability, and why are the other two tests, if they do not measure ability, introduced at all into the statistical analyses? How should the reader interpret findings about the interaction between schooling and ability when, as in the analysis of the Talent data, certain tests are termed "specific achievement tests" at one point in Hause's discussions and "specific *ability* and achievement"[2] at another point? With the four Project Talent tests— whatever they measure—showing significantly different associations with earnings at different schooling levels, and without a basis for discriminating among the tests so as to determine which is a "better" measure of the concept of ability, what should the reader make of the diverse findings?

[2] Emphasis added to this and the following quotations from Hause.

And, since test scores generally vary by level of educational attainment, with the level of schooling affecting the test scores and also being affected by them, what can we learn from Hause's analyses about the interactive effects of ability and schooling?

Whenever statistical analyses are performed, the question arises as to how results should be interpreted when they run counter to expectations. Even if one grants the usefulness of the ability measures used by Hause, the fact is that many of the results reported in the paper are contrary to what he anticipated. Rather than examine the possibilities that his general hypothesis is either in error or is less widely applicable than he believed, Hause repeatedly presents ad hoc explanations to rationalize these contrary findings as being consistent with his a priori expectations. Thus, regarding the surprising negative coefficient of ability for doctors in the NBER-Thorndike sample (table 4), we are told that this "*could* arise because the more able invest in more-specialized training and have not caught up with others by this time." Then, when the interaction between IQ and years of schooling is found to be statistically *in*significant (table 6), we are told that the small sample size is the culprit: "If the Rogers sample could be expanded [sixfold] to the same size as the NBER-Thorndike sample *while maintaining covariances*, the interaction coefficient would have a *t*-value exceeding 2.5." Of course, a sufficient increase in sample size will always make any coefficient significant *if* the covariances are maintained.

In table 8, regarding the "negligible effect" of IQ on 1965 earnings of high school nongraduates, we are told that "it is *possible* that high school nongraduates with very low IQ scores did not respond to the sample questionnaire." Later, turning to the Project Talent data, we are told that the fact of mean earnings for high school graduates not being higher than for nongraduates "*may be* due to a differential response bias favoring nongraduates with high earnings, although there is no direct evidence." Finally, in connection with the Husén sample Hause says: "The drop in the coefficient of the university graduates for the TST38 coefficient [table 12] *could be* a peculiarity of the quite small sample, or it could arise from decisions to get a university degree being less dependent on expected earnings." Each of these speculations is plausible, but so are others.

John Hause has tackled an important but most difficult area for analysis. We can all agree with him that there is no chance for economists and others concerned with ability-earnings relationships to be "mentally unemployed" for some time. To this prediction I would add the hope for more strenuous efforts to define "ability" (as well as "motivation") at the conceptual level, as a precondition to devising operational tests of the quantitative impact of both on earnings.

Equity Implications of State Tuition Policy and Student Loans

Robert W. Hartman

Brookings Institution

Many economists have for some time now advocated tuition increases, complemented by expanded student loan programs, at state-supported colleges and universities. The present system of state support, it is argued, does not contribute to economic efficiency in at least two senses. First, relative prices, facing the student consumer, between the public and private education sectors distort the true cost ratios in the two sectors. Second, the social benefits of higher education are doubtful (or of low value); therefore it is improper to drive a wedge between public and private rates of return to higher education.

Most recently, the attack on subsidized state tuitions has rested on equity grounds: Not only do we have an inefficient system, but the poor are paying for it. Thus, many economists—and, more important, legislators—have argued that substituting loan programs for subsidized tuition will not only cure inefficiency but also will improve the equitability of our system of financing higher education.

This paper is focused only on the equity effects of removing state tuition support and introducing loan finance. The efficiency arguments either are self-evident or depend heavily on the political and social values one brings to the evaluation of social benefits. The discussion of equity effects of a low-tuition policy has been flawed in three ways:

1. The distribution of benefits and costs has been measured in terms of transfers from the taxpaying public to children whose parents are of prime earning age, thus failing to specify the permanent income of beneficiaries and payers.

2. The criterion of equity being used has not been made clear. If transfers are intergenerational, what constitutes equity? Is the gain in income by some to be weighted differently from the losses of others?

I am grateful to Joseph A. Pechman for advice and to John Yinger for computer assistance and helpful comments. Dan Sullivan and Mary von Euler provided research assistance.

3. The attempt to combine the tax side and the subsidy side to derive a net-benefit measure has obscured issues more than it has clarified them (Hansen and Weisbrod 1971*b*, pp. 363–74).

An attempt made in this study to overcome some of these problems includes the design of a model which traces one cohort of high school seniors through higher education and later earnings. The gains in earnings from this cohort alone are used to measure the benefits of state subsidy or loan programs. The pattern of future taxes to be paid (or loan repayments to be made) by this cohort is assessed. Finally, several measures of equity, including one of social mobility, are discussed.

Part I of the paper provides an illustrative example of what the system of state support that has prevailed in the past might be expected to produce in the future. Then a format is described, in Part II, for illustrating the gross effects on future income distribution of an increase in tuitions at state institutions. There I also explore the magnitude of changes which would be occasioned in future income distribution by offsetting some of the losses of higher tuition through expanded loan programs. Finally, I consider, in Part III, how the tax system used to support low tuition and the repayment system used for student loans might be evaluated and compared on equity grounds.

I. Future Implications of Low State Tuitions

To spell out the income distribution effects of the continuation of low-tuition policies at publicly supported colleges, as a basis for discussion of changes in that policy, we have developed a grossly oversimplified model of the income-generating process. In essence, our model takes a census survey of male high school seniors in 1965 and traces the cohort through college entry, completion, and future incomes, using data from various sources.

All data are standardized to a cohort of 100,000 male high school seniors in 1965, whose rates of high school completion were estimated by the Bureau of the Census in 1967.[1] Then the high school graduates, grouped into seven family-income (parental-income) classes, were allocated into two postsecondary attendance categories dependent on whether they were or were not attending college. For the "do attend" college category, students were allocated to four types of schools: public 2-year, private 2-year, private 4-year, and public 4-year institutions.[2] Students from each family-

---

[1] Data for males were made available by the Bureau of the Census in a set of unpublished tables (1968). A description of the sample and data for males and females has been published (Bureau of the Census 1969*b*).

[2] The 4-year college attendants were divided between public and private by income class on the basis of an October 1966 census survey, based on both males and females (Bureau of the Census 1969*a*, table 4). Two-year college students in each income class

income class differed in the mix of institutional types attended with a larger proportion of students from low-income families attending public and 2-year institutions.

The college attendants were then assigned educational attainments, by applying a completion rate to each institutional type. For example, the subgroup of students who attend 4-year public colleges was allocated among the classes: (1) did not complete 1 year, (2) completed 1-3 years, (3) completed 4 or more years of college.[3] Different allocations were made for 2-year colleges and for 4-year private schools. (It should be noted that these completion rates were based entirely on institutional type and not on family income or ability within institutional type.) Students who did not complete a year of college were reassigned to the category "high school graduate."

The process of assignment of the cohort of 100,000 students to high school graduation, college attendance, institutional type, and completion paths allowed the identification, for each parental-income class, of four final education-attainment categories: (1) not high school graduate, (2) high school graduate, (3) 1-3 years of college, and (4) 4 or more years of college.

To estimate the future income-distribution implications of existing patterns of educational attainments by parental-income class, I applied the census distributions of total money income in 1967 (Bureau of the Census, 1969c) by education and age, using the "years of school completed" census categories corresponding to the four educational-attainment groups just listed.[4] The census tables for "all males" were employed in the age brackets 25-34, 35-44, 45-54, 55-64, and 65 years and over, to generate income distribution over time for the entire cohort.

Thus, the distribution of income for the cohort depends on the initial mix of male high school seniors by family-income class,[5] high school gradu-

---

were distributed between public and private institutions by the proportion of males in each control category in 1966 (U.S. Office of Education 1967, table 3).

[3] Continuation rates were set as follows: Trent and Medsker (1968, p. 81) estimate that 17 percent of college entrants drop out during the first year. This rate was used for all institutional types. Relative B.A. completion rates were derived from Trent and Medsker (1968, table 21, p. 79). It was assumed, on the basis of studies cited in Folger, Astin, and Bayer (1970, pp. 170 ff.), that 50 percent of all 4-year public college entrants complete 4 years. When combined with the relative completion rates from Trent and Medsker, this gives completion rates of 0.18, 0.50, and 0.76 for all 2-year schools and for 4-year public and private schools. Most of the dropout data used were for males and females; Summerskill (1962, p. 631) indicates that differences in dropout rates between the sexes are small.

[4] For the "not high school graduate" group, I used "1-3 years of high school," as given in the census tables.

[5] The cohort on which the results in the text were based is derived from a 1965 survey of high school seniors. Persons who dropped out of school prior to the twelfth grade are thus omitted, and this leads to a truncation of the future income distributions, since no one, by definition, has education attainment of less than 1-3 years of

ation rates in each class, college attendance rates in each class, type of college attended by college entrants, and completion rates by type of college attended (with all of these yielding educational attainment by family-income class), plus income distribution by educational attainment and age.

Table 1 shows the college attendance patterns of the cohort. The well-established result that college attendance rates are greater for the rich than for the poor is quickly confirmed: more than 80 percent of the male high school seniors from the highest family-income class attend college, while less than 20 percent from the lowest-income class enroll. The results confirm another fact which has received less attention: children of middle- and upper-income classes are more likely to attend a *public* institution than those from low-income backgrounds. The probability of attending a public school is over three times as great for a student from the highest family-income category as for the lowest, although the concentration of private-school attendance in the upper-income class is shown in that the probability of attending *any* college is over four times greater in the highest class than in the lowest.

Tables 2 and 3 summarize the final educational attainments of our cohort of students. Once again the contrasts among the seven family-income classes are pronounced. Only 15 percent of the male high school seniors from the lowest-income bracket complete 1 or more years of college while over two-thirds of the children from the uppermost bracket complete that much schooling. Put another way, the probability of earning a bachelor's degree is almost six times greater for the children of the rich than for the progeny of the poor.

From the educational attainments just presented, income distributions at 30 (the census category 25–34 years), 40, 50, 60, and 65 years of age were computed for the cohort, by assuming that the 1967 distribution of income (Bureau of the Census 1969c) by education and age for males applies equally to all family-income subgroups, given their educational attainment.

Table 4 gives an overview of the income distribution through the lifetime of the cohort. It shows the familiar increase in incomes up to age 50 (the census category 45–54) and a decline thereafter. The low absolute

---

high school. Unfortunately, data on pre–twelfth grade dropouts, comparable with the high school senior sample, are not available by income class. Using the best available data, it is estimated that approximately 10 percent of the age cohort of males drops out before the high school senior year, in addition to the 8 percent who drop out in the senior year. This estimate is derived as follows: In 1959, 15.8 percent of the age cohort of males dropped out during the senior year of high school and 19.6 percent prior to that year (Nam and Cowhig 1962, p. 14). Thus for every senior-year male dropout, there were 1.24 presenior dropouts (19.6/15.8 = 1.24). If the ratio of presenior to senior dropouts held the same for the 1965 cohort, and if the dropout rate during the senior year in 1965 was 8.9 percent (calculated on the base of male seniors), then 10.0 percent of the male cohort would have dropped out before the senior year and 8.0 percent during the senior year.

TABLE 1

College Attendance of Cohort of 100,000 Male High School Seniors in October 1965 by Class of Family Income

(Number of Students)

Family Income	Total	Do Not Attend College		Attend College				
		High School Graduate	Not High School Graduate	Public		Private		Total
				2-Year	4-Year	2-Year	4-Year	
Under $3,000	10,707	7,022	1,686	680	792	80	447	1,999
$ 3,001–$ 3,999	7,586	3,871	1,390	1,144	752	134	294	2,325
$ 4,000–$ 5,999	19,883	11,169	1,491	3,318	2,386	389	1,130	7,223
$ 6,000–$ 7,499	15,604	7,562	1,367	1,747	3,206	205	1,518	6,676
$ 7,500–$ 9,999	19,074	8,114	1,290	3,580	3,893	420	1,777	9,671
$10,000–$14,999	19,820	6,193	1,219	3,568	4,907	419	3,515	12,409
$15,000 and over	7,325	587	422	1,248	2,381	146	2,540	6,315
Total	100,000	44,517	8,865	15,286	18,317	1,793	11,222	46,618

TABLE 2

EDUCATIONAL ATTAINMENT OF COHORT OF 100,000 HIGH SCHOOL SENIORS IN
OCTOBER 1965 BY CLASS OF FAMILY INCOME
(NUMBER OF STUDENTS)

Family Income	Total	Not High School Graduate	High School Graduate	1–3 Years College	4 or More Years College
Under $3,000	10,707	1,686	7,362	787	873
$ 3,001–$ 3,999	7,586	1,390	4,267	1,100	830
$ 4,000–$ 5,999	19,883	1,491	12,397	3,276	2,719
$ 6,000–$ 7,499	15,604	1,367	8,696	2,433	3,108
$ 7,500–$ 9,999	19,074	1,290	9,758	4,009	4,017
$10,000–$14,999	19,820	1,219	8,302	4,457	5,843
$15,000 and over ...	7,325	422	1,661	1,870	3,372
Total	100,000	8,865	52,442	17,932	20,761

TABLE 3

EDUCATIONAL ATTAINMENT OF COHORT OF 100,000 HIGH SCHOOL SENIORS
IN OCTOBER 1965 BY CLASS OF FAMILY INCOME
(PERCENTAGE)

Family Income	Total	Not High School Graduate	High School Graduate	1–3 Years College	4 or More Years College
Under $3,000	100	16	69	7	8
$ 3,001–$ 3,999	100	18	56	14	11
$ 4,000–$ 5,999	100	7	62	16	14
$ 6,000–$ 7,499	100	9	56	16	20
$ 7,500–$ 9,999	100	7	51	21	21
$10,000–$14,999	100	6	42	22	29
$15,000 and over	100	6	23	26	46
Total	100	9	52	18	21

TABLE 4

INCOME CHARACTERISTICS OF COHORT REACHING SPECIFIED AGES

Age	Mean	Gini Coefficient	% Over $15,000	% Over $25,000
30	$7,555	.269	3.6	0.7
40	$9,533	.287	11.0	2.5
50	$9,929	.321	15.0	3.8
60	$9,052	.370	13.1	4.2
65	$5,240	.500	6.2	2.0

level of the mean incomes reflects of course, our use of cross-sectional
data; and we have not, therefore, accounted for the effects of price inflation
or the productivity-induced upward shift in age-education income profiles.
Two summary measures of the income distribution are given in table 4.
A conventional Gini coefficient, calculated for each age, rises as the cohort
ages, reflecting the greater variation in income at later stages of careers.
In addition, the table shows the proportion of the entire cohort falling
in the two top future-income categories. The probability of earning over
$15,000 (about 50 percent above mean income between 40 and 60 years
of age) peaks at age 50, where the ratio stands at 15 percent.

What we are most interested in, of course, is the comparison resulting when the high school senior cohort is broken into original family-income categories. To illustrate, a set of measures similar to those just
described was calculated for the various original family-income groups
at age 50. (Hereafter, all distributions will be for the original cohort at
age 50, since perusal of the data indicates that all results would be true
at other ages as well.)

Table 5 shows the results at age 50. These indicate that the average
member of the low parental-income group earns about 10 percent less than
the average member of the entire cohort and that the average member of
the wealthiest original bracket earns about 15 percent more than the
cohort average.

More relevant to the question of social mobility is the finding that the
chance of earning $15,000 or more (read "moving to a high-status posi-
tion") is only 9.9 percent for children of the poor but 23.6 percent for
children of the rich—more than a two-to-one advantage in status attainment for the privileged classes.[6]

Overall this is not the picture of an educational system producing anything like egalitarian results. Moreover, the model that generated these
results almost certainly understates the inequalities that the real world of
higher education will actually produce. The major, glaring omissions that
would have made the resulting distributions more disparate by income
class are: (1) the absence, in the cohort, of any student who dropped out
before the senior year of high school, and such students are surely concentrated in low parental-income classes; (2) the assumption of a common

[6] While children of wealthy families have nearly a six-to-one advantage in college
graduation, the two-to-one advantage arises for the following reason: At age 50, the
1967 census reports a 39 percent chance of male college graduates earning over
$15,000, 16 percent for those with some college, 8 percent for high school graduates,
and 3 percent for non–high school graduates. Males from the wealthiest income class
have a 46 percent chance of graduating from college, a 26 percent chance of attaining some college, a 23 percent chance of being high school graduates, and a 6 percent
chance of less than high school graduation, producing a chance of earning $15,000 or
more of $(0.39)(0.46) + (0.16)(0.26) + (0.08)(0.23) + (0.03)(0.06) = 24$ percent.
Children from homes where incomes are under $3,000 have corresponding estimates
of $(0.39)(0.08) + (0.16)(0.07) + (0.08)(0.69) + (0.03)(0.16) = 10$ percent.

TABLE 5

Income Distribution of Cohort at Age 50 by Original Family Income

	Original-Family-Income Categories							All Families
	$0–$3,000	$3,001–$3,999	$4,000–$5,999	$6,000–$7,499	$7,500–$9,999	$10,000–$14,999	$15,000 and Over	
Mean at age 50	$9,001	$9,218	$9,556	$9,851	$10,025	$10,500	$11,427	$9,929
Gini	...	...	...	...	...	...	...	.321
Proportions:								
Over $15,000	9.9	11.2	12.8	14.5	15.4	18.2	23.6	15.0
Over $25,000	2.6	2.9	3.3	3.7	3.9	4.6	6.0	3.8

dropout rate in a particular type of college, for it is certain that students from low-income homes are more likely to fail completion within a given category of school; and (3) the assumption that anyone who reaches a given educational-attainment level is equally as likely as anyone else to earn over X dollars, for surely children from high-income homes who get a bachelor's degree will, in fact, earn more than others with like degrees.

So, the status quo is surely inegalitarian. We now ask what would happen if public institutions were to raise tuition.

II. The Effect of Tuition Increases on Education Attainment, Income Distribution, and Mobility

A substantial increase in tuition at public institutions could affect the future incomes of high school seniors in the cohort by: reduction in the rate of high school graduation, since the option value of high school completion would be lowered; a lowered entry rate into public institutions through the operation of both income and price effects; some offsetting diversion into private institutions because of their lowered relative price; and a reduction in completion rates at public institutions due to the higher annual cost of attendance.

Little empirical evidence exists on the size of any of these effects that could be expected if tuitions at public institutions were raised by such a large sum as $1,500 per annum (a tuition increase of this magnitude for public institutions would cover full costs [Cheit 1971, p. 32] and would represent a cost increase of about one-third to the public-college student, counting both opportunity earnings and existing student charges in the base).

To estimate the effects of increased tuition at public institutions of higher education on the cohort's future income, it was assumed that the tuition increase of $1,500 had no effect on high school graduation rates. Second, the percentage reduction in the number of entrants to public institutions was assumed to be an inverse function of original family income.[7] Third, it was assumed that students discouraged from entering public institutions would enter private schools to the following extent: 5 percent in the lowest family-income category, 10 percent in the second-lowest category, 15 percent in the next, and 20 percent in all family-income classes above $6,000. Fourth, the completion rate for 4 or more years of college was assumed to be reduced by 20 percent in public institutions. Finally, it was assumed that a tuition increase of this magnitude would discourage

[7] The equation in the program reads: $E_i = b(\Delta T/Y_i)$, where E_i is the percentage reduction in public school entrants of income class i, $\Delta T =$ tuition increase = $1,500, and Y_i is the mean income of class i. The program is constrained so that E_i cannot exceed 98 percent. For a similar approach see Radner and Miller (1970).

90 percent of the public school entrants whose family incomes are below $6,000.

It is appropriate at this point to stress the arbitrary nature of most of these assumptions. The reader should interpret those results which follow as a plausible set of outcomes of an experiment, rather than as a prediction of future events.

The educational-attainment results of this experiment are shown in table 6. Lines 3, 4, and 5 show the levels and changes in the level of attainment of 4 or more years of college in each original family-income class. (Similar results obtain for 1–3 years of college.) The experiment was so structured that the percentage reduction in rates for attainment of a bachelor's degree would be greater in low-income classes. In the range of variation shown, 53 percent fewer low-income males eventually graduate, while only 11 percent fewer wealthy offspring fail to complete college. The implied elasticity of completion of college with respect to a cost increase of 33 percent is also shown.[8]

What are the effects of the changes in educational attainment on the distribution of income and mobility?

Table 7 shows the income-redistributional implications of the state-institution tuition increase. In a nutshell, the effects on the overall distribution of income of the cohort at age 50 are negligible. The Gini coefficient for the incomes of the entire cohort is unchanged from the low-tuition situation. Similarly, the low-family-income students have average earnings of about 90 percent of the cohort average, both before and after the tuition change; high-family-income males earn about 15 percent, on average, more than the cohort, before and after tuition rises.

The absolute levels of earnings differ somewhat more significantly among the parental family-income groups. The proportion of male progeny of families with incomes below $6,000 who will receive over $15,000 income is reduced more than 16 percent, while the proportion of the highest family-income class earning that much is reduced by about 6 percent (table 7). Both of these results straddle the 11 percent average reduction, for the whole cohort, in number of high earners.

What are the equity implications of these changes?

For those who think that higher public-institution tuitions and attendant attainment changes in higher education will significantly affect the overall distribution of income, our model suggests that this is not the case. Enrollment and completion of college among children of the poor is so

---

[8] A strong believer in the public benefits of higher education would presumably stop here. Table 6 shows 22 percent fewer college graduates (and about 23 percent fewer people completing 1–3 years of college, a fact not shown in the table). These results would lead to a reduction of those social benefits associated with the fraction of the population that receives higher education.

TABLE 6

Changes in Educational Attainment of Cohort Resulting from Tuition Increase of $1,500

				Original-Family-Income Class				
	Under $3,000	$3,001–$3,999	$4,000–$5,999	$6,000–$7,499	$7,500–$9,999	$10,000–$14,999	$15,000 and Over	Total
Original number with B.A.	873	830	2,719	3,108	4,017	5,843	3,372	20,761
Original percentage with B.A.	8	11	14	20	21	29	46	21
Final number	411	448	1,880	2,398	3,170	4,950	3,012	16,269
Final percentage	4	6	9	15	17	25	41	16
Percentage change	−53	−46	−31	−23	−21	−15	−11	−22
Implied elasticity*	−1.6	−1.4	−0.9	−0.7	−0.6	−0.5	−0.3	−0.7

Note.—See text for explanation of assumptions used in these calculations.
* The percentage change in number of B.A.'s divided by a price increase of 33 percent.

TABLE 7

Changes in Income Distribution and Mobility of Cohort Resulting from Tuition Increase of $1,500

| | Original-Family-Income Class | | | | | | | |
	Under $3,000	$3,001–$3,999	$4,000–$5,999	$6,000–$7,499	$7,500–$9,999	$10,000–$14,999	$15,000 and Over	All Families
Mean income at age 50	$8,680	$8,818	$9,235	$9,557	$9,740	$10,239	$11,179	$9,631
Gini	...	...	...	...	...	...	...	.317
Proportions:								
Over $15,000* ..	8.1 (−18)	9.0 (−20)	11.0 (−14)	12.8 (−11)	13.8 (−11)	16.6 (−8)	22.1 (−6)	13.2 (−11)
Over $25,000* ..	2.2 (−15)	2.4 (−17)	2.9 (−12)	3.3 (−11)	3.5 (−10)	4.2 (−8)	5.6 (−7)	3.4 (−10)

* Parentheses enclose the percentage change from table 5.

small (table 3) that even large reductions in that small number do not much affect the future incomes of the entire low-parental-income cohort. At the same time, high-income groups, which do participate heavily in public institutions, are little affected by the tuition increase (by assumption, to be sure). As a result, overall income distribution cannot be said to worsen as a result of the abandonment of low-tuition policies.[9]

But is the overall distribution what we care about in assessing equity implications of higher education finance? I think not. Support of higher education has little or nothing to do with the low end of the future-income distribution. It is unlikely that anyone could advocate college training as a poverty-averting policy.

A more plausible case can be made for the effects of state supported low tuitions on social mobility. Here the equity issue is how potent tuition policy is in opening doors to high-income positions. On this score our illustrative model does show significant results. The equity-increasing aspect of state-tuition subsidies inheres in the fact that removal of such benefits will induce a differentially larger reduction in high-income earners among children of low-income families than among children of high-income backgrounds. If upward mobility is considered an important social value, substantial rises in tuition will have to be offset. One obvious offsetting policy would be to raise tuition and channel the revenues into grants to financially needy students. In this way social mobility could be preserved and might even be increased (Hansen and Weisbrod 1971a). Barring this possibility, what are the prospects of increased access to loans as an offset to raised tuition?

Suppose, for example, that tuitions were raised by $1,500 and all students were guaranteed access to $1,500 loans at market interest rates.[10] The change in net cost to the student must be equal to $1,500 plus the *difference* between the discounted present value of the future repayments as valued by the student and $1,500. Only if the student's discount rate is infinity can this difference be equal to $1,500. (In other words, if the student treats the loan as a grant, a "loan" will offset an equal rise in price.) The same condition holds even if the interest rate on the loan is subsidized at below-market rates: the tuition increase raises the net cost to the student by less than its nominal total, but by a positive sum unless the student's discount rate is infinite.

Existing federal student loan programs, the largest of which are the National Defense Education Act student loan program (NDSL) and the 1965 Higher Education Act guaranteed loan program, are of this character. They limit the student to borrowing no more than $1,000–$1,500

[9] We remind the reader that we are dealing with a truncated income distribution here because of the omission of students who never reach high school senior status.

[10] Suppose that market interest rates were what would ensue under a government-guaranteed (against default) loan plan.

per year, and they contain provisions for limited-interest subsidies. For those NDSL borrowers who become teachers of disadvantaged children, the entire loan may be cancelled and thus fulfill the requirement for a perfect offset against a tuition increase.[11]

In the case of income-contingent loans, where repayments are based on a contracted fraction of gross income, the net change in cost to the student must be positive unless expected income is zero.[12] Naturally, the net-cost increase would be relatively less for those whose income expectations are low under income-contingent loans. So, in general, access to loan programs, complementing a rise in tuition, increases the net cost to the student, but by less than the nominal rise in tuition. Only in improbable cases do loans *fully offset* tuition increases.

Increased tuitions coupled with loan programs offering students access to loan amounts in excess of the tuition increase could reduce the perceived net cost of attending college under certain circumstances. For example, if tuition were to increase by $1,500 and all students were offered $3,000 loans, the net price of college to the student would decline if he valued his repayments at less than $1,500. Such a valuation could occur, if market rates of interest were charged, only if the student's discount rate were much higher than the market rate of interest (and the loan were for a long term) or if the student loans featured heavily subsidized rates of interest (in this last case, it might be noted, we would have achieved precisely the kind of effect subsidized tuitions produce: a subsidy for all borrowers regardless of need).

Income-contingent loans in per capita amounts considerably in excess of tuition increases could reduce net costs of higher education to those students whose expected repayments fall far short of the amount borrowed. This possibility will be realized only if students are permitted to borrow substantially more than the tuition increase and if the income-contingent repayment schedule is very progressive. For example, Yale University's recently announced tuition-postponement option imposed a tuition increase of $500, coupled with an option for undergraduates to borrow up to $800 (Yale 1971). This will result in a net decrease in cost only to those students who value the expected repayments on an $800 loan at less than $300. Since Yale's repayment terms are sufficiently liberal to future low-earners, it is conceivable that some students will have enjoyed a net drop in costs (as they see it) as a result of the new program.[13]

On balance, the impact of increased access to loan programs coupled with

---

[11] Even in this case, the student borrower may be uncertain whether he will in the future become eligible for teacher cancellations and thus may not treat the loan as if it were a grant. On the subject of federal loan programs, see Hartman (1971).

[12] An exception to this is exemption of low-income levels from any repayment requirement, as in the Ohio Plan discussed below.

[13] But this set-up raises the prospect that high earners will not participate.

a tuition increase of X dollars can best be analyzed by treating the loan program as reducing X dollars by some fraction. An attractive loan program coupled with a tuition increase of $1,500 might be equivalent to a tuition increase of only $800; a less attractive loan program would imply a perceived tuition rise of $1,100 and so on. Under these assumptions, the introduction of better loan opportunities on the distribution of income (given a tuition rise) would result in income-distribution effects somewhere between the original model and the uncompensated tuition increase of $1,500 discussed above. Loan access would restore the social-mobility payoff of low tuition only if children of low-income families were to evaluate the combined tuition increase and loan access as amounting to no net change in the cost of higher education. As indicated above, this condition requires that the implicit subsidy in the loan program (the difference between the present value of the repayments discounted at the student's rate of discount and the principal value of the loan) be equal to the tuition increase. Table 8 shows the discount rate the student would have to be using in order for loans of various magnitudes and maturities to produce sufficiently large implicit subsidies to offset a tuition increase of $1,500. The table is constructed on the assumption that the student borrows at a nominal rate of interest of 8 percent.

As the table shows, low-income students would have to apply very high discount rates to their repayments—even for loan amounts appreciably in excess of the tuition increase—if conventional loan programs are to leave unchanged their net cost of higher education. Given the present slim knowledge about the economic calculus of students from low-income families, there would seem to be appreciable risk of losing the present equity gains if loans replaced subsidized tuition. Only if the loans were available in very large per student amounts, at lengthy maturities, and possibly with

TABLE 8

DISCOUNT RATE REQUIRED TO PRODUCE SUBSIDY OF $1,500
IN 8 PERCENT LOANS OF VARIOUS AMOUNTS AND MATURITIES

Borrowed Amount	Maturity (Years)	Discount Rate Required to Offset Tuition Increase of $1,500 (%)
$3,000	35	17
	30	18
	20	20
$2,500	30	22
	20	>25
$2,000	30	>35
$1,500	All	∞

subsidized interest rates,[14] could one confidently expect that loan programs would be an adequate substitute for price subsidies (or direct grants) for low-income students. Under conventional loan programs these subsidies would have to come from taxpayers; in an income-contingent program such subsidies to (future) low-income persons might be collected from successful borrowers, but there are, of course, some difficulties in raising subsidies from borrowers.

III. Paying for Higher Education through Taxes or Loan Repayments

I turn now to a consideration of the equity and redistributiveness of the tax and loan methods of financing higher education, following the above discussion of the behavioral parameters on which tax or loan support depends and how they work through entry and continuation rates to educational attainment and income.

Imagine that the high school seniors in the cohort described earlier are responsible for paying for their own higher education throughout their working lifetimes. If you like, assume that the cohort "imports" educational services while going to school and then finances, through compulsory taxation or loan amortization, "exports" to the outsiders during working lifetimes.

We can distinguish several aspects of the equitableness of the tax or loan-repayment mechanisms, including the temporal distribution of payments, treatment of users and nonusers, and vertical equity.

1. The Timing of Payments: Intertemporal Distribution of Income

Ignoring in this section interpersonal comparisons of tax burdens, the first question to ask is, What will be the time pattern of the cohort's exports under tax finance versus loan finance?

Under tax-financed higher education, the financial burden can be spread over the lifetime of the assets acquired. In our example, the imports of education services are paid for over the taxpaying (postschool) years. We can imagine that some given fraction of the cohort's annual state tax payments are set aside for payment to outsiders; thus, higher education tax burdens would approximate the time pattern of cohort income.

Some research (Thurow 1969, p. 329) would seem to indicate that people would like to consume more in their younger (up to age 40–45) years, and are willing to consume less when they are of more advanced age. If these findings can be made to apply to the temporal pattern of

---

[14] If a student were allowed to borrow $3,000 for 30 years at a 5 percent nominal interest rate, an implicit grant of $1,500 would be implied if the student's discount rate is 13 percent.

taxes, a case can be made that tax burdens are too high in the cohort's twenties and thirties. A more income-elastic state tax system (or a pattern of age-specific tax rates suggested by Thurow) would be preferable. Nonetheless, it seems reasonable to conclude that state tax-financed payments for higher education probably come close to minimizing the burden of paying over time.

Turning now to loan programs, it is useful first to describe repayment features of existing federal student loan programs:

1. The 1965 Higher Education Act guaranteed loan program provides for repayment installments, commencing about a year after the borrower is no longer a student, over a period of "not less than five years (unless sooner repaid) nor more than ten years" (Higher Education Act 1965, p. 1239). Moreover, the legislation governing this program stipulates that the annual repayment of any borrower must be at least $360. As a practical matter, this means that all borrowers whose aggregate debt is less than $2,500 must pay $360[15] and will have repayment cycles of less than 10 years. Borrowers with a larger debt most commonly pay the equivalent of a constant annual sum in repayment of their loan (Hartman 1971, p. 3).

2. National Defense Education Act loans are 10-year loans, with repayments commencing a little less than a year after student status is terminated. The legislation provides for repayment of the principal amount, together with interest thereon, in equal annual installments (National Defense Education Act 1958, p. 1285). There are administrative reasons, relating to teacher cancellation provisions of the loans (Hartman 1971, pp. 94–95), that have impelled many institutions to write repayment schedules such that a constant amount of principal is repaid each year plus the interest on the outstanding balance. The first repayment is, therefore, the largest. Moreover, the law governing this program also stipulates a minimum annual repayment of $180, implying that borrowers whose debts aggregate less than about $1,500 will have to pay the minimum.

It does not take much to see that virtually all of the repayment provisions in these loan programs run counter to our best guess as to the welfare-maximizing temporal pattern of repayments. All the costs in both loan programs are concentrated in the youngest age bracket. Small borrowers, who are most likely to be dropouts and to face the lowest lifetime incomes, are forced to accept the most concentrated repayment periods. In the National Defense loan program, the highest repayments occur in the first years of repayment.

Proposed loan programs usually have features designed to mitigate the worst temporal aspects of existing federal programs. First, such proposals usually provide for repayment periods lengthened to 30–40 years (Carnegie

---

[15] Most repayment schedules for students are based on a ceiling interest rate of 7 percent per annum. The constant annual sum repayment for a 10-year schedule is $142 per $1,000 borrowed.

Commission 1970; Shell et al. 1968; U.S. Department of Health, Education, and Welfare 1969) or at least to 15–20 years (Danière 1969), as in the Nixon administrations proposal (Higher Education Opportunity Act 1971, sec. 408, p. 36). The effect of lengthened terms combined with constant annual payments would be to reduce, compared with existing loan programs, repayment burdens in early postcollege years. Second, many of the proposed loan programs stipulate a repayment scheme in which each borrower's repayment would be proportional to his income (that is, a fixed "tax rate" on gross income [Shell et al. 1968]). Under such a scheme, the cohort's temporal pattern of repayments would be very similar to the state tax pattern.

Recently, the governor of Ohio has promulgated the "Ohio Plan," which would require that students who attend public universities pay a special tax to "repay" the state for instructional subsidies. Repayments commence no sooner than the first year in which the student receives $7,500 in taxable income; the repayment schedule provides for no liabilities under $7,000 adjusted gross income and a mildly progressive tax between $7,000 and $105,000, adjusted gross income (Ohio House Bill no. 930).[16] The temporal distribution of receipts from the Ohio Plan would conform closely to Thurow's (1969) estimate of the optimal pattern; a large fraction of the cohort of borrowers would be exempt from any tax under age 35, and repayments would move with income thereafter.

In summary, as far as the welfare effects of temporal payment patterns are concerned:

1. Present federal loan programs almost certainly are unattractive to the student. They concentrate repayments in the earliest, lowest-income years. Any cohort of borrowers would probably reject such a payment scheme if it had a choice.

2. To the extent that the state tax system can be viewed as spreading payments over a working lifetime, more or less in keeping with the pattern of cohort income, the major weakness (in temporal welfare) would seem to be the tax burden at ages up to 45.

3. Long-term loans, especially those based on income, would have temporal characteristics similar to a state tax system. The Ohio Plan has the merit of lessening repayment burdens in immediate postgraduate years.

2. *Users versus Nonusers*

No equity issue has raised more attention than the transfer of resources through the state tax system from nonusers to users of public higher edu-

---

[16] Repayment ceases when the state subsidy is repaid *without* interest. Taxpayers would still be heavy subsidizers of the program. A similar bill providing for repayment with interest on the subsidy has been introduced in Oregon (Oregon State Senate Bill no. 735).

cation. (Note that I do not equate "users" with "gainers"; if there are public benefits to higher education, nonusers will also be gainers.) A tuition increase, coupled with extending capital markets, goes a long way toward rectifying this alleged inequity. The price of correcting the inequity is, of course, the changes in social mobility described in earlier sections.

I want to attempt to clarify the nature of the transfer from nonusers to users. Previous studies have analyzed the transfers from the taxpaying public (of various ages) to the families of public-college attendants, thus failing to correct for age or extent-of-use differences between the two groups. The method used here of looking at one cohort through life avoids this pitfall. Table 9 shows the number of students from the original cohort, classified by use or nonuse of public education and by income at age 50 under the present system of public support. Nonusers have been divided into those who do not attend college and those who attend private college, since there is reason to believe that the latter group for the most part chose not to use public college services while the former group may not have had any real choice.

Suppose, now, that public higher education were financed by a head tax. Then tax receipts for higher education would be proportional to the number of people reported in table 9. Under this assumption, two-thirds of the tax burden would be carried by people who never used the public system of higher education. Moreover, half of the cohort never attended any college at all, and a substantial number of persons must have been prevented from using this public service because of admissions policies or lack of financial means. Finally, looking at the income levels of taxpayers under this head tax, only about 37 percent of the tax load would be carried by people with above-average incomes.[17] Fully 45 percent of the taxes

TABLE 9

DISTRIBUTION OF 100,000 USERS AND NONUSERS OF PUBLIC
HIGHER EDUCATION BY INCOME AT AGE 50
(NUMBER OF PERSONS)

| | | NONUSERS | |
INCOME	USERS	No College	Private College
Under $3,000	1,862	3,797	653
$ 3,001–$ 5,999	4,074	10,802	1,294
$ 6,000–$ 9,999	11,209	25,218	3,693
$10,000–$14,999	8,798	10,117	3,453
$15,000 and over	7,470	3,646	3,866
Total	33,413	53,580	12,959

NOTE.—Total does not add to 100,000 due to rounding.

[17] Average income of the cohort at age 50 is about $10,000. See table 4.

would be levied against people who did not use the system and also had less than average income.[18]

A head tax is a regressive extreme. As an alternative, we can assume that the marginal tax used to finance public higher education is a proportional share of the state and local tax burden in each income class.[19] Under this assumption, tax liabilities for higher education are shown in table 10. Even here, nonusers pay more than 60 percent of the cost of higher education. Moreover, over 30 percent of the taxes are collected from people who are both nonusers and below-average earners.

Finally, suppose that tax dollars supporting higher education are collected only from above-average earners—those with incomes in excess of $10,000. Nonusers of public higher education comprise 57 percent of the population in that income class, so even under this extreme assumption nonusers would pay more than users.

Looking at the spectrum of possible assumptions about tax sources to finance higher education, it seems reasonable to conclude that nonusers pay somewhere between 57 and 66 percent of the costs of higher education. If charging nonusers is justified by external benefits received from the subsidies granted to users, those subsidies should be generating benefits to nonusers at least equal to 57–66 percent of their annual value. To give some perspective to these numbers, it should be noted that in 1966–67 state and local governments contributed about $5 billion to the revenues of institutions of higher education.[20] This sum represents about 0.8 percent of personal income in that year. Thus, the question to ask about 1966–67

TABLE 10

DISTRIBUTION OF STATE AND LOCAL TAXES BY USER STATUS
AND INCOME AT AGE 50 (PERCENTAGE)

INCOME	USERS	NONUSERS	
		No College	Private College
Under $3,000	0.5	1.0	0.2
$ 3,001–$ 5,999	2.2	5.9	0.7
$ 6,000–$ 9,999	9.0	20.3	3.0
$10,000–$14,999	10.9	12.5	4.3
$15,000 and over	14.7	7.2	7.6
Total	37.3	46.9	15.8

[18] The reader is reminded that our cohort excludes those who never became high school seniors. Thus, the nonuser/no-college column is understated.

[19] The tax-burden distribution used in this illustration was taken from the estimates prepared by David Ott (*Economic Report of the President*, 1969, chart 11, p. 161). Data underlying the chart are given in Pechman (1969).

[20] Derived from Becker (1970).

is whether the transfer of about 0.5 percent of personal income from non-users to users produced at least $3 billion in benefits to the nonuser group. This, of course, is a minimum condition. One can always think of public programs that are more efficient and equitable (such as grants to low-income students) and others that are less so.

If loan programs were to replace state-subsidized tuitions, the beneficiaries of reduced tax burdens would be the large group of relatively low-income non–college attendants and the small, affluent group which attends private college under the present system. Loan repayments under such a policy shift become analogous to tax burdens, and some recent proposals have tried to improve the equity effects of loan repayments. To these we now turn.

3. Interpersonal Redistribution through Loan Repayments

Redistribution under loan financing is an almost undiscussed topic; all we have to rely on are various assertions that income-contingent loan programs would have "good" redistributive effects. Before taking a closer look at that contention, it might be useful to summarize the distributive effects of present federal programs.

Table 11 presents some relevant data on how well the principal federal loan programs accomplish the goal of providing capital-market access to students from various parental-income classes. The data on loan volume in 1967–68 indicate that, compared with all families with college-age children, recipients were somewhat more likely to be from the upper half of the income distribution. In comparison with the distribution of *students*, however, the loan programs (especially National Defense student loans) are somewhat targeted toward lower-income groups. Similarly, the implicit

TABLE 11

REDISTRIBUTION UNDER GUARANTEED LOAN AND NATIONAL DEFENSE
STUDENT LOAN PROGRAMS 1967–68 (PERCENTAGE)

Gross Income Class	All U.S. Families with College-Age Children (1969)	Dollar Volume of Guaranteed and National Defense Loans	Implicit Subsidies in Loan Programs
Under $3,000	10.6	13.1	13.2
$ 3,001–$ 5,999	23.0	15.0	15.1
$ 6,000–$ 7,499	13.0	11.8	11.9
$ 7,500–$ 8,999	11.7	10.8	10.9
$ 9,000–$11,999	16.6	19.0	19.1
$12,000–$14,999	13.1	15.3	15.4
$15,000 and over	11.9	15.1	14.4

SOURCE.—Hartman (1971), tables 12 and 13, pp. 49–51.

subsidies[21] that were provided in these programs in 1967–68 show some tendency of direction toward better-off parental-income groups. By 1968–69, the reduction in the interest subsidy[22] under the federal guaranteed loan program, which serves a higher-income clientele than National Defense loans, shifted the pattern of subsidies toward lower-income groups, but not enough to offset the previous conclusions.

In short, when redistribution of benefits of existing loan programs is looked at according to the parental-income distribution, the conclusions are very similar to those reached on low state tuitions: a disproportionate share of the benefits accrues to higher-income classes.

Repayments of federal loans will affect the interpersonal income distribution depending on the amounts borrowed by *future* income class. To determine the rate of repayment by future-income class, data showing the average annual amount borrowed and the frequency of borrowing (the product of which is "debt") by future-income class would be needed. To my knowledge, no such data exist. There is evidence that the average federal loan rises somewhat by *parental*-income class.[23] In view of this and the greater educational attainment of students from higher-income families, one could expect to observe higher repayment obligations in the upper end of future-income cross-sections.

The repayment format under long-term income-contingent loans has been taken by some people to be self-evidently pro-poor. By their nature, income-contingent repayment loans mean that families with no income make no repayments while families with high earnings pay substantial sums. In fact, it is self-evidently true that, if a fixed repayment tax rate is applied per $1,000 borrowed, if everyone borrows the same amount, and if everyone participates, the repayment tax will be strictly proportional among users of higher education.

But, in fact, all potentially practical income-contingent loan schemes involve some provision for borrowers who realize very high incomes to "opt out," that is, to treat their repayments as if they were based on a conventional loan. When repayments (based on income) just requite the conventional loan at the "opt-out interest rate," further repayments are

---

[21] Implicit subsidies here mean only the dollar value of the difference between the market interest rate (taken as 6 percent in 1967–68) and the rate paid by students in the federal programs in that year (zero during enrollment and 3 percent in the repayment period for both programs). The omission of teacher cancellation subsidies probably understates the subsidy to poorer-income classes. On the other hand, an assumption, for all income classes, of the same in-school period in which no interest is paid probably results in understatement of the subsidy to the wealthier students.

[22] Beginning in 1968–69, students were required to pay a ceiling of 7 percent interest during the repayment period, a level that governs the program today.

[23] But not very much. In 1968–69, the average borrower from families with incomes below $6,000 borrowed about $700, while the average borrower from the $15,000-and-over class borrowed about $900 (Hartman 1971, appendix D).

excused. The "opt-out" provision has been written into loan proposals to insure that those who expect high incomes participate and generate the "profits" that provide the cushion necessary for the lender to subsidize the low-income attainers whose repayments will not suffice to repay their loans.

The provision of a maximum interest rate introduces a regressive element into the income-contingent loan-repayment pattern. To illustrate this point, consider a variable-term loan program with the following provisions: Students may borrow $1,000 if they promise to repay 0.8 percent of their annual income for up to 30 years. If, prior to 30 years, the sum of their repayments is sufficient to repay a conventional $1,000 loan at 9 percent interest ("opt-out" rate), their repayments will cease. If at the end of 30 years their repayments have been insufficient to requite a 9 percent loan, any remaining balance is forgiven. Suppose, finally, that the lending agency raises its funds at a cost of 7 percent interest; the margin of 2 percentage points between the lending agency's borrowing rate and the "opt-out" rate finances the unpaid balances of those who reach the 30-year maximum term. (It should be noted that these parameters are not entirely fanciful; they are rounded-off versions of an actuarial estimate of what a zero-profit program might look like, based on U.S. census data (Dresch and Goldberg 1972).

Now let us examine the repayment flow of five students under such a program. To keep the arithmetic simple, it is assumed that each student's income profile over time is perfectly horizontal—he reaches his "permanent income" level immediately and stays there forever. Each student accumulates a $1,000 debt.

Table 12 shows the permanent income and the annual payment (0.8 percent of income) of the five students. Column 3 shows how many years of repayment each student will take before discharging his obligation; students A and B remain in the program for the full term, while C, D, and

TABLE 12

REPAYMENT INCIDENCE OF 30-YEAR VARIABLE-TERM LOAN PROGRAM

Student	Permanent Income (1)	Annual Payment (2)	Years to Pay (3)	Present Value of Repayment at 7% (4)	Col. 4 ÷ Col. 1 (%) (5)
A	$ 3,000	$ 24.00	30	$ 298	9.93
B	$ 12,167	$ 97.34	30	$1,208	9.93
C	$ 19,478	$ 155.82	10	$1,094	5.62
D	$ 71,059	$ 568.47	2	$1,028	1.45
E	$136,250	$1,090.00	1	$1,019	0.75

NOTE.—Tax rate = 0.008; interest rate = 0.09.

E all "opt out" early, as their repayments are sufficient to repay a 9 percent loan. Column 4 shows the present value of repayments, calculated at a 7 percent discount rate,[24] to make the streams of repayments of the different students comparable. Student A is, in fact, subsidized under the income-contingent loan program. Only 30 percent of his loan is paid off; the remaining $702 is a (deferred) gift or an insurance benefit. Students B, C, D, and E all pay an excess amount for their loans over and above what they would pay for a conventional 7 percent loan. Student B's excess payment, however, is the largest for any "taxed" student.

Loan repayment data can be made comparable with the standard tax-incidence studies by computing the ratio of the present value of loan repayments to the "permanent incomes" of the five students (table 12, col. 5). It is clear from these data that the repayment scheme under an income-contingent loan program is like a proportional tax at all incomes up to that of student B[25] and is regressive at all higher income levels. In fact, the resemblance between this incidence pattern and that of the Social Security tax is striking: proportionality up to a maximum wage base and regressivity thereafter.

Yale's loan program has overcome part of the regressivity problem by, in effect, raising the maximum-wage base. Under Yale's repayment program, a very low tax rate was selected: 0.4 percent of income per $1,000 borrowed. This low tax rate (and the programs' 35-year repayment period) is compensated for in Yale's plan by the imposition of a very high "opt-out" interest rate over a maximum term of 35 years.[26] Yale's repayment scheme requires that a borrower *repay 150 percent of his original loan plus accumulated interest on this sum.* Yale loan contracts specify that the interest rate used be equal to Yale's cost of borrowing (say 7 percent). The actual interest rate paid, based on the original sum borrowed, will vary from borrower to borrower and will be greatly in excess of 7 percent for many whose loans terminate before 35 years. For example, a student who

[24] We use 7 percent, the borrowing rate of the lender, rather than 9 percent, the "opt-out" rate, because 9 percent represents a charge that includes both a pure interest rate and an "income insurance premium." It is the excess over the borrowing rate of the lender that makes it possible to insure that borrowers whose incomes are small (or whose lives are short) will not have to pay off their loans in full (A's "gift" of $702 is paid by the excess payments of B, C, D, and E). In calculating present values, we are interested in the rate at which consumers convert income flows of different periods, and that rate has nothing to do with income insurance. For this reason, the appropriate consumer discount rate is less than the "opt-out" rate. Whether 7 percent or some interest rate between 7 and 9 percent is appropriate depends on whether the lender's borrowing rate is lower or the same as the consumer's borrowing rate over his lifetime. A 7 percent interest rate rests on the implicit assumption that they are the same.

[25] Student B's repayments just repay his loan at the "opt-out" rate at the end of the full contractual payment period. He is the marginal "opt-outer."

[26] For a discussion of profit trade-offs of tax rates, interest rates, and repayment periods, see Dresch and Goldberg (1972).

borrows $1,000 and whose repayments terminate in 1 year would repay $1,605 ($1,500 times 1.07) in that year. The actual interest rate paid on the loan is about 60 percent! (Before reacting too strongly to the loan shark rate, it should be noted that such a student would have to earn $401,250 in that first year in order for his tax to automatically reach a level of $1,605.) Students whose repayments terminate in longer periods would pay progressively lower, true implicit interest rates. For example, the borrower whose repayments just meet Yale's termination condition in 35 years (Student D_1, in table 13) pays an implicit interest rate of about 11 percent.

Table 13 illustrates the positive association under the Yale Plan of "opt-out" interest rates and high income in the effect on six hypothetical student borrowers. Yale's program extends the range over which the repayment scheme is proportional to permanent annual income to a level of about $29,000. After that, it is regressive.[27]

The redistributional "goodness" of Yale's program in contrast with the variable-term loan and with a conventional 25-year loan at 7 percent interest can best be seen in figure 1. Here, the ratio of the present value of repayments discounted at 7 percent to permanent income is plotted for each loan program.[28]

The figure makes clear that a conventional long-term loan is the most

TABLE 13

ILLUSTRATIVE ANNUAL REPAYMENTS FOR STUDENT LOANS UNDER THE YALE PLAN

Student	Permanent Income (1)	Annual Payment (2)	Years to Pay (3)	Present Value of Repayments at 7% (4)	Col. 4 ÷ Col. 1 (%) (5)
A	$ 3,000	$ 12.00	35	$ 155	5.2
B	$ 12,167	$ 48.67	35	$ 630	5.2
C	$ 19,478	$ 77.91	35	$1,008	5.2
D_1	$ 28,963	$ 115.85	35	$1,500	5.2
D_2	$ 53,393	$ 213.57	10	$1,500	2.8
E_1	$401,250	$1,605.00	1	$1,500	0.4

[27] Yale's program specifies that if an entire cohort repays the loans in less than 35 years, borrowers who still have liabilities will be excused beyond that point. The illustrations ignore this provision.

[28] The Yale Plan was based on income projections different from those used in the variable-term loan case. Thus, part of the reason that the Yale Plan curve is low is that the repayment profiles were richer than those in the variable-term program described above. A Yale Plan—low tax rate, high "opt-out" interest, long maturity—applied to a lower-income cohort would have a shape similar to the Yale curve in figure 1, but it would be displaced upward by a few percentage points.

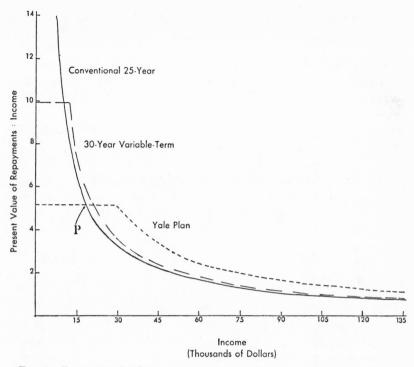

FIG. 1.—Repayment incidence of 30-year variable-term, conventional 25-year 7 percent, and Yale Plan loans.

regressive repayment plan and is more regressive than existing state-local tax structures as well. The mildly redistributive variable-term loan is less regressive (proportional) at low incomes but is regressive over the broad range of incomes that college graduates are likely to earn in future years. This loan program imposes a fairly minor penalty on higher-income persons relative to what they would pay under a conventional loan; therefore it is likely to attract a broad spectrum of students. It is a feasible program, with mildly favorable repayment incidence at low incomes. Yale's plan is far and away the least regressive program of those so far delineated. Both in terms of limiting burdens on the future poor and on socking it to the future rich, the Yale Plan is the most equitable. The Yale Plan favors both low and very high incomes and imposes higher burdens on a broad spectrum of "middle incomes."

The unfortunate thing about Yale's program is that Yale is not the government and cannot compel participation. A prospective borrower at Yale must ask whether participation in the Yale Plan is superior to alternative methods of finance that are open to him. Although there are not now available 7 percent, 25-year loans for students, we shall use that as an alternative simply because it is a likely option open to many *Yale parents* (for example, refinancing a mortgage). A Yale parent counseling his child could, in effect, reason as follows from figure 1: "If our best guess is that the future income of the student will exceed about $20,000, we would be better off refinancing our mortgage, unless we place very heavy negative values on the possible shortfall of income below that level, compared with the possible earnings above that level." In short, the only students who are likely to participate in Yale's program are those who confidently expect low incomes, those with average expectations but strong aversion to risk, and those with no or decidedly inferior alternatives.[29]

The Yale Plan is hardly likely to attract really wealthy students; if a program with these characteristics were introduced in place of low-tuition policies at state institutions, the same nonparticipation of the rich could be expected. From a redistributive point of view, the major significance of this result is that state taxes now collected from the rich would be lost for the support of others in higher education.[30]

There are two obvious ways to keep the rich in the program, contributing some substantial sum to the educational costs of future low-income students:

First, it is possible to conceive of a repayment format that would essentially follow the incidence pattern of Yale up to point P in figure 1 and follow the conventional loan-repayment schedule thereafter. Under these circumstances, no one would be worse off under the income-contingent loan program than under a conventional loan and all would presumably sign up for the plan. The implication of this repayment schedule is that *somebody has to be willing to subsidize it*, for the insufficient payments of the low-earners are not in this case made up for by a tax on the well-to-do borrowers. If public funds are to be used for the purpose, the policy question is: Is the subsidy better used here to improve the redistributiveness of the repayment plan, or would it be better used in the first place to keep tuitions low? In terms of the impact of financing on the social mobility of children from low-income homes, the answer to this question depends on the responsiveness of such students to the higher tuition charge versus their responsiveness to the generous subsidization of those who earn low incomes in the future.

The second avenue to more equitable repayment schemes is to remove voluntarism from the picture altogether and compel high-income users of public higher education to contribute financially to the education of their low-earning classmates. This would be the result of a plan in which *all*

---

[29] In addition, of course, some people will be willing to pay for the more convenient time pattern of repayments under income-contingent programs. Also, favorable tax treatment of interest paid under income-contingent plans could shift students into that form of borrowing. Our discussion implicitly assumes that these effects would be overwhelmed by the repayment comparisons discussed here.

[30] For an estimate that these taxes are not insignificant, see Pechman (1970).

students who use public higher education would be required to repay low tuition subsidies according to a progressive income tax schedule. Such a scheme might, however, shift students who expect high earnings to the untaxed private sector; thus a case could be made for providing that sector with instruction subsidies as well.[31] Such a system could be made more progressive than any existing state tax system.

The only possible drawback to this arrangement is its effects on social mobility: Will the rate of social mobility be significantly lessened by the repayment requirement? Again we refer to the Ohio higher education bill. Along with the new Ohio Plan tax for users of higher education, the bill would supply grants to low- (parental-) income students. On pure equity grounds it would be hard to beat this proposal. If we were to imagine a four-cell matrix based on low-high parental income and low-high future income, the Ohio Plan would aid all students in any "low" cell. The only omitted cell would include those with both high parental and high future incomes. Perhaps that is why the proposal was greeted by the executive director of the American Association of State Colleges and Universities with the statement that the Ohio Plan would be "a reversal of what public higher education has stood for for more than 100 years" (Crowl 1971, p. 1).

Final Comments

The principal conclusions reached in this paper are:

1. Under seemingly plausible assumptions as to the responsiveness of students to a substantial rise in tuition levels at state institutions, there is a significant reduction in educational attainment of children from families with incomes under $6,000 and some reduction in social mobility.

2. Greater access to loan programs could be expected to modify this result, but it would probably not offset it, unless loans were available in amounts in excess of a tuition increase.

3. The distribution of pretax income, in any global sense, would not be overwhelmingly changed by a shift from low tuition to loan financing.

4. Present federal loan programs are almost certainly inferior to state tax finance in the temporal allocation of the burdens of paying for higher education.

5. State-supported low tuitions transfer resources from nonusers to users. Even under a progressive tax system nonusers would be paying a substantial share of the cost.

6. State tax systems are regressive. Conventional loan repayments are even more regressive. Variable-term loans, with small internal redistribu-

---

[31] This extension of subsidy to the private sector can best be defended on efficiency grounds: if there are social benefits to higher education, they exist in the private sector as well as in the public.

tions, are superior to state tax systems on equity grounds, especially at low incomes. At high incomes they may be worse than state tax systems. The Yale Plan would be a superior money raiser on equity grounds. But high-earners might not participate.

7. The social mobility benefits of low tuition could be attained (and bettered) by a system of grants to students from low-income families. If coupled with a progressive state tax on users to repay higher education subsidies, greater equity could be expected.

References

Becker, Ernst. "Financing of Higher Education: A Review of Historical Trends and Projections for 1975–76." In *Trends in Postsecondary Education.* U.S. Office of Education, pp. 97–180. OE-50063. Washington: Government Printing Office, 1970.

Bureau of the Census. "All High School Seniors of October 1965 in Follow Up Survey." Washington, 1968.

———. *Characteristics of Students and Their Colleges, October 1966.* Current Population Reports, ser. P-20, no. 183. Washington: Government Printing Office, 1969. (*a*)

———. *Factors Related to High School Graduation and College Attendance: 1967.* Current Population Reports, ser. P-20, no. 185. Washington: Government Printing Office, 1969. (*b*)

———. *Income in 1967 of Persons in the United States.* Current Population Reports, ser. P-60, no. 60. Washington: Government Printing Office, 1969. (*c*)

Carnegie Commission on Higher Education. *Quality and Equality: Revised Recommendations, New Levels of Federal Responsibility for Higher Education.* New York: McGraw-Hill, 1970.

Cheit, Earl F. *The New Depression in Higher Education: A Study of Financial Conditions at Forty-one Colleges and Universities.* New York: McGraw-Hill, 1971.

Crowl, John A. " 'Ohio Plan' Creates a Storm; Would Require Students to Repay State for Education in Public Colleges." *Chronicle Higher Educ.,* March 29, 1971, p. 1.

Danière, André. "The Benefits and Costs of Alternative Federal Programs of Financial Aid to College Students." In *The Economics and Financing of Higher Education in the United States: A Compendium of Papers,* pp. 556–98. Congress, Joint Econ. Committee, 91st Cong., 1st sess., 1969.

Dresch, Stephen P., and Goldberg, Robert D. "Variable Term Loans for Higher Education—Analytics and Empirics." *Ann. Econ. and Soc. Measurement* 1 (January 1972): 59–92.

Economic Report of the President, January 1969. Washington: Government Printing Office, 1969.

Folger, John K.; Astin, Helen S.; and Bayer, Alan E. *Human Resources and Higher Education: Staff Report of the Commission on Human Resources and Advanced Education.* New York: Russell Sage Found., 1970.

Hansen, W. Lee, and Weisbrod, Burton A. "A New Approach to Higher Education Finance." In *Financing Higher Education: Alternatives for the Federal Government,* edited by M. D. Orwig, pp. 117–42. Iowa City, Iowa: American Coll. Testing Program, 1971. (*a*)

————. "On the Distribution of Costs and Benefits of Public Higher Education: Reply." *J. Human Resources* 6 (Summer 1971): 363–74. (*b*)

Hartman, Robert W. *Credit for College: Public Policy for Student Loans.* New York: McGraw-Hill, 1971.

Higher Education Act of 1965. Public Law 89-329. 79 *Stat.* (1965): 1219–1270.

Higher Education Opportunity Act of 1971. H. R. 5191. 92nd Cong., 1st sess., 1971.

Nam, Charles B., and Cowhig, James D. *Factors Related to College Attendance of Farm and Nonfarm High School Graduates: 1960.* Series Census-ERS (P-27), no. 32. Washington: Bureau of the Census, 1962.

National Defense Education Act of 1958. Public Law 85–864. 72 *Stat.* (1958): 1580–1605.

Ohio House Bill no. 930. 119th Ohio General Assembly, reg. sess., 1971–72.

Oregon State Senate Bill no. 735. 57th Oregon Legislative Assembly, 1971.

Pechman, Joseph A. "The Rich, the Poor, and the Taxes They Pay." *Public Interest,* no. 17 (Fall 1969), pp. 21–43. Brookings Inst. reprint no. 168.

————. "The Distributional Effects of Public Higher Education in California." *J. Human Resources* 5 (Summer 1970): 361–70.

Radner, R., and Miller, L. S. "Demand and Supply in U.S. Higher Education: A Progress Report." *A.E.R.* 60 (May 1970): 326–34.

Shell, Karl; Fisher, Franklin M.; Foley, Duncan K.; and Friedlander, Ann F. "The Educational Opportunity Bank: An Economic Analysis of a Contingent Repayment Loan Program for Higher Education." *Nat. Tax J.* 21 (March 1968): 2–45.

Summerskill, John. "Dropouts from College." In *The American College: A Psychological and Social Interpretation of the Higher Learning,* edited by Nevitt Stanford, pp. 627–57. New York: Wiley, 1962.

Thurow, Lester C. "The Optimum Lifetime Distribution of Consumption Expenditures." *A.E.R.* 59 (June 1969): 324–30.

Trent, James W., and Medsker, Leland L. *Beyond High School: A Psychosociological Study of 10,000 High School Graduates.* San Francisco: Jossey-Bass, 1968.

U.S. Department of Health, Education, and Welfare, Office of the Assistant Secretary for Planning and Evaluation. *Toward a Long-Range Plan for Federal Financial Support for Higher Education: A Report to the President.* Washington: Dept. Health, Educ., and Welfare, 1969.

U.S. Office of Education. *Opening Fall Enrollment in Higher Education, 1966.* Washington: Office Educ., 1967.

Yale University. "Questions and Answers: The Yale Tuition Postponement Option." Brochure. New Haven, Conn., July 1, 1971.

Comment

Douglas M. Windham
University of North Carolina at Greensboro

My dissatisfaction with Robert Hartman's present effort stems from (1) a feeling that he has either purposefully or accidentally asked the wrong questions about tuition policy and loan programs, and (2) that even the questions asked have not been answered in the most meaningful way. This latter objection is less vital because it may be easily rectified through an improved formulation of the analytical model along lines Hartman himself suggests.

The uses to which the model is put I find more disconcerting than the structure of the model itself. The attempt to separate tuition effects from any other change in the system is the weakest form of incomplete analysis. The effect of higher tuition must be, initially, to replace public financial support with private monies, and thus free funds for the governmental unit controlling the educational system (Windham 1971). These funds can allow for a tax reduction, be used for a new form of expenditure within the higher educational system, or be spent on some other public activities. Studying only the effect of a tuition increase and ignoring these other prospective effects biases the results. Although there is no way of predicting the uses of tax savings from a tuition increase, a newly funded public service would have to be *even more* progressive in its benefits than is the present public higher education system for low-income (and possibly middle-income) families not to benefit from the alternative financing system.

This brings one to the question of what is the relevant comparison to make with the status quo. No one would seriously suggest that tuition increases alone were a means to greater equity. However, it has been suggested that full-cost tuition, combined with an aid program which fully funds financial need, is an attractive solution to the crisis in higher educational finance. While Hartman does not offer a model of such a program, his present model could easily be adjusted to produce it.

Rather, in his paper he expresses concern for the effect of loan-repayment plans on present consumers of higher education. Obviously, those who are now receiving tuition subsidies will be worse off if their subsidy is changed into a loan. Hartman himself has noted, however, that the valid basis of comparison is between users and nonusers of the present system. If a fully funded program utilizing loans increases, as may be expected, the utilization of the system by present nonusers, gains in both efficiency and equity may result.

Students from lower-income families would find it easier to get into school *and to stay there*. The latter effect would be apparent in lower attrition rates as low-income students are relieved of financial pressures while in school. The current users of the higher educational system may be viewed as consisting of the well-to-do and the prospectively well-to-do. It is the present nonusers who deserve society's concern.

The criticism of present loan programs as "unattractive" is applicable, again, mainly to individuals already in the system. If this money were more available to those who presently do not have adequate resources with which to finance their education, the consensus concerning "attractiveness" would be altered. The improvement of capital markets is one of higher education's greatest needs. Longer repayment formats would help. However, loans granted on a basis other than of need will involve the same misallocation of funds that tuition subsidies presently cause.

The final result of this confusion about which models should be compared appears when Hartman notes: "A tuition increase, coupled with extending capital markets, goes a long way toward rectifying this alleged inequity. The price of correcting the inequity is, of course, the changes in social mobility described in earlier sections." There is no proper reason for the author to make this statement. The "price" of such a program has nothing to do with the effects upon mobility which result from a tuition increase *without* capital-market effects. Attempting to cite such effects as the consequences of the combined tuition/loan model results in a serious error of analysis. The true "price" of the program will be borne by those who, given a determinable ability to pay for their own education, are then required to do so.

A tuition increase/loan system should have the effect of changing general subsidies based simply upon college attendance into specific subsidies based upon need. Given the present limited availability of funds for higher education, it appears nonsense to do otherwise. While the advantage of a system of specific rather than general subsidies may appear obvious, there is nothing to indicate that Hartman feels that this is an important consideration.

The discussion of full-cost tuition is certain to raise the specter of the "social benefits" of higher education. The term "specter" is used advisedly, for the supposed social benefits are amorphous at best. I have yet to see a satisfactory objective delineation of even the nature of these social benefits; their quantitative evaluation must await such a delineation. The form of social benefits cited in the Hartman paper is embarrassingly subjective and inadequate.

The existence of social benefits in higher education does not affect the validity of the full-cost tuition, fully funded aid program. First, social benefits should result in subsidies only where the lack of such subsidization may be expected to reduce the production of the social benefits. It seems quite fair to expect that students from higher-income families will educate themselves (in return for substantial private benefits) even if tuition subsidies are removed. Second, any social benefits which do exist are not generated exclusively during the educational period itself. If, for instance, teachers or chemists are needed, it appears more efficient to supplement pay scales than to subsidize tuition. The often-criticized "teacher scholarship" plans in various states have shown that teachers depart, taking with them whatever hypothetical social benefits existed, if market rewards are not sufficient to retain them in an occupation.

Another matter of concern to many is that full-cost tuition may drive a large number of students into private schools. The dangers in this are not obvious. There is no reason to believe that private schools cannot generate social benefits as well as public schools, and the public schools would save money by no longer being required to subsidize such students. The probability of a dramatic change in the public/private mix differs greatly from state to state depending upon, among other things, family-income distributions and the relative quality of the two educational systems.

At the beginning, I noted that I felt the present form of Hartman's model was weak in certain areas. The inegalitarian effect of the status quo is underestimated by the omissions Hartman noted at the end of Part I. However, the strong contribution of this paper is in the presentation of a model for analyzing the lifetime effects of higher education upon income distribution. That some of the present assumptions are questionable is a function of the different opinions of researchers and the awesome paucity of data that Hartman must have faced. The lifetime-income effect is most important in measuring the income-redistributive effects of higher education because it shows the relative homogeneity within the group of users of the system versus the heterogeneity between user and nonuser groups.

A refined model, tooled to compare our present system with one of full-cost tuition and fully funded financial aid (as well as any new alternative proposals), should be the result of Hartman's work. If such a model is generated, the students of the economics of education will be greatly in his debt.

Reference

Windham, Douglas M. *Fiscal Capacity, Tax Effort, and Financial Aid in North Carolina.* North Carolina Financial Aid Studies, 1970, pt. 4. Atlanta: Southern Regional Office, College Entrance Examination Board, February 1, 1971.

Comment

Luther Tweeten

Oklahoma State University

Robert Hartman concludes that when the benefits of existing loan programs for students are examined in relation to parental-income distribution, a disproportionate share of benefits accrues to higher-income classes. This conclusion is similar to the Hansen-Weisbrod and Windham findings relative to low tuition in California and Florida, respectively. In fact, the tendency is widespread indeed for benefits from public programs of varied types to be distributed regressively within the group eligible for the program. I have noted evidence (Tweeten 1970, chap. 13; Tweeten and Schreiner 1970) to support this principle in federal programs of farm price and income supports (ASCS), farm loans (FHA), economic development (EDA), and special schooling (Head Start and aid to deprived children under the Elementary and Secondary Education Act of 1965).

Unless I misread history and current pronouncements, the originators and current administrators of land-grant universities and other state universities and colleges have believed they promote equity. The evidence suggests that higher education in fact receives high marks for serving the cause of economic efficiency but receives low marks for serving the cause of equity. It appears that the failure to promote equity has grown not out of intent but out of misunderstanding and lack of information. Efforts by economists to increase understanding have not yet been very successful. The Ohio Plan described by Hartman would promote greater equity in distributing the net benefits of higher education. Yet the plan is said by the director of the American Association of State Colleges and Universities to be "a reversal of what public higher education has stood for for more than 100 years." (Only partly in jest one can ask whether those who object are worried that the tax will drive alumni from the state.)

Why do people so widely support zero or low tuition if its effects are regressive? One reason may be the "Irish Sweepstakes" syndrome. Low-income parents who are aware the odds are against their child nevertheless choose to view their child (though perhaps yet unborn) as somehow special and able to beat the odds and someday attend the state university.

The principle that public program benefits tend to be distributed regressively within the group eligible for benefits begs explanation. I propose that explanation lies not in the perverse intents of administrators but rather in a ubiquitous and fundamental conflict between serving goals of equity and efficiency with public programs. The conflict grows out of limited public funds and the desire to use these funds to generate the most income possible. The funds generate the greatest income per public dollar spent when focused on persons who are highly motivated and able. But these individuals frequently prosper in the absence of the program, and they (or their parents) are likely to be at the upper-income end of the group eligible for the program. Furthermore, funds gravitate in their direction because these individuals are frequently vocal and effective in the political arena and hence are useful in keeping appropriations alive.

Economists have not effectively communicated the concept of regressive-income effects of higher education, partly because the concept is not well defined and articulated. Hartman also testified that the data need to be refined to provide fit fuel for such powerful analytical engines as simulation. Data cited by Hartman indicate that the probability of attending college is four times as great for youth from the highest than the lowest class of family income. By simulating successive generations, it is possible to observe the distribution of income if this pattern is continued for an extended period, with children from higher-income families receiving more schooling and, in turn, generating more income which enables their children to obtain more schooling. Hartman, in his simulation model, emphasizes the impact of loan programs used to finance schooling. More emphasis on the impacts of grants to low-income students would be instructive. He should examine, for full-cost and other tuition levels, the impact of a given subsidy budget allocated in alternative ways to the youth from various parental-income groups. His reason for not doing so (because political prospects for it are slim) is inadequate. Quantifying the impact on attendance of higher tuition coupled with tuition grants to low-income students is one way to articulate and perhaps "sell" the proposal to the public.

In devising new forms of financing higher education, one confronts the difficulties of administering a means test and obtaining reliable data on family income and wealth from which to practice tuition "price" discrimination. Also, a loan program alone may not induce the socially desirable level of investment in schooling—some subsidy may be necessary. Data for 1959 indicate a social rate of return of 10 percent to investment (public plus private) in college; this might be regarded as the marginal decision, since elementary and secondary schooling is widely viewed as a "must" investment.[1] This return is in line with rates of return to alternative investments and suggests, on the average, economic efficiency in schooling. The private rate of return to college investment for the individual was 13 percent. This is a very favorable economic payoff (very few capital investments available to individuals provide a rate of return this high); it should have led to overinvestment in schooling but apparently did not, in terms of the social rate of return. A high private return to the individual made possible by a public subsidy may be necessary to overcome imperfections in the market and induce sufficient investment to result in the socially desired return of 10 percent.

References

Hines, Fred; Tweeten, Luther; and Redfern, J. Martin. "Social and Private Rates of Return to Investment in Schooling, by Race-Sex Groups and Regions." *J. Human Resources* 5 (Summer 1970): 318–40.

Tweeten, Luther. *Foundations of Farm Policy.* Lincoln: Univ. Nebraska Press, 1970.

Tweeten, Luther, and Schreiner, Dean. "Economic Impact of Public Policy and Technology on Marginal Farms." In *Benefits and Burdens of Rural Development: Some Public Policy Viewpoints,* Center for Agricultural and Econ. Development, pp. 41–76. Ames: Iowa State Univ. Press, 1970.

[1] Data for white males are from Hines, Tweeten, and Redfern (1970).

On Tuition and the Costs of Higher Education: Prolegomena to a Conceptual Framework

Marc Nerlove

University of Chicago

> "Who is the expert in perfecting the human and social qualities? I assume from the fact of your having sons that you must have considered the question. Is there such a person or not?"
> "Certainly," said he.
> "Who is he, and where does he come from?" said I, "and what does he charge?"
> "Evenus of Paros, Socrates," said he, "and his fee is twenty guineas."
>
> PLATO, *The Apology*

What role can and should tuition play in the economics and financing of higher education in the United States? Central to my approach to this question is the belief that tuition is not now, but should be, a price in an economic sense. By this I mean that tuition should perform the function of rationing the available supply of higher educational services *and* of allocating scarce resources between the sector producing higher educational services (including graduate education and basic research) and the rest of the economy, as well as among different types of institutions of higher education, and even among different parts of the same institu-

The work on which this essay is based was supported under a grant from the National Science Foundation to the University of Chicago and under a grant for the study of the economics of population and family decision making from the Rockefeller Foundation. Some of the work was done during August 1971 when I was a visiting professor at the University of British Columbia. John Perry Miller graciously supplied a compendium of materials on the Yale Tuition Postponement Option. For helpful preliminary discussions on matters covered by this essay, I am indebted to Robert W. Fogel, Edward H. Levi, Walter Y. Oi, and T. W. Schultz. Robert McC. Adams, Denis De Tray, Richard B. Freeman, Stanley Fischer, Robert J. Gordon, Zvi Griliches, D. Gale Johnson, Harry G. Johnson, Reuben A. Kessel, Edward H. Levi, T. Paul Schultz, T. W. Schultz, George J. Stigler, Virginia K. Thurner, and James Tobin have commented extensively on an earlier draft. Needless to say, none of these generous people is responsible for such errors as remain, and many do not share the opinions expressed.

tion. To say this does not constitute a case against subsidizing higher education in a variety of ways, however. I believe that, at a given level of tuition paid by individual students, the demand for higher educational services will tend to be below socially optimal levels, and that, at the "price" represented by a given level of tuition, a less than socially optimal level of resources may be devoted to higher education unless society also subsidizes basic research.

Loan programs, especially the proposed "Educational Opportunity Bank" and the "Yale Tuition Postponement Option," in which there is so much current interest, are considered in a sequel to this paper.

1. Is Tuition a "Price" in an Economic Sense? Should It Be?

The role of prices is, on the one hand, to ration available supplies of a good among those who demand it and, on the other, to allocate scarce productive resources to the industry and/or firms which supply the good. Does the tuition charged by American colleges and universities for undergraduate and other postsecondary education now perform, or could it conceivably perform, the allocative functions of a "price" in an economic sense? Since the time of Adam Smith economists have been aware that, under fairly stringent assumptions to be sure, free markets and prices which perform these functions will lead to socially optimal results. The chief sources of difficulty which arise have to do with so-called externalities, with uncertainty which cannot be covered by insurance, and with certain intergenerational welfare comparisons which may not be adequately made in current-generation markets. Such barriers to effective functioning of markets and prices are especially important in analyzing the demand for and supply of products produced by the higher educational sector.

The higher educational sector in the United States is exceptionally complex and produces a bewildering variety of products. This sector consists of many different types of "firms," which range from proprietary vocational establishments and 2-year junior colleges to 4-year liberal arts colleges and the great public and private universities with their penumbra of associated professional schools and research institutes. Among its products are narrowly directed vocational training and undergraduate education—varying in quality from little better than what is offered in many secondary schools to the equal of anything offered anywhere in the world in any era—graduate education (also of varying quality), applied and basic research, and public service and extension.[1] Despite the under-

---

[1] An impression of the complexity of the industry, its incredible diversity of products, and the role which the sector plays in American society as a whole can be found in Jencks and Riesman (1968); Bolton (1969) presents a more quantitative view.

lying complexity of reality, the analysis that follows makes use of the concept of "units of undergraduate education" of constant quality, as if it were really possible to put a credit hour at Podunk State on a comparable basis with one at the University of Chicago. The special problems posed by graduate and professional education are neglected, although the framework can and should be extended to cover these types of educational services.

The major public and private universities of this country produce research and graduate education *jointly* with undergraduate education. To a lesser extent this is also true of 4-year liberal arts colleges, although the nature of the research done is a little more difficult to define. Many institutions of higher education produce no research of any discernible value at all, although, in some cases, other social functions may be performed. For such institutions, it is relatively simple to assess the extent to which tuition and student fees cover the costs associated with the production of the good conveyed; in general, of course, these costs are not covered by tuition and fees. They are supported, in part, through gifts, through income from endowments that are the result of past gifts, and by the general public, directly through taxes or indirectly through tax exemptions. For institutions in which undergraduate education and research and graduate education are jointly produced, it is much less clear how to measure the extent to which the tuition and fees charged undergraduates (apart from student aid) fail to cover the costs of providing that education. Many would regard the commodity supplied by these institutions as qualitatively rather different from that supplied by institutions which produce nothing else. That they fail to cover costs, however, is the inescapable conclusion reached by all who have examined the problem. The tuition and fees charged by public instiutions are quite consciously set below any plausible estimate of what it costs to educate a student; the same is as true of high-quality liberal arts colleges as it is for the major private and public universities. The *rationing*, by selective admission, of places in both public and private institutions to those who seek attendance suggests that tuition does not cover the costs of production of the quality of commodity demanded, nor does it serve the traditional economic function of rationing the available supply among those who would consume it or of calling forth additional supplies to meet these unmet demands.[2] Moreover, because a substantial number of universities

---

[2] O'Neill (1971) confirms, for the institutions included in the U.S. Office of Education surveys, Bowen's (1968) findings for major private universities, namely, that, even netting out expenditures for "organized" (separately funded) research, instruction and departmental research costs are rising far faster than tuition and fees. O'Neill's study is notable for her attempt to include capital costs (rarely taken into account) and to make some adjustments for quality differences in output. The papers by Jenny and Wynn (1969a, 1969b) attempt a detailed analysis of expenditures in a group of small, private, 4-year liberal arts colleges and provide further confirmation, although they do not allow for capital expenditures.

charge students substantially less than cost, they may restrict entry to the industry, reduce in some dimensions the diversity of the products that are produced, and perpetuate misallocations of resources among the "firms" comprising the higher educational sector.[3]

Tuition and fees are not the only costs to a student of obtaining an undergraduate education. Such an education is, in fact, a commodity, partly capital good and partly consumption good, which is *produced* by a student using his own time and a variety of services supplied by the higher educational sector. Thus, the demand for the services of the sector is a *derived demand,* that is, a demand for a factor of production rather than for a good valued for itself; and this is the case irrespective of whether an undergraduate education is regarded primarily as an investment in human capital or as something which contains significant quantities of current consumption. The costs associated with the time involved are the earnings foregone because the student must devote much of his time to his studies, leaving less for paid work and reducing his wage during those hours he does work below that which he might have received in full-time employment. The foregone-earnings component is not easy to measure because employment opportunities differ by region, race, sex, and other characteristics, and because many students do work part-time, thus reducing the amounts foregone. There are other costs associated with going to college that are not due to tuition and fees nor to the time involved; for example, the extent to which board, room, and incidentals exceed that which would have been spent had the student not sought a higher education is a cost attributable to going to college. Various estimates are available that suggest that the foregone-earnings component may amount to more than half the total cost paid by a student attending a prestigious and expensive private institution and, of course, a correspondingly greater fraction for one attending a zero-tuition or low-tuition public institution (Hansen and Weisbrod 1969, pp. 41–54; Schultz 1971, pp. 82–95, 102–15). Other expenses account for a much smaller, but presumably nonnegligible, fraction of the total (Hansen and Weisbrod 1969, pp. 49–51). Because substantial other costs, principally foregone earnings, are incurred by a student in the production of the human capital and consumption represented by a college education, the level of such costs and variations therein will affect the derived demand for the services of the higher educational sector and, of course, the consumption of college education and investment in human capital which takes place over time.

---

[3] Harry Johnson points out that diversity may be increased in some directions because the products produced are not subject to market discipline. The point is that once the market tie is broken, decisions as to what a university or universities will produce lie with a smaller, more homogeneous group than would otherwise be the case. Imposition of the particular set of standards and values of this group on society as a whole must tend to reduce freedom of choice.

Tuition clearly does not now function as a price in an economic sense throughout the higher educational sector, although it may do so for a small and rather unimportant subsector that does not include any of the major private or public universities, or indeed public instiutions of any kind or most private 4-year colleges. Whether tuition should be a price in an economic sense depends on the role tuition might play in the market determination of demand and supply and how and why a market mechanism might break down from a social point of view.

2. Tuition and the Demand for Undergraduate Education

What would be the effects of using tuition to ration the available supplies of different undergraduate educational services produced by the higher educational sector among those who demand those services? In particular, for a given structure and level of tuitions and fees, will the demand for the "products" of the higher educational sector be optimal from a social point of view? Or will the demand be too great or too small and will the composition of demand for the different types of products be socially undesirable? Are there socially undesirable effects from using nonmarket mechanisms to allocate available supplies?

If undergraduate education were purely a consumption good and if a student's consumption of it made only himself better off and no others in society, the problem of the adequacy of demand from a social point of view would be easy to analyze. College education is not merely a current consumption good, however, but, in part, a durable producers' good enabling those who have acquired it to achieve both higher pecuniary and higher psychic incomes. Moreover, there may be important benefits accruing to others in society, of the current generation or of future generations, benefits which are not captured by the individual educated. In addition, the production process by which an individual transforms the services of the higher educational sector, his own time, and his own abilities into human capital "in place" and current consumption is, at best, poorly understood, thus further complicating the analysis. Recent discussions of the problem among economists have emphasized the investment character of a college education, have de-emphasized the current consumption component, and do not appear to have considered fully the issues raised by the notion that the demand for the services of the higher educational sector is, in fact, a derived demand for a factor of production.

The Importance of Understanding the Technology of the Educational Transformation

Not using tuition as a means of allocating resources among "firms" producing different products or products of different qualities in the higher educational sector may lead to restriction of diversity within the sector or to diversity in undesirable directions. Moreover, since demand is rationed by other means, students themselves do not have the opportunity, assuming *they* do understand the transformation process, to combine inputs in the most productive way. A certain number of hours of class per week for 4 years, with summers off, and in such and such combination of subjects, may simply not be the best way for everybody, or perhaps anybody, to achieve the desired transformation of himself. There may be, to be sure, a substantial informational gap: neither a student nor his parents nor his advisors may be in a position to judge the various products offered or the manner in which those products will interact with his particular abilities and interests. Informational gaps of this sort lead in other areas such as medical care to nonmarket control by licensing and other forms of certification. It is not clear, however, that the transformation process is much better understood by those who do the licensing (accreditation) in the higher educational sector than by those who utilize the services produced by the sector, although it is possible that the "gatekeepers" who actually ration available supplies may have superior knowledge.

The question, it would seem, is whether any useful function may be served by not allowing full freedom of the choice of which types of higher educational product are purchased, even from a "suitably" restricted menu. This is a question not of the level of aggregate demand but of its composition. If it is assumed that the severe informational problems connected with the nature of the product have been solved, there is only one argument which I find cogent: A substantial part of what a prestigious private university or college has to offer may depend on the sort of students it can attract. Thus, the consumption of the product of such an institution by a student with the qualities desired (say exceptional intellectual or athletic ability) enhances the quality of the institution's output and, hence, its attractiveness to similar students. Perhaps it is only by charging a relative tuition too low to ration the supply of places among potential occupants that the institution can ensure an adequate supply of the sort of student who generates the appropriate externalities. Scholarships and other forms of student aid also may be used for such effects and to achieve those mixtures of student types believed to enhance the quality of the education produced. Indeed, it is possible that a regime of high tuition and substantial student aid could simultaneously enhance both the selectivity of the institution and its revenue, but it is doubtful that an individual institution could achieve such a happy state of affairs unilaterally.

That a higher education, indeed any education at all, is produced, in a sense, by each student by means not only of the services of the higher educational sector but also by inputs of his own time, efforts, and abilities, is an important consideration not only in the analysis of the composition of the derived demand for educational services but also of their level in aggregate. Opportunities for alternative employment may significantly affect the costs of acquiring a college education, especially for low-income groups. Uncertainty about the results of going to college, stemming from the individual's uncertainty about his own abilities, the quality of the educational services he may receive, or the effect of a higher education on his own income prospects may reduce demand below socially optimal levels. Quite apart from the compositional aspect of demand, the aggregate demand may be expected to be below a socially optimal level at any level of tuition sufficiently high to ration the supply of services provided by the higher educational sector.

Effects of Imperfections in Capital Markets

In his now classic paper in which he made the first suggestion of an income-contingent loan-repayment program for the financing of higher education, Friedman (1955, reprinted 1962) pointed out that an important reason for the insufficiency of demand is a particular sort of imperfection in the capital market:

> Investment in human beings cannot be financed on the same terms or with the same ease as investment in physical capital. It is easy to see why. If a fixed money loan is made to finance investment in physical capital, the lender can get some security for his loan in the form of a mortgage or residual claim to the physical asset itself, and he can count on realizing at least part of his investment in case of default by selling the physical asset. If he makes a comparable loan to increase the earning power of a human being, he clearly cannot get any comparable security. In a non-slave state, the individual embodying the investment cannot be bought and sold. . . . A loan to finance the training of an individual who has no security to offer other than his future earnings is therefore a much less attractive proposition than a loan to finance the erection of a building: the security is less, and the cost of subsequent collection of interest and principal is very much greater. [1962, p. 102]

Such reasoning lies behind many of the existing and proposed tuition-loan programs.[4]

In view of the substantial magnitude of the foregone-earnings com-

---

[4] Hartman (1971) describes existing and proposed programs and analyzes their effects on existing capital markets, the distribution of their benefits, and various aspects of alternative terms and implicit elements of subsidy. A subsequent paper of my own will deal with income-contingent loan-repayment programs in more detail.

ponent, existing loan or loan-guarantee programs are too restricted in their terms, length of repayment period, and size of loan, to offer many lower- and middle-class young people an opportunity to borrow against future earnings to the extent necessary to achieve adequate levels of demand even for the educational services of virtually free public institutions. Some part of a college education may be pure present consumption, or future psychic income. To the extent that it does not, on the average, result in higher pecuniary earnings to those who obtain it, it is unreasonable to expect the capital market to provide the wherewithal to finance it on terms different from those through which other forms of consumption are financed. But clearly a large part of a college education does represent investment in human capital which does result in higher financial rewards to those who acquire it. The degree to which rates of return to this form of investment exceed those on other assets (apart from risk) is indicative of the gap between actual demand and a socially optimal level. Because of the special problems which the riskiness of the investment in human capital raises, however, it is not clear with what rate of return the returns to a college education ought to be compared in order to assess the extent to which capital-market imperfections reduce demand below optimal levels.

Effects of Risk and Imperfections in Information Flows

The process of obtaining a college education is not only costly but quite risky as well. A particular student does not really know, in any precise way, the quality of the services he will receive from an educational institution. Moreover, these services are only one of several inputs to the educational transformation. The student is also likely to be at least partially ignorant concerning his ability to make use of what the higher educational sector provides and, more important, of the value of the product produced by those inputs and with his own efforts and abilities. Some types of education are narrowly vocational in character; much professional education at the postgraduate level in medicine, law, business, and engineering may also be of this nature, as recent events bring home. The demands by the economy for particular sorts of educated people are constantly changing; to the extent that a college education specifically "fits" an individual for a particular profession or occupation or specifically prepares him for postgraduate training which does so, an element of substantial risk is introduced into the calculation of the worth of an investment in a college education.[5] To the extent that a "liberal"

[5] For a careful analysis of the dynamics of the market for college-trained manpower see Freeman (1971). Freeman (pp. 202–26) presents evidence that students do have realistic income expectations, do consider foregone earnings in their educational plans, and do alter their career choices on the basis of additional information regarding income prospects and other occupational characteristics during the course of

education, a perfection of "the human and social qualities" which may be inherent in every human being, enables the student to adapt more flexibly to the economic environment in which he may find himself over his lifetime, the acquisition of an education reduces the economic risks to which the student may be exposed. Certain kinds of education may be regarded as an "insurance policy" against unemployment, against technological obsolescence of one's skills, and against low income. There are really two types of risks involved in the acquisition of a higher education: (1) the risk that each student faces, of not having the requisite abilities to benefit, and (2) the risk that what he does acquire will not provide him with higher income or better employment opportunities. Even if the latter risk were minimal, the former would still exist.

There are substantial numbers of people who like to gamble, not only at roulette wheels and racetracks, but on commodity exchanges, on stock markets, and in the foundation of new enterprises and the production of new products. On the average, however, people are risk-averse. Higher average rates of return must be paid on more risky, as compared with less risky, investments; people do purchase insurance; and, in general, they must be compensated for bearing risk, although some groups may be willing to bear risks at lower costs than others. This has important consequences for answering the question of whether the aggregate demand for the services of the higher educational sector will be large enough from a social point of view at any level of tuition that serves to ration available supplies. (Risk is also an important, but not the only, reason why the market mechanism will not call forth a socially optimal volume of research, both basic and applied.)

In the absence of insurance against acquisition of unwanted skills or lack of ability to complete an educational transformation to the fullest extent (and thereby failure to acquire the maximum number of "units" of a college education even though purchasing the requisite number of inputs from the higher educational sector), rates of return to investments in college education will have to be higher than to other, less risky investments. In calculating such rates of return, the current consumption component should be deducted from the cost and the nonpecuniary income stream valued and added to the future stream of money income; existing calculations do not make these adjustments and thus tend to understate the true rates of return to private individuals investing in college educations. Is it optimal from a social point of view that the rate of return to investment in higher education should be so high, or does the presence of substantial risk suggest that, in the absence of insurance or subsidies,

---

their career preparations. This is not to say that students consider only potential pecuniary benefits, but rather that they appear to be quite conscious of the "trade-offs" between money income and other career benefits.

aggregate demand will be deficient from society's standpoint? Do existing or proposed loan programs even begin to cope with this problem?

Two aspects of risk must be considered: Some individual risks can be pooled so that the aggregate risk is much less than the individual risk. This reduction in variance for sums of independent events is, of course, just what insurance companies sell. To the extent that the risks associated with investment in a college education can be pooled away in this sense, they are *private* but not *social* risks; if individuals are not made to bear them, they will, on the average, invest more in their educational transformations, and the allocation of resources among investments in human capital, investments in physical capital (and knowledge), and current consumption will be more socially optimal. Observed rates of return to different forms of investment will tend to be closer to one another after adjustment for nonpecuniary elements. Uncertainties associated with the way in which time, abilities, and the inputs provided by the higher educational sector are combined to produce the educational transformation are perhaps largely of this "poolable" character. The risks associated with society's changing demands for skills and college-educated manpower are not primarily, however, of a "poolable" sort, since the individual events which combine to form the aggregates are not independent of one another. These are *social* risks which must be borne by someone, although not necessarily solely by the individual students who are exposed to them. Such risks do require that rates of return to investments subject to them should be higher than those on riskless investments in order to achieve an optimal allocation of resources in the economy as a whole. But who should bear the risk on society's behalf and why cannot an individual risk-averse student transfer some of the risks for a price to someone or some group less risk-averse than he? As Tobin and Pugash (1971) so neatly put it: "When both parties stand to gain, there is room for a deal. This is the simplest and most fundamental principle of economics."[6]

The existence of insurance markets in connection with the uncertainties associated with the educational transformation would permit both a reduction in risk due to pooling and a transfer of risk from those less willing to bear it to those more willing to do so. Unfortunately, except in a very rudimentary sense in connection with the Yale Tuition Postponement Option, such insurance markets do not exist. Arrow (1971, p. 184) comments:

> The nonexistence of markets for the bearing of some risks in the first instance reduces welfare for those who wish to transfer those risks to others for a certain price, as well as for those who

[6] At Chicago, we would regard it as the *second* simplest and most fundamental principle, the first being that there is no such thing as a free lunch!

would find it profitable to take on the risk at such prices. But it also reduces the desire to render or consume services which have risky consequences; . . . these commodities are complementary to risk-bearing. Conversely, the production and consumption of commodities and services with little risk attached act as substitutes for risk-bearing and are encouraged by market failure there with respect to risk-bearing.

Thus, the failure of society to provide a means for pooling and shifting the risks associated with obtaining a college education reduces demand at any tuition below a level which would be socially optimal. Why has such a failure occurred and what bearing do these reasons have on the possibility of providing nonmarket alternatives?

Not all the risks of fire and death, which it might be socially desirable to provide a mechanism for shifting, can be shifted through insurance. Limitations on the size of policies, direct controls over those insured, insistence on elements of coinsurance, and the bankrupty and limited liability laws are all nonmarket responses to the absence of an appropriate market mechanism. The most important reason that the market fails to provide insurance or, when it does provide it, limits it in ways which prevent full shifting of risk, is the so-called moral hazard. This is the danger that the insurance policy itself changes incentives and affects the probability of the contingency against which the insurance is sought.

"The problem is that the insurer, or more broadly, the risk-bearer cannot completelv define his risks; in most circumstances he only observes a result which is a mixture of the unavoidable risk, against which he is willing to insure, and human decision. . . . But the insurance policy may . . . lead to a motive for increased loss, and then the insurer or risk-bearer is bearing socially unnecessary costs" (Arrow 1971, p. 142). In the case of an investment in a college education, the moral hazard that the insured will take a job that is not monetarily remunerative after graduation is compounded by the difficulties of assessing intrinsic abilities to begin with and the outcome of the educational process at the end. This problem is especially complicated for women. (*Pace!*)

Income-contingent Loan-Repayment Programs

The existence of a severe moral hazard and the discrepancy between the information possessed by an individual student and that which could be known to an insurance company are presumably reasons why the market economy has not provided institutions for shifting the risks involved, but this does not mean that the same moral hazard would exist for society as a whole, or that at least partial insurance would not be desirable from a social point of view. Indeed, a form of coinsurance or limited liability

Friedman suggested in his seminal paper is the basis for all income-contingent loan-repayment programs such as the Educational Opportunity Bank (U.S. Panel on Educational Innovation 1967; Shell et al. 1968; Shell 1970) and the Yale Tuition Postponement Option Plan (Brewster 1971; Tobin and Pugash 1971; Yale University 1971): "The device adopted to meet the corresponding problem for other risky investments is equity investment plus limited liability on the part of the shareholders. The counterpart for education would be to 'buy' a share in an individual's earning prospects; to advance him the funds needed to finance his training on condition that he agree to pay the lender a specified fraction of his future earnings. In this way, a lender would get back more than his initial investment from relatively successful individuals, which would compensate for the failure to recoup his original investment from the unsuccessful" (Friedman 1962, p. 103).

Of course, it is only to the extent that pecuniary benefits are obtained from a college education that an income-contingent loan-repayment scheme can contribute both to the problems arising from imperfections in the capital markets and to those arising from risks that cannot otherwise be shifted. To the extent that the gains from a college education are in the form of future psychic income or current consumption, neither imperfections in the capital market nor those in the risk-bearing market can be corrected in this way. Moreover, the difficulty which prevents a market solution to the risk-shifting problem is certainly not removed entirely by an income-contingent loan-repayment program, especially one operated by a single university. Those who have poor income prospects, either because of self-recognized lack of ability or because they feel likely to choose low-paying occupations on account of the value they place on the nonpecuniary benefits associated with such occupations, are more likely to borrow under such schemes to finance their educations than are those with exceptionally good income prospects because of their economic and social background, self-recognized ability, or prospective choice of occupation. This is the problem of adverse selection, which should be carefully distinguished from the moral hazard. The former is ex ante; the latter is ex post.

The insurance afforded by an income-contingent loan-repayment program may greatly alter the incentives of the women who participate in the program to participate later in the labor force, since their pecuniary income is more heavily "taxed" under such a program than it might otherwise be.[7] There may be a good reason for society to subsidize the

---

[7] Thus, an income-contingent loan-repayment program might, after allowing for the effects of increased education of women, have the unfortunate social consequence of increasing fertility. There is considerable evidence that, *ceteris paribus,* anything which diminishes the incentives for a woman to work outside the home enhances the probability that she will have a large family. In the absence of such a change in

education of women (beyond any level at which it might be desirable to subsidize higher education generally), so that this particular moral hazard might well be considered bearable by society as a whole.

One fear that has been expressed concerning the income-contingent loan-repayment programs is that they may alter the incentives for alumni gifts. Such gifts already are subsidized by the federal government, since they are deductible on federal tax returns. It is not possible to say how the repayment of a fixed, but small, percentage of one's income, part of which would also be deductible as interest, would alter the incentive of an alumnus to donate to his alma mater. Large donors, who have buildings or professorships named after them, presumably would be affected relatively little; moreover, the evidence is that small donors may contribute rather little over their lifetimes.

Income-contingent loan-repayment plans (see Hartman 1971, pp. 61–92) have been much discussed in the last few years. Many ingenious devices have been suggested for dealing with the special problems of women, with the problem of adverse selection, and with the moral hazard involved in the insurance element, and for introducing various elements of subsidy deemed desirable. A sequel to this paper deals with some of these schemes. Suffice it here to say: (1) The problems of administering the programs, enforcing whatever repayment plan is adopted, and ensuring that the magnitude of the program and the size of the loans granted thereunder are sufficient to remove imperfections in the capital and risk-bearing markets for nearly all students who would otherwise be prevented from utilizing a socially optimal level of higher educational services are greatly mitigated by a program national in scope. Beyond "leading the way," what can be accomplished by an individual private university is very small indeed. (2) The problem of adverse selection facing an individual institution is much greater than that facing society as a whole, and the possibility for reduction of aggregate risk through pooling of individual risks is much less. (3) The element of subsidy and the question of whether it is desirable to subsidize the utilization of the services of the higher educational sector at all is quite separable from the issue of the desirability of introducing income-contingent loan-repayment plans on a large scale. Without such plans it is clear that, at any tuition level representing the costs of supplying those services, demand will be below socially optimal levels. An economist would say that, without such a program and if there were no subsidies, the entire demand function lies below the welfare-maximizing demand function: At least some people can be made better off by an income-contingent loan-repayment program

---

incentives, one might expect increased education for women to lead to a decline in fertility, since such education enhances the income possibilities of labor-force participation.

without, at the same time, making any member of the current generation worse off.[8]

Externalities of Higher Education and the Case for Subsidies to Students

If a college education improves the economic productivity of an individual and if he can capture that benefit through higher earnings, he has an incentive to acquire those skills. The individual and the social interest coincide; beyond ensuring that market imperfections do not impede his quest, society has no interest in further rewarding him in order to induce him to use still more scarce resources that might be devoted to other valuable endeavors. But if a college education for one person contributes to the welfare of others in a way which cannot be appropriated by that individual in the form of higher current consumption or future earnings, both psychic and pecuniary, then removal of market imperfections will not ensure a socially optimal level of demand for the services of the higher educational sector. We call such nonappropriable, "third-party" benefits *externalities* or *external effects.*

The externalities of elementary school education are manifest and universally obvious. None would deny that literacy and a reasonable arithmetic facility are essential to the functioning of American society and that such social benefits go far beyond any individual's ability to capture them in the form of higher earnings. The external benefits of secondary education are perhaps less obvious and some would even go so far as to say that since the era of the "melting pot," when the secondary (and elementary) schools served a homogenizing function and, at the same time, provided a mechanism for social mobility, there have been few externalities of any magnitude. It is still more difficult to identify the externalities of college education. (Note that we must distinguish here between the external effects of producing inputs for college education in the higher educational sector—for example, research—and externalities in the utilization of those inputs.)

The kinds of externalities that one hears much about are benefits to society as a whole in such forms as training for citizenship and for community leadership, creation of a group with "human and social qualities" that may serve as an example to others, providing a mechanism for social mobility, or ensuring the continuation of social and cultural values.[9]

---

[8] Because of possible fertility effects, future generations may be made worse off. There are reasons to believe, however, that providing the present generation with more education will tend to make future generations better off, so that the net effect on future generations is not clear.

[9] Harry Johnson points out that higher education may have negative externalities in the form of greater social instability. Of course, what is negative in the short run may be positive in the long run; the capacity for change may be enhanced by a certain amount of instability, although too much might destroy society altogether.

Indeed, it is difficult for me to believe that such externalities are not important in view of the substantial amount of long-standing public and private subsidization of higher education. Yet it is probably true, as Friedman (1968, p. 111) suggests, that there has been "no serious attempt to identify true external effects systematically in such a way as to permit even a rough estimate of their quantitative importance—of how large a subsidy, if any, can be justified on these grounds." Admitting that we are far from being able to measure the external benefits of post-secondary education is *not*, however, the same thing as denying that such benefits exist; it is wrong to conclude that "until this is done, the demand for subsidy in the 'public interest' must be regarded as special pleading pure and simple." Nor can one argue on this basis for eliminating such subsidies as there are. The lack of measurement is not even an argument for decreasing the level of subsidy. It is an argument for trying to find out what the extent of the externality is and why there has been so much subsidization in the past.

Higher education will undoubtedly continue to receive substantial public and philanthropic subsidies. It is important that such subsidies are made in a way which only increases the utilization of higher educational services and the resources devoted to their production and does not distort the allocation of resources in other ways which may be socially undesirable.

One of the major sources of confusion in thinking about subsidies to higher education is the redistributive effect which such subsidies often have. We believe that more equality of income is a good thing, but, perhaps harking back to an earlier era, equality of opportunity is still more important. To the extent that the acquisition of a college education increases the future income of one who acquires it, subsidizing him to do so in one way increases his income relative to what it would have been in the absence of a subsidy, although not necessarily in relation to that of others. Such subsidies may, therefore, have the effect of reducing income inequality, although it is likely that they will in fact increase inequality because the overall returns to education will be reduced. There are other ways to reduce income inequality, and it is clear that public support of higher education may have rather different effects in this direction than are intended by those who argue for such support. Even with progressive general taxation, for example, it is clear that public support of low- or zero-tuition public institutions redistributes income primarily from low- and very high-income groups to middle-income groups.[10] Public support of undergraduate education in private institutions (say, through the subsidy of buildings of various sorts) not only

---

[10] Some of the subsidy may be recaptured through higher taxes on the higher incomes resulting from the increased education of those subsidized.

may distort the sector's use of resources, because of the selective nature of the subsidy, but tends even more to redistribute income away from those in society who have least. The point is that there may be more efficient ways to redistribute income than through subsidies to higher education, and the issues associated with income distribution should be separated in our thinking from those associated with the desirability of subsidies to the sector.

Equality of opportunity is a thornier problem, as Harry Johnson has pointed out (in this Supplement). To some extent inequalities of opportunity to acquire the larger lifetime income streams afforded by access to higher education are simply the result of imperfections in the capital and risk-bearing markets, and, to the extent that they are, the solution to the problem of increasing equality of opportunity is not to subsidize students but to improve these markets. Inequality of opportunity results not only from differences in material inheritance but also from the unequal inheritance of genetically determined ability and from more elusive nonmaterial elements in the family backgrounds of children. Very few would argue either for the equalization of genetically determined opportunities or for the means which would be necessary to create more equality in this dimension, although an argument could be made for compensating those who were unlucky enough to be born with less wit and intelligence than average.[11] The difficulties in distinguishing between inherited and acquired abilities are manifold—indeed, the distinction is becoming increasingly blurred—but I take it for granted that the nonmaterial elements in the family backgrounds of children *are* important to their opportunities and, more particularly, to their ability to engage in the educational transformation.

Although modern welfare economics does not appear to have satisfactorily resolved the intergenerational problem or recognized the social, as opposed to individual, interest in future generations, society has many institutions for assuring its own continuity and the welfare of its members yet unborn. The chief among these is the family.

Intergenerational Externalities and the Case for Subsidizing the Education of Women

More than 50 years ago, Frank Knight (1921, pp. 374–75) wrote some words about the interest of society in the continuity of the social order, the role of the family, and the possibility of equality of opportunity, which are worth remembering:

> The personal powers of individuals . . . obstinately resist

[11] See Denison (1970). It is terribly difficult for an academic to argue this position, but, of course, that does not make it wrong.

generic separation from material goods in their economic bearings. Innate ability, in the sense in which there is such a thing, is inevitably hereditary, and nothing can be done about it except to modify the conception of the individual's property rights to his own powers. But culture in all its subtle significance, as well as education and training in their cruder forms, are also more or less transmissible and more or less subject to voluntary bestowal, and the factor of personal influence or "pull" can by no means be left out of account. The significance of control over these things is very great. . . . It seems that real equality of opportunity, a true merit system, is hardly conceivable, and that no very close approach to such a consummation can be expected in connection with the private family. Plato, of course, recognized this fact, which most of his modern successors have a tendency to blink.

The ultimate difficulties . . . center around the problem of social continuity in a world where individuals are born naked, destitute, helpless, ignorant, and untrained, and must spend a third of their lives in acquiring the prerequisites of a free contractual existence. The distribution of control, of personal power, position, and opportunity, of the burden of labor and of uncertainty, and of the material produce of social industry cannot easily be altered. . . . The fundamental fact about society as a going concern is that it is made up of individuals who are born and die and give place to others; and the fundamental fact about modern civilization is that it is dependent upon the utilization of three great accumulating funds of inheritance from the past, material goods and appliances, knowledge and skill, and morale. Besides the torch of life itself, the material wealth of the world, a technological system of vast and increasing intricacy and the habituations which fit men for social life must in some manner be carried forward to new individuals born devoid of all these things as older individuals pass out. The existing order, with the institutions of the private family and private property (in self as well as goods), inheritance and bequest and parental responsibility, affords one way for securing more or less tolerable results in grappling with this problem.

Many things have changed since Knight wrote, but in American society the family is still the central institution ensuring continuity of the social order. Women have achieved far greater equality with men and participate in the labor force to a much greater degree and on better terms than they did 50 years ago, but for all the strident protest of the women's liberation movement, the woman remains the center of the family and its most important component in the intergenerational transfer of acquired ability. The family and its central figure are, at the same time, the most important source of social continuity and the greatest source of inequality of opportunity. Evidence is accumulating that the educational attainment of the mother is among the most important determinants of a child's future academic and economic success. The education of women enhances the educability of the next generation, and greater equality among women should tend to reduce the inequality of opportunity inherent in the intergenerational transfer of acquired ability through the family and to increase the efficiency of the family as an institution which helps to maintain the continuity of the social order. Needless to say, the extent to which elementary, secondary, and higher education contribute to these goals is not easily quantified, nor, to my knowledge, has anyone come close to measuring these effects.

In the modern theory of family decision making, as developed in economics, the welfare of the children and other members of the family is assumed to enter the utility function of a single decision maker (not always the husband and father!), thus obviating the necessity for assuming a "family utility function" with all the concomitant problems of social utility functions in general. It might be argued—and has been—that the benefit to succeeding generations and to society in terms of social continuity is internalized; that is, it "accrues in large part to the parents in terms of satisfactions" (Schultz, in this Supplement). Since no one has yet measured this effect, it is just as easy to argue that a substantial part is *not* internalized and that a social optimum would not result if each family simply maximized its own welfare subject to a set of market prices. Indeed, there is good reason to suppose that each individual's concern for others diminishes with distance in both time and space, and that the reason for many institutions of society is precisely to ensure that the interests of future generations will be adequately guarded by the present.[12]

By withdrawing from market activities to devote herself to her family, a woman may deprive society of the benefit of certain other sorts of externalities which higher education may generate. These must be offset against the intergenerational externalities which may be generated within the family. However, many of the sorts of externalities of higher education which come readily to mind do not depend upon market activities

---

[12] It is possible, of course, that a part of society invests too much in future generations. Wealthy families may bequeath too much material capital to their progeny and force their children to undertake larger than optimal investments in human capital. This does not mean, however, that the investment of society as a whole is optimal or that it is properly distributed between human and nonhuman capital. Low-income parents, in particular, may be prepared to invest far less than would be socially desirable in the education of their children.

for their realization, and these would not disappear if a woman did not participate in the labor force.

The traditional role of women in American society is changing, and perhaps the roles of men and woman are becoming less differentiated; but, to the extent that the woman remains the center of the family and its prime component in the transmission of some acquired abilities and of an important part of culture, I believe a case can be made for subsidizing the education of women over and above any subsidy deemed appropriate for the education of men. To the extent that both men and women play an equal role in the intergenerational transfer that takes place within the family and to the extent that individual utility maximization cannot guarantee the adequacy of this transfer, subsidy to the education of both men and women woud seem to be desirable from the point of view of society. As indicated above, what is being made is a case for all education, not just higher education. The contribution of the latter to the social goals outlined here has not been measured; it may be slight or great. Moreover, if the skills acquired through higher education are used later in the market and to enhance the income, pecuniary and psychic, of the family unit, lesser intergenerational externality exists and there is less of a case for a subsidy, differential or absolute.

3. Tuition and the Supply of Undergraduate Educational Services

What kinds of supply effects may be expected from the use of tuition to allocate scarce resources between the higher educational sector and the rest of the economy and among "firms" in this "industry"? Does it make sense to use tuition to allocate resources within colleges and universities as well as among them? What is the nature of production in the higher educational sector? How do research and undergraduate education interact, and what is the role of different disciplines? All of these are questions connected with the supply of undergraduate educational services.[13]

Product Diversity and Accreditation

There are important similarities between medical care and the services provided by the higher educational sector to those seeking an undergraduate education. In both cases, the service provided is informational in character. While it is true that one can envisage situations in which the value of a piece of information is well-defined even though the information itself is not known, in most situations the value of the information is not precisely known until the information itself has been acquired.

---

[13] Recall that the simplification of counting undergraduate educational services in quality-adjusted units has been adopted.

This may be the case with medical and other professional services. One of the most important nonmarket responses to uncertainty of this sort in the professional sphere is *licensing;* in higher education this takes the form of *accreditation,* which is basically a form of quality control designed to compensate for the lack of a market mechanism for shifting the risks and uncertainties associated with the purchase of an informational commodity. Just as the uncertainty about the prospects of medical treatment is socially handled by rigid entry and licensing requirements for physicians, so the uncertainty about higher educational services is socially handled by more or less rigid accreditation requirements for specific programs and restrictions on the entry of colleges and other institutions of higher education into the sector as defined by those requirements.

As I pointed out in the first section of this essay, one of the consequences of not allowing tuition to assume the role of a price in an economic sense may be a restriction in the variety of services offered by the higher educational sector. Essentially the argument is that the decision on what is to be produced is confined to a narrower group with more homogeneous preferences than society at large.[14] In a market context, the preferences of the consumers of the product or products are expressed through their effects on prices, but when prices cease to function so as to ration demand among consumers, they also cease to function in such a way as to allocate resources among firms producing different products or to provide incentives to produce goods desired by consumers. Restriction of the decision to a small group may lead to greater diversity than would be desirable from a social point of view if the preferences of the group are sufficiently bizarre, but, on the whole, it is plausible that product diversity will be diminished in at least some directions.

Because of the informational nature of the product, a great deal of uncertainty is bound to be associated with the use of higher educational services. To some degree it may be possible to shift a portion of the risk through income-contingent loan-repayment programs, but, for the reasons discussed in detail in the previous section, it will never be possible to shift all of the risks because so much of the return to the individual is nonpecuniary. Moreover, moral hazards exist on the supply as well as the demand side; even were society as a whole to assume a large part of the burden of risk, direct controls would no doubt still be imposed. Use of tuition as a price in an economic sense would undoubtedly increase the diversity of products offered by the higher educational sector, and the right sort of loan programs would mitigate some, but not all, of the uncertainty; accreditation and some restriction of entry might still be

---

[14] The same point also is made in a somewhat different context by Buchanan and Devletoglou (1970, p. 39); they argue that the quality and characteristics of the product will be chosen so as to reflect maximization of the utility of its producers rather than of its consumers.

desirable from a social point of view, although much could be done to increase informational flows without restricting entry.

Widespread below-cost pricing and accreditation interact in a most unfortunate way to exacerbate the lack of diversity in American higher education and to force homogeneity in a particularly inappropriate direction. The recent cases of Parsons College and Marjorie Webster Junior College illustrate this point. The case of Marjorie Webster Junior College is particularly instructive. Marjorie Webster, a 2-year institution incorporated and run as a business organization in Washington, D.C., had periodically requested accreditation from the Middle States Association of Colleges and Secondary Schools. It had been repeatedly refused review on the grounds that the association grants accreditation only to "a non-profit organization with a governing board representing the public interest." Finally, Marjorie Webster brought suit against the association in the U.S. District Court for the District of Columbia and was granted an injunction forbidding enforcement of the association's rule (Manne 1969; Koerner 1970).[15] The initial decision was reversed on appeal and, sad to say, the Supreme Court refused to review it, but the arguments and the judge's opinion in the initial case are most instructive in connection with this discussion. Middle States argued that the "profit motive . . . threatened the integrity of the proprietary institution by diverting it from the basic responsibilities of an educational institution." The judge's reply as reported by Manne (1969, p. 8) and Koerner (1970, p. 53) was:

> Educational excellence is determined not by the method of financing but by the quality of the program. Middle States' position, moreover, ignores the alternative possibility that the profit motive might result in a more efficient use of resources, producing a better product at a lower price. Additionally, an efficiently operated proprietary institution could furnish an excellent curriculum whereas a badly managed non-profit corporation might fail. Defendant's assumption that the profit motive is inconsistent with quality is not supported by the evidence and is unwarranted. There is nothing inherently evil in making a profit and nothing commendable in operating at a loss.

Unfortunately, as reversal of the lower court's decision illustrates, there may be an inevitable conflict between the delegation and trust implicit in the social institution of accreditation and licensing designed to reduce the uncertainty about the quality of the product and profit maximization. This is as true in medicine or law as it is in education, and it is doubtful

---

[15] For a detailed discussion of the parallel in the supply of medical services and medical education, see Kessel (1970).

that the conflict can be entirely removed by any program designed to lead to greater diversity in the higher educational sector. Greater knowledge of what actually takes place in the educational transformation could, however, lead to more enlightened accreditation policies and a greater diversity in American higher education.

Joint Production in Higher Education

It is assumed for the sake of this argument that only two products are produced by the higher educational sector, basic research and graduate education, on the one hand, and undergraduate education, on the other. Variations in quality are here taken account of by counting higher quality research or undergraduate education as a larger number of units than that of lower quality.[16]

Graduate education and basic research seem to me to be inextricably intertwined, so that treating them as Marshall's knife blade and handle—perfectly complementary—as a first approximation does little violence to the reality. Applied research is of a somewhat different character, and much, especially the more applied, can be successfully accomplished without the presence of students. Certain research organizations such as the RAND Corporation and the Brookings Institution are attempting to incorporate rudimentary graduate programs in their existing research structures; others, such as the National Bureau of Economic Research, Battelle, and Stanford Research Institute have long had university ties; and the large governmental research units tend to function most effectively in the natural sciences, where the institution of postdoctoral training is most firmly established so that they do in effect have students. This suggests that there is a substantial area of basic research and perhaps some part of applied research (which, after all, shades off rather gradually from the pure) where graduate students are such an important part of the process that their training cannot really be treated separately from the ongoing research program of which they are a part.

Professional education in such fields as medicine, law, engineering, social work, or business presents more difficult problems. For a long time,

16 Such simplification not only ignores some incredibly difficult measurement problems but also implicitly assumes that different types or qualities of educational services or research services are perfect substitutes for one another (for example, that some number of years at low-quality college x is equivalent to 1 year at Harvard). Not only does the assumption of perfect substitutability do violence to my intuitive sense of what is involved in the educational transformation (different types of experience are valuable to different sorts of people), but it is not obvious that the marginal rates of substitution between years x and years at Harvard ought to be independent of the *amounts* of each which are available. If there were a lot more Harvard years than there are, college x years might be worth *relatively* more. Still, one has to draw the line somewhere in the degree of complexity which can be introduced, and I draw it here for the time being.

training in many of these fields was carried out separately from university programs in graduate education and basic research, but it is now concentrated in university professional schools or university-related schools.[17] This suggests, too, a certain complementarity. Such complexities are largely ignored in the discussion which follows, although the analysis does suggest a way of looking at the problem of additional joint products such as professional education, applied research, and, perhaps research administration, which is frequently undertaken by individual universities or consortia of universities.

That basic research (and the graduate education associated with it) is typically a joint product produced with undergraduate education is a fact which needs to be explained and may even provide some argument for subsidizing certain kinds of undergraduate education (Kaysen 1960, pp. 56–57; Weisbrod 1962, p. 120). I argue below that there is indeed a strong case for public subsidy of the basic research which takes place in the higher educational sector, even at certain types of institutions not usually thought of as being in the "basic-research circuit," so to speak, but that this does not necessarily entail a subsidy to undergraduate education and may actually make such education more costly to society.

Universities such as Johns Hopkins, which was originally founded primarily for the purpose of doing graduate education and basic research, have, over time, gradually incorporated undergraduate programs of substantial size relative to the programs originally emphasized. Conversely, Harvard and Yale, where undergraduate education was once paramount, have become increasingly active centers of basic research and graduate education. To some extent these developmnts may have been due to the changing pattern of support for higher education in this country; to some extent they are surely due to the complementarity among different fields, the nature of basic research in the humanities, and the complementarity between basic research (and the graduate education associated with it) and the production of undergraduate educational services.

One of the central reasons why a university is more than a collection of departments is the existence of strong complementarities among fields and disciplines, both with respect to research and with respect to undergraduate teaching. It is difficult to conceive of good research being done, for example, in political science or sociology without strong programs in anthropology, economics, and history, or in economics without strength in statistics and mathematics, or in astronomy without corresponding activity in physics. This is even more the case with research and training

[17] Historically, of course, many colleges and universities in the United States grew out of professional schools, especially schools for the training of individuals for the law and for religious ministries.

which takes place in professional schools, and, although there are many great universities without an extensive set of associated professional schools, the reverse feedbacks are too often neglected by those who attempt to understand the nature and working of a university. Thus, a variety of research and teaching activities are mutually supportive and more efficiently carried on (using fewer scarce resources) together than apart.

There is some difficulty in distinguishing true jointness in production from scale effects. The various activities of a university use common facilities, such as buildings, libraries, and computers. One of the reasons that different disciplines are pursued and both research and undergraduate teaching are done together is to gain more efficient use of these common facilities. If, for example, the scale of operation of any one activity were sufficiently large, it could be that any supposed complementarity would disappear. I think, however, there are deeper reasons for jointness in production.

In the natural sciences, especially the physical sciences, it is remarkable how frequently senior scientists of great eminence teach the most elementary undergraduate courses. The same is true to a lesser degree in the biological and social sciences.[18] It may well be that surveying one's whole field quite broadly, or trying to make clear the structure of a discipline to the "uninitiated," or showing how a discipline would attack a particular scientific, social, or philosophical problem, is inherently "educative" to someone engaged in basic research. To this extent research and undergraduate instruction are complementary in production and best carried on within the same institution and by the same people. (This is true in a *gross* sense but, as argued below, will not be true at the *margin*, where, indeed, research and the provision of undergraduate educational services must be substitutes if resources are allocated efficiently.)

The Special Nature of the Humanities

What appears to be true of the sciences, to a greater or lesser degree, depending upon which particular discipline is considered, is, in a sense, fundamentally true of the humanities. I can claim no expertise within this group of disciplines beyond that afforded by a good—and by now somewhat old-fashioned and outmoded—general, liberal education, but it has always seemed to me that the humanities are concerned, in one way or another, with the meaningful reinterpretation of man's past and his works to each succeeding generation. They are concerned in a very

[18] Curiously, casual observation suggests such participation in undergraduate teaching is rarer among distinguished humanists than among distinguished scientists. If such is indeed the case, it is not consistent with my view of the nature of the humanities as expressed herein.

fundamental sense with the intergenerational transmission of culture and of values. Directly or indirectly, therefore, they are deeply bound up with undergraduate education and the "educational transformation."[19] Modern culture contains a large component of science, too, of course, and, to the extent that natural and social scientists are concerned with making the scientific part of our heritage meaningful to succeeding generations, they too are humanists in my sense. The undergraduate college is to the humanist what the laboratory is to the natural scientist and the survey and the census are to the social scientist. It is impossible to conceive of basic research in the humanities being carried out without a considerable direct or indirect involvement in the whole process of undergraduate education. This does not mean, of course, that the two must be carried out by the same individual, or even at the same institution, but only that meaningful research in the humanities cannot be separated from undergraduate education somewhere in the system.

The Case for Subsidizing Basic Research

As remarked above, information has a number of peculiarly uncomfortable properties from an economic point of view and cannot easily be considered as a commodity in the ordinary use of that term. Some information results in benefits, pecuniary or nonpecuniary, to the producer himself; a number of institutions (the patent system, copyrights) have been developed in our economy to increase the scope of appropriability of the gains from the production of new knowledge. In general, the more applied a piece of research, the greater the appropriability or potential appropriability of its benefits. New knowledge, especially of a more basic character, has benefits, however, which are so widely diffused throughout society that it is difficult, if not impossible, to invest the producers of such knowledge with appropriate property rights in the information.[20] It is what economists would call a "public good," a commodity the consumption of which by one individual does not reduce the amount available for the consumption of others; indeed, in the case of knowledge, individual consumption may, in a sense, enhance the availability for other persons. Fundamental or basic research is, almost by definition, an input

[19] For a similar view, see Roush (1969, p. 641).

[20] Hirschleifer (1971) distinguishes between "foreknowledge" and "discovery" and shows that, in general, no incentive need to be provided to those who obtain the former type of information and that, indeed, there may be socially undesirable overinvestment in the acquisition and dissemination of such knowledge. "Discovery," on the other hand, creates speculative opportunities which may or may not enable the discoverer to capture part of the value of the new knowledge. In the case of basic research the uncertainties are so great, and the chains by which the discoveries produce real world effects so long, that it is doubtful that any speculative opportunities provide sufficient incentives to engage in the activity.

for further research (Arrow 1971, pp. 154–55): "To appropriate information for use as a basis for further research is much more difficult than to appropriate it for use in producing commodities; and the value of information for use in developing further information is much more conjectural than the value of its use in production. . . . Thus basic research, the output of which is only used as an informational input into other inventive activities, is especially unlikely to be rewarded [by the market mechanism]."

Again, basic research in the humanities presents special problems just because such research is so intimately tied up with the educational process and the intergenerational transmission of culture and of values. To the extent that such research is not immediately rewarding to its producer, however, there would appear to be an even clearer case that its benefits cannot be privately appropriated.

From a social point of view, moreover, it would also seem that various devices which have been introduced in order to invest individuals with certain property rights in knowledge may have the effect of reducing the general welfare. Once basic knowledge or information has been created, the social product will be greater if all have access to it merely for the costs of transmitting it. Artificial barriers to its use designed to convey some part of the social benefit of new knowledge to its producers and so give them an incentive to invest scarce resources in its acquisition can only have the effect of reducing the ultimate benefit to society as a whole.[21] But, without such incentives, private individuals, motivated only by the direct satisfaction of discovery, will tend to invest too little in the production of new basic knowledge. Clearly, it is in the public interest to subsidize collectively the acquisition of new knowledge, especially that of a fundamental or basic character. To some degree, private philanthropy may fill the gap between what individuals would do for their own satisfaction and what would be socially optimal, but such an exact coincidence of public and private interests would be fortuitous. Indeed, the benefits of basic research to society may be so great and so uncertain in character and extent that reliance on individuals' maximizing their own satisfactions may be exceedingly undesirable from a social point of view.

Not only are the gains from basic research largely unappropriable by those who do the research, but the process itself is a highly risky one (Arrow 1971, p. 138): "The outcome of any research project is necessarily uncertain, and the most important results are likely to come from projects whose degree of uncertainty to begin with was greatest. The shifting [and presumably pooling as well] of risks is thus most needed

---

[21] As Hirschleifer (1971) points out, overinvestment in the acquisition and dissemination of "foreknowledge" or opinion can easily occur. The discussion here, however, is restricted to the type of knowledge generally acquired within the educational sector, and one hopes the speculative component is not large.

for what is very likely the most profitable of activities from society's point of view."

Both the "public" nature of the good produced and the riskiness of the research process, coupled with the uninsurability of these risks, suggest that too little basic research will be carried out in an economy which relies purely on the market mechanism. This may be true as well for much applied research. Moreover, institutional devices for making the gains from basic research privately appropriable not only do not mitigate the deficiency in the activity due to its riskiness but also have the unfortunate feature of reducing the use of the fundamental knowledge gained below socially optimal levels. It is not surprising, therefore, that the great bulk of basic research has been carried on in universities, in nonprofit institutions, by the government, and by private individuals who derive satisfaction from the process itself. The role of colleges and universities has been an especially important one, in part because of the complementarity between teaching and basic research. Such complementarity does not, however, imply that a socially optimal level of basic research activity will be undertaken by the higher educational sector in the absence of subsidy, nor does it imply that subsidies directly for research or indirectly through subsidies to students have equivalent effects or benefits to society.

The Complementarity of Research and Teaching and the Effects of Subsidizing Research

That basic research and graduate training and the provision of undergraduate educational services are carried on within the same institution and frequently by the same individuals, as already noted, suggests that the two activities are complementary in production in the sense that fewer scarce resources are needed to produce given amounts of the two goods if they are produced together rather than separately. Indeed, there is some doubt that certain kinds of basic research, for instance in the humanities, can be produced independently of undergraduate education at all. But this does not imply that the provision of undergraduate educational services should therefore be subsidized. I argue here that if society does pay for basic research so that a socially optimal quantity is produced, it may well have the effect of making the provision of undergraduate educational services more expensive, but this increase in cost is desirable from society's point of view. A few diagrams are helpful in the elucidation of this argument. Figure 1 shows the various combinations of research and graduate education, on the one hand, and undergraduate educational services, on the other, which can be produced with two different levels of resources in the higher educational sector. The boundaries of the feasible regions for given levels of resources are called transfor-

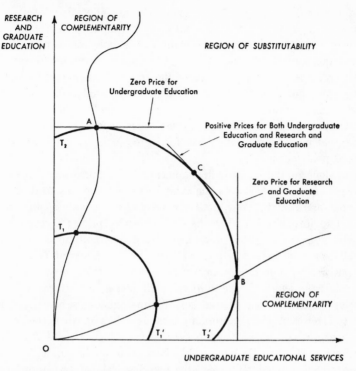

FIG. 1.—Combinations of undergraduate education and of research and graduate education showing the regions of complementarity and the region of substitutability.

mation curves; the curve $T_1 T_1'$ represents a lower level of resources than the curve $T_2 T_2'$. The sections of the transformation curves that bend outward, for example, between the abscissa and point B or between the ordinate and point A on the curve $T_2 T_2'$ represent a region in which more of both teaching and research can be obtained without using additional scarce resources; that is, they are regions in which teaching and research are complementary. If "firms" (educational institutions) in this country behave optimally, we will never observe them operating to the left of a point such as A or below a point such as B, since to the left of A more teaching can be obtained as a by-product of research without any further expenditure of resources, and, conversely, below B more research can be obtained as a "free" by-product. Nonetheless, the existence of such regions in the transformation curves explains why we will generally observe teaching and research being done together.

Even if society pays nothing for basic research, some of it will be undertaken in connection with undergraduate education, since more of the latter can be obtained from a given volume of resources if some of the former is also produced. Remember that I have adopted the simplification that both research and undergraduate educational services are measured in "quality-adjusted" units, so that what is here expressed as an increase in the quantity of teaching may simply represent an increase in the quality of teaching. Thus, at a zero "price" for research, the sector will operate at a point along the transformation curve such as *B,* where some quantity of research is nonetheless produced. This research, however, is of positive benefit to society as a whole; collectively, society should therefore be willing to pay for it. Moreover, it has been argued above that unless society *does* pay for it, too little will be produced from a social point of view.

The slope of the straight line tangent to the transformation curve at points *A, B,* or *C* represents the ratio between the prices paid for teaching and for research. Thus, at *A* the slope is zero, implying that nothing is paid for teaching but that there is a positive price for research; conversely, at *B* the slope is infinite, implying that nothing is paid for research but that there is a positive price for teaching; at *C* both prices are positive. *If a price per unit of research is set in such a way that it represents the value to society of an additional unit of research,* then the relative prices represent the socially optimal trade-offs between teaching and research.[22] A social optimum, then, is achieved when the price line is tangent to the transformation curve, for at such a point the quantity of teaching which would have to be given up to obtain an additional unit of research for given resources (the marginal rate of transformation between teaching and research) is exactly equal to the relative value which society places on the two products. Thus, if society subsidizes the higher educational sector to produce research in a socially optimal way, the sector will always operate at a point such as *C,* where teaching and research are substitutes in the sense that for a given level of resources devoted to higher education more research can only be obtained by providing fewer undergraduate educational services, and conversely.[23]

[22] If these trade-offs depend on how much of each product is produced and consumed, the lines will be curved. It may be argued, however, that they will be convex when viewed from the origin, and thus that none of the conclusions reached by approximating such trade-offs by constant "price" ratios is altered.

[23] This is simply an expression of the well-known principle that when only two products are produced, we will only observe profit-maximizing firms producing at a point at which the two are substitutes. If three or more products are produced, however, it is possible to observe their production at points where certain pairs may still be complementary, in the sense that more of both could be produced for a given level of resources, but only, of course, by giving up some of the third good. A three-good model would be appropriate if, for example, we were to treat graduate education and research as separate activities, but then it would be difficult to argue that research and *undergraduate* teaching were the complementary pair. The addition of professional and preprofessional educational services to the product mix, however, does complicate matters quite a bit. Nonetheless, the conclusions reached on the basis of the two-commodity model hold, in broad outline, and should provide a firm basis for subsequent analysis of more complicated models.

In general, of course, a subsidy to basic research and graduate instruction carried out in the higher educational sector will cause additional resources to flow into the sector. The extent to which this occurs will determine whether more or fewer undergraduate educational services will be supplied with than without such a subsidy to research. Figure 2 illustrates the two possibilities. If no subsidy to research is provided, the level of resources drawn into the higher educational sector will be sufficient to produce combinations of teaching and research along the transformation curve $T_1 T_1'$; in fact, a quantity OA of undergraduate educational services will be produced. If research is now subsidized, the price line will be twisted from its original vertical orientation and more resources will be drawn into the educational sector, shifting the transformation curve outward. If very few additional resources are drawn in, the transformation curve will shift outward only a very little, say to $T_2 T_2'$; at the particular relative price for teaching and research represented by the relationship between the research subsidy per unit and

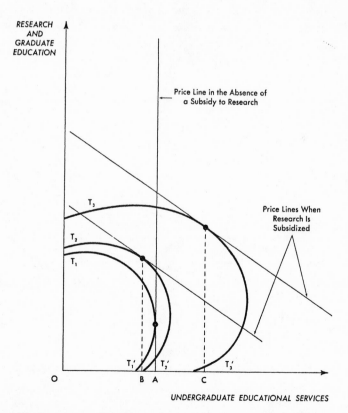

Fig. 2.—Illustration of two possible effects on the supply of undergraduate educational services resulting from a subsidy to research.

tuition, *less* undergraduate educational services—an amount *OB* rather than *OA*—will be provided. Of course, in general the provision of less teaching will cause a movement along the demand function for undergraduate educational services, so that, in a free market, tuition will rise, twisting the price line toward the vertical a bit so that somewhat more would be provided by the sector. On the other hand, if a great many resources flow into the higher educational sector as a result of the subsidy to research, the transformation curve will shift outward by a lot, say to $T_3T'_3$; at the relative price for teaching and research reflected in the slope of the price line, more of both, an amount of teaching represented by *OC* rather than *OA*, will be supplied. The greater supply of undergraduate educational services would, in a free market, however, cause a movement along the demand function so that tuition would fall, twisting the price line more toward the horizontal; the sector would operate so as to produce an amount between *OA* and *OC*.

Figure 3 illustrates how the interaction between tuition and the research subsidy would function in a free market situation. The curve $S_1S'_1$ is the supply curve of undergraduate educational services when research is unsubsidized; the upward slope of $S_1S'_1$ reflects the need for higher

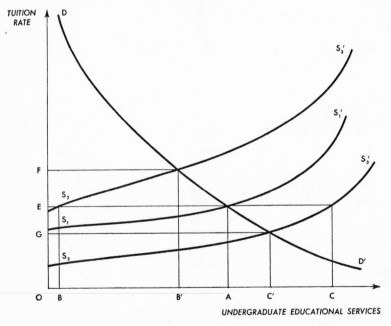

Fɪɢ. 3.—Illustration of the possible effects on tuition and the equilibrium quantity of undergraduate educational service when basic research is subsidized. Supply curves: $S_1S'_1$ = unsubsidized research; $S_2S'_2$ = subsidized research, resources in inelastic supply; $S_3S'_3$ = subsidized research, resources in elastic supply.

levels of tuition to call for a greater supply because scarce resources must be drawn into the higher educational sector from other productive uses in order to produce the additional quantity. If the demand for undergraduate educational services is represented by the curve DD', it can be seen that the market equilibrium tuition rate will be OE and the equilibrium quantity produced by the sector and used by students will be OA. For tuition rates below OE more undergraduate educational services will be demanded than are supplied; and for tuition rates above OE the sector would be prepared to supply more than students would want to use. When research is subsidized, more resources will be drawn into the higher educational sector, but now undergraduate educational services must compete within the sector for the use of these resources. Whether the supply curve for undergraduate educational services will rise or fall in relation to the supply curve when no subsidy is provided to research depends upon two factors: (1) how easy it is to substitute research for teaching within the sector and (2) how easily additional resources are drawn into the sector.

If the resources used by the higher educational sector are very scarce and/or exceptionally valuable in alternative uses, they will be *in inelastic supply* to the sector. It will require a large subsidy to research to attract additional resources, and the more easily research can be substituted for teaching, the more resources from the inadequately supplemented total will be drawn away from teaching in the sector. When resources are *in inelastic supply,* the supply curve for undergraduate educational services will lie above the curve for unsubsidized research, as $S_2 S_2'$ does. When resources are easily drawn into the educational sector, because either the right sort are not particularly scarce or because these resources are not exceptionally valuable in alternative uses, they are *in elastic supply.* Then a small subsidy to research will draw forth a great many additional resources; even though some of these are diverted to research, so many additional resources are available that more teaching *and* more research are both produced. In the case of an elastic supply of resources to the educational sector, the supply curve for undergraduate educational services will lie below the curve for unsubsidized research, as $S_3 S_3'$ does. Of course, the subsidy may alter the whole shape, not just the position of the curves as I have drawn them in figure 3; and it is possible for the curve for subsidized research to lie above that for unsubsidized research for part of its length and below it for the rest.[24]

___

[24] Since we would expect resources to become increasingly scarce as the sector expands, they might be in elastic supply for low levels of tuition and subsidy and in inelastic supply at high levels. This would have the effect of making the unsubsidized supply curve rise more rapidly and might cause the subsidized curve to rise still more rapidly, so that the curve for subsidized research would start out below the unsubsidized curve but would cross it at some point and continue above it. The

If resources are in inelastic supply, so that the supply curve becomes S_2S_2', the quantity of undergraduate educational services supplied will not fall to OB but only to OB' because tuition will rise to OF, causing some substitution away from research. Conversely, if resources are in elastic supply, subsidizing research will cause the supply curve to shift downward and to the right; but the quantity of undergraduate educational services will not rise to OC but only to OC', since the tuition rate will fall to OG, causing some of the increase to resources to be drawn out of teaching and into research.

I must candidly admit that I do not know what the elasticity of supply of resources to the educational sector is or how easy it is to switch resources in the educational sector from teaching to research (at least at the margin where the switch counts). The substitutability of resources within the sector depends on the production function for the various outputs produced by the sector. Provosts may have some intuitive notion of what this function is like for their own institutions, but I doubt that anyone has a clear grasp of the function for the sector as a whole. My own guess is that *at the margin* it is in fact easy to substitute, since many of the same people tend to do both undergraduate teaching and research. However, I would also guess that quality resources are not easily drawn into higher education in the short run, but in the long run they are; hence, subsidizing research in the short run will put a strong upward pressure on tuition rates, but in the long run it will not and may even tend to reduce them somewhat per constant-quality unit of undergraduate educational services supplied. The answer to the question of how market pricing of educational services would interact with subsidies to research depends heavily on quantitative knowledge which we simply do not now have.[25]

If society subsidizes basic research, such a subsidy may have the effect of making undergraduate education more expensive. Does this give rise to an argument for subsidizing the production of undergraduate educational services as well? Provided society does not subsidize basic research excessively, I think the answer is unequivocally "no." The resources used by undergraduate educational activities are in this case more expensive from society's standpoint, which now includes the provision of basic research as well as all the other alternatives to which the resources used in the higher educational sector could be put; and these resources should

---

analysis of the effects of a subsidy would then depend on the point at which the demand curve crossed the unsubsidized supply curve, above or below its intersection with the subsidized supply curve.

[25] Since there has been a very large expansion of higher education in the past two decades and, at the same time, only a modest increase in the *relative* incomes of professors and researchers, it would seem that the labor supply is quite elastic. Labor, of course, accounts for a large part of the resources used by higher education. I owe this point to D. Gale Johnson.

be valued accordingly even if, on other grounds, subsidies to undergraduate education are provided. The proper way to determine the subsidy to basic research constitutes, however, a grave difficulty. Presumably the subsidy should be set so that the expected rate of return to dollars invested in the last project undertaken is just equal to the rate of return on the next best alternative project, public or private. The measurement of such return, however, and proper allowance for risk from a social point of view raise problems which seem far from solution. It is possible that research will, under these circumstances, be overly subsidized, so that some case might be made for a compensating subsidy to undergraduate education if, indeed, subsidizing basic research caused the cost of obtaining such an education to rise. Too much at this point is unknown, however, for continued rational speculation.

Public and Private Institutions

Tuition, of course, does not function in anything like the way it would have to function in order to allocate resources between teaching and research in the manner described above. Not even in private institutions does it represent the value of resources used in teaching at the margin. The situation is far more serious for the allocation of resources among different types of institutions, particularly between the so-called public institutions, which charge little tuition or none at all, and private colleges and universities, which are generally subsidized in other ways and may receive a large measure of public support but which of necessity charge a good deal more for the undergraduate educational services they provide. Because most public support is channeled through institutions which pass the subsidy along in the form of below-cost charges to those lucky enough to qualify for admission, the public sector of higher education has grown spectacularly relative to the private sector. In 1950 approximately 50 percent of undergraduate enrollment was in publicly controlled institutions; by 1967–68 the percentage had risen to nearly 70 percent (O'Neill 1971, p. 71).

Former Chancellor Lawrence Kimpton of the University of Chicago is reported to have once said that is is difficult to sell a product when they're giving it away down the street for nothing. Not only has public support of higher education through markedly below-cost tuition at publicly controlled institutions effectively redirected scarce resources into the public sector of the industry, but it has surely had a depressing effect on the level of tuition private institutions have been able to charge. The downward pressure on tuition at private institutions has had several socially undesirable effects.

Most obviously, of course, rapid development of the public sector in the form of extremely low-tuition institutions has contributed to the serious financial condition in which private institutions now find themselves, both by holding down the revenues of private institutions and by increasing their costs by bidding up the prices of scarce factors of production. Much of the bidding up of prices would have occurred as the result of increased support to the sector as a whole in any case, but the manner in which that support has been directed has had the effect of virtually strangling the private part, which is caught between rising costs and its own inability to raise the prices it charges for its product. Much has been said about the advantages of a pluralistic system of higher education in America; it is believed by many that private institutions are more innovative and freer from political control and can supply a more diverse, if not a better, product. While this is not necessarily the case, to the extent that a pluralistic system does have value to society, destruction of the private sector is socially undesirable.[26]

Another, more subtle, effect of the downward pressure on tuition has to do with the nature of the product produced by the private sector. Major private institutions typically "rebate" a large fraction of the tuition income they receive to students in the form of aid. Partly this may be done out of sheer altruism—the desire that at least some poor but bright boys will have the opportunity to attend a Harvard or a Yale—but in part it is done to achieve a particular type of student body. A large part of what happens during the educational transformation, or at least some kinds of educational transformation, comes about through the contact of the student with others of similar age but dissimilar background and ability. Intelligence has, at least until recently, been thought to be the most important characteristic of a student who generates large external effects of this sort in other students around him. Since bright people are always in short supply, private institutions tend to "bid" for them by selectively reducing the costs of attending college. By holding down tuition levels at private universities, public support of higher education through publicly controlled institutions has reduced the possibility of such price discrimination and thereby the ability of private institutions to supply the distinctive product that results from the externalities generated by certain types of students. To be sure, these same students may continue to generate externalities in the public sector, but scale effects are surely important here, and it may be difficult to generate the kind of critical mass needed for the effect in a large public institution. Recent educational experiments in the public sector are, however, directed rather explicitly to solution of this problem.

[26] The undesirable redistributive effects of public support through low tuition have been mentioned earlier. As indicated, these effects may consist largely of an income transfer from low- and high-income groups to middle-income groups.

4. Policies and Directions for Research: Some Conclusions

> I felt that Evenus was to be congratulated if he really was master of this art and taught it at such a moderate fee. I should certainly plume myself and give myself airs if I understood these things; but in fact, gentlemen, I do not.—PLATO, *The Apology*

I must confess that when I began this study I had hoped that a policy paper, in the best sense, would emerge, but now I find what is largely a research proposal has come out instead. This section summarizes the main problems on which further research appears most needed and draws together some tentative conclusions of the preceding analysis for public policy.

Policies

There is a clear case for a national loan program with an income-contingent repayment plan to mitigate the worst effects of imperfections in the capital market and the market for risk-bearing. Without such a program, national in scope, students cannot finance higher education on terms comparable with investment in physical capital, nor can they insure themselves against the risk of a low lifetime income from which to repay an ordinary loan. Without such a program, the demand for undergraduate educational services will be below the level desirable from society's standpoint. Programs on a university-by-university or college-by-college basis cannot begin to solve the problem of demand deficiency due to market imperfections.

Loan programs by themselves, however, may not increase demand sufficiently in view of possible externalities of higher education. To the extent that further subsidies are found socially desirable, they should go directly to the students and not, except under most unusual circumstances, to institutions for disbursement or for general support of undergraduate educational facilities at below-cost tuition. Special consideration should be given to the possibility of subsidizing women's education so long as the private family remains a central institution of our society and women continue to play the central role in the family that they have in the past. Such subsidization has as its goal greater equality of opportunity among members of succeeding generations, as well as their enhanced educability.

It is in the best interest of society and private institutions of higher education that there be full marginal cost pricing of undergraduate educational services. Publicly supported and controlled institutions will lose from such a policy, although their losses may be substantially mitigated by removal of demand deficiency due to market imperfections. A policy for all institutions of equal prices for equal services should be encouraged, leaving open, however, the possibility of systematic price discrimination among individual students through selective aid, if such a pricing policy is necessary to achieve a certain quality of product. The aid given to some students, however, should be fully covered by higher charges to their fellow students, who benefit from the higher-quality education the presence of those aided makes possible.

Accreditation agencies need to be controlled, publicly or by institutions of higher education themselves, so that they do not stifle imaginative and innovative solutions to higher education's problems and prevent the immense diversity of which American higher education is capable from occurring.

Public support for basic research in all disciplines (not just those momentarily fashionable) through individual project support or through institutional support seems warranted; however, the appropriate level of support will depend on the expected benefits to society of such research, and these benefits are not now measurable with any degree of confidence, let alone precision.

Finally, it would seem both appropriate and desirable for the major national research universities to mount a sizable research program designed to discover answers to some of the questions about the nature of education and its production which, unanswered, preclude more definitive policy recommendations.

Directions of Research

Two and a half millenia ago Socrates strove to understand the nature of the educational transformation. It left him puzzled and his contemporaries in worse condition. What was it beyond training in specific skills that happened to a human being? It is easy to understand the training of a horse or a dog, but the education of a person is not so well defined. What are the contributions of inherited abilities, family background, previous training and education, surroundings, teachers, fellow students, time, and effort? What differences do the educational services provided by a college or university make? Is the transformation impeded by high student-faculty ratios for some people but not for others? Are particular educational environments better for some people and different ones better for other people? Are there different kinds of educational transformations? Is what happens quantitatively measurable along a single axis, or are several dimensions needed to quantify the result? Can it be quantified at all? We have made little progress in the last 2,500 years in answering these questions.[27] It is possible that many of them are unanswerable; yet

---

[27] Two examples of the sort of thing which has been done in recent years are Astin (1968) and Griliches and Mason (in this Supplement). The Astin paper is

these questions lie at the very heart of the economic issues discussed in this essay and are central to many social issues of fundamental importance.

A related series of questions concerns the role of the family in the intergenerational transmission both of acquired ability and of values and culture. Do we understand this process? Can we disentangle genetically determined abilities and characteristics from acquired ones? It used to be thought that the answer to this question was simple; now we know better. To what extent does a model based on the maximization of a single "decision maker's" utility function, containing the utility or consumption of other family members, explain family behavior, especially its behavior with respect to numbers of children, investment in them, and allocation of the woman's time? If such a model does account for observed family behavior, can it also be used to measure the degree to which the current generation's investment in their children falls short, if it does, of what the next generation would have invested in themselves had they been in a position of control? How does the investment take place and what is the role of each parent? Have these roles been changing, and how will such changes as have been taking place affect the intergenerational transfer and the extent to which it is optimal from a social point of view? Can we formulate a clear and consistent set of principles for determining the social interest and its possible divergence from the private interests of the current generation? Economists working on growth have been seeking such a set of principles for some time, but I do not find an adequate formulation in any of the literature with which I am familiar.

What are the externalities of higher education? Can they be measured? This is Friedman's challenge. Economists have made some progress in recent years in identifying and measuring the external effects of elementary and secondary education, but the externalities of higher education, if any, are much more subtle and elusive. It seems certain that they are of a generally noneconomic character, and their elucidation and measurement may require quite different ways of looking at human and social behavior than those which economists find congenial. Unless, however, the external benefits to society can be measured and valued, even if only crudely, the case for subsidies to higher education remains weak.

Another area in which both conceptual formulation and measurement are required is in the analysis of the production function and process in the higher educational sector. It may be necessary to distinguish among different types of institutions, and it is certainly necessary to distinguish a variety of outputs of different qualities. Can the quality differences

---

relatively naïve from a statistical point of view, overlooking the serious problems arising from the simultaneous determination by several relationships of a number of variables involved in the analysis. The Griliches-Mason paper is more sophisticated statistically, but the authors encounter severe measurement problems in the data they analyze.

be quantified? What are the trade-offs, for instance, between research and graduate education, undergraduate educational services, professional educational services, and applied research? How do different disciplines interact within the same institution? Do the trade-offs differ from one discipline to another, or is there a common structure? How can the different outputs be measured? What is the relationship of these outputs to the inputs of such scarce resources as senior faculty, junior faculty, secretarial and clerical support, administrative services, library and computer facilities, laboratories and equipment? Numbers of classroom hours at various levels (graduate, undergraduate, seminar), numbers of doctoral dissertations supervised, degrees awarded—these are readily available; some universities collect data on such other faculty outputs as papers and books published, outside lectures given, and editorial work. While individual data of this sort are likely to be quite unreliable ("noisy"), departmental statistics may be better. Inputs at the departmental level— types of faculty, supporting services, expenditures in various categories— can be assembled. Allocation of overhead facilities does cause problems, however; how are the library and computer facilities to be charged, and what account needs to be taken of the outputs of other departments in the inputs of a particular one? Could sufficient comparability across some category of colleges and universities for a given discipline (say, for the twenty major departments of economics) be obtained to permit estimation of a multiple-product production function?[28] Despite obvious imperfections in the degree to which these different measures represent actual outputs and inputs and lack of comparability in terms of quality, is it clear a priori that such an investigation would produce results of little or no value?

Finally, what are the characteristics of the supply of factors of production to the higher educational sector? Are faculty resources in elastic or inelastic supply to the sector? How do career choices depend upon expected incomes? What are the rates of response to changes in relative income expectations? Recent work on the supply of doctorates and the demand for holders of the doctorate by other sectors of the economy is largely deficient in that it neglects or gives little consideration to price effects. Freeman's work (1971, esp. pp. 160–79) is a notable exception in this respect. We are closer to answers here than to any of the other

[28] For an example of the estimation of a production function where "output" is defined in terms of a vector of quantities rather than a single homogeneous commodity, see Eads, Nerlove, and Raduchel (1969). Note that, although this paper involves estimation of the cost function rather than the production function itself, the Shephard-Uzawa duality theorem permits inference about the production function from the cost function. Despite a number of quite difficult statistical problems, the results do allow an analysis of the trade-offs between different "bundles" of outputs, defined in terms of types of aircraft used and a number of separate characteristics of local air service.

questions raised above, but the answers to this set of questions need to be put together with an analysis of the production process in the higher educational sector in order to understand the effects of subsidies to research, full-cost tuition, and the changing structure of the demand for trained manpower in the economy as a whole.

References

Arrow, Kenneth J. *Essays in the Theory of Risk-Bearing.* Chicago: Markham, 1971.

Astin, A. W. "Undergraduate Achievement and Institutional 'Excellence.'" *Science,* August 16, 1968, pp. 661–68.

Becker, Gary S. *Human Capital: A Theoretical and Empirical Analysis with Special Reference to Education.* New York: Nat. Bur. Econ. Res., 1964.

Bolton, R. E. "The Economics and Financing of Higher Education in the United States." In *The Economics and Financing of Higher Education in the United States: A Compendium of Papers,* pp. 1–104. Congress, Joint Econ. Committee, 91st Cong., 1st sess., 1969.

Bowen, William G. *The Economics of the Major Private Universities.* Berkeley, Calif.: Carnegie Commission Higher Educ., 1968.

Brewster, Kingman. Statement on the Yale Tuition Postponement Option. Press release. New Haven, Conn., February 6, 1971.

Buchanan, J. M., and Devletoglou, N. E. *Academia in Anarchy.* New York: Basic, 1970.

Denison, Edward F. "An Aspect of Inequality of Opportunity." *J.P.E.* 78 (September/October 1970): 1195–1202.

Eads, George; Nerlove, Marc; and Raduchel, William. "A Long-Run Cost Function for the Local Service Airline Industry: An Experiment in Nonlinear Estimation." *Rev. Econ. and Statis.* 51 (August 1969): 258–70.

Freeman, Richard B. *The Market for College-trained Manpower: A Study in the Economics of Career Choice.* Cambridge, Mass.: Harvard Univ. Press, 1971.

Friedman, Milton. "The Role of Government in Higher Education." In *Economics and the Public Interest,* edited by Robert A. Solo, pp. 123–44. New Brunswick, N.J.: Rutgers Univ. Press, 1955. Reprinted as chap. 6 of Friedman, M. *Capitalism and Freedom.* Chicago: Univ. Chicago Press, 1962.

———. "The Higher Schooling in America." *Public Interest,* no. 11 (Spring 1968), pp. 108–12.

Hansen, W. Lee, and Weisbrod, Burton A. *Benefits, Costs, and Finance of Public Higher Education.* Chicago: Markham, 1969.

Hartman, Robert W. *Credit for College: Public Policy for Student Loans.* New York: McGraw-Hill, 1971.

Hirschleifer, J. "The Private and Social Value of Information and the Reward to Inventive Activity." *A.E.R.* 61 (September 1971): 561–74.

Jencks, Christopher, and Riesman, David. *The Academic Revolution.* New York: Doubleday, 1968.

Jenny, H. H., and Wynn, G. R. "Expenditure Expectations for Private Colleges." In *The Economics and Financing of Higher Education in the United States: A Compendium of Papers,* pp. 440–64. Congress, Joint Econ. Committee 91st Cong., 1st sess., 1969. (*a*)

———. "Short-Run Cost Variations in Institutions of Higher Learning." Ibid., pp. 261–94. (*b*)

Kaysen, Carl. "Some General Observations on the Pricing of Higher Education." In *Higher Education in the United States: The Economic Problems*, edited by S. E. Harris, pp. 55–60. Cambridge, Mass.: Harvard Univ. Press, 1960.

Kessel, R. "The A.M.A. and the Supply of Physicians." *Law and Contemporary Problems* 35 (Spring 1970): 267–83.

Knight, Frank H. *Risk, Uncertainty and Profit*. Boston: Houghton Mifflin, 1921.

Koerner, J. D. "The Case of Marjorie Webster." *Public Interest*, no. 20 (Summer 1970), pp. 40–64.

Manne, Henry G. "Scholars vs. Profits." *Barron's*, August 25, 1969, p. 1.

O'Neill, June. *Resource Use in Higher Education*. Berkeley, Calif.: Carnegie Commission Higher Educ., 1971.

Orwig, M. D., ed. *Financing Higher Education: Alternatives for the Federal Government*. Iowa City, Iowa: American Coll. Testing Program, 1971.

Plato. "The Apology." In *The Last Days of Socrates*, translated by Hugh Tredennick, pp. 45–76. Baltimore: Penguin, 1959.

Roush, G. J. "What Will Become of the Past?" In "The Future of the Humanities." *Daedalus* 98 (Summer 1969): 641–53.

Schultz, Theodore W. *Investment in Human Capital: The Role of Education and of Research*. New York: Free Press, 1971.

Shell, Karl. "Notes on the Educational Opportunity Bank." *Nat. Tax J.* 23 (June 1970): 214–20.

Shell, Karl; Fisher, Franklin M.; Foley, Duncan K.; and Friedlander, Ann F. "The Educational Opportunity Bank: An Economic Analysis of a Contingent Repayment Loan Program for Higher Education." *Nat. Tax J.* 21 (March 1968): 2–45.

Tobin, James, and Pugash, James. "The Economics of the Tuition Postponement Option." *Yale Daily News*, February 10, 1971.

U.S. Panel on Educational Innovation. *Educational Opportunity Bank* (Zacharias Committee Report). Washington: Government Printing Office, 1967.

Weisbrod, Burton A. "Education and Investment in Human Capital." *J.P.E.* 70, suppl. (October 1962): 106–23.

Yale University. "1971–72 Tuition Postponement Option Plan," and "Questions and Answers: The Yale Tuition Postponement Option." Brochures. New Haven, Conn., July 1, 1971.

Schooling and Inequality from Generation to Generation

Samuel Bowles

Harvard University

I. Introduction

For at least half a century schooling has been the chosen instrument of American social reformers. More and better schooling has been seen as an antidote to the brutalization of industrial life. More equal access to schooling has been sought as a powerful vehicle for the equalization of economic opportunity, the redistribution of income, and the elimination of poverty.

Until recently, the choice of education as the instrument of those who sought greater equality in the United States has not been based on any direct evidence of its efficacy in bringing higher incomes to the children of the poor. Rather, the popularity of educational reform among liberals and progressives stemmed from more political considerations: educational equalization seemed to offer a strategy for achieving the greater social equality that was politically viable. More equal education, it was confidently asserted, could achieve significantly greater equality of economic opportunity and incomes without challenging the basic economic institutions of society and without requiring any major redistribution of capital.

Yet over the past decade, important empirical support has been forthcoming for those who see education as—to quote Horace Mann—"the great equalizer." First, the *possibility* of more equal schooling achieving a more equal distribution of income seemed to be confirmed by studies of the determinants of individual earnings.[1] The earnings functions estimated in these studies demonstrated a strong relationship between years of school-

This paper represents part of a larger work on alienation, class, and schooling that I am undertaking jointly with Herbert Gintis. I gratefully acknowledge his help and that of Valerie Nelson and Janice Weiss. The work presented here has been financially supported by the Social and Rehabilitation Service of the U.S. Department of Health, Education, and Welfare. An earlier draft of this paper was presented at the Far Eastern Meetings of the Econometric Society in Tokyo in June 1970.

[1] Hanoch (1967); Mincer (in press) is the most comprehensive and recent study.

ing and earnings. For white males 25–34 years old, for example, each additional year of schooling appeared to result in around $350 additional annual income.[2] It seemed obvious that if more schooling could be given to the children of the poor, a significant increase in their incomes would result.

Second, the *actual role* of schooling as an equalizer seemed to be confirmed by recent studies of the intergenerational transmission of economic status. The social background of individuals was shown to exercise a relatively minor impact upon the number of years of schooling attained. Measures of parents' occupational and educational status appeared to explain only between a quarter and a third of the variance of years of schooling attained (Blau and Duncan 1967; Duncan 1968; Duncan, Featherman, and Duncan 1968; Hauser 1969, 1970). Further, the same studies seemed to show that additional schooling exerts a major effect upon earnings or occupational status *independent of the social class background of the individual.* This last finding is of central importance, for it seems to lay to rest a common objection to the early earnings functions, namely, that the apparently large impact of schooling upon earnings might be a statistical artifact resulting from the positive correlation between the social class background and the level of schooling of individuals.

These recent studies ran contrary to a large and venerable body of sociological literature on the relation between social class and schooling. Earlier studies had asserted that social class was a major determinant of the amount, quality, and vocational orientation of the educational experience of individuals (for example, Warner, Havighurst, and Loeb 1944; Hollingshead 1949). Yet the more recent work of the Duncans and their associates was based on far larger, more comprehensive samples, and used more rigorous and systematic statistical techniques. The older view of social class and schooling has gradually been discredited.

The confidence in education inspired by the demonstration that schooling is a major determinant of earnings underlay the basic strategy of the U.S. government's effort to combat poverty. In addition, the earnings-functions studies gave strong support to what has been called the human capital interpretation of inequality (Mincer 1958; Becker 1964). Education and training programs consumed the lion's share of War on Poverty funds. Underlying this allocation of resources was a new view of poverty. It explains the poverty of the poor by their low productivity, and this, in turn, is attributed to their low levels of schooling and training (Schultz 1966). Inadequate education is seen as the problem, and more education as the solution.

The empirical basis for this position, strong as it seemed at first, is no

[2] The figure is an average over all years of schooling (Hanoch 1967) and refers to the nonsouthern region.

longer uncontested. Evidence has begun to accumulate challenging the efficacy of schooling as an equalizer of incomes. Hanoch (1967) found that the internal rate of return to increased schooling (except for graduate studies) was considerably lower for blacks than for whites. Extending Hanoch's work, Weiss (1970) estimated earnings functions for black workers having 12 or fewer years of schooling. He found no statistically significant monetary return to additional schooling except for workers in the 35–44-year age group. Harrison's work (1969) with more recent data has done nothing to overturn the impression of negligible monetary returns to education for blacks. But low returns to schooling evidently are not confined to blacks. Using data on draft rejects—a group not atypical of the poverty population—Hansen, Weisbrod, and Scanlon (1970) estimated that the difference in annual earnings associated with an additional year of schooling was a paltry $62.[3]

To evaluate the conflicting evidence on the role of schooling as a vehicle for the equalization of opportunity and income I have estimated a model of individual earnings determination and intergenerational transmission of economic status. Specifically, I estimated a recursive model similar to that used by Duncan and his associates:

$$\text{EDUC} = ax, \tag{1}$$

$$\text{INC} = b_1\text{EDUC} + bx, \tag{2}$$

as well as the reduced form equation:

$$\text{INC} = cx. \tag{3}$$

The following notation is used: EDUC = respondent's years of schooling; INC = respondent's annual income; x = a vector of variables measuring the respondent's socioeconomic origins. All variables are expressed in normalized form. In each equation there is a stochastic disturbance term which I have omitted here for simplicity of presentation.

I will consider three measures of the relationship among social class, schooling, and income. The first is the fraction of variance of EDUC explained by the socioeconomic background variables—a measure of the extent to which an individual's years of schooling is predetermined by his social and economic origins. The second is b_1, the regression coefficient of years of schooling in the earnings function. The third is the difference in the fraction of variance explained in equations (2) and (3), or the increment in the R^2 associated with the introduction of the years-of-schooling variable. Because of the unambiguous causal ordering of the variables, this third measure is a legitimate indicator of the extent to which the dispersion of years of schooling is associated with the dispersion of income

---

[3] The figure is the regression coefficient of years of schooling in an equation predicting income. Other variables in the equation are age and race.

independently of the causally prior dispersion of socioeconomic background.[4]

While the estimated model presented below must be seen as provisional and based to some extent on conjecture, two conclusions of general importance seem warranted:

First, failure to adequately measure the social class background of individuals has led a number of researchers to premature and probably seriously misleading conclusions concerning the role of schooling in the process of income determination. The inadequate measurement of social background has arisen both from excluding important dimensions of social class and from erroneously measuring aspects of class actually incorporated in the models. I will deal with these two problems in Sections II and III, respectively. The results presented in Section IV—even bearing in mind their conjectural nature—are sufficient to recommend considerable skepticism concerning the credibility of estimates that take inadequate account of the twin problems of specification bias and erroneous measurement.

Second, my estimates—both of the model itself and of the remaining biases due to errors of measurement and specification—suggest that social class background is considerably more important as a determinant of both educational attainment and economic success than has been indicated in recent analogous statistical treatments by Duncan and others. Likewise, my results seriously question the putative efficacy of schooling as an instrument for the equalization of incomes. The economic return to additional schooling for individuals of a given social class background will be shown to be considerably less than the simple relationship between schooling and earnings would suggest.

II. The Specification of Socioeconomic Background

I will begin with an obvious point: assessment of the role of schooling in the intergenerational transfer of economic status requires a rather complete understanding of the ways in which the transfer of status takes place. More specifically, estimation of equations (1)–(3) is likely to yield biased results unless we are able to specify fully those characteristics associated with a person's family background that might have some plausible direct or indirect causal relationship to the likelihood of the person earning high income in his adult life.

Equations (1)–(3) can be estimated as a recursive system only because the relationship represented by equation (1)—the determination of years of schooling attained—is postulated as causally prior to that represented by equation (2)—the determination of income. While this seems a reasonable assumption, the unbiased estimation of equation (2) requires the

---

[4] The three measures M_1, M_2, and M_3 are not independent: $M_3 = M_2^2 (1 - M_1)$.

highly unlikely complementary assumption that the error term in the first equation is uncorrelated with that in the second. The most obvious source of bias is that some dimensions of the social background of the individual exert a positive direct effect upon both the level of schooling attained by the individual and his later income. If these aspects of the social background are not measured by the socioeconomic background variables, the level of schooling achieved (EDUC) will serve as a proxy for these unmeasured variables in equation (2). For this reason the coefficient of EDUC will be overestimated. For example, if parental wealth has a direct positive effect both upon the level of schooling attained and the later income of the individual, the coefficient of the schooling variable in the income-determination equation will represent not only the direct effect of education upon income, but part of the direct effect of unmeasured parental wealth upon the respondent's income as well. Thus unless we are able to completely specify and accurately measure all of the relevant background variables, x, all three of our measures of the role of schooling in income determination will be biased: The proportion of variance of years of schooling attained explained by social background will be underestimated, the regression coefficient of the years of schooling variable will be overestimated, and the increment in the explained variance of income associated with the introduction of the schooling variable will be overestimated.

Because available data do not allow the complete specification of the relevant social background of individuals, existing estimates of the role of schooling in the intergenerational transfer of economic status are biased, as I will show in this section. More concretely, I will argue that the absence of measures of family income, parental wealth, and the position of the parents in the hierarchy of work relations has systematically biased the resulting estimates in the direction of showing schooling to have a powerful effect upon income independent of the socioeconomic background of the individual. In the next section, I will show that even those variables that *are* frequently included in studies of income determination—father's occupational status score and father's educational level—are measured with a substantial degree of error, thus exacerbating the above biases due to specification errors.

Family income and wealth are obvious candidates for inclusion in the equation predicting years of schooling attained. Both measure the ability of parents to finance the direct and indirect costs of their children's education. Both probably are associated with dimensions of the value orientations and aspiration levels of the home not fully captured in the available socioeconomic status variables measuring father's occupation and education. Likewise, no compelling argument can be adduced for their exclusion from the income-determination equations. Quite the contrary. A direct relation of parental wealth to individual income—operating through inheritance— would seem an obvious aspect of the process of the intergenerational transmission of economic status. Moreover, plausible conjectures suggest that the relationship between parental wealth and respondent's income may be of considerable magnitude.

Consider the following model, with all variables expressed in normalized form: $NW = f_0\ PNW$; $INC = f_1\ NW + f_2\ EDUC + fx$; and the reduced form: $INC = f'_0\ PNW + f'x$, where $NW =$ respondent's net worth, and $PNW =$ parents' net worth. All other variables are as defined in the Introduction. Notice that the model postulates no direct relation between parents' net worth and the income of the respondent; the influence of PNW upon INC is totally mediated by NW; likewise, the linear additive form precludes interaction between PNW and EDUC and x. Last, I have not postulated a direct partial relation between PNW and EDUC. If we now assume that the variance of PNW explains 25 percent of respondent's net worth, $f_0 = .5$. Further assume an average rate of return, i, of 7 percent, and that the standard deviation of NW is roughly three times as large as that for income. (This latter assumption is based on data from the 1967 Survey of Economic Opportunity [see Cromwell, in preparation].) Then $f_1 = i\ (S_{NW}/S_{INC}) = .21$, and the normalized regression coefficient of PNW in a reduced-form income equation is $\partial_{INC}/\partial_{PNW} = f'_0 = f_0 f_1 \approx .10$. Incorporation of even a small direct partial relation between parental net worth and respondent's years of schooling would raise f'_0 to above .15, or only slightly less than the normalized partial regression coefficient of father's occupational status on son's income (estimated in Section IV).

The biases resulting from the exclusion of parental income and wealth measures would be minor if these variables were highly correlated with the parental occupation and education variables on which data are ordinarily available. But this is not the case. In the sample used here and originally studied by Duncan and his associates, the respondents' occupational status score and educational level together explain only 32 percent of the variance of income of non-Negro males of nonfarm background, aged 35–44 years.[5]

The statistical association between net worth and the socioeconomic status variables ordinarily used is similarly weak, as the correlation coefficients in table 1 indicate, for occupational status and years of schooling together explain only 5 percent of the variance of net worth.[6]

A third excluded dimension of the socioeconomic background of respondents is the parents' position in the hierarchy of work relations. The importance of this dimension can best be understood in the framework of the following model of intergenerational status transmission:[7]

---

[5] Correlations from Duncan et al. (1968) have been adjusted upward to account for errors in measurement of all three variables. This particular age group seems most relevant to our concerns here as it is the group most likely to have young children in the home.

[6] These figures would be somewhat higher if the measurement errors in the variables were taken into account.

[7] The model outlined here is developed in more detail in Bowles (in press).

TABLE 1

ZERO-ORDER CORRELATIONS AMONG MEASURES OF SOCIOECONOMIC STATUS,
NORTHEAST CENSUS REGION, NONFARM HOUSEHOLDS
HEADED BY MALES, AGED 25–44

Variable	(1)	(2)	(3)	(4)
1. Income	1.0	...	...	...
2. Years of school	.375	1.0	...	...
3. Occupational SES	.384	.556	1.0	...
4. Net worth	.314	.184	.177	1.0

SOURCE.—Cromwell (in preparation). Data based on the 1967 Survey of Economic Opportunity tapes made available by the U.S. Office of Economic Opportunity. Households headed by males in the military service or enrolled in school are excluded. The sample size is 596. I am grateful to Cromwell for making these data available to me.

The social relations of production characteristic of advanced capitalist societies (and many socialist societies) are most clearly illustrated in the bureaucracy and hierarchy of the modern corporation.[8] Occupational roles in the capitalist economy may be grouped according to the degree of independence and control exercised by the person holding the job. The degree of occupational self-direction is positively associated with, but by no means completely determined by, the worker's position in the hierarchy of work relations. The personality attributes associated with the adequate performance of jobs in occupational categories defined in this broad way differ considerably, some apparently requiring independence and internal discipline, and others emphasizing such traits as obedience, predictability, and willingness to subject oneself to external controls.

These personality attributes are developed at a young age in the family and, to a lesser extent, in secondary socialization institutions such as schools. They are reinforced in the day-to-day experience of adults. Because people tend to marry within their own class, both parents are likely to have a similar set of these fundamental personality traits. Thus children of parents occupying a given position in the occupational hierarchy grow up in homes where child-rearing methods and perhaps even the physical surroundings tend to develop personality characteristics appropriate to adequate job performance in the occupational roles of the parents.[9] The

[8] Max Weber referred (1946) to bureaucracy as the "most rational offspring" (p. 254) of discipline, and remarked that "military discipline is the ideal model for the modern capitalist factory" (p. 261).

[9] Much of the evidence for this assertion is from three major studies of occupational self-direction and parental values by Melvin Kohn which he summarized in 1969. He concludes: "Whether consciously or not, parents tend to impart to their children lessons derived from the conditions of life of their own class—and thus help to prepare their children for a similar class position . . . . The conformist values and orientation of lower- and working-class parents . . . are inappropriate for training children to deal with the problems of middle class and professional life. . . . The family, then, functions as a mechanism for perpetuating inequality" (p. 200). On class differences in child rearing with respect to the importance of obedience, see Dolger and Ginandes (1946) and Kohn (1964). See also the study of differences in child-rearing practices in families

children of managers and professionals are taught self-reliance within a broad set of constraints (Winterbottom 1953; Kohn 1963); the children of production-line workers are taught obedience.

While this relation between parents' class position and child's personality attributes operates primarily in the home, it is reinforced by schools and other social institutions. Thus, for example, the authoritarian social relations of working-class high schools complement the discipline-oriented early socialization patterns experienced by working-class children. The relatively greater freedom of wealthy suburban schools extends and formalizes the early independence training characteristic of upper-class families.

In this interpretation, the educational system serves less to change the results of the primary socialization in the home than to ratify them and render them in adult form. The complementary relationship between family socialization and schools serves to reproduce social class differences in personality development from generation to generation.

The operation of the labor market translates these differences into income inequalities and occupational hierarchies. The personality traits, values, and expectations characteristic of different class cultures play a major role in determining an individual's success in gaining a high income. The apparent contribution of schooling to higher income, far from being the result of the independent role of schooling in the development of cognitive capacities, seems to be explained primarily by the personality characteristics of those who have higher educational attainments.[10]

In this view, the hierarchy of work relations is replicated in social class differences in values and child rearing. Because of the important role of affective characteristics as determinants of success both in school and on the job, class differences in parental values and child-rearing practices play an important role in replicating the class structure in the next generation. If this interpretation is correct, the failure of studies of income determination to adequately measure the parents' position in the work hierarchy results in an underestimate of the impact of socioeconomic background upon adult economic success and an overestimate of the effects of schooling.

Once again, the exclusion of a measure of the parents' position in the hierarchy of work relations would be of little import if this dimension of family background were highly correlated with the socioeconomic status score of the parents' occupation or with the parents' education. But this does not appear to be the case. Melvin Kohn has shown (1969, p. 166) that the relation between occupational self-direction and parental values (self-

---

headed by bureaucrats as opposed to entrepreneurs by Maccoby, Gibbs, et al. (1954) and Miller and Swanson (1958). While the existence of class differences in child rearing is supported by most of the available data (but see Lewis 1965), the stability of these differences over time has been questioned by Bronfenbrenner (1963).

[10] This view is elaborated in Gintis (1971). For other studies stressing the noncognitive dimensions of the schooling experience, see Parsons (1959) and Dreeben (1968).

direction vs. conformity) is statistically significant even when the occupational status score of the parents is controlled.

The existence of biases in estimates of the schooling-income-socioeconomic-background relationship arising from the failure to consider relevant dimensions of socioeconomic background does not by itself require that the estimates be rejected. But on the other hand, one cannot place much confidence in the existing estimates unless a compelling argument can be made that these biases are small. No such case has been made—or even seriously attempted—by the main contributors to the literature on intergenerational status transmission and individual income determination.

I have attempted to eliminate one source of specification bias by hypothesizing a parents' income variable and developing estimates of the relevant row and column in the product-moment matrix on the basis of data from a variety of sources. The methods used are described in the Appendix. The crucial assumption used in the estimation is that the zero-order correlation between parents' income, on the one hand, and respondent's income, on the other, is equal to the correlation between father's occupation and respondent's occupational status.[11]

Available data do not allow use of variables even hypothetically measuring parental wealth and the position of the parents in the hierarchy of work relations.

I turn now to the problem arising from erroneous measurement of those socioeconomic background variables ordinarily available.

III. Measurement Errors

The above biases are due to the incomplete specification of the model and would arise even if the variables I am forced to use were accurately measured. Unfortunately, the available data contain serious inaccuracies.

The presence of errors in measurement in the variables used lowers the explanatory power of the equations, and ordinarily biases downward the regression coefficients of the erroneously measured variables. Because the degree of error in the measurement of the father's occupation and education variables greatly exceeds that in the respondent's own years-of-schooling variable, we are led to expect that failure to take systematic account of these errors will lead to an underestimation of the importance of socioeconomic background as an influence upon educational attainments and later income. The relative importance of schooling as a determinant of income will be correspondingly overestimated.

---

[11] The resulting raw (uncorrected) correlation is .202, or slightly lower than the value of .258 found for this correlation (from the matrix used by Conlisk [1968]) in the small sample used by the Berkeley Guidance Study. That study somewhat supports the figures used in this essay, nonetheless the conjectural nature of this aspect of the exercise should be obvious.

In this section I attempt to estimate the magnitudes of the error components in each variable and to develop a method of estimating equations (1) and (2) that will reduce the biases due to the errors-in-variables problem.

I will use these estimates in Section IV to eliminate some of the measurement-error bias from a model of intergenerational status transmission and income determination.

The data used in this essay are from a U.S. Census survey of slightly more than 20,000 males 20–64 years of age in 1962.[12] Respondents were asked to report their own occupation and level of educational attainment (in years) as well as the occupation and educational level of their father or family head. Additional data collected included the number of siblings of the respondent and his income in the year previous to the survey. Because the importance of family size has been stressed by many students of mobility, I have included the number of siblings reported by the respondent as a measure of social background. The occupation of the respondents' fathers was scaled according to the Duncan socioeconomic status index. An index of years of schooling is the sole measure of educational attainment.

These data were collected by surveys and often required the respondent to provide retrospective information such as his father's occupation when the respondent was 16 years old. Quite apart from errors in responses likely in these cases, some of the data do not correspond exactly to the models which I seek to estimate. This errors-in-variables problem is to be distinguished from the problems associated with the inadequate specification of equations in the model due to the above-mentioned incomplete measurement of the social class of the respondent. Confining attention to the incomplete set of variables on which we do have data, we find that the data available often do not measure what they purport to measure, and further, that the measure itself, even if accurately observed, does not correspond to the variable in our model. For example, in a model of the effect of education upon economic success, we would like to measure respondent's permanent income, yet our observations purport to measure only annual income. We may generalize the problem as follows: For each variable, x, and for any individual observation, i, we have

$$x'_i = x_i + u_i, \tag{4}$$

where x_i = the true value of the variable, x'_i = the observed value of the variable, and u_i = the error in measurement. We know that errors of this type will bias the least-squares estimates of the regression coefficients as well as the coefficient of determination.

[12] Blau and Duncan (1967, pp. 10–19) give a more complete description of the sample properties. I will discuss estimates only for the group 25–34 years of age.

In order to eliminate the biases arising from the discrepancies between the observed and true values of the variables used, I will estimate the zero-order correlation coefficients among the true variables and use these corrected correlation coefficients to estimate the model of mobility.[13] If we assume that the errors, u_i, are uncorrelated with the true values, x_i, then it follows that[14]

$$\mathrm{var}(x') = \mathrm{var}(x) + \mathrm{var}(u). \qquad (5)$$

Now define r_j, the correlation of the true value of x_j, with its observed value, as

$$r_j = \sqrt{\frac{\mathrm{var}\, x_j}{\mathrm{var}\, x'_j}}, \qquad (6)$$

or the square root of the fraction of the variance of x'_j, the observed measure, which is accounted for by the variance of x_j, the true measure. Then the observed correlation between any pair of variables x_k and x_j, r'_{kj}, may be written as a function of the true correlation, r_{kj}, the correlations between the true and observed variables, r_k and r_j, and the correlation of the errors in the two observed variables, r_{ukj}:

$$r'_{kj} = r_{kj}\, r_k\, r_j + r_{ukj}\sqrt{1 - r_k^2}\,\sqrt{1 - r_j^2}. \qquad (7)$$

The corrected correlation coefficients, r_{kj}, will be used as the normalized $X'X$ matrix to estimate the model of class immobility. (See Appendix for corrected and uncorrected correlation matrices.)

For each variable I attempt to introduce independent data concerning the degree of error in the measures that I have used in my regression equations. While the information used to estimate the accuracy of the measures is itself subject to serious question arising from differences in samples, ages of respondents, and variable definitions, I believe that the errors arising from erroneous estimates of reliability are considerably less serious than those which would result if I were simply to use the uncorrected data.

I will consider the error in each variable in turn, and then deal with those pairs of variables for which the errors are likely to be correlated. (The somewhat complicated processes of estimating these values are described in more detail in the Appendix.)

I turn first to problems concerning the definition and measurement of income. Abstracting from inaccuracies in the respondents' reported income, I have already noted that annual income is not the correct variable

[13] This method is formally equivalent to that suggested by Johnston (1963) and others (see Appendix).

[14] To adopt a more realistic assumption would greatly complicate the task of calculating corrected correlation coefficients and would require unavailable data.

to use in a model of the intergenerational transfer of economic attainment. Most available studies do not allow us to distinguish between the variance in annual income due to year-to-year transient variations, on the one hand, and simple reporting errors, on the other. However, there are a number of estimates of the fraction of the variance of observed income that is accounted for by both reporting errors and the transient component in annual income. The estimate most consistent with the available data implies that only 70 percent of the variance of observed income is due to the variance of permanent income.[15] The' square root of the figure, .84, is the estimate of the correlation of permanent and observed income which appears in column 3 of table 2.

I turn now to questions concerning the accuracy of respondent's reports of their own educational attainments. Immediately following the 1950 census, a postenumeration survey was conducted to check the accuracy of census responses (Bureau of the Census 1960). A comparison of the respondents' reports to both the census and the Post-Enumeration Survey allows an estimate of the correlation of the true and reported values. I have calculated a number of values of this correlation based on alternative assumptions concerning both the relative accuracy of the census and the

TABLE 2

ESTIMATED ERRORS IN VARIABLES MEASURING SOCIOECONOMIC
BACKGROUND, INCOME, AND EDUCATIONAL LEVEL

Variable Required (1)	Measure Used (2)	Estimated Correlation of Observed Measure with True Value of Variable Required (3)
1. Respondent's permanent income	Respondent's annual income	.84
2. Respondent's educational attainment	Respondent's years of school attained (index)	.91
3. Occupational status of the father or family head of respondent	Duncan's status score for the occupation of father or family head	.80
4. Educational atttainment of father or family head of respondent	Years of school attained (index) by father or family head	.80
5. Parent's permanent income	Parents' annual income	.84
6. Family size	Number of siblings	.96

SOURCE.—See Section III and Appendix.

[15] The choice of this figure is explained in the Appendix, where a series of alternative estimates are given.

Post-Enumeration Survey and the correlation of errors in reporting to the two surveys (see Appendix for method of calculation and the alternative estimates). The most plausible assumptions yield a correlation of .91 between the true and observed values of the index of educational attainments. These correlations are reported in column 3 of table 2.[16]

Note that while I have estimated the degree or error in reporting one's educational attainments (col. 3 of table 2), I have assumed that years of schooling is an accurate measure of the level of educational attainment. Years of schooling attained should not be construed as an accurate measure of the total school resources devoted to a respondent's schooling. While the amount of resources "enjoyed" per year is associated with the years of school eventually attained, the correlation is far from perfect. Whatever bias arises due to this discrepancy operates—though not necessarily with equal force—for both the respondent's schooling and that of his parents.[17]

Consider now the accuracy of the respondents' reports of their parents' occupation and education. The data used here are from a survey in which respondents were asked to report the highest level of schooling attained by the father or family head, as well as the occupation held by the father or family head at the time the respondent was a teenager.

As part of their survey of intergenerational mobility, Blau, Duncan, and their associates administered a survey of 570 males in Chicago; the usual questions concerning parents' status were asked, along with an item eliciting the respondent's address when he was 16 years old (Blau and Duncan 1967, pp. 457–62). The decennial censuses nearest to the respondent's sixteenth birthday were then searched to extract the census report of the respondent's father's occupation.[18]

The zero-order correlation between the occupational status as reported by father and by son was found to be .74. There is a downward bias in this measure, as the census years from which the father's own reports were taken did not correspond exactly to the sixteenth year of age of the respondent. On the other hand, an upward bias is implicit in the method by which the sample to be studied was selected. The study automatically excluded respondents who could not correctly recall another retrospective

---

[16] The correlation between the true and observed values of respondents' occupational status score calculated in the same manner was .92.

[17] See the next section for a discussion of biases arising from the inadequate measurement of schooling.

[18] Of the original 570, only 137 cases could be used in the study. Inclusion required that the respondent had correctly recalled his address and had responded to the question concerning father's occupation, and also that his father had responded to the census question on occupation. A study of the matched responses then compared occupation of the father as reported by the respondent with that reported (presumably by the father or mother of the respondent) to the census. Then those reporting farm occupations to both surveys were eliminated, reducing the total to 115, and the occupations were scaled by the Duncan status score.

fact (their address at age 16), as well as those who did not answer the question concerning father's occupation and those whose father also had not replied to that question when asked by the census enumerator. While these considerations would seem to point on balance to an upward bias in the estimated accuracy of the responses, use of the figure is consistent with the data on cohorts collected by the 1962 Occupational Changes in a Generation Survey, as well as with other census data (see Appendix). I have, therefore, used this figure, and, as I did not have independent evidence on the accuracy of reports of parents' educational attainments, I applied the figure to that variable as well.

Use of this reliability estimate in conjunction with independent census data implies a negligible correlation of errors in reporting occupational and educational attainments (see Appendix).

The estimate of the accuracy of reports of number of siblings is based on the following reasoning: Duncan reports a correlation of .96 between mothers' census and reinterview reports of number of children ever born. Making the extreme assumption that the reinterview was totally accurate and that adults report number of siblings as inaccurately as they report number of children ever born, the correlation between the reported and actual number of siblings is .96.[19]

The evidence of this and the previous section points unambiguously to the existence of shortcomings in the specification of socioeconomic background, for errors in the measurement of some variables appear to be significant. Furthermore, as was indicated in the previous section, important socioeconomic background variables are omitted altogether.

A test proposed by Duncan et al. (1968) provides independent evidence on these shortcomings of measurement and specification. Because brothers ordinarily share a common socioeconomic background, estimates of the equation predicting years of schooling also allow the prediction of the degree of correlation between the educational attainments of brothers.

If we rewrite equation (1) for the respondent, with variables in normalized form $EDUC = ax$, and assume that siblings share a common socioeconomic background and similar relations between educational attainment and socioeconomic background, then the predicted correlation between brothers' years of schooling, $\hat{r}*$, will be:

$$\hat{r}* = \sum_{i=1}^{n} a_i r_{\text{ieduc}}, \tag{8}$$

where a_i is the normalized regression coefficient of the ith socioeconomic background variable from the equation predicting EUDC, and r_{ieduc} is the

[19] If the reinterview mentioned by Duncan was as inaccurate as the census and the errors are uncorrelated, a figure of .98 would be more appropriate.

zero-order correlation between the brother's years of schooling and variable i (assumed equal to that for the respondent himself).[20]

If the predicted correlation $\hat{r}*$ falls short of the actual correlation, $r*$, we must conclude that the factors influencing the respondent's level of schooling have been inadequately specified or erroneously measured, or both. The observed correlation for the sample of males, aged 25–34 years, studied here is .54 (Duncan et al. 1968, table B.5). After correcting this observed coefficient for errors in reporting,[21] this coefficient rises to .65. Using the equation as estimated by Duncan et al. (1968, p. 54), uncorrected for errors in variables and including only father's occupational status and educational level and respondent's number of siblings as measures of socioeconomic background, the predicted coefficient is .26, less than half of the observed coefficient. A discrepancy this large suggests not merely that biases exist, but that they are likely to be significant.[22] In the next section I will subject my own estimates to a similar test.

IV. An Empirical Model of Schooling and Income Determination

The estimates of reliability of the socioeconomic status, education, and income variables have been used to calculate a correlation matrix among the true values of the variables. (This correlation matrix, along with recalculated standard deviations of these variables, appears in the Appendix.) I have used the corrected correlation matrix to estimate equations (1), (2), and (3). The resulting estimates can tell us little about the magnitude of the biases arising from inadequate specification of the socioeconomic background of individuals. The only adjustment for this problem is the hypothetical introduction of a variable representing parents' income. Yet the estimated equations, as presented in table 3, do cast some light on the seriousness of the errors-in-variables problem.

The following characteristics of the results should be noted: First, the measures of family background explain 52 percent of the variance of the

[20] The value of $\hat{r}*$ is thus equal to the fraction of variance in sons explained by equation (1).

[21] I am assuming, conservatively, that the respondent's reports of brother's educational attainment are no more error prone than reports of his own educational attainment.

[22] Of course, the omitted variables may not measure dimensions of the socioeconomic background of the individual. The only other potentially important common aspect of background which may be conceived of as exogenous in this model seems to be the common (but not identical) genetic inheritance of brothers. Duncan et al. (1968) explicitly measured the effect on educational attainments of differences in childhood IQ, and thus were able to extend the above calculations to take some account of the common genetic inheritance of siblings. The resulting value of $r*$ for non-Negro native men 25–64 years of age was .34, still far short of .573, the observed correlation for this sample.

TABLE 3

REGRESSION EQUATIONS FOR MODEL OF SOCIOECONOMIC BACKGROUND, SCHOOLING, AND INCOME, U.S. NON-NEGRO MALES WITH NONFARM BACKGROUNDS, 25–34 YEARS OLD

DEPENDENT VARIABLE	NORMALIZED REGRESSION COEFFICIENTS OF:*					R^2
	Father's Occupational Status	Father's Years of Schooling	Parents' Income	Respondent's Number of Siblings	Respondent's Years of Schooling	
1. Respondent's years of schooling	.155 (58.8)	.204 (108.6)	.412 (832.3)	−.181 (185.6)	...	.517
2. Respondent's earnings	.112 (29.5)	†	.112 (27.7)	−.059 (10.9)	.203 (76.2)	.151
3. Respondent's earnings	.173 (77.3)	†	.197 (105.7)	−.102 (33.8)	...	.130

NOTE.—Refers to experienced civilian labor force, 1962, as represented by the occupational changes in a generation survey sample.

* F-statistics in parentheses.

† In a prior estimate this coefficient was insignificantly different from zero. The equation presented here was estimated without this variable.

234

years of schooling obtained by the respondent.[23] Second, years of schooling attained appears to be a significant determinant of the earnings of the respondent. The estimated increment in annual income associated with an additional year of schooling is $265. Yet this partial relationship of schooling to income net of socioeconomic background is less than 60 percent as large as the gross return indicated by the simple relationship between the two variables.[24] This finding suggests that much of the apparent economic return to schooling is in fact a return to socioeconomic background.[25]

Third, the variance of earnings explained by the social background variables alone is only slightly less than that explained by these variables along with the educational attainments of the respondent. The social background variables alone explain 13.0 percent of the variance of earnings.[26] The additional variance explained by years of schooling is only 2.1 percent. I infer from this result that years of schooling attained exerts a comparatively minor independent influence on earnings independent of social background. Most of the impact of years of schooling on earnings appears to be a direct transmission of economic status from one generation to the next.[27]

As an internal check on the plausibility of the correction for errors in measurement, I can now calculate the correlation between brothers' years of schooling predicted by my estimate of equation (1).[28] The predicted correlation, .52, still falls short of the true (corrected) .65. Nonetheless this calculation suggests that the correction for errors in variables has resulted in a considerable improvement in prediction.[29]

Returning to table 3, it might be argued that the explanatory power of the schooling variable would be increased if I had a measure of the quality as well as the duration of schooling. While this is undoubtedly true, the

[23] This is almost twice the fraction of variance explained by the uncorrected variables in Duncan et al. (1968).

[24] This calculation is based on the normalized regression coefficient of years of schooling in equation (2), the corrected zero-order correlation coefficient between schooling and income, and the corrected standard deviation of the two variables.

[25] It is shown below, in an extension of this work, that introduction of a measure of early IQ reduces the apparent net effect of schooling still further (see Bowles and Gintis 1972).

[26] The social background variables here include number of siblings. If that variable is excluded, the R^2 falls to .12. Using the uncorrected data from Duncan et al. (1968), the R^2 is .054 with number of siblings in the equation and .045 without.

[27] This does not appear to be the case when the respondent's occupational status is used as the dependent variable. The results suggest that while education exerts a major independent influence on occupational attainment, this influence does not translate into a major independent influence on earnings. The discrepancy between these results may be explained by the wide dispersion of earnings within occupational categories.

[28] The predicted correlation is calculated as described in the text using correlation coefficients from table A3 and normalized regression coefficients from table 3.

[29] Gintis and I show elsewhere (1972) that the introduction of a hypothetical variable measuring childhood IQ in this model raises the predicted correlation to a value slightly below the actual (corrected) correlation.

importance of this point is easily exaggerated. It is difficult to conceive of operational measures of school quality which will be at the same time important in their influence on adult economic success and not highly correlated with years of schooling attained and the social class of the respondent. The most commonly suggested—average school resources per year of schooling—would seem to be highly correlated with both years of schooling and social class background. A second measure—scholastic achievement—appears to fail on all counts. To the extent that we can explain the variance among individual students in scholastic achievement, the social class of the student seems to be the main explanatory variable. The increment in the explained variance of scholastic achievement scores associated with the introduction of school policy and resource variables in an equation already including crude measures of the social background of the student is ordinarily very small.[30] Better measures of school policies and resources would undoubtedly alter the picture somewhat, but even a substantial change would not be of great import as long as the scholastic achievement scores themselves are highly correlated with the number of years of schooling attained. If the Armed Forces Qualification Test (AFQT) may be taken as a proxy for a scholastic achievement test, we arrive at an estimate of .68 for this correlation,[31] suggesting that a substantial part of the variance of scholastic achievement is already measured by the years-of-schooling variable.

The more serious problem involved in the use of the achievement score (or its relatives such as the AFQT score) is that there is very little evidence that the effect of schooling upon economic success operates to any significant degree through the effect of schooling upon the types of cognitive development measured in these tests. If the sole medium through which schooling operated was cognitive development as measured by achievement tests, then we would expect to find that the addition of an individual's test score to an equation using years of schooling to predict individual earnings would result in the coefficient of schooling falling to zero. On the other hand, if education contributed to earnings entirely independently of its effect on cognitive development, the coefficient of years of schooling would be reduced by a relatively minor amount.[32]

[30] See Coleman et al. (1966) and Bowles (1970). This statement does not imply that variations in school policy or resources have no effect on scholastic outcomes, but rather that school policy and resources as conventionally measured exercise very little influence not already measured statistically by the social class variables. For a discussion of this problem, see Bowles and Levin (1968a, 1968b).

[31] The correlation refers to U.S. males 25–34 years old and is corrected for errors in both variables. The test-retest reliability of the AFQT is about .95. The uncorrected correlation is from Duncan (1968). Other sources report a considerably higher correlation between AFQT score and years of schooling completed. See Personnel Research Division, Adjutant General's Office (1945) for evidence on this correlation as well as on the reliability of the AFQT.

[32] The reduction in the coefficient of education in this case would be explained by

Evidence from unpublished studies by Cutright, Conlisk, and Griliches, summarized by Gintis (1971), indicates that the regression coefficient of years of schooling is only slightly reduced and remains highly significant upon the introduction of a measure of cognitive development to a function predicting individual earnings or income. Though preliminary, these results suggest that schooling exerts an influence upon earnings largely independent of its contribution to scholastic achievement.[33]

In summary, the importance of biases arising from the exclusion of school quality variables cannot be adequately estimated, in part because of our inability adequately to specify what we mean by school quality. We cannot exclude the possibility that these biases may be large. Nonetheless, the above considerations lead me to doubt that important modifications in the results would follow the successful inclusion of a school quality variable in the model.

V. Conclusion

Given the available data and restrictive assumptions required in the analysis, my own estimates are unavoidably subject to considerable error. Two possible sources of error in my treatment of the errors-in-variables problem seem to be particularly important: the assumption that errors in the main variables are uncorrelated with the true values, and the fragmentary nature of some of the evidence concerning the reliability of the variables and the correlation among errors in the variables. Moreover, while the direction of the specification biases seems reasonably certain, its real magnitude cannot be inferred with any confidence from the estimated coefficients of the hypothetical parents' income variable. We must await real data on this variable and on the other relevant aspects of family background before much of a quantitative nature can be said about this problem.

Nonetheless, the above estimates of correction for errors in variables, along with the earlier discussion of specification bias, leave little doubt that the estimation of models of social mobility and income determination which confine the measurement of socioecenomic background to respondents' reports of their parents' occupation and education level will result in significant biases. It is equally clear that these biases systematically understate the importance of social class in the determination of income and educational attainment.

Yet even having corrected for errors in measurement of the limited range of variables on which data are available, and having eliminated at least

the assumed positive correlation between the level of cognitive development and the noncognitive variables that, in this model, are hypothesized as the medium through which education affects earnings (see Gintis 1970).

[33] This argument is based on Gintis (1969).

some part of the specification bias, I have estimated a set of equations which, while explaining a large portion of the variance of years of schooling, explains relatively little of the variance of income. Of course to some extent the limited explanatory power of equations (2) and (3) may be explained by the remaining shortcomings in the specification of the model—the omission of measures of parental wealth, the parents' position in the hierarchy of work relations, and perhaps other dimensions of social class as well as the quality of schooling. Furthermore, Mincer's work (in press) suggests that a substantial increment in explained variance of income would result from the introduction of measures of work experience and on-the-job learning.

Yet the low R^2 in equations (2) and (3) may be the result of a mechanism in the individual income-determination process, the implications of which have, to my knowledge, been entirely ignored by economists and sociologists interested in income inequality and stratification. One's social class and educational level do not determine one's income; rather, they determine (presumably subject to some random influences) one's opportunity. Opportunity takes the form of a choice among jobs, each offering a different configuration of monetary and nonmonetary rewards. The income received by an individual is thus the result of a choice—a choice constrained by what could be called the occupational opportunity set. Only if preferences for various attributes of jobs are independent of socioeconomic background and level of schooling will the estimation of equations (1)–(3) yield unbiased estimates of the relations between social class, schooling, and real income, or equivalently, the *opportunity* to earn high money incomes. Yet this does not appear to be the case. There is considerable evidence that rich, high-status parents place a larger value on the nonmonetary aspects of work and a lower value on monetary returns than poorer, lower-status parents. Further evidence indicates that the job preferences of teen-age children show a similar relationship to socioeconomic status (Hyman 1966). The biases which arises in this case are illustrated in figure 1. Each job is characterized by an expected money income and a level of nonmonetary benefits (or costs) of the associated work.[34] The occupational opportunity set *oab* indicates the jobs available to an individual from a family of low socioeconomic status who has attained relatively few years of schooling. The opportunity set *oa′b′* refers to the job opportunities of an individual from a high-status family who has attained relatively many years of schooling.[35] Now if preferences for the monetary and nonmonetary aspects of work are associated with social class or with years of schooling, the occupations chosen may be illustrated by points *x* and *x′*. The money-income difference between the two individuals

[34] Nothing is lost by assuming (unrealistically) a single dimension for the nonmonetary aspects of each job.
[35] The opportunity loci *ab* and *a′b′* need not, and in general will not, be parallel.

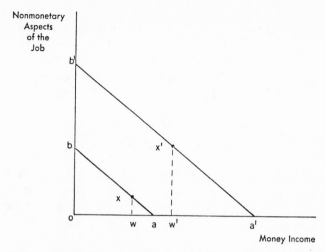

FIG. 1.—Occupational opportunities with endogenous preferences

$(w' - w)$ thus understates the differences in real income or opportunity, which may be measured on the money income axis as $(a' - a)$. As a result, the power of equations (2) and (3) to explain money income may greatly understate the relationship between real income or job opportunity on the one hand, and social class and schooling on the other. If the main determinant of job preferences is socioeconomic background, then the relative importance of the background variables as an influence on economic opportunity will be underestimated. Similarly, if education is the main determinant of job preferences, the coefficient of the years-of-schooling variable will be underestimated.[36]

Considering the biases arising from the problem of endogenous occupational preferences, along with the biases due to incomplete specification of family background, the results reported in table 3 demonstrate a surprisingly strong relationship between socioeconomic background on the one hand, and educational attainments and income on the other.

The substantial impact of even the limited measurement of socioeconomic status possible in this study can be illustrated as follows: Define a composite social class index, S, as the equally weighted sum of the three socioeconomic status variables.[37] Now we may ask: What is the expected difference in educational attainments and income for two hypothetical white males, ages 25–34, one originating from a high-status family and

[36] The greater explanatory power both of schooling and parental socioeconomic status in predicting the occupational status of the respondent (results calculated in a manner similar to equations [1]–[3] are not reported here; see also Duncan et al. [1968]) may be due in part to this association among job preferences, social class, and schooling. See also n. 27 above.

[37] That is: $S = 1/3$ FED $+ 1/3$ FOCC $+ 1/3$ PARinc.

the other from a low-status family? Let us define high- and low-status families as those scoring exactly one standard deviation above or below the mean on the three family-status scores.[38] By this definition, the high-status individual's origins—at the eighty-ninth percentile of the composite social class (S) distribution—are translated into an advantage of 4.6 years of schooling over the respondent whose low-status origins place him at the eleventh percentile.[39] Further, even in the evidently unlikely event that both individuals attained the same years of schooling, the individual of high-status origins could expect to earn $1,630 more annually over the ages 25–34.

Calculated in terms of the probability of receiving either a relatively high or low income, the impact of social class on income determination is even more striking. Taking account of the direct impact of socioeconomic background on income as well as its indirect effect via the relationship between social class and years of schooling attained, the high-status individual has 2.8 times the probability of receiving an income over $10,000 annually than the low-status individual. Analogously, the low-status individual is 2.8 times more likely to receive less than $1,200 annually.

While these calculations must be taken as only illustrative of orders of magnitude, they do suggest that substantial inequality of economic opportunity exists in the United States and that the educational system is a major vehicle for the transmission of economic status from one generation to the next.

Appendix

Methods Used to Estimate the Corrected Correlation Matrix

1. *Equivalence to the More Familiar Errors-in-Variables Approach*

I will first show that the method used is equivalent to the generalized errors-in-variables approach as described by Johnston (1963). First write the normal equations in the form

$$\sum_{i=1}^{n} \hat{b}_i M'_{r_i r_k} = M'_{r_k r_j} \qquad (k = 1 \ldots n \text{ equations}), \quad (A1)$$

[38] Assuming a normal distribution of S in the population under study, and utilizing the correlation coefficients in table A3, an individual whose family scored a standard deviation above the mean on all three status scores will be 1.21 SD above the mean on S, or at the eighty-ninth percentile of the social class distribution. Analogous calculations for an individual whose family scored a standard deviation below the mean place that person at the eleventh percentile.

[39] The impact (in standard deviation units) of a 2 SD difference in each socioeconomic background variable is calculated from equations identical with those in table 3, except that the number-of-siblings variable has been omitted so as to isolate the direct and indirect (via family size) effect of social class upon educational attainments and income. The equations omitting the NSIBS variable are virtually identical with those reported in table 3, and may readily be calculated from the corrected zero-order correlation matrix. The corrected standard deviations of years of schooling and income used to translate the normalized impact into raw figures appear in table A5.

where $\hat{b}_i$ is the estimated regression coefficient of variable i in an equation predicting variable j, and

$$M'_{x_i x_k} \text{ and } M'_{x_k x_j}$$

are the observed second-order sample moments. If the variables are measured with error (uncorrelated with the true variables), we may estimate unbiased regression coefficients using n equations which appear in the form

$$\hat{\hat{b}}_1 \left(M'_{x_1 x_1} - \text{var } u_1 \right) + \sum_{i=2}^{n} \hat{\hat{b}}_i \left(M'_{x_1 x_i} - \text{cov } [u_1, u_i] \right)$$

$$= M'_{x_j x_1} - \text{cov } (u_j, u_1), \quad (A2)$$

etc., where $\hat{\hat{b}}_i$ are the unbiased regression coefficients and u_i is the error term in the observed variable x'_i. Expressing equation (A2) in standard deviation units of the true variables yields the system

$$\begin{bmatrix} 1 & M_{12} & \ldots & M_{1n} \\ \cdot & & & \cdot \\ \cdot & & & \cdot \\ \cdot & & & \cdot \\ M_{n1} & \ldots & & 1 \end{bmatrix} \begin{bmatrix} \beta_1 \\ \cdot \\ \cdot \\ \cdot \\ \hat{\beta}_n \end{bmatrix} = \begin{bmatrix} M_{1j} \\ \cdot \\ \cdot \\ \cdot \\ M_{nj} \end{bmatrix}, \quad (A3)$$

where β_i is the unbiased estimate of the normalized regression coefficient of variable i, and where

$$M_{ij} = \frac{M'_{x_i x_j} - \text{cov } (u_i, u_j)}{\sigma_{x_i} \sigma_{x_j}}. \quad (A4)$$

Rearranging, we have

$$M_{ij} = \frac{M'_{x_i x_j}}{\sigma'_{x_i} \sigma'_{x_j}} \cdot \frac{\sigma'_{x_i} \sigma'_{x_j}}{\sigma_{x_i} \sigma_{x_j}} - \frac{\text{cov } u_i u_j}{\sigma_{x_i} \sigma_{x_j}}. \quad (A5)$$

Using the notations introduced in the text, and noting that

$$(\sigma'_{x_i} \sigma'_{x_j}) / \sigma_{x_i} \sigma_{x_j} = (r_i r_j)^{-1},$$

it follows from the fact that

$$\text{cov}(u_i, u_j) = r_{uij} \sigma_{ui} \sigma_{uj},$$

and,

$$1 - r_i^2 = \frac{\sigma_{u_i}^2}{\sigma_{x_i}^2}$$

that

$$M_{ij} = \frac{r'_{ij}}{r_i r_j} - \frac{\sqrt{1 - r_i^2} \sqrt{1 - r_j^2}}{r_i r_j} \cdot r_{uij}, \quad (A6)$$

which is identical with equation (7).

2. The Accuracy of Reported Annual Income as a Measure of Permanent Income

Various estimates of the ratio of the variance of permanent income to observed annual income are available. The first is Friedman's estimate based on the elasticity of consumption with respect to income.[40] Friedman's estimates for nonfarm or urban families in 1935–36 and 1941 appear as lines 1 and 2 of table A1.

We arrive at a second estimate if we define permanent income as that measured by the weighted sum of the income in a number of years, and then inspect the fraction of variance in any individual year's income explained by the incomes of other years. Using 3 adjacent years' income for a sample of 24,738 whites, we arrive at the estimates which appear in lines 3–5 of table A1. Alternatively, we may use the correlation of incomes in adjacent years. Assuming that both

TABLE A1

ANNUAL INCOME AS MEASURE OF PERMANENT INCOME

Sample	Method	Fraction of Observed Variance in Annual Income Due to Variance in Permanent Income
Nonfarm or urban families:		
1. 1935–36	} Income elasticity of consumption	.82*
2. 1941		.87*
White veterans:		
3. 1962	} Fraction of variance of each	.73†
4. 1963	year's income explained by	.71†
5. 1964	} 3 other years' incomes	.77†
Urban spending units:		
6. 1947, 1948	{ Correlation of adjacent years' incomes	.83‡
White veterans:		
7. 1962, 1963	} Correlation of adjacent years'	.83†
8. 1963, 1964	} incomes	.83†
All Wisconsin taxpayers:		
9. Average of six coefficients for all consecutive pairs of years, 1929–35	{ Correlation of adjacent years' incomes	.84‡
White veterans and Wisconsin taxpayers:		
10. Various years ...	{ Best estimate in explaining correlations among incomes at times separated by various numbers of years, assuming serially correlated errors	.70§

* From Friedman (1957), p. 67.
† Calculated from correlations of yearly income found by Cutright (1969). The additional year was 1958.
‡ From Friedman (1957), p. 187.
§ Data from Friedman (1957) and Cutright (1969). Method described in text.

[40] Friedman (1957) shows that the elasticity of consumption with respect to income is an estimate of the fraction of the variance of observed income attributable to the variance of permanent income. This estimate is based on the assumption that the transient components in annual income are not serially correlated.

income figures are imperfect measures of the underlying permanent incomes, and that the errors in each are uncorrelated, this correlation coefficient is an estimate of the portion of variance of observed income which is due to variations in the permanent income. Various estimates on this basis appear as lines 6–9 in table A1.

It seems likely that the transient components in annual income will be serially correlated. This possibility is indicated by the fact that the correlation coefficients among annual incomes for given individuals decline as the number of years intervening between the years increases (Friedman 1957; Cutright 1969). Thus we may assume that the estimates in lines 1–9 represent overestimates of the fraction of the variance of observed annual income due to variations in permanent income.

Gintis has attempted to deal with the problem of serially correlated errors in a recent unpublished paper (1970). He used the following basic model: Let

$$y^i_t$$

be the observed annual income of the ith individual in year t;

$$y^i_p$$

is the permanent income of the ith individual, and

$$e^i_t$$

is the deviation from the permanent income in year t. Then

$$y^i_t = y^i_p + e^i_t \tag{A7}$$

and

$$e^i_{t+1} = p\, e^i_t + u^i_{t+1} \tag{A8}$$

where the u^i are serially correlated. Gintis then showed that the correlation between incomes in h years apart, r_h, will be a function of the autoregressive pattern as described by p, and $\mathrm{var}(e)/\mathrm{var}(y_p)$, the ratio of the variance of e to the variance of permanent income. Thus,

$$r_h = \frac{1 + p^h\,[\mathrm{var}(e)/\mathrm{var}(y_p)]}{1 + [\mathrm{var}(e)/\mathrm{var}(y_p)]}. \tag{A9}$$

Using this equation and the data from Friedman and Cutright, I have arrived at the following estimates: $\mathrm{var}(e)/\mathrm{var}(y_p) = .43$ and $p = .5$. These estimates imply that 70 percent of the variance of observed income is attributable to the variance of permanent income.[41] The discrepancy between this estimate and those mentioned previously is explained by the fact that the lower estimate is based on the assumption that errors in observed income are serially correlated. Because the Gintis model fits the data so well,[42] I conclude that the assumption of serially correlated errors is appropriate. I will therefore use

[41] In arriving at this estimate I have eliminated observations based on correlations with an income reported very early in the work experience of the respondent. It seems likely that the error variance of this early year's reported income is atypically large, and that the average annual rate of increase of observed income over this period is quite high. Both of these characteristics of the pattern of earnings in the early years will cause estimates based on expression (A9) to overstate the size of the error component in annual income.

[42] Simple models in which, assuming serially uncorrelated errors, $(p = 0)$ would

$$.84 \ (= \sqrt{.70})$$

as the estimated correlation between observed and permanent income[43] (see col. 3 of table 2).

3. *Errors in Reporting Education and Occupation*

On the basis of the 1950 Post-Enumeration Survey, the Census Bureau published matrices recording responses to the original census enumerators and to the Post-Enumeration surveyors. I have scaled these responses using the Duncan occupational status scale, as well as his educational attainments scale, and correlated the two responses. The correlations were .86 for educational attainment and .83 for occupational status.[44]

In order to use these correlation coefficients to estimate the error variance as a fraction of the variance of observed occupational status and educational attainment, two basic assumptions must be made: one concerning the accuracy of the original census relative to the Post-Enumeration Survey, and the other concerning the degree to which errors in reporting to the original census are correlated with errors in reporting to the Post-Enumeration Survey. Because the *Current Population Survey* data upon which my mobility estimates are based were collected by highly trained census enumerators, I think it reasonable to assume that these data are about as accurate as the Post-Enumeration Survey which also was conducted by a well-trained staff, and that both are highly reliable by comparison with the general census data. Because the Post-Enumeration Survey took place very shortly after the census, it also seems reasonable to assume that the errors in both sources are positively correlated. I have estimated various measures of the accuracy of the Post-Enumeration Survey, based on alternative assumptions concerning the degree of correlation of errors, and the relative accuracy of the Post-Enumeration Survey and the census. These estimates are presented in table A2. I have chosen the middle assumptions for each as the basis for the estimate of the correlation between observed and true variables for educational attainment and for occupational status.[45] These figures appear in column 3 of table 2.

4. *Correlation of Errors and Internal Consistency of the Reliability Estimates*

The evidence from the Duncan and Blau census follow-up study (1967, pp. 457–

---

not predict the observed pattern of correlation coefficients, even as a rough approximation.

[43] Data from the 1950 Post-Enumeration Survey of the U.S. census suggests that the correlation of reported incomes in the same year to two separate surveys is .80. This figure presumably represents pure reporting error, as it does not contain transient year-to-year variations in income. If we assume that the error component in the census is twice as great as in the Post-Enumeration Survey, and further that the correlation between errors in reporting to these two surveys is .5, the estimated correlation between reported and actual annual income is .87. This calculation suggests that most of the "error" in reported annual income is due to erroneous reporting rather than to transience of annual income.

[44] Although the respondents' occupational status score is not used in the estimated equations, the estimated reliability of this variable will be used in calculating other reliabilities.

[45] Let r_p and r_c represent the correlations between the true measure and that measured by the Post-Enumeration Survey and the census, respectively. Further, define r_{pc} as the correlation between census and Post-Enumeration responses, and r_u as the correlation of errors in the two measures. Then (using equation [7]) we have

$$r_{pc} = r_p r_c + r_u \sqrt{1 - r_c^2} \sqrt{1 - r_p^2}.$$

TABLE A2
Estimated Correlation of True and Observed Values for Respondents' Reports
of Own Occupations and Years of Schooling

ERROR VARIANCE OF CENSUS/ ERROR VARIANCE OF PES	CORRELATION OF ERRORS IN CENSUS AND PES REPORTS		
	.0	.5	.7
	Occupation		
1.0	.935	.870	.770
1.0	.959	.923	.882
2.0	.970	.950	.930
	Education		
1.0	.930	.850	.730
2.0	.953	.910	.865
3.0	.965	.940	.920

62) yielded the figure .8 as the estimate of the correlation between the observed and true occupational status of parents. It was further assumed that the figure of .8 also represents the correlation between reported and real educational attainments of parents. It remains to be shown, first that these estimates, together with other evidence on reliabilities and with the fragments of independent evidence available, imply a negligible correlation of errors in reporting occupational status and parents' income. Second, I will show that the reliability estimates themselves are consistent with the available data and with each other.

In order to do this I adopt the following procedure: First define r_{oe} as the correlation between the true occupational status and true educational attainment. Let a superscript p indicate that the correlation refers to the father or head of household of the respondent. Let the superscript prime ($'$) indicate the observed correlations, and the subscript u indicate that the correlation refers to the correlation of error terms rather than the variables themselves.

Using equation (7), I can now write the observed correlations as a function of the true correlations, the correlations of the observed with the true variables, and the correlations of the error terms. Thus:

$$r_{oe}^{p'} = r_{oe}^{p} \, r_{o}^{p} \, r_{c}^{p} + r_{uoc}^{p} \sqrt{1 - r_{o}^{p2}} \sqrt{1 - r_{c}^{p2}} \qquad (A10)$$

$$r_{oe}' = r_{oe} \, r_{o} \, r_{e} + r_{uoc} \sqrt{1 - r_{o}^{2}} \sqrt{1 - r_{c}^{2}}. \qquad (A11)$$

We have some independent information on the trend in the correlation between occupational status and educational achievement. This evidence, in turn, will allow some inferences about the relationship between

$$r_{oc}^{p}$$

and r_{oe}. The evidence of a cohort analysis of the occupational changes in a generation sample suggest no trend in the correlation between occupational status and educational attainment.

Because the respondent's own occupational status is reported for different points in the individual life cycle for different age cohorts, not much can be inferred from the correlations between respondent's own occupational status and educational attainment. However, respondents were asked to report their parents' occupational status at a roughly similar time in the life cycle of the parents, namely, when the respondents were about 16. Thus the correlations among the parents' variables provide evidence largely independent of the position in the life cycle. For the four 10-year age cohorts from 25 to 64, the correlations are (from oldest to youngest): .5313, .4863, .5300, and .4885. There is no apparent secular trend, thus motivating the assumption that[46]

$$r_{oe} = r^p_{oe}.$$

Assuming that

$$r_{uoc} = r^p_{uoc}$$

it can be seen from equation (A10) and (A11) that our estimated reliabilities and the assumption that $r_{oe} = r^p_{oe}$ imply that the correlations of errors

$$r_{uoe} \text{ and } r^p_{uoc}$$

are negligible. It is assumed on this basis that the correlation of errors in reporting education and income is also zero. Assumption of a (perhaps more plausible) positive correlation of errors would lower the corrected correlation between schooling and income and would thus result in a lower estimate of the independent effect of schooling upon income.

The evidence that there has been no secular trend in the relationship between occupational status and educational attainment may be further checked in a manner which provides evidence on the consistency of the no-trend assumption with our estimated correlations of true and observed variables.

If there has been no trend in the relationship between occupational status and educational attainment, and *if* our estimate of the accuracy of the respondent's reports of his own and his parents' occupations and education are accurate, then the corrected correlation of educational attainment and occupational status for the 25–34-year-old respondents' parents should be roughly equal to the analogous correlation for the 35–44-year-old respondent's own occupation and education. (The latter age group is selected as that which is most likely to have 16-year-old children, and thus to correspond to the parents' status retrospectively reported by the 25–34-year-old respondents referring to the period roughly 9–19 years ago when they were 16.) The corrected correlation for the 35–44-year-olds is .7676, while that for the parents of 25–34-year-olds is .7633. It should be stressed that the striking similarity of these two correlations demonstrates only the consistency of our estimates. Other estimates might also be consistent, although a little experimentation will show that an alternative set of consistent estimates is not easy to come by.

Table A3 summarizes the corrections; see also tables A4 and A5.

[46] These are the observed correlations reported in Duncan et al. (1968, p. 51). Folger and Nam (1967) present evidence that the degree of association between educational attainment and occupational status declined over the period 1940–60. The Folger and Nam results must be seriously questioned, however. It may be seen from equations (A10) and (A11) that any significant decline in this relationship, namely,

$$r_{\hat{o}e} < r^p_{oe}$$

implies a large negative correlation of errors in reporting occupation and educational attainment. This seems to be highly unlikely.

TABLE A3
Corrected Zero-Order Correlations among Main Variables for Non-Negro Males, Aged 25–34, with Nonfarm Backgrounds in Experienced Labor Force, 1962

Variable	(1)	(2)	(3)	(4)	(5)	(6)	(7)
1. Income	1.000	.4345	.3004	.3566	−.1889	.2283	.3004
2. Occupation	.840/.923	1.000	.4786	.7751	−.2793	.4632	.4786
3. Parents' income	*	*	1.000	.6031	−.1811	.4018	.4900
4. Years of schooling ..	.840/.910	.933/.91	.840/.91	1.000	−.3734	.5518	.5677
5. Number of siblings ..	.840/.960	.923/.96	.840/.960	.910/.96	1.000	−.3504	−.2982
6. Father's education ...	.840/.800	.923/.80	.840/.910	.910/.80	.96/.8	1.000	.7633
7. Father's occupation ..	.840/.800	.923/.80	.840/.923	.910/.80	.96/.8	8/.8	1.000

NOTE.—Corrected coefficients appear above the diagonal. The first and second number in the cells below the diagonal are the estimated correlation between the true and observed variables denoted by the column and row headings, respectively (for sources see tables 2 and A4).
* Corrected correlations for these cells are assumed to be equal to the respective corrected correlations of father's occupation with respondent's income and occupation, respectively.

TABLE A4

Zero-Order Correlations among Main Variables for Non-Negro Males, Aged 25–34 with Nonfarm Backgrounds in Experienced Labor Force, 1962
(Original Data and Sources)

Variable	(1)	(2)	(3)	(4)	(5)	(6)	(7)
1. Income	1.000	.3369	...	.2726	−.1523	.1534	.2019
2. Occupation	*	1.000	...	.6510	−.2475	.3420	.3534
3. Parents' income	*	..	1.000	.4610	−.1460	.3071	.3799
4. Years of schooling	*	*	†	1.000	−.3262	.4017	.4133
5. Number of siblings	*	*	‡	*	1.000	−.2691	−.2290
6. Father's education	*	*	‡	*	*	1.000	.4885
7. Father's occupation	*	*	‡	*	*	*	1.000

* From Duncan et al. (1968), p. 51.

† Data provided by the California Guidance Study. I am grateful to Marjorie Honzik and the Institute of Human Development at the University of California (Berkeley) for making these data available to me, and to John Conlisk for drawing my attention to the data source and assistance in acquiring the data. These correlations are estimated for a sample of about seventy individuals and their families.

‡ From Duncan et al. (1968), p. 51. These figures are the actual correlations for 55–64-year-old respondents' own income, education, and occupation.

TABLE A5

MEANS AND STANDARD DEVIATIONS OF MAIN VARIABLES FOR NON-NEGRO MALES, 25–34,
WITH NONFARM BACKGROUNDS IN EXPERIENCED LABOR FORCE, 1962

		STANDARD DEVIATION	
VARIABLE	MEAN*	Uncorrected*	Corrected†
Income	$6,140	$4,290	$3,604
Years of schooling	12.38	3.04	2.77
Number of siblings	3.49	2.86	2.75
Father's education	9.17	3.53	2.82
Father's occupation	34.59	22.35	17.88

* From Duncan et al. (1968), p. 51.
† Estimated standard deviation of the true variable, calculated as the product of the uncorrected standard deviation and the estimated correlation between the true variable and the observed variable (from table 2).

References

Becker, Gary S. *Human Capital: A Theoretical and Empirical Analysis with Special Reference to Education.* New York: Nat. Bur. Econ. Res., 1964.

Blau, Peter M., and Duncan, Otis Dudley. *The American Occupational Structure.* New York: Wiley, 1967.

Blau, Peter M., and Gintis, Herbert. "Social Class, IQ, and the Inheritance of Inequality." Mimeographed. Harvard Univ., 1972.

Bowles, Samuel. "Towards an Educational Production Function." In *Education, Income, and Human Capital,* edited by W. Lee Hansen, pp. 11–61. Studies in Income and Wealth, vol. 35. New York: Nat. Bur. Econ. Res., 1970.

———. "Unequal Education and the Reproduction of the Social Division of Labor." *Rev. Radical Polit. Econ.* 3 (Fall-Winter 1971): 1–30.

Bowles, Samuel, and Levin, Henry. "The Determinants of Scholastic Achievement: An Appraisal of Some Recent Evidence." *J. Human Resources* 3 (Winter 1968): 3–24. (*a*)

———. "More on Multicollinearity and the Effectiveness of Schools." *J. Human Resources* 3 (Summer 1968): 393–400. (*b*)

Bronfenbrenner, Urie. "Socialization and Social Class through Time and Space." In *Education and Society,* edited by W. Warren Kallenbach and Harold M. Hodges, Jr., pp. 171–77. Columbus, Ohio: Merrill, 1963.

Bureau of the Census. *The Post-Enumeration Survey: 1950.* Technical Paper no. 4. Washington: Bur. Census, 1960.

Coleman, James S., et al. *Equality of Educational Opportunity.* Washington: Government Printing Office, 1966.

Conlisk, John. "A Bit of Evidence on the Income-Education-Ability Interrelation." Mimeographed. Univ. Calif., Los Angeles, September 1968.

Cromwell, Gerald. Ph.D. dissertation on the relationship between economic growth and income distribution, Harvard Univ. (in preparation).

Cutright, Phillips. "Achievement, Military Service, and Earnings." Mimeographed. Harvard Univ., May 1969.

Dolger, Laura, and Ginandes, Janet. "Children's Attitudes toward Discipline as Related to Socioeconomic Status." *J. Experimental Educ.* 15 (December 1946): 161–65.

Dreeben, Robert. *On What Is Learned in School.* Reading, Mass.: Addison-Wesley, 1968.

Duncan, Otis Dudley. "Ability and Achievement." *Eugenics Q.* 15 (March 1968): 1–11.

Duncan, Otis Dudley; Featherman, David L.; and Duncan, Beverly. "Socioeconomic Background and Occupational Achievement: Extensions of a Basic Model." Project No. S-0074 (EO-191). U.S. Department of Health, Education, and Welfare, May 1968.

Folger, John K., and Nam, Charles B. *The Education of the American Population.* Washington: Bur. Census, 1967.

Friedman, Milton. *A Theory of the Consumption Function.* Nat. Bur. Econ. Res. Gen. Series no. 63. Princeton, N.J.: Princeton Univ. Press, 1957.

Gintis, Herbert M. "Alienation and Power: Towards a Radical Welfare Economics." Ph.D. dissertation, Harvard Univ., 1969.

———. "Regressions on Income Where the Dependent Variable Follows an Autoregressive Pattern." Mimeographed. Harvard Univ., 1970.

———. "Education, Technology, and the Characteristics of Worker Productivity." *A.E.R.* 61 (May 1971): 266–79.

Hanoch, Giora. "An Economic Analysis of Earnings and Schooling." *J. Human Resources* 2 (Summer 1967) 310–29.

Hansen, W. Lee; Weisbrod, Burton A.; and Scanlon, W. J. "Schooling and Earnings of Low Achievers." *A.E.R.* 60 (June 1970): 409–18.

Harrison, Bennett. "Education and Earnings in the Urban Ghetto." Mimeographed. Univ. Maryland, 1969.

Hauser, Robert M. "Schools and the Stratification Process." *American J. Sociology* 74 (May 1969): 587–611.

———. "Educational Stratification in the U.S." *Sociological Inquiry* 40 (Spring 1970):102–29.

Hollingshead, August de Belmont. *Elmtown's Youth: The Impact of Social Classes on Adolescents.* New York: Wiley, 1949.

Hyman, Herbert H. "The Value Systems of Different Classes." In *Class, Status, and Power: Social Stratification in Comparative Perspective,* edited by Reinhard Bendix and Seymour Martin Lipset, pp. 488–99. 2d ed. New York: Free Press, 1966.

Johnston, John. *Econometric Methods.* New York: McGraw-Hill, 1963.

Kohn, Melvin L. "Social Class and Parent-Child Relationships: An Interpretation." *American J. Sociology* 68 (January 1963): 471–80.

———. "Social Class and Parental Values." In *The Family: Its Structure and Function,* edited by Rose Laub Coser, pp. 472–96. New York: St. Martin's, 1964.

———. *Class and Conformity: A Study in Values.* Homewood, Ill.: Dorsey, 1969.

Lewis, Hylan. "Child-Rearing among Low-Income Families." In *Poverty in America,* edited by Louis A. Ferman, Joyce L. Kornbluh, and Alan Haber, Ann Arbor: Univ. Mich. Press, 1965.

Maccoby, Eleanor E.; Gibbs, Patricia K.; and the staff of the Laboratory of Human Development. Harvard University. "Methods of Child-Rearing in Two Social Classes." In *Readings in Child Development,* edited by William E. Martin and Celia Burns Stendler, pp. 380–96. New York: Harcourt Brace, 1954.

Miller, Daniel, and Swanson, Guy. *The Changing American Parent: A Study in the Detroit Area.* New York: Wiley, 1958.

Mincer, Jacob. "Investment in Human Capital and Personal Income Distribution." *J.P.E.* 66 (August 1958): 281–302.

———. "Schooling, Age, and Earnings." In *Human Capital and Personal Income Distribution.* New York: Nat. Bur. Econ. Res., in press.

Parsons, Talcott. "The School Class as a Social System: Some of Its Functions in American Society." *Harvard Educ. Rev.* 29 (Fall 1959): 297–318.

Personnel Research Section, Classification and Replacement Branch, the Adjutant General's Office. "The Army General Classification Test." *Psychological Bull.* 42 (December 1945): 760–68.

Schultz, Theodore W. "Investment in Poor People." Seminar on Manpower Policy and Programs, Office of Manpower Policy Evaluation Research. Washington: Dept. Labor, 1966.

Warner, W. Lloyd; Havighurst, Robert J.; and Loeb, Martin B. *Who Shall Be Educated?* New York: Harper, 1944.

Weber, Max. *From Max Weber: Essays in Sociology.* New York: Oxford Univ. Press, 1946.

Weiss, Randall, D. "The Effect of Education on the Earnings of Blacks and Whites." *Rev. Econ. and Statis.* 52 (May 1970): 150–59.

Winterbottom, M. "The Sources of Achievement Motivation in Mothers' Attitudes toward Independence Training." In *The Achievement Motive*, David C. McClelland, John W. Atkinson, Russell A. Clark, and Edgar L. Lowell, pp. 294–304. New York: Appleton, 1953.

Comment

Gary S. Becker

University of Chicago

Economists have long argued that family background—I eschew the term "social class" because its meaning is obscure and because its recent use in economics has impeded clear thinking—is an important determinant of preschool training, schooling, on-the-job training, and other investments in what is now called "human capital." Thus, background has been considered a major *indirect* determinant of earnings and occupation. Much less importance has been attached, however, to the *direct* effects of background on earnings and occupation.

The empirical evidence developed by Samuel Bowles[1] clearly supports, indeed reinforces, these conclusions, except that family background is alleged also to have an important direct effect on earnings. Although Samuel Bowles's paper is fragmented and somewhat disorganized, he attacks a significant problem with resourcefulness and thought. My discussion concentrates on the one apparent conflict between his findings and received opinion, and on the mechanism by which family background affects the amount invested in human capital and earnings.

Bowles argues that the importance of family background has been underestimated in previous empirical studies, partly because measures of only a few of the possibly relevant dimensions of background have been available. Part of the effect of the omitted dimensions is either lost or picked up by nonbackground variables such as education. This argument, however, also can be made for every other variable: No complete empirical counterpart of any variable is ever available. To maintain objectivity, one must adopt a skeptical attitude until evidence is provided. Since Bowles does not provide any evidence, he wisely does not dwell on this argument. Instead he dwells on errors of measurement in the included dimensions, and this is the main contribution of the paper. Scattered evidence is used

---

[1] I have based my comments throughout on the version of Bowles's paper presented to the COBRE workshop.

to estimate the measurement error in each variable, and then all the regression and correlation coefficients are corrected for these errors. Since the error in measuring family background is estimated to be greater than that in other variables, of course the relative importance of family background is raised by his corrections.

I tend to agree that family background is more poorly measured than most other variables in these studies because persons have been asked to recall such information as the education and occupation of parents who usually do not live in the same household and are frequently deceased. Although Bowles uses considerable ingenuity, his estimates are based on small and unreliable samples, and thus they are a poor substitute for data that combine education and other characteristics directly reported by parents with various characteristics reported by their children.

Regressions run on such data probably would differ considerably from those derived by Bowles, even if he correctly estimates the size of each measurement error. He has assumed that the error in measuring a variable is not only uncorrelated with its own true value but also with the true values of the dependent variables. Yet I suspect that the errors are systematic, and especially that errors in reporting family background are positively correlated with variables measuring "own achievement." If so, errors in measuring family background may have increased, rather than decreased, the statistical contribution of these variables.

Even if Bowles's estimates of measurement error are accepted, his discussion overstates the direct effect of family background on earnings. For one thing, he does not explain why the direct effect on occupation is so small; we know that discrimination, which analytically is closely related to family background, affects earnings primarily by affecting occupation. For another, the statistical procedure used is not legitimate. He argues that "own education" adds relatively little to the R^2 in the earnings regressions when it is introduced after the family background variables. But the relative importance of correlated independent variables cannot be evaluated in that manner: they operate jointly, not sequentially. Otherwise, why not reverse Bowles's procedure, add family background after "own education," and reduce the contribution of background?

When all variables are considered jointly, "own education" has a larger normalized coefficient and F-value than any other variable in the earnings regression; in particular, it has a larger direct effect on earnings than any single background variable and probably one greater than all combined. If the variables are considered sequentially, it should at least be noted that introducing "own education" into the regressions greatly lowers the coefficients and the significance of the background variables.

By playing up the direct impact of family background on earnings and playing down that of "own education"—more generally, that of "own human capital"—Bowles does little justice to the latter. He uses linear regressions whereas human-capital theory implies a semilog form; his discussion of the quality of schooling is incomplete[2] and marred by the same illegitimate statistical procedure already criticized, and of greatest significance, he essentially neglects preschool and postschool investments.

A few years ago Chiswick and I (1966) suggested that regression estimates of the impact of schooling on earnings have been too low because postschool investments have been ignored. Less-educated persons generally have spent more time on postschool investments than more-educated persons of the same age because the former leave school at an earlier age. The resulting downward bias in the estimated effect of schooling on earnings would be particularly large at younger ages, such as those considered by Bowles, because more-educated persons would not have had much time to catch up.

In an outstanding work (in press), J. Mincer finds that schooling and rough estimates of postschool investment jointly explain about 35 percent of the variation in earnings; schooling's contribution is considerably increased, not decreased, by including postschool investments.[3] Schooling alone explains about one-third of the variation in earnings of persons with about 8 years of postschool experience. In the light of these calculations, family background, even after all of Bowles's adjustments, appears to have a minor direct effect on earnings.

I suspect that even the relatively small, apparent direct effect of family background on earnings is not mainly due to nepotism, "contacts," or "class" collusion, but to the effect of background on preschool and other nonschooling investments. One piece of evidence is that the labor-force participation of educated women is higher than that of other women, except when young children are present; then it is considerably lower. A plausible interpretation is that educated women withdraw to invest in their children because these women have a comparative advantage in preschool and other home investments. This implies that a mother's education has a larger effect on earnings than a father's education (Bowles uses father's education), and that part of the return to a mother's education is reflected in the productivity of her children.

The strong positive relation between family background and schooling that Bowles finds is, presumably, partly explained by this positive relation between background and home investments since these investments ease the access to schooling opportunities. Of course, a wealthy background also provides the financing for foregone earnings and other school expenditures. Moreover, public support of education often favors persons with better backgrounds (a favoritism that may not be unintentional).[4] For example,

[2] For example, he does not mention the study by Hunt (1963).

[3] A summary of some of the results is in Mincer (1970).

[4] For a discussion of the relation between political coalitions and various redistributive measures, see Stigler (1970).

probably the main effect—perhaps intent too—of the segregated school system in the South (and the North?) has been to discriminate against black children in educational expenditures; also, many state systems of higher education redistribute resources from poor to middle- and upper-income families. Unfortunately, little is known about the relative importance of home investments, ability to finance, and public subsidies in explaining the strong positive relation between family background and schooling.

References

Becker, Gary S., and Chiswick, Barry R. "Education and the Distribution of Earnings." *A.E.R.* 56 (May 1966): 358–69.

Hunt, Shane J. "Income Determinants for College Graduates and the Return to Educational Investment." *Yale Econ. Essays* 3 (Fall 1963): 305–57.

Mincer, Jacob. "The Distribution of Labor Incomes: A Survey with Special Reference to the Human Capital Approach." *J. Econ. Literature* 8 (March 1970): 1–26.

———. "Schooling, Age. and Earnings." In *Human Capital and Personal Income Distribution.* New York: Nat. Bur. Econ. Res., in press.

Stigler, George J. "Director's Law of Public Income Redistribution." *J. Law and Econ.* 13 (April 1970): 1–10.

Note on the Intergenerational Transfer of Public Higher-Education Benefits

Joseph A. Pechman

Brookings Institution

The traditional way of looking at the burdens and benefits of higher education is to distribute the net benefits received by students by the income
classes of parents (taxpayers). This sweeps the problem created by the
intergenerational nature of the benefit transfer under the rug. It seems to
me that a more useful way of looking at the problem is to acknowledge
that the benefits of public higher education are received by one generation
while the costs are paid by another and that there is no way of merging
benefits and costs in one distribution to evaluate the equity of the system.

The benefits of higher education are received by the students who attend
college (although their parents may also feel better knowing that their
children are being educated). The costs are shared by the parents, who pay
for most of the out-of-pocket costs (tuition and room and board), the
taxpayers, who subsidize higher education, and the students, who bear the
cost of foregone earnings. Let us omit foregone earnings for the moment.
The remainder of the costs are borne by a generation of people (either
parents or taxpayers) who are, in effect, making a gift to those who are
going to a public college or university. Of course, there is an understanding
that each generation of earners will pay for the higher education of the
succeeding generation. There is no practical way of obtaining a distribution
of net benefits (or net burdens) by income classes in such a system, because the persons who receive the benefits are not the same persons
who pay the costs.[1]

The views expressed herein should not be attributed to the officers, trustees, or other
staff members of the Brookings Institution.

[1] This problem is analogous to that of estimating the net benefits of the Social
Security system. Benefits are received by the aged while earners pay costs of the
system (Pechman, Aaron, and Taussig 1968, pp. 180–81). In that study, distributions,
by income classes, of the burdens and benefits of social security are shown separately
for the earners and the aged, respectively, and no attempt is made to net one out
against the other.

On this reasoning, the "fairness" of the method used to finance the costs of public higher education cannot be judged by comparing the taxes and tuition paid by parents with the benefits received by college students. If society decides that higher education should be a public activity, the costs of that activity should be allocated in accordance with the tax system it judges to be best or fairest. If that tax system happens to be regressive, the fault is not that students (or their parents) are paying too little for their education. Society always has the option to improve its tax system to pay for public services of all sorts, including higher education.

Whatever the verdict on the tax side, there is a real question as to whether the benefit side of the system is equitable. If it is observed, as is the case, that children from low-income families either do not go to college or go to inferior schools, the system of distributing the benefits of public higher education is inequitable. Clearly, individuals who happen to be born into poor families should receive as much from this public service as do children who are born into middle- and high-income families. To correct this inequity, it is necessary to change enrollment practices and other discriminatory techniques now used against those who come from poor families so that they will have the same opportunity to go to college as those coming from higher-income families.[2]

Given the unequal precollege education, the equalization of educational opportunity at the college level would involve a number of costly steps. First, it would be necessary to invest heavily in compensatory education for those with deficient elementary and secondary education. Such education is now provided in a few schools, but it is clearly inadequate in numbers, quality, and scope. To overcome the educational handicap of poor children of college age in this country would require a staggering investment in compensatory education as compared with present programs. Second, youngsters from poor families cannot rely on their families to pay *any* out-of-pocket expenses, and in any case, they should not work much, given their academic preparation. They should be given grants that would be sufficient to pay these costs as well as instructional costs. Third, the earnings foregone by poor students may be a real burden for their families. To offset this cost, it may be necessary to supplement the incomes of the poor families to alleviate this burden. Finally, since not all children will be able, or will wish, to go to college, it would be inequitable to confine the educational subsidy to those among the 18-year-olds who choose college. The only way to handle this problem is to establish a one-time grant or drawing account for all individuals reaching the age of 18, to be used only for education purposes. Those who go to college could apply their grant

[2] Not the least of these needed changes is a method which would compensate for the deficient elementary and secondary school education given to children from poor families.

to college costs; the others would be allowed to use these grants for vocational or other types of training any time after they reach 18 years of age.[3]

So far, nothing has been said about tuition charges. (It is assumed that, whatever the tuition policy, students from poor families will be given grants that would be sufficient to pay tuition as well as other costs.) Whether or not tuition should be charged and, if so, how much of total instructional costs such charges should cover, depend on the degree to which higher education generates public benefits (in the Samuelson sense). Ideally, foregone earnings, plus tuition, plus out-of-pocket costs should pay for the private benefits of higher education and the remainder should be paid out of taxes. Estimates of the total higher-education costs privately paid differ, but they are clearly well in excess of 50 percent if foregone earnings are counted as a cost. Those who would charge full-cost tuition assume that higher education generates only private benefits; those who argue for free tuition assume that other costs (foregone earnings and out-of-pocket costs) are roughly proportional to private benefits. There is no way to settle this issue empirically. My own view is that the public benefits of higher education are significant and that it would, therefore, be unfair to impose the entire cost of higher education on students (and their families). Furthermore, the distributional effects of full-cost tuition are unlikely to be acceptable, even if generous public grants were available to students coming from low-income families. Full-cost tuition would have virtually no effect on enrollments of students from wealthy families, but it would certainly discourage enrollments of students from the low- and middle-income classes who would not be eligible for grants.

There remains the question of public versus private higher education. Many (but not all) of the private colleges in this country provide the same type of education as is provided in the public colleges. Thus, the two types of schools probably generate the same types of benefits, both public and private. A good case can be made, therefore, for subsidizing private as well as public higher education. Private institutions already receive a major subsidy in the form of their own income tax exemption and the deduction and exemption of charitable gifts and bequests to colleges and universities under the income and estate taxes, respectively. (The same tax benefits are available to public institutions, but they are not as important for them as they are for private institutions.) Part of the difference in costs between public and private institutions is due to the relatively more expensive type of education (for instance, smaller classes and better facilities) provided by the private institutions. It is doubtful that this difference should be subsidized by the public. But, for the "nonquality" related costs, if anyone could measure them, some move toward parity of treatment of public and private institutions of higher learning is warranted.

[3] This is a proposal by Tobin (1968).

References

Pechman, Joseph A.; Aaron, Henry J.; and Taussig, Michael K. *Social Security: Perspectives for Reform*. Washington: Brookings Inst., 1968.

Tobin, James. "Raising the Incomes of the Poor." In *Agenda for the Nation*, edited by Kermit Gordon, pp. 77–116. Washington: Brookings Inst., 1968.

Equity and the Finance
of Higher Education

W. Lee Hansen

University of Wisconsin

The many new proposals advanced during the past few years for financing higher education have been promoted, almost without exception, by appealing to their important and favorable equity consequences. What is meant by the term "equity"? To what degree will various proposals help achieve greater equity, however equity is defined? What kinds of side effects might these proposals produce in the process of achieving greater equity? Questions like these are difficult to answer because no systematic framework for analyzing equity and equity effects has evolved. Traditionally, equity has been viewed as a normative matter, and consequently, little attention has been given to developing the tools required to analyze it. The need for answers to the questions posed persists, however, and this paper offers a starting point in the search for answers. It might best be viewed as an essay on equity as applied to the provision and finance of higher education.

This paper focuses on undergraduate higher education. While there is jointness in the production of undergraduate education and such activities as graduate and professional education, research, public service, and the array of other activities known as higher education, it is also quite apparent that most undergraduate students are enrolled at institutions almost exclusively concerned with undergraduate teaching. It is not inappropriate, therefore, to concentrate only on undergraduate education. The focus is, moreover, on students rather than instiutions of higher education, because public policy presumably seeks to benefit students by producing more or less higher education.

In viewing the financing of undergraduate education, I focus, further, on the distinction between public and nonpublic sources of support—that is, between support by taxpayers and by students and their parents. I shall be less concerned with the important policy issue of whether public support comes from federal, state, or local government. Finally, I shall emphasize undergraduate education obtained in public institutions, where some of the most interesting equity issues arise.

I

What distinguishes "education" from other goods and thereby justifies the public financing (and usually the public provision) of undergraduate education? There are two quite different answers, one of which centers on efficiency and the other which emphasizes equity. Moreover, the answers are not unrelated, since the pursuit of equity may have some effects on efficiency and vice versa.

The conventional allocative efficiency justification is that significant external benefits are produced as individuals seek to enhance their own private welfare through undergraduate education (see West 1965). Without public subsidies, goes the argument, a less than optimal quantity of education would be purchased, and consequently, society as a whole would suffer. The provision of subsidies reduces private costs and thereby raises the marginal private rate of return to the level of the social rate of return. To determine the appropriate subsidy level, of course, the value of the external benefits must be known.

Evidence supporting this external-benefits argument for the public financing of undergraduate education is woefully weak. Bold assertions are made about the existence and size of "social" benefits from "higher education," and the distinction between graduate and undergraduate education often is blurred as these are considered. The long list of presumed benefits includes everything from "improved citizenship" to "enhancing manners and refinement of conduct" (Bowen 1971). But there is virtually no firm evidence on whether or not these benefits exist. And if they do exist, how valuable are they and to whom are they valuable?

The most frequently stated equity justification is that many young people cannot afford to pay the costs of college so that public subsidies should be provided to assist them. Without these subsidies, it is argued, access is contingent upon unequally distributed parental income and wealth rather than on ability to benefit from college. By setting an appropriate schedule of subsidies, the effects of differential economic well-being can be offset.

This view of equity differs considerably from what is produced by the subsidies provided through the present system of financing. Since the typical approach not only in the United States but in many other countries is to provide uniform subsidies to *all* students, those students (families) willing to pay the unsubsidized cost gain a windfall while others who are unwilling to pay the unsubsidized cost but willing to pay the lower, subsidized cost can now attend college. Still other students are unwilling to attend even at the partially subsidized price. They, along with the rest of the population, gain no direct benefits from the subsidy program. Thus, the presence of a subsidy program alters the immediate, as well as the prospective, distribution of real income.

There are, as suggested above, both a priori and empirical bases for evaluating the direct impact of this subsidy. But little can be said about who bears the burden of the taxes required to finance the subsidies. There is no ready way to determine what proportion of the taxes paid by people in different income classes supports any particular public expenditure program (see Hansen and Weisbrod 1971c). However, if changes in subsidies are accompanied by changes in tax rates, then it may be possible to infer how different groups or classes are affected. Such clear-cut cases rarely occur. Various categories of public expenditures are changing simultaneously, and a variety of considerations enter into determining how the tax changes will be distributed across income groups. Taken together, this makes it fruitless to try to link higher-education subsidies with the taxes paid "for" higher education so as to find out exactly whether individual benefits and individual payments balance out. Clearly, some redistribution is taking place through the way we finance higher education, but it cannot be isolated without recourse to highly arbitrary assumptions.

The objective of promoting greater equity might well conflict with such other objectives as economic efficiency. For example, providing subsidies sufficient to offset the limited resources of poorer students' families would require either larger tax revenues or reduced subsidies for wealthier students, or some combination of the two. The possible effects that might result range from reductions in the amount of work effort supplied (because of tax increases) to reduced rates of college attendance for wealthier students (because of their higher tuitions).

II

Real difficulties arise in discussing equity because the term has no clear-cut definition comparable to that of efficiency; the concept of equity discussed above is only one of several that might have been used. Views about what is equitable differ widely among individuals, and as yet there is no consensus yielding an operational criterion by which to assess the equity in higher education or in its finance. This has led people to examine, from a variety of viewpoints, the distributional effects of the present system and of alternatives to it, and they have then been free to draw their own conclusions.

What people mean by "equity" might be partly clarified by examining various proposals designed to achieve it. Four distinctly different objectives emerge from such proposals. They call for changing the distribution of (1) student input to the educational system, (2) student output of the system, (3) subsidies among students, and (4) incomes. In each case, the extent to which the system provides greater equity in the treatment of individuals classified and cross-classified by various background characteristics merits observation. Consider each of these objectives in turn.

Equity in the distribution of student input to undergraduate education forces an explicit consideration of the distinction between eligibility to attend college and actual attendance. Eligibility involves an ex ante determination of the extent to which attendance opportunities are indeed open to all, whereas actual attendance is an ex post determination of the extent to which these opportunities are realized.[1] Actual attendance patterns differ considerably among population groups. Many forces create a gap between opportunities and their realization; among them are student interest, aptitude, and motivation, plus the financial barriers which reflect limited student (parent) resources to finance college costs. Earlier some of these same forces also may have affected qualification for access. Hence, there is a choice of criteria to use in evaluating how effectively proposals meet the objective of altering the student mix.

If the objective is that of equity in the distribution of student output of the system, then a distinction must be made between opportunities for achievement and actual achievement. This distinction is exemplified in discussions of equality of opportuntiy in this country's elementary and secondary schools (Bowles 1968; Coleman 1968). The potential for student achievement is considerable; yet wide differences in achievement levels exist, even though attendance is almost universal. So far, less interest has been evidenced in this objective at the undergraduate level, perhaps because of the assumed high correlation between attendance and achievement. On the other hand, little is known about achievement—or learning—differences among different students at different colleges and universities. We probably know even less about the connection between what is achieved and the cost of the resource inputs used up.

Still another objective, and a not unrelated one, is equity in the distribution of the subsidies provided through the higher-education system. Where there is more than one type of public higher-education system (junior colleges, state universities), students attending different institutions will gain different amounts of subsidies. The duration of attendance will also affect the total amount of subsidies received.

Another objective is that of greater equity in the distribution of income of the population. To the extent that more postsecondary education leads to greater earning power, the future distribution of income and the position of particular people in that distribution will be affected by decisions on who attends college, how long they attend, and how much they achieve. The higher-education system can be visualized as operating so that the inter-

---

[1] This distinction is made effectively in a report of the Carnegie Commission on Higher Education (1970, pp. 11–14).

generational distribution of income remains largely unchanged or, alternatively, so as to shift about the position of family members in the income distribution from one generation to the next.

The extent to which one or another of these equity objectives is now being realized can be sketched out briefly.[2] To simplify the presentation, I shall focus largely on students classified by income or socioeconomic status (SES).

The evidence clearly shows that the higher the family's income and/or its SES, the more likely the children are to plan to attend college, to actually enroll in college, and to complete college. And within each income or SES class, the greater the academic ability (class rank, for example) of students, the more likely they are to plan to enroll in and attend college. Nevertheless, sizable numbers of apparently qualified young people (in the upper half of their high school classes) from less affluent families (the bottom two quartiles) do not attend college, while substantial numbers of apparently less qualified young people (in the bottom half of their high school classes) from more affluent families (the top two quartiles) do attend college. Since financial barriers affect who goes to college and for how long, the current system is nonneutral in its treatment of people.

This nonneutrality results even though tuition averages only about a quarter of the full cost of undergraduate education and large amounts of student financial aid are disbursed. While low tuition reduces the financial barrier for all students, including some to whom full tuition would be no barrier, students from lower-income families may be "able" to attend college only if they obtain additional financial aid to help offset the out-of-pocket costs and, perhaps even more important, the pressure to augment family income (the foregone-earnings costs of college). The currently available financial aid is, however, grossly inadequate to meet total student financial "need" as generally defined. All financial aid—in the form of grants, work, and loans—at best adds up to less than 40 percent of financial need as it is conventionally measured.

There appears to be no evidence whatsoever on how levels of achievement differ among various classes of college students. There is, however, some evidence on the distribution of subsidies For California, Weisbrod and I (Hansen and Weisbrod 1969) found that undergraduate subsidies vary considerably among the three higher-education systems (junior colleges, state colleges, and the university) and that the high-subsidy institutions enrolled, on the average, students from higher-income families.[3] In Wisconsin, by contrast, there is virtually no difference among the amounts of the annual subsidies offered in the three systems of higher

[2] Much of the evidence reported in the following four paragraphs is drawn from Hansen (1970a).

[3] For a critical review, see Pechman (1970) and Hartman (1970). Also see Hansen and Weisbrod (1971b).

education, even though the average family incomes of the students enrolled in those systems do differ (Hansen 1970*b*). Yet in Wisconsin, too, the ex post distribution of subsidies favors students from families with higher incomes because those students are more likely to complete their undergraduate programs.

Whether or not education speeds up the process of intergenerational income mobility—and speeds it up compared with what—is not known. We do know that college attendance of children is associated with college attendance of their parents, even after controlling for income; we also know that children, on the average, exceed the educational attainments of their parents. But the extent to which students and parents differ in their relative position in the income distribution from generation to generation is not known.

This brief review indicates that, while there are some criteria by which to judge the equity of the system, the data are still inadequate. Yet we may be able to salvage something. First, assume that for reasons of equity it is argued that more students from lower-income families should be assisted in going to college. If there were limited spaces, then college would probably replace the less able but affluent students with the more able but financially poorer students. On the assumption that higher achievement in high school is more likely than higher parental income to be correlated with high productivity (or income) subsequent to college attendance, resource allocation would be improved by effecting this shift in the composition of the college student body. Thus, an action deemed to help achieve greater equity holds out the promise of being more efficient as well. Such an action, however, would involve not only increasing "access" among certain students but decreasing it for others; restricting opportunities for higher-income families would be controversial, particularly if additional tax revenue had to be sought to provide the financial aid for the new group of students. It would surely not be seen as "equitable" by those families who would be denied the opportunity to use the market system to purchase the higher education they wanted.

Second, if student financial aid is viewed as including the student subsidies now provided through below-cost tuition, then total student financial aid actually exceeds, rather than falls short of, total student financial need. Even if we assume that an enrollment increase among lower-income students is brought about by the increased available financial aid funds, total aid would still meet at least two-thirds of the total financial need, and that would be well above the present 40 percent (Hansen 1970*a*). Thus, by simply reallocating the public resources already used to support undergraduate education, the existing financial barriers could be largely offset. And by the reasoning presented in the previous paragraph, this would probably lead to greater equity and efficiency.

These interesting results should alert us to the fact that proposals for

266

financing undergraduate education may well have favorable equity and efficiency effects. They also suggest that objectives of equity and efficiency need not always conflict, although they often do.

III

Proposals for promoting greater equity in higher education—and that is what most of the proposals for financing higher education emphasize—are of two kinds. One kind involves the extent to which there are likely to be intergenerational transfers of resources: from taxpayers and private donors to students and their parents, and from taxpayers, donors, and parents to college students. The other kind involves the extent to which there are intragenerational transfers which take direct account of the investment nature of college expenditures. I will not attempt here to review the gamut of financing plans, for this has already been done by others (Wolks 1968; Orwig 1971).

Proposals of the first kind take several forms. One is to provide equal treatment to all students, irrespective of their differing characteristics and financial conditions. This might involve (a) full instructional cost tuition charges (no subsidy for anyone attending college); (b) zero tuition charges (an equal but partial subsidy for all who attend college); (c) full grants to students to cover all institutional and opportunity costs of attendance (an equal and complete subsidy for all who attend); and (d) a fixed grant of the "GI bill" variety for education and training (this could be a full or partial subsidy to all who seek postsecondary education and training).

Common to proposals (b) and (c) is the provision of approximately equal-sized subsidies to all eligibles even though their family resources may differ widely. This means that subsidies as a proportion of income fall as family income increases. At the same time, the wider the gap between the private costs of education and the subsidy, the smaller will be the percentage of lower-income students availing themselves of the subsidy. As a result, the average ex post subsidy received per eligible person may rise with income level over some range, although whether the average subsidy as a fraction of family income exceeds, equals, or falls short of income depends upon the price and income elasticities of demand.

Such proposals for equal treatment ignore the different initial circumstances in which students and their families find themselves. Students from higher-income families have access to more resources to help pay for the costs of college; many of them would attend even if there were no subsidy. Lower-income students, by contrast, find themselves unable to afford college even with substantial subsidies. Thus, proposals (b) and (c) generate support because they reduce the impact on attendance of differential ability to pay.

These proposals differ widely in how their costs are shared. With full student grants, proposal (c), all undergraduate education costs are borne by taxpayers and donors. With a system of full-instructional-cost tuition charges, proposal (a), taxpayers and donors make a zero contribution while students and their parents share the instructional costs and the income foregone during attendance. Zero tuition, proposal (b), is an intermediate proposal, one which differs only in degree from (c). Fixed grants, proposal (d), by covering a much larger group of individuals, become more expensive to taxpayers than (a) unless the size of the grant is scaled down to where students and their parents have to share in the costs.

These proposals will have differing incentive effects. The larger the size of the subsidy, the greater will be the private rate of return to investing in undergraduate education; a higher rate of return will stimulate an increase in enrollments, thereby raising the cost of the proposal to taxpayers. The sensitivity of the private rate of return to alternative tuition policies can be illustrated with some recent unpublished calculations for Wisconsin.[4] Assume that the private rate of return (for males only) to a 2-year degree program in Wisconsin is 11.5 percent. If, instead of paying tuition amounting to approximately 30 percent of total instructional costs, the student were charged zero tuition, then the rate of return would rise, but only slightly, to 12.0 percent. With tuition set at full instructional costs, the rate of return would drop to 10.3 percent. These results give some notion of the low sensitivity of private rates of return to alternative tuition policies. The principal reason is that even full-cost tuition comprises only a small fraction of the costs of college; foregone income constitutes the major cost element. Changes in tuition costs will, of course, have no short-run effect on the rate of return to total resource costs. Over the longer run, as the number and quality of the student body change in response to tuition changes, we might expect the social rate of return to change somewhat.

Another variant of the first kind of proposal calls for special "equalizing" treatment for all students, that is, treatment which by differentiating among students places them on an equal financial footing in overcoming the financial barriers to college attendance.[5] The variants on this kind of proposal involve either financial aid grants based on student financial need or financial aid grants and work opportunities based on student financial need. The principal difference between these variants is in the extent to which students must work to help earn their college expenses and to which students must allocate some of their time to work effort.

Under these proposals, student grants based on "need" might cover any amount ranging from tuition, or some part of it, to the full out-of-pocket costs of college attendance, and might even include some allowance for foregone income. Thus, the grants would vary inversely with family income.

[4] These calculations were made in collaboration with David Witmer.
[5] For fuller treatment of this type of proposal, see Hansen and Weisbrod (1971a)

Because the grants would help to offset financial barriers, we would expect them to reduce the differences between the number of eligible students and the number enrolled—the reduction being inversely related to family income.

The cost-sharing effects of these proposals bear mention. The higher the student-grant maximum and the lower the tuition, the greater will be the cost of the program. But if we assume, for example, that full-cost tuition is charged, then those students who cannot demonstrate financial need and their parents will bear all of the costs of college. Those students demonstrating full financial need will have their instructional costs (full-cost tuition) borne by taxpayers; students and their parents will share the remaining costs, unless the grant maximum is set high enough to include an allowance for foregone income. By a judicious setting of the grant schedule, a program can be designed that will not increase taxpayer cost of undergraduate education but will result in a reduction of subsidies in favor of students from lower-income families.

The incentive effects of these proposals are strikingly different from those discussed earlier. While the social rate of return to total resource costs will behave as mentioned above, the private rates of return will change. With unchanged tuition, the rate of return will increase for students receiving financial aid and remain the same for those not receiving financial aid. But if full-cost tuition is charged, the rate of return will rise even more for students receiving financial aid (they now receive a greater subsidy) while it falls for those without financial aid (their subsidy has been decreased). The shifts in rates of return made possible by direct grants or subsidies to students will stimulate greater enrollment by qualified students with financial need but will possibly reduce somewhat the enrollment by students without financial need. Actually, the enrollment response is not fully clear inasmuch as students with no financial need are viewed as "financially able" to pay the costs of college; hence, they might be expected to continue enrolling at essentially the same rate. The demand elasticity for higher income students is, however, not known.

Under these proposals, then, the structure of student grants would be such as to insure equal opportunities for students of comparable ability but with different family circumstances, in overcoming the financial barriers to attendance.

Proposals in the second broad category recognize that expenditures on undergraduate education represent an investment which is highly likely to result in greater earning capacity, and hence young people should have equal access to investment funds which they can repay later in life. Becker and Chiswick (1966) proposed this as a criterion for assessing equity ("equality of opportunity") in the market for higher education.

The task—given this interpretation of "the problem"—becomes one of improving the capital market for educational loans. Of the numerous proposals, some are national in scope (the Zacharias proposal [U.S. Panel on Educational Innovation 1967]) while others are very limited (Yale's new tuition-postponement option [Tobin and Pugash 1971]). The effects of loan schemes have been analyzed by Hartman (1971),[6] so there is no need to describe these proposals in any detail here.

What kinds of equity effects are likely to result under a loan plan? We would expect a continuation of intergenerational transfers of resources from parents to children, depending upon a family's ability to pay. The higher the family income, the more likely it is that the student will not need to take the loan. Lower-income students, by contrast, will more likely borrow because of the inability of the family to transfer any large amounts of resources to them. So what we are likely to observe is approximately the same subsequent incomes of students from higher- and lower-income families but different net incomes after allowance for annual interest and principal repayments.

What these plans mean for incentives is difficult to say. Undoubtedly, larger numbers of qualified lower-income students will wish to make use of loan funds, although the terms of the loans and the extent of the subsidy built into them presumably would be important variables. How sensitive these students will be to the amount of the loan they must take out and the interest charges they must pay, particularly as tuition rises toward full instructional cost (a likely occurrence, I would guess), is much more difficult to say. One reason for this uncertainty is that, whatever the private rate of return, the perceived net benefits may differ appreciably, depending upon whether the out-of-pocket costs of education are financed largely through transfers from parents versus student borrowing that requires future repayment.

The cost-sharing effects are clear. To the extent that tuition is still subsidized, the only additional cost to taxpayers will be the interest subsidy, if there is one, and that cost should not be large. More likely, as noted above, tuition will gradually increase so that the relative costs of undergraduate education to taxpayers will decline. Students and, in part, their parents will absorb the increase.

IV

When alternative methods of financing higher education are discussed, particularly those which move far toward offsetting the financial barriers confronting qualified lower-income young people, there is considerable concern about who will pay the costs. If additional resources are required, this will mean an increase in taxes or a reduction in expenditures on other

[6] A part of Hartman's (1971) study, prepared for the Carnegie Commission on Higher Education, appears in Orwig (1971, pp. 117–42).

programs. Rarely, however, is there any discussion of the incidence of the additional taxes or of which other programs would have to be cut. While someone will have to pay, who that will be and how much they will have to pay are unclear. On the other hand, if existing resources are to be reallocated, as in the full cost-grant scheme Weisbrod and I proposed for Wisconsin, then it is quite clear who will bear the brunt of the costs and how much they will have to pay. It will be students (families) in the middle- and upper-income groups, and they are likely to object.

Objectors to any shift in financing higher education often fail to recognize that *current* family income is not the sole measure of a family's ability to pay their children's educational costs. Families also have recourse to their net worth, at least some portion of which was probably accumulated specifically for purposes of college financing (Lansing, Lorimer, and Moriguchi 1960). This reserve of net worth, with its ratio to income rising as income increases, means that the ability to pay out of some combination of current income and net worth rises more sharply than is indicated by looking at family income alone (Hansen and Weisbrod 1968).

The role of wealth in affecting college attendance is an intriguing one, because it has important implications for the extent to which different financing schemes will bring about changes in the distribution of income from one generation to the next. Parental financing of undergraduate education can be viewed as one of several methods for transferring wealth from generation to generation; two other methods are via cash or in-kind gifts during the lifetime of the parents and via inheritance later.

Educational purchases appear to be a preferred form of transfer,[7] and upon reflection, the reasons become apparent. Foremost is the parental view that education becomes embodied in the child and thus cannot be taken away or easily destroyed or lost; hence, by this purchase, parents exert a permanent influence on the child and help to insure the child's continued livelihood through the earning power this education will generate. In addition, supporting a child through college yields some tax saving through the exemptions for dependents permitted under the tax laws; also, gift and inheritance taxes are avoided. More important, perhaps, is the leverage that such expenditures provide in helping parents achieve their wishes for the future life-style of their children. By providing tuition and other out-of-pocket costs, parents can easily tap the public subsidy that accompanies enrollment in public colleges and the subsidy of endowments at private colleges. The wise parent may also enlist the efforts of the child to offset some of the out-of-pocket costs by working while he attends school. All of these forces combine to strengthen the desire to transfer wealth, or at least some minimum amount of it, via education investment.

The ability to transfer wealth in this way is facilitated by the structure

[7] For some evidence, see Guthrie (1963).

of education, with its relatively weak emphasis on academic standards as a condition for admission to college. As some have remarked, there is a college for everyone: a person with even the lowest academic credentials will be admitted to a college somewhere, the only difficulties being finding the college and financing the costs. This characteristic of American higher education makes it easier for wealthy families to effect wealth transfers to their children through education purchases than in most other nations.

Taking account, then, of the desirability as well as the ability to transfer wealth from generation to generation via educational purchases, we would not expect the present method of financing higher education to do much to alter the shape of the income distribution from one generation to the next or to affect the relative income position of the successive generations. The reason is found in the effect of college attendance itself on lifetime incomes. We know that, on the average, the incomes of college graduates exceed those of high school graduates and, given the assumption (for which there is some evidence) that the ratio of wealth to income is higher for the college educated, that the ability to pass on more education to their children rises more than proportionately with the educational attainment of parents. Hence, we find that educational attainment, through its effect on income, and, in turn, its effect on wealth, works to limit the way in which the distribution of income from generation to generation is altered.

What can we now say about the several major types of financing proposals advanced earlier? If across-the-board subsidies were increased, the intergenerational distribution of income would change only insofar as additional lower-income students are induced to attend. If a system of grants which met student financial need were implemented, the chances for qualified lower-income students to rise in the distribution relative to their parents would increase. If at the same time tuition were set at full cost with grants increased commensurately, there would be an even more substantial effect. Not only would more lower-income students find their way into and through college, but the diminished subsidies resulting from higher tuition to upper-income students would reduce the relative payoff to college for them; hence, a greater amount of intergenerational shifting might be expected. If a system of loans were introduced, opportunities for lower-income students to improve their position in the income distribution would increase. But this change might be illusory; what is important is not gross but net income (gross income less debt repayment), and this, for college students who borrow heavily, might not be much greater than the gross income of high school graduates.

V

Much remains undiscussed in this paper. Almost nothing has been said about the effect of making subsidies available only for formal instruction of the kind now designated as "higher education." Other important human-

272

investment options not now subsidized—proprietary training, on-the-job training, apprenticeship, and the like—might on equity grounds qualify for subsidies of the kind provided via formal higher education. In addition, the difference in treatment of students attending public and private institutions of higher education requires analysis. And whether the interests of equity are better served by providing subsidies to individuals rather than via institutions must be studied. Finally, some interesting parallels could no doubt be drawn between equity in higher education and that in other public programs.

The concept of equity—whether in the financing of higher education or of other programs—remains an elusive one. At the same time, growing concern about equity is forcing us to address this topic. Out of all of this we can only hope that an analytical framework will emerge to help us deal more systematically with equity questions.

References

Becker, Gary S., and Chiswick, Barry R. "Education and the Distribution of Earnings." *A.E.R.* 56 (May 1966): 358–69.

Bowen, Howard R. "Finance and the Aims of American Higher Education." In *Financing Higher Education: Alternatives for the Federal Government*. edited by M. D. Orwig, pp. 155–70. Iowa City, Iowa: American Coll. Testing Program, 1971.

Bowles, Samuel. "Towards Equality of Educational Opportunity." *Harvard Educ.* 38, special issue (Winter 1968): 89–99.

Carnegie Commission on Higher Education. *A Chance to Learn: An Action Agenda for Equal Opportunity in Higher Education*. New York: McGraw-Hill, 1970.

Coleman, James. "The Concept of Equality of Educational Opportunity." *Harvard Educ. Rev.* 38, special issue (Winter 1968): 7–22.

Guthrie, Harold W. "Intergenerational Transfers of Wealth and the Theory of Saving." *J. Bus.* 36 (January 1963): 97–108.

Hansen, W. Lee. "Financial Barriers to College Attendance." In *Trends in Postsecondary Education*. U.S. Office of Education book OE-50063. Washington: Government Printing Office, 1970. (*a*)

———. "Income Redistribution Effects of Higher Education." *A.E.R.* 60 (May 1970): 335–40. (*b*)

Hansen, W. Lee, and Weisbrod, Burton A. "An Income Net-Worth Measure of Economic Position." *A.E.R.* 58 (December 1968): 1315–29.

———. "The Distribution of Costs and Direct Benefits of Public Higher Education: The Case of California." *J. Human Resources* 4 (Spring 1969): 176–91.

———. "A New Approach to Higher Education Finance." In *Financing Higher Education: Alternatives for the Federal Government*, edited by M. D. Orwig, pp. 117–42. Iowa City, Iowa: American Coll. Testing Program, 1971. (*a*)

———. "On the Distribution of Costs and Benefits of Public Higher Education: Reply." *J. Human Resources* 6 (Summer 1971): 363–74. (*b*)

———. "Who Pays for a Public Expenditure Program?" *Nat. Tax J.* 6 (December 1971): 515–17. (*c*)

Hartman, Robert W. "A Comment on the Pechman-Hansen-Weisbrod Contro-versy." *J. Human Resources* 5 (Fall 1970): 519–23.
————.*Credit for College: Public Policy for Student Loans.* New York: McGraw-Hill, 1971.
Lansing, John B.; Lorimer, Thomas; and Moriguchi, Chikashi. *How People Pay for College.* Ann Arbor: Survey Res. Center, Inst. Soc. Res. Univ. Mich., 1960.
Orwig, M. D., ed. *Financing Higher Education: Alternatives to the Federal Government.* Iowa City, Iowa: American Coll. Testing Program, 1971.
Pechman, Joseph A. "The Distributional Effects of Public Higher Education in California." *J. Human Resources* 5 (Summer 1970): 361–70.
Tobin, James, and Pugash, James. "The Economics of the Tuition Postponement Option." *Yale Daily News*, February 10, 1971.
U.S. Panel on Educational Innovation. *Educational Opportunity Bank.* Zacharias Committee Report. Washington: Government Printing Office, 1967.
West, E. G. *Education and the State.* London: Inst. Econ. Affairs, 1965.
Wolks, Ronald A. *Alternative Methods of Federal Funding for Higher Education.* Berkeley, Calif.: Carnegie Commission Higher Educ., 1968.

Comment

O. H. Brownlee

University of Minnesota

I am in no particular disagreement with the position taken by Lee Hansen. He claims that both increased equity and greater efficiency than now exist in financing higher education are compatible up to a certain point, in spite of the different interpretations that reasonably can be assigned to efficiency. I believe that this contention is correct, although the evidence in support of it is largely casual.

However, instead of examining various schemes that might be more equitable and appraising their efficiencies in comparison with existing arrangements, it seems easier to consider eliminating some obvious inefficiencies that now exist and to see whether the outcomes are likely to be more inequitable according to any of the various reasonable definitions of equity.

If a subsidy to higher education is to be provided, it should be paid directly to individuals, rather than to institutions as is generally the case at present and as has generally been recommended by the educators and study commissions advising the federal government. Payment to individuals rather than institutions permits us to abandon discussion about how high tuition ought to be and to focus directly on how much should be given to persons in various circumstances and how the money for such transfers should be raised. The expected increased efficiency that would accompany such an institutional change has been discussed by Friedman, Alchien, Buchanan, and many others. Among the expected outcomes are: more nearly minimizing the cost of producing whatever is provided, greater diversity of curricula, and greater specialization among institutions. I do not see how such a change need make the distribution of the subsidy less equitable than that resulting from present arrangements.

A determination of how much ought to go to whom should raise the question of benefits that accrue to persons other than those receiving the schooling. If these "externalities" are no different from those resulting from other forms of investment, there is no reason for making the subsidy conditional upon its being used for education. If there are benefits to the society as a whole that result from investment in higher education and that would not accrue from other forms of investment (it seems unlikely that they would be equally important in all of the various possible forms of such education), then, apart from whatever subsidy is to be provided to more nearly equalize resource endowments among individuals, the amount of the subsidy should differ according to the type of training chosen by the individual.

I agree with Hansen that the evidence in support of the contention that higher education merits a subsidy because of these "externalities" is very weak. However, even those who purport to find such externalities would agree that they are virtually nonexistent in professional and graduate education. I have not heard claims that morticians or dentists are better citizens than other persons with comparable incomes. Doctors, engineers, lawyers, and veterinarians are not usually credited with marginal social products that exceed their marginal private ones. In fact, the "externalities" argument is most often applied to training in the social sciences and education, but the evidence seems to me no better with respect to these fields than those listed above.

In any event, although Hansen's discussion deals only with undergraduate education, we ought to be able to agree to abandon the subsidy to graduate and professional education. If, as Schultz has contended in his paper here, graduate education and research are joint products, with the difference between the cost of providing the education and the charges made for it being about equal to the graduate student's contribution to research, the differences among fields and universities probably are large. Direct payment for the research and marginal cost pricing for the training would be more efficient than the present practice.

If there are "externalities," surely they are not large enough to warrant a subsidy as large as higher education is now receiving. The transfer confined to investment in education thus becomes difficult to justify. If its purpose is to more nearly equalize resource endowments, transfers should be available for any form of investment. If individual preferences are to really count, a transfer should also be available for current consumption, if the individual wishes to use it in that manner. Educational subsidies are of no benefit to those who cannot take advantage of them and can make the distribution of income more unequal than if they did not exist. The absurdity of an income-equalizing measure of zero tuition at universities with admission requirements that can be met only by those with incomes high enough to pay the full costs of secondary education ought to be obvious. Nevertheless, such a condition exists in some less developed countries and is frequently justified as a measure to help the poor catch up with the rich! Policy in the United States is not so extreme, but ability to attend a university is positively correlated with income.

A more rational transfer scheme would make the net transfer vary inversely with potential income or wealth. This is an outcome of equal grants to all financed from proportionate or progressive income taxation. However, the amount of the gross transfer required to accomplish a given degree of equalization is larger when it is given to all (on their eighteenth birthdays?) than if the grants were inversely related to potential income or wealth, and the incentive effects due to higher marginal tax rates are thus more adverse. The costs of administering effective means tests have to be compared with those of reduced incentives. If such a system subsidized the dull and penalized the bright, would we buy it? My guess is that we would not. However, this is what many definitions of equity imply.

Comment

Finis Welch

National Bureau of Economic Research

Lee Hansen has done a thorough job of (1) laying out a smorgasbord of schemes for funding college education and (2) highlighting some of the main equity considerations. He observes that efficiency arguments based upon external benefits lack empirical footing, and then proceeds to the analytically less ambiguous but equally unsubstantiated equity issues. Here the very range of his discussion serves to emphasize the diversity of objectives and the lack of factual knowledge. To quote an earlier comment at this workshop: "We can speculate so freely because we know so little."

Frankly, I find it hard to criticize the paper for sins of commission or, given the state of the data, for sins of omission. Alternatives are reported generally without taking sides, and I cannot fault the report. Instead of serving as critic in the traditional sense, let me summarize a few points and then add to the speculation.

First, my impression is that Hansen feels that the present financial system is highly variable but that greater absolute benefits accrue to families with higher incomes. Further, the distribution of attendance viewed as attendance probabilities by parental-income class is more equal than it would be in a system of full charge without accompanying loan programs.

Basically, the idea is that the fraction of children attending college in all parental-income classes is a negative function of the tuition rate. Too, the tuition level that induces a given enrollment rate, say of 50 percent, rises with family income. Here the alternative model from which Hansen's distributional conclusions are drawn is clearly a world of full-cost tuition without capital-market intervention. But note that even with capital-market imperfections these conclusions need not hold. If, for example, private schools offer lower subsidies and have higher quality and if the demand for quality is elastic vis-à-vis family income, the distributional effects are indeterminate. It is possible that substitution responses between high- and low-quality schools, respectively, both private and public, are so small that greater subsidies would in fact accrue to middle-income families. I imagine that few would argue that New York's public elementary schools result in higher subsidies to higher-income families.

One of the main issues begged in this analysis is the quality of schooling. In fact, I submit that the main reason the Hartman profile of average future income by family-income class is so flat is that he ignores completion probabilities as a function of parental income and, more important, that he ignores positive correlations between schooling quality and parental income. The evidence cited by Bowles of correlations between family background and income, holding nominal school completion constant, reflects, in part, schooling quality.

Next, Hansen offers the tantalizing example of what I call a Schultzicism —a "free [policy] lunch" in which equity and efficiency are compatible— when he states that, "on the assumption that higher achievement in high school is more likely than higher parental income to be correlated with high productivity (or income) subsequent to college attendance, resource allocation would be improved by effecting this shift in the composition of the college student body." Lower-ability, but affluent, students would be dropped in place of higher-ability, but financially poor, students.

Notice that reference is to high school achievement rather than to "raw" ability, so that by the time high school is completed we would expect much confounding with parental status. Notice also that if John Hause is right—that if there is positive interaction between the return to ability and education—the case for this kind of shift is strengthened.

Hansen appears to come out in favor of a policy that insures equal opportunities for students of comparable ability but different family circumstances.

Here I quibble briefly. First, the origin of ability should be specified. Is it raw or innate? Or, is it ability after high school achievement? If the former, what of efficiency, and if the latter, what of equity?

I conclude with two points relevant to further research. First, I suspect that instances of Schultzicisms are not too uncommon and a search may be fruitful. For example, the "benefit" to college attendance may be related to peers. It may be that students of high socioeconomic standing gain from the presence of colleagues of low socioeconomic standing, so that some price discrimination may be efficient. It does not matter that the relationship is symmetric; it only matters that, to insure "balance," affluent students may have to bribe others to attend their schools. Last, although loan programs have been touted here, I for one am dubious about their possibilities in changing income distributions. Obviously, they cannot be faulted on classical efficiency grounds, but as a device for permitting the redistribution of income, there is the obvious point that at the margin you "gotta" pay for what you get. More important, I think, is that we have lost sight of the consumption aspects of education.

Viewed only as an investment, a loan program that reduces capital-market frictions should improve the *efficiency* of the distribution of education. But when consumption aspects are considered, if the demand for children's education is family-income-elastic, agreement between educational attainment and family income might be greater under a full-loan program than it is now.

This, of course, is not "bad." Barring the ever-illusive "externalities," the case for subsidizing families by bribing their offspring to go to college is probably weaker than the case for food stamps: black markets would likely be less efficient in the case of schooling.

The Alternatives before Us

Harry G. Johnson

London School of Economics and Political Science and University of Chicago

The function of this paper is, presumably, to pull together the detailed discussions that have taken place during the four days of this conference on higher education and the personal distribution of income. These discussions have ranged widely over many issues both of philosophy and of economic theory and also over the proper way to extract the maximum of information from the minimum amount of statistically usable data. From them, however, should emerge a set of issues that can be shaped into some sort of rough agenda for future research and theorizing.

I begin with some fairly elementary but, I hope, relevant comments on the motivation of the conference. Two quite different themes have motivated the large and long-standing literature of social concern and social reformism with respect to the personal distribution of income.

One concern has been with what is variously termed "the need for a social minimum" and "the poverty problem." Those who have expressed this concern, and thought about it, have shared the general philosophical position that inequalities of income and wealth resulting from differences in productive input into the economic system of society are necessary and justified by their contribution to the efficiency and the dynamic progress of the economy and hence to the general well-being. Nevertheless, they feel that those who are more fortunately placed by reason of their superior productive power have an obligation to ensure that their less fortunate fellow citizens do not fall below some socially determined standard of decency, in terms of level of consumption of goods and services. This position, in its less sophisticated version, leads to the recommendation of income redistribution through the fiscal process and provision of social services and security designed to ensure a "social minimum" for every citizen by virtue of his being a citizen. In its more sophisticated versions, the approach leads to uneasiness about the extent to which the prospects of innocent children are determined by the accidents of their parentages, and to consequent recommendation of policies designed, on the one hand, to prevent children of a particular generation from obtaining too great a head start over their peer group and, on the other hand, to prevent others from suffering too much disadvantage because their parents were economically unsuccessful. Specifically, this has in the past involved considerable interest in progressive inheritance taxation and, more recently, concern about "equality of opportunity" in the educational system. Whether unsophisticated or sophisticated, this approach soon gets involved in conflicts between a belief in the necessity of economic incentives to motivate economic contributions and accumulation and a recognition that completely free play for economic incentives produces results considered humanly and socially and even morally unjustifiable.

The other approach has been concerned with "equality" rather than with the "social minimum." The two, of course, do not necessarily overlap: a society could have no poverty but great inequality; or it could have equality for the majority and so satisfy most statistical definitions of equality, while still being characterized by widespread poverty. But the two approaches do tend to overlap and become confused with each other because poverty only becomes noticeable and apparently remediable when a sufficiently small proportion of the population (Roosevelt's one-third, Johnson's one-fifth of the nation) is subject to it, while inequality only becomes a source of serious social concern when its existence leads to a significant proportion of the population—who may themselves be either "poor" or "rich"—believing that the existing degree of inequality is unjust. Philosophically, a concern with inequality raises as intractable problems as does a concern with poverty, and perhaps even more difficult problems. For it rests on the a priori proposition that all men are in some sense either equal or potentially equal. While this proposition can be satisfied fairly cheaply in the political sphere by giving each person one vote and not inquiring too closely into how he chooses to spend it, the achievement of economic equality raises far more difficult problems, especially of cost. Moreover, just as concern about poverty has both a less and a more sophisticated version—reallocation of existing income versus reallocation of existing opportunity toward the poor—so concern about equality has both a less and a more sophisticated version: equalization of existing incomes through fiscal transfers and equalization of income-earning opportunities through rearrangement of the availability of opportunities. And just as concern about poverty faces a conflict between a social judgment of "fairness" or "decency" and an economic understanding of the laws of economic incentives, so concern about equality faces a conflict between a social judgment of fairness in the provision of opportunities and an economic judgment of the adequacy of the responses of differently situated individuals to these opportunities.

Further, there is in both cases the problem of the intergenerational dimension of the question. Is poverty in the sense of some indecently low-income receivers tolerable if it is not passed on to the second generation, as part of the economic incentive system, or must no poverty be tolerated anywhere at any time? Is "from shirt-sleeves to shirt-sleeves in three generations" a satisfactory definition of an equalitarian system—as it used to be considered in nineteenth-century America, as applied to those who were lucky in their own generation—or should it be rewritten into "no shirt-sleeves for anyone, ever!"?

Economics used to be a branch of moral philosophy before it became independent and emerged through the title of "political economy" into the status of a self-styled social science. At least in the hands of its best practitioners in the intervening years, it sought to temper economic logic and the doctrine of laissez faire by an understanding of how these economic forces impinged on society as it was actually organized—namely, not by unfettered free enterprise but by families which, for good or ill, arrived from generation to generation by a process of inheritance which involved a triad of material property, genetically determined innate ability (or, perhaps more cautiously expressed, potential ability), and something occasionally referred to as "family character." Frank Knight used scornfully to dismiss equalitarianism with the argument that it was impossible by public policy to equalize the nonmaterial family backgrounds of children. I would venture the thought that compulsory conscription of children into state-run orphanages might do the trick—and this has sometimes been suggested, and even practiced in small communities by utopian socialists, though the proposal has few modern proponents among social philosophers. But every time I use this assumption to set up a simple model of a human-capital–oriented society (I cannot use a slave society to exemplify the principles of rationality with respect to human capital in this day and age), the laughter of my students reminds me of how unrealistic politically the suggestion is.

I should add that one of Knight's major points in this connection, and one I have never forgotten, is that the inegalitarian economic consequences of unequal inheritance of genetically determined ability or of family character are just as morally indefensible as the inegalitarian economic consequences of unequal inheritance of material property. Yet one of the basic problems confronting us in this conference in the policy area has been that our society discriminates sharply in favor of both genetical inheritance and the capacity of well-to-do parents to give their children an inheritance of culture, time, patience, and travel in substitution for an inheritance of material property. This substitution possibility continues to frustrate inheritance taxation designed to increase equality within the next generation. As academics we typically lack either the reasoning power or the intellectual frigidity to pursue that point to its logical conclusion. In particular, we are typically unwilling to contemplate the idea that, regardless of whether poverty or inequality is our focus of concern, material capital can be substituted for human capital, and if we want to equalize opportunities for income earning among children of different inheritances (with respect to both total and composition), we should in all honesty consider the possibility of giving them money instead of education, rather than seeking only to use money to buy them educational equality.

Much of the work that has been presented at this conference appears to have been slowly fumbling its way back to insights into the social aspects of higher education that the older-style economists—Adam Smith and Alfred Marshall on one side of the Atlantic, Thorstein Veblen and Frank Knight on the other—already had, though one has to interpret them with insight and modernize their language. The concepts of different supply and demand curves for education by upper- and lower-income groups, of different search costs and risks, of differing entrepreneurial requirements, of differences between innate and acquired capacity for education on the part of children from richer and poorer families, of ability and motivation as opposing forces governing the ultimate performance of the educated, are all concepts that one could acquire, if one tried, by reading a few novels by Jane Austen or Charles Dickens—or, for that matter, by Horatio Alger. I do not say that these economic concepts are uninformative or unenlightening when applied to the problems of the relation between education and income distribution—quite the contrary. But I would say that the need to develop and emphasize them is the consequence, on the one side, of an excessively naïve view of the democratic, equalitarian, and other characteristics that American society likes to attribute to itself, a view emphasized during the post–World War II period by the assumed threat to the American way of life posed by what every European immigrant to America had been taught to regard as the monster threat to European civilization—the barbarous Russian empire, the Byzantine deviant from the true Catholic religion. This view has only gradually been dispelled by the recognition that the Russians are really failed Europeans like ourselves and that the real threat to our civilization now comes from the mysterious East. On the other hand, the need for the new concepts has been created by our own conception, developed since the 1930s, of our subject as a "science," philosophically, socially, and ethically neutral, and requiring mathematical theorizing for its intellectual base and econometric testing to furnish plausibility and what Veblen called "ceremonial adequacy." Science demands the submergence of social conscience in a welter of statistical squabbles. Economists with a feel for society have had both to learn a different language and to adapt its grammar and semantics to cover situations excluded from consideration by the tri-

umphant simplicity of the scientific core of the subject, in order to return
to the discussion of things that concern them as human beings and as
members of society.

I have dwelt so long on these preliminaries as a prelude to reminding
you that since the early 1960s we have moved very rapidly—and mostly
in response to the social and intellectual dynamics of this country rather
than to any inner logic of the unfolding of the scientific development of
our subject—from supreme self-confidence in the power of economics to
solve all conceivable problems to considerable self-questioning about how
much it really has to say about important problems. And sometimes we
have made near-desperate efforts to make it say something about problems that are of the utmost social concern but about which we may not be
able to say very much, no matter how hard we try, though we may be
able to hide that fact successfully from ourselves and our colleagues by
juggling with the semantics of our subject and deploying the full set of
our hard-won statistical techniques. In the early sixties, the national
mood of the United States changed from confidence to self-questioning.
I will not discuss the reasons in detail but, in my judgment, they had a lot
to do, on the one hand, with the United States overreaching itself in its
assumed responsibilities to the rest of the world, particularly for setting
Europe straight on American melting-pot lines and defending it from the
Russian threat, and, on the other hand, with the change in the immigration laws in the 1920s. I believe the latter change had tremendous long-
run social consequences: it protected the average U.S. citizen from
competitive pressures to conform with the melting-pot tradition in order
to survive in the United States, and at the same time it made other countries an easier haven for refugees grateful to have escaped an oppressive
regime and culture. Americans who were capable of observing reality and
testing social hypotheses against it began to proclaim, and not merely
suspect, that all was not well with American democracy and the American
free enterprise system—and indeed that American society might itself be
an unduly oppressive regime.

Initially, the criticism was that, while the United States was still the
greatest country in the world—even obscenely disgusting for its affluence—
it was flawed because a substantial number of its citizens unaccountably
failed to share in the affluence that had been assumed to be every
citizen's right. Hence the launching of the war on poverty, to whose in-
frastructure in economic research many people present at this conference contributed at the time.

But the concern about the prevalence of poverty is only a superficial
symptom of malaise and one highly correlated with the business cycle.
A society with a small minority of poor and a vast majority of presumably nonpoor can cure its ills with a relatively small expenditure of

conscience money, though the rich are always grudging in spending money if it will actually succeed in removing the occasion for their charity or render their clients genuinely independent.

The American social conscience, however, has moved on rapidly, largely under the impact of military reverses abroad and related social discontent and intellectual ferment at home, to a far more sweeping condemnation of the economy and the society, one which concentrates on inequality among citizens in general rather than on poverty among a minority of them. Concern about this problem has indirectly motivated the calling of this conference. One of our major problems has been to work back from both the known territories of welfare economics and human-capital theory and the techniques and limitations of regression analysis to the real but ambiguously and poorly defined concerns of the nation's wider intellectual community with its emotionally strongly felt, but operationally opaque, ideas about what the problem of inequality in American society is. It is easy to think of theoretically and even statistically meaningful aggregative definitions of inequality in the personal distribution of income. It is much harder to relate these to the real subjects of public concern about the income distribution.

In the papers for this conference, leaving aside all the matters of detailed technical debate, there have been, in my judgment, two central questions in dispute:

First, what is inequality? Most of us would, I think, agree on two basic points. One comes from the theory of human capital and is by now familiar: inequality is to be measured not by the labor incomes of individuals undifferentiated by age and education but by the lifetime earnings (or with greater theoretical accuracy, consumption) profiles of these individuals. The other is a rather newer and more slippery point: real and socially important inequality is associated with the differences among children of differentially situated parents in the degree of access to opportunities to acquire such lifetime income streams.

Such differences in opportunity raise two different kinds of problems. The first is that to define a standard for a tolerable degree of inequality of opportunity facing individuals of the same age cohort, it is necessary to refer to the life history of a family over more than one generation. The difficulties we have with the welfare economics of this problem are associated with the neglect in our basic welfare economics theory, of the fundamental realities of parental choice and parental ambitions—or lack of them—for children. We also ignore the realities of childrens' appreciation both of the limitations of their parents and their own opportunities to exploit their parents' useful qualities while escaping from parental limitations.

Second, the intergenerational utility function that defines familial welfare is not a constant. It shifts over time and always involves the problem of social choice that welfare economists have been studying intensively but without clear and simple results.

In a largely immigrant America, parents' ambitions typically were both to offer opportunities to their children and to force compliance with the costs of those opportunities. The children typically saw those costs as externally imposed and their parents as qualified by their position in society to be paternalistic decision takers. In a stable second- or third-generation America, however, the costs of compliance appear on both sides to be internally imposed by the family and necessary to parental self-respect, but not necessary to the children's survival and prosperity in the society. The children do not even feel the immigrant's self-chosen obligation to accept the society. The problems involved cannot really be solved satisfactorily purely by juggling with the pricing system for education, though that pricing system creates a host of unnecessary and confusing problems, to an important extent because it places such a heavy emphasis on the exercise of paternalism not by parents but by the educators themselves.

The second central question is: What is the role of higher education in the generation of inequality? The formulation of this question is associated with certain important characteristics of American society as set by history—and particularly the crucial role that education has played in American society. Earlier, education kept civilized and cohesive a colonial population forced to cope with a barbarizing environment and needing both replacement of the intellectual tools of superiority over the surrounding savagery and reminder of the religious beliefs that justified their own responsive barbarism. Later it was a way of integrating into an English-speaking and English-cultured community the first- and second-generation refugees from non-English-speaking European countries that for a historically short period the United States welcomed to its Atlantic shore. As a result of this tradition and of a set of ideas on the social value of education held in common with most European countries and derived in part from the recruitment needs of the monastic celibacy of the Middle Ages, American public opinion has always accorded a special place to education as a solvent for social problems. The educated person—even though when employed as a teacher he was frequently criticized and persecuted for rising above his station as a mere babysitter for the potential pioneers who would eventually do the real work of American society—always enjoyed residual respect as the former and preserver of the society's human capital. The educational system also served as the filter through which the heterogeneous raw human material provided by immigration was assigned to its proper place in society, as determined by its potential productive contribution.

It is, therefore, natural enough that American society, and particularly American intellectuals, should look to the putative defects of this educational system as the root source of the flaws in the society, and look to reform of the educational system as the solution to these problems. Serious flaws can easily be found whether one looks primarily as a social critic or as an economist.

To the social critic, a system that selects the future recipients of income streams from human capital according to their success in passing tests devised and imposed by its educators is both selecting in large part on the basis of parental resources, culture, effort, and familial ambition and relying on a selection process that may be neither socially nor economically effective. The process may be appropriate to a society welcoming immigrants and then sorting them out into the useful and the nonuseful, according to an agreed-upon concept of what the society needs in the way of useful citizens, by selectors whose qualifications also were agreed upon. This was an essentially self-confident imperialist society, bent on political and economic expansion, regardless of its rhetoric of freedom. It is much more questionable for a mature society that protects its wealth by the exclusion of immigrants and purports to guarantee every citizen a due share of its riches. (Incidentally, one of the most ominous characteristics of contemporary American society, particularly of its radical intellectuals, is a general unawareness that what the citizenry would like to spend for social or for radical purposes is a product of past effort and current monopoly that could be easily either squandered or eroded, or both, by international competition.)

It is equally easy to look at the pure economics of a system in which at least minimum-quality education at every level is provided nominally free, or nearly free, to all candidates suitably qualified—though without regard to the foregone earnings to which human-capital theory has quite rightly called attention—and to point out that the combined results of the inevitable fiscal limitation on the total quantity provided, the equally inevitable dependence on rationing by the educators who control admissions, and the availability of privately provided education at an extra price, are economic nonsense in almost every dimension of economic theory.

The direction of the final outcome of economically nonsensical financial arrangements for higher education, however, is more difficult to determine than appears at first sight. As Anne Krueger commented on T. W. Schultz's paper, we have generally been trying to find "third-and-a-half-best" but politically feasible solutions to a "fourth-or-fifth-best" problem, and it is not easy to tell where we stand. Let me illustrate some of the difficulties by reference to the British higher education system. Weisbrod and Hansen have shown that California's educational system redistributes real resources from the lower- to the higher-income groups. Krueger argued, using a model that allowed for the presence of private universities that have to be paid for by parents in addition to the taxes they pay for state universities that they do not patronize with their children because quality is too low, that the income redistribution might go the other way and that there might, in consequence, be either overallocation or underallocation of resources to higher education as a whole.

In the United Kingdom there are no really private universities that support themselves by fees plus private endowments; most of the funds come from the government. There are two kinds of overallocation of resources and students to these universities. On the one hand, middle class parents probably overspend on preuniversity supplementary education aimed at getting their children into the "free" state university places by buying them an edge in passing the requisite examinations. Overspending in this connection includes not only direct costs of private schools or supplementary coaching but choice of work location and type of job to maximize chances of obtaining university scholarships, the number of which per eligible student varies among localities. On the other hand, children of all classes confronted with the choice between going to work on completion of high school and going to a university are faced with working for wages, paying taxes, and escaping from paternalism into freedom, or paying the price of university paternalism in order to live for 3 years at public expense in an environment in which university teachers regard it as a failure on their part to flunk out a student they have once admitted. Everything encourages cleverness at yearly examinations, idleness between them, and the postponement of a career decision. As against these incentives to overallocation of the supply of trainable students, there is a severe restraint imposed on the total number of university places by the immense budgetary cost of the system. This restraint operates not only to restrict numbers but to adulterate educational quality through the imposition of standard rules governing such disparate matters as office sizes and ratios of junior to senior staff. Whether the net result of these conflicting pressures is too much or too little higher education is an open and unresolved question. Inefficient the system certainly is from an economic and, I would judge, from a social point of view.

The point I would like to stress in this connection, however, is not so much the many problems of inefficiency raised by the present system of finance of higher education in the United States, but the limitation of the American assumption that the key to the solution of such social problems as poverty or inequality or the "just society" is to be looked for in reforms of the financial or administrative aspects of the secondary and higher education system. The educational system, and especially the university system, obviously has inherently inefficient and generally conservative biases. One could reduce these biases by putting the whole apparatus on a price-system basis. But if one argues for this, one must go the whole hog —and here I would disagree with T. W. Schultz, who is, I think, wrong to concede an argument for providing educational subsidies to the children of poor parents. By the time they get to the stage of university admission, they are probably already out of the poverty or deplorably unequal class. If poverty or inequality is considered a problem, one should recognize that the poorest among us, and the one most deserving of help from his fellow men, is the one whom nature forgot to endow with brains —and that the way to make it up to him is not to exclude him from school and tax him to pay part of the cost of educating his intellectually well-endowed and no-longer-poor peer group among the children of poor parents, but to give him money in lieu of the brains he lacks. Superior intelligence or skill is undoubtedly more economically useful than the absence of it, but discriminating in favor of it by fiscal subsidization will not necessarily produce a more democratic and poverty-free or egalitarian society.

I have not sought explicitly to produce a neat list or "menu" of the alternatives before us, as they emerge from the state of the art of economic analysis of higher education. The technical questions of measurement are extremely difficult, and I have refrained from discussing them. As I see it, the really tough questions are three: First, how far do we really believe in the ability of economic analysis to set up socially relevant standards of inequality in the educational field, standards which correspond to what the public is really worried about, and if we do, how could we improve the situation? Second, how far can we insist on a competitive cost-oriented system to finance higher education? This raises a question I have not dealt with because I can see no way to grapple with it, and that is the vexed issue of whether higher education produces significant social and economic externalities that are worth subsidization, even indiscriminate subsidization. Third, if we insist on applying competitive principles to higher education, are we prepared to recommend cash redistributions of income to solve the poverty or the inequality problem, and insist on that too? If not, we may implicitly be accepting a retrogression from a "fourth-best" to a "fifth-best" performance with respect to a widely accepted social goal.

These points, I hope, though presented in a somewhat rhetorical and unscientific way, are some of the important alternatives for discussion that now lie before us.

Some Reflections

Edward F. Denison

Brookings Institution

I heartily concur with nearly everything in Harry Johnson's thoughtful paper that bears upon current problems of providing equity in education. However, I cannot quite concur in his description of the history of education in America and Europe. Differences were more basic than Johnson allows, and Horatio Alger merits more than a mention.

Native as well as foreign-born Americans typically believed that a child should and could rise above the station of his parents and that the most effective route was to obtain more education than his parents had. School attendance requirements were lax, but vast numbers of students chose to remain in school after departure was legally permitted. Parents demanded expansion of facilities to accommodate them. The different aspects of the process were constantly interacting. Because schools were locally controlled, it was unnecessary to wait for a national consensus and national financing to extend educational opportunities; the richer localities and those whose voters were most enthusiastic about education moved ahead. Other districts then tried to catch up with the leaders, who by now were again moving forward.

In Europe, in contrast, the vast majority lacked faith in economic and social advancement through education. Elementary education laws, viewed as necessary for citizenship, were strict and enforced; but, except for small numbers planning to continue through the university, students left school as soon as departure was legal even if opportunity existed for further education. Pressure to extend educational opportunities was weak, and with national systems schooling could be extended only when a national consensus was reached and national financing was available. Recently, European attitudes and practice have moved rapidly toward those in America, but history has left America with a distribution of its labor force by level of education that is greatly dispersed from bottom to top, and European countries with a distribution extremely concentrated at a point corresponding to past legal requirements for school attendance.

I should now like to try to set out, rather baldly, a set of seven propositions. Our discussions suggested they might receive rather general assent among us, but I mean to commit no one but myself.

1. Equity in the expenditure of public funds for higher education can be examined without trying to relate the distribution of taxes for education to benefits from education.

2. Public funds obtainable for higher education, or more generally for investment in young people, are limited. Much larger expenditures on those now benefiting least or not at all would necessitate smaller expenditures on those now benefiting most.

3. Of the several aspects of economic inequality and/or inequity in our economy that may disturb us, it is the distribution of opportunity to secure lifetime income to which examination of investment in young people is chiefly germane.

4. Young people's prospects for securing future income vary widely. The important characteristics that both bear upon future income *and* are sufficiently observable to form a possible basis for discriminating among the young in the expenditure of public funds are limited to: economic position of family, as indicated by income or wealth; academic appitude or achievement at particular ages, as measured by IQ aptitude, achievement tests, or school grades; race; place of residence; and sex.[1] If young people are classified by any of these characteristics, the per capita public expenditure per young person is bigger for the group already having the better income prospect. (Because of marriage, the sex classification, however, is tricky, and I exclude it henceforth.)

5. From the standpoint of equity, it is unconscionable to invest the most public funds in those with the best prospects. The minimum requirement for equity is to spend as much for those with worse as for those with better prospects, which would call for an equal per capita expenditure. Some wish to reverse the present discrimination to give extra help to those with the dimmer prospects.[2]

6. Much of the inequality stems from higher education, but this does not mean that a program to equalize public expenditures for investment in youth should be limited to higher education. Not only other forms of education but also cash grants or annuities must be considered. Formulation of an equitable program should also consider efficiency and individual

[1] I disregard small groups with pronounced physical handicaps or exceptional athletic ability.

[2] One danger should be recognized. The characteristics available for use in discrimination are only some of the determinants of future income, and once we leave grouped data and consider individuals, they are not necessarily the most important characteristics. Much of the observed earnings differential among individuals is not explained by them. Departure from equal expenditures for all by discriminating in favor of those with the worst prospects as indicated by these characteristics will introduce new discrimination against those whose future is not bright for other reasons.

preferences. Assuming options are provided, the question remains: Who should make the decisions—the child, the parent, school authorities, or the state?

7. The only form of discrimination in favor of those with the best income prospects that is seriously defended is concentration of expenditures for higher education on those most academically talented. The case, which rests on efficiency grounds, is not impressive. Analyses presented here indicate the earnings increment from higher education to be only moderately greater for those with high academic aptitude than for others; hence, concentration of higher education has only a moderate effect on total national income insofar as the gains are private. Moreover, private gains—those we can measure—do not justify discrimination. The argument must rest on the allegation of external benefits to others. Our discussion suggested general skepticism that external benefits are large, and extreme skepticism that they are so much larger when public funds are concentrated on the academically talented, rather than distributed more equally, that those not now attending college are better off under the present arrangement. The justification requires a showing that the few academically talented students who attend college now, but would not if they had to pay or repay more of the cost of their education, contribute so much to the welfare of the others that the latter are better off under the present system than if their share of public funds were invested for them directly. This would be even less likely than now if opportunity for loans were further improved.

Time and agenda permitted only fragmentary discussion of other aspects of efficiency in the investment of either public or private funds in young people. Keen interest in all aspects of the topic was coupled with uncertainty about how best to proceed, except that improvement of capital markets for investment in human capital and perhaps introduction of greater competition in the education industry seemed likely routes to improvement.